Eastern Canons

Companions to Asian Studies

Wm. Theodore de Bary, Editor

EASTERN CANONS:

To Ainslie T. Embree
Teacher to the core

Contents

Preface

If a forum is the classic setting for the discussion of public issues, this book serves as a forum on an educational issue much before the public today: the status of the "classic" itself. The funny and paradoxical thing that has happened on the way to this forum, however, is the growing challenge in the academy—traditionally the custodian of the classic canon—to any concept of a classic or canon at all, while in the popular mind there persists such a powerful hankering for tradition and all things classic, as witness, even in so unlikely an arena as the world of sports, the spectacular proliferation of tournaments called "classics," purporting to preserve as enduring monuments of human achievement anything that aspires to become more than a one-time event. If, in such wise, athletic contests can be thought classics, the folk wisdom behind it may owe something to the idea that repeated trial and testing—the ability to survive perennial struggle and gain renewed strength from it—is what establishes something as truly "classy" (the original meaning of the Latin *classicus*).

At Columbia University in 1987, on the fiftieth anniversary of the required core course in the Humanities, a symposium was held on "The Humanities as Contested Ground." Later the forum was extended to include, in 1988, the fortieth anniversary of the sequential Oriental Humanities course. As it happens, too, the year 1989 marks the thirtieth anniversary of an earlier symposium on the Oriental Humanities, published in 1959 under the title *Approaches to the Oriental Classics*. That book, now out of print, contained essays on classics of the major Asian traditions, and comments on their significance for education by such non-orientalists as Jacques Barzun, Lyman Bryson, and Mark Van Doren.

The comparatively open and expansive view of the canon which these earlier essays bespoke, allowing for the possibility of a plurality of canons in a multicultural world, stands in some contrast to the educational hostilities that have broken out since. In the confusions of the contemporary debate there is still to be heard, no doubt, some resistance to such a liberal and expansive view, but the real issue today, at its deepest, is not one of conflicting cultures or conservative versus liberal views. The challenge now, even when offered in the name of so-called "non-Western" cultures, is revealed in this very negative and incoherent formulation of the matter itself, for "non-Western" is not a concept that stands for anything in itself and is meant less to affirm the positive value of these alternative traditions than to call into question the validity of any tradition at all. Indeed today we face nothing less than a radical, cultural-revolutionary challenge to any kind of canon, Eastern or Western.

Such of course is not the point of this book, which tends to reaffirm the practical validity of a multicultural canon as a working concept in the core curriculum. If, however, the book still claims to serve as a genuine forum, rather than simply as a defense of some established position and practice, it is because we do not start from a preconceived definition of the canon, which is then projected out and superimposed on other cultures, but proceed inductively to examine what other traditions have considered classic, and from this empirical base develop criteria, both old and new, that may contribute to an enlarged conception of the humanities. Such a view of the canon may still be thought of as a working, contestable construct for educational purposes.

This book then aims to address two main questions: What is the place of Asia in the humanities curriculum today, and how may classics of the major Asian traditions illustrate the values and genres honored in those traditions. In chapter 2 a rather full list of classic works—by no means a fixed or complete canon—is given. From this larger list a few examples are taken, representing each of the four main traditions, and discussed in brief interpretive essays intended to introduce them to the general reader. Here two points should be kept in mind. First, we have not necessarily chosen the best-known works, because much has already been written about them, but have often picked ones less known or at least less accessible to the average reader. Second, the essays are aimed at the nonspecialist. We have not striven for originality of interpretation—though some of that appears in these pages—but rather for what is most central and commonly understood about these works in their own tradition, what it is that has made them classics by general consensus over the centuries, and what it is that can still speak to us most directly today.

The present volume represents an updating of the earlier *Approaches to the Oriental Classics* (1959), and reproduces a few of the essays originally published therein. For the most part, however, its contents are new. They either address the new educational challenges of the late '80s and the '90s, or offer fresh approaches to the individual classics that always invite reexamination and in this process win renewed appreciation. Some essays too have already appeared in the *Great Ideas Today*, 1987, Chicago, Encyclopedia Britannica/Great Books Foundation, 1987, and are reprinted with the permission of the editors, Mortimer Adler and John Van Doren.

The undersigned wish to acknowledge the invaluable assistance of Paul Anderer and Ruth Levenson in the planning and conduct of the anniversary observances documented herein, as well as the great help of Marianna Stiles in preparing these essays for publication. Beyond such specific contributions, this book draws on the collective efforts and experience of many members of our staff over the years. Among them the editors wish particularly to recognize the long-standing and very distinguished service of Ainslie Embree and John Meskill.

Wm. Theodore de Bary
Irene Bloom

Eastern Canons

1 ASIA IN THE CORE CURRICULUM

Wm. Theodore de Bary

In the debate which erupted during the spring of 1988 over changes in the Stanford core course on Western civilization, the political heat generated, and the attendant confusion of issues as these were aired in the media, did little to advance the cause of education. The cast of characters in this much publicized controversy had the so-called "fundamentalists," William Bennett, Allan Bloom, and others who claimed to speak for traditional values and the Great Books, ranged against those who would infiltrate third world politics, feminism, and cultural relativism into the sanctuary of Western learning. Among those who defended Stanford's innovations were some who insisted that the whole idea of a privileged canon was a latter-day imposture of Ivy League WASPS, making icons of "dead white boys" so as to protect the sacred turf of the Western (or, as some would put it, the East Coast) academic establishment. For liberationists the need to include feminist issues, "ethnic cultures," and minority studies in the core curriculum would justify, if it came to that, even the dropping of Homer, Aristotle, Dante, Shakespeare, Darwin, Mill, and Freud from the list of required readings.

Few would deny that there are real issues at stake here. This is not much ado about nothing, blown up out of all proportion by political partisans of the right and left. Many of the views expressed are seriously held by persons in a position to affect the course of American education. Nevertheless, between the confrontational politics of some, and the unyielding defensiveness of others, there seems to have been little disposition to engage in any fundamental reexamination of educational needs or exploration of new curricular possibilities. Equally valid goals have been needlessly set at cross-purposes, and the scoring of polemical points has substituted for what one might have hoped would become a "great debate" on the most basic issues.

One need not imagine it possible to isolate such a debate from all politics or ideology, nor suppose that education itself can be entirely free of indoctrination. Better instead that the premises and purposes of an educational program be made explicit, and that faculties openly take responsibility for the values their curriculum is meant to serve. Better still, however, if faculties, in meeting this challenge, accept the needs of students themselves as the prime consideration, rather than the promoting of some political or social program or the pursuit of the faculties' own special interest—as well as their most natural instinct—to replicate their own academic species.

THE NATURE OF THE CORE CURRICULUM

Most experienced college teachers, or scholars who have given real thought to problems of a core curriculum as distinct from the training of students in particular disciplines, would not, I think, deny the need for education to transmit essential civilizational values, and to do so, at least to some degree, in a manner that would show their bearing on problems of compelling contemporary concern. Students expect of a college education that it will equip them not only with the specific skills needed to make their way in the world but also with some understanding of themselves and how they can make a meaningful contribution to the increasingly complex society in which they live.

The hope of achieving this in any reasonable measure today—of providing some combination of competent instruction in specific disciplines and mature guidance in their preparation for life—must proceed from a recognition that for most students, whether in specialized training or general education, the best that they can realistically hope to accomplish in college is to make a good start at what will become a lifetime work. For this the core curriculum must be well-defined at the start, properly structured as it develops, and open-ended in facing the future.

In most colleges today, dominated as they are by practitioners of specialized disciplines and by departmental structures, there is consciousness enough of the need for systematic, sequential training in such disciplines, and for the setting of priorities by those competent to judge what will contribute to a sustained, cumulative learning experience. Yet when it comes to general education, there is little awareness that a like need exists—for a definite structure and orderly progression toward intellectual maturity. Too often general education is thought of simply as a brief moment of intellectual adventure before the grim business of specialization takes over. Important as is this lively sense of exploration, its pursuit should be nurtured, sustained, and cultivated rather than allowed to drift aimlessly or become diffused through random exposure to a variety of unrelated, undirected learning experiences. Nor should its free exercise be thought of simply as part of a "broadening" process, after which one settles down to concentrate on a major. A distinction is in order between free electives, which serve the student's independent growth as long as the individual accepts his or her own responsibility for them, and requirements legitimately imposed to serve the shared needs of the community. For this deliberate infringement on the student's freedom the institution itself must take responsibility and be prepared to offer some justification.

For the student simply to be exposed to new ideas and experiences, valuable though these might be in themselves, is not enough. Nor can such exposure be justified purely for its shock value, as if the outcome were a matter of indifference and the experience one that could just as well lead anywhere or nowhere. Such indiscriminate openness is certainly liable to the charge of moral or cultural relativism, and may only be disorienting to the student if the teacher thinks his job goes no further than to disabuse the student of his previously held convictions, leaving him with the kind of "open mind," empty of any convictions, that Allan Bloom sees as effectively closed to any genuine value commitment.

Indeed, there would be in this no basis for a valid claim on the student's time in the form of a required course. Nor, without any sense of relatedness to what has gone before or coherence with what comes after, can such a learning experience qualify as part of a core curriculum—much less as education, which always involves some "leading" on the part of the teacher and, with that, like it or not, some leadership and decision-making responsibility.

In many places exposure to something other than one's major is sought through a "distribution requirement," an arrangement that appeals to the student's desire for freedom of choice, while at the same time it suits the disposition of most faculty to share with students a taste of their own discipline, so long as such teaching does not require the scholar to step very far outside his or her own field. Keeping essentially within departmental limits, such instruction is likely to be highly controlled, as it must be for the introduction of any discipline, and academically quite "respectable." Nevertheless it leaves important educational needs unmet.

Many of life's problems, and society's too, fit poorly into disciplinary grooves. Often students feel at a loss, having no sense of how to relate what they call "academics" to the pressing contemporary problems of which they cannot be unaware. Under such a regime students' intellects tend to develop in a value-free, sanitized, laboratory environment, largely detached from normal human sympathies. Their moral sentiments and aesthetic sensibilities undergo no comparable process of refinement, nor are their judgmental faculties adequately exercised in regard to value questions. Left in this condition of immaturity, students' consciences are easily played upon, or preyed upon, by others with strong ideological opinions or fundamentalist convictions, only too ready with simple answers to urgent questions of the day.

The usual academic response to questions of laymen about contemporary issues is that the matter—whatever it is—is more complicated than the layman supposes. The realities of a problematic situation, so the familiar lines goes, do not lend themselves to simple yes or no answers, black/white solutions. No doubt this is true, and not simply an academic cop-out as it often appears to be, yet its effect is to leave the questioner more impressed with the superior knowledge of the expert than confident of his or her own ability to grapple with the issues.

Even much of general education today falls victim to the respect for genuine academic competence. Competent scholars often disqualify themselves from teaching general education courses, supposedly as a matter of intellectual responsibility and honesty. Or, if they cannot extricate themselves entirely from this duty, they ask to be allowed some leeway, in required courses, to teach at least something from their own particular field of specialization. Yet, in the absence of any comparable concession to students' personal predilections, once such allowance is made for the instructor, students understandably sense an asymmetry in what is demanded of both parties. The suspicion arises that there is some arbitrariness in the fixing or relaxing of criteria for the "core" and from this students begin to feel that their own preferences, even though not informed by the same academic competence, should be entitled to like consideration. Before long, as further concessions are made, the common core ceases to be either common or core.

"General education," a term which gained currency from the

much publicized Harvard Red Book "General Education in a Free Society" (1945), expressed a need to offset the trend toward increasing departmentalization of learning. "General" in this case meant the opposite of specialization, and at its best could be taken to represent a balanced undergraduate program. Yet, whatever the balance achieved, the vagueness of the term "general" lent itself to a wide latitude of interpretation, ranging from a more or less well-defined distribution requirement to a virtual guarantee of the student's right to freedom of choice. There was, at the center, no core, if by this one meant that students should be exposed to a common body of problems, materials, and shared discourse. Whether for such reasons or not, what developed at Harvard, later to be ratified by the Rosovsky Report of 1977, was a kind of smorgasbord of specially tempting departmental delicacies, offered to a general audience by star lecturers, who could be counted on to impress and captivate the minds of undergraduates, even if the program did not generate a common body of thoughtful discourse among either faculty or students of the college as a whole.

At Columbia, where the basic elements of a core curriculum had been put together in the twenties and thirties, the term "general education" did not come into use until much later, with Daniel Bell's report on *The Reforming of General Education* (1967). Before that, at least in the late forties and fifties, "core curriculum" was the term most frequently used. Initially the program itself was identified with a required Contemporary Civilization course, quite openly and directly addressed to contemporary problems and making no pretence at conveying the essence of Western civilization or defining traditional values. Yet it did present these contemporary problems in historical perspective, as products of a long evolution in Western society and as central problems of human society which had occupied the best minds of the West for centuries. Institutional history and source readings from major Western thinkers provided much of the content, while discussion in small classes, involving direct student engagement with the material (especially the source readings) provided the indispensible complement, as a flexible instructional method, to the prescribed content of the common core.

Alongside of CC developed the Honors course of John Erskine, which had a different provenance: in important respects it sought to preserve the benefits of old-fashioned classical learning after the abandonment of the language requirements in Latin and Greek, based now on the reading and discussion of classic works *in translation*. As an Honors course this could perhaps be thought "elitist," and insofar as it sought to perpetuate the liberal values of a classical education, in the manner of eighteenth- and nineteenth-century gentlemen in England, Europe, and (in Columbia's case) the remnants of the old Hudson Valley aristocracy, one could think of it as perpetuating an elite tradition.

But demographic changes, the influx of large immigrant populations into New York, and Columbia's early accessibility to bright young Jews, Italians, Irish, and blacks, meant that its student body by this time had become quite diverse and "democratic," as compared to other Ivy League institutions. And when the Honors colloquium was transformed in 1937 into a Humanities course required of all freshmen, it had already become part of a larger movement, at first centered in New York and later spread to Chicago, with a distinct populist flavor. Its early teachers did their work not only in Columbia classrooms but in "people's institutes," Cooper Union, adult education centers, union halls, and in the best New York high schools, where highly talented, upwardly mobile children of immigrant and refugee families demonstrated their scholarly promise. Mortimer Adler was no WASP, and when he took the message of what he called "The Great Books" to Chicago, and thence throughout the country, his strong commitment was to democratic education, to the reform of American education at large, on all levels. Ironically, had he been less of a populist and popularizer Adler might have spared himself the condescending criticisms of a real elitist, Allan Bloom, who would later deprecate Adler's efforts as bordering on vulgarization and hucksterism.

It is ironic that Adler's practical, enterprising spirit in the packaging and sale of the Hundred Great Books, with the Syntopican as guide, and the Hundred Great Ideas as the agenda for discussion, together constituting his populist program of education, should have given such defined form to the Great Books program that it assumed the monumental proportions of a fixed canon. At Columbia meanwhile, in what had begun as an experimental program, the works referred to as "classics" or "important books" (rarely as "Great Books"), have won their place on the Humanities reading list, and re-won it year after year, not by being elevated and safely enshrined out of the reach of any tampering, but by proving themselves in a dialogue perennially challenging to students and teachers alike.

Confirmation of the inherent appeal and impressiveness of the works themselves comes not only from generations of students and alumni—inveterate defenders of the Humanities course—but from the larger place these texts have won even in the older Contemporary Civilization course. Though CC is more historically and topically oriented, experience over the years has shown that texts representing great minds and major historical figures are better suited to issue-oriented discussion than are the secondary studies and historical essays originally prepared for CC. It would seem that personal confrontation with issues and alternative ways of viewing them is more effectively induced by the individual's encounter with great thinkers. Projecting oneself into past encounters of ideas, weighing possible courses of action, and considering the historical consequences, the student mentally exercises a certain freedom of choice, practices taking responsibility for his own judgments in dialogue with others, and develops his own independence of mind. Indeed, so effective and so prevalent has this practice become in CC, and so central the discussion of major texts, that those responsible for the direction of the course, while not wishing to dampen students' enthusiasm for the "great books," feel some need now to redress the balance, to direct more concerted attention to historical background, lest the discussion became elevated to an almost timeless realm.

It is true enough to say that the "canon" of classics of great books, as known in America today, is the creation of a particular age and educational movement, with quite precise origins, even though its character as the product of a given class or ethnic group is not easily defined, inasmuch as the era in question was one of rapid social change. No less true, however, is the fact that the creators of this modern curriculum, as educated, cultured men, were dedicated to perpetuating a long-standing tradition of classical learning formed by others quite different from themselves in race, class and religion.

Moreover it is a tradition that has stood the test of time—both time past and time present—consisting of works marked indeed by the circumstances of their original creation but also surpassing them. What has survived is not the product of a unilinear development, identifiable with any given establishment or even any one tradition. The so-called Western tradition, at its inception, drew heavily on "Oriental" sources in the Near and Middle East. Much of Greek philosophy came into the hands of the medieval West through the good offices of Muslim Arabs, who recognized the importance and responded to the challenge of Greek thought at a time when it had been eclipsed in Europe during the so-called Dark Ages. Long before there were any WASPS in the world Aristotle stood as a formidable presence in the minds of the great Islamic philosophers, al-Ghazālī and Ibn Khaldūn, as much later he would again in the eyes of modern East Asians. Plato, Aristotle, St. Augustine, Dante, Shakespeare, and Dostoyevsky, when once made available to educated Japanese and Chinese, quickly established themselves as classic thinkers and writers of universal stature.

It is not just that "each generation chooses its own ancestors" as the saying goes, and thus has its own part to play in the process of canon criticism, canon redefinition, or even—if it comes to that—iconoclasm, but that certain works perennially survive translation and critical scrutiny across time as well as cultures. This is what marks them as "classics"—worthy of serious consideration by each new generation—and thus claimants to some priority of attention in any structured curriculum.

In this way the core at Columbia has come to be defined through practical experience more than by an abstract definition or ideological design. Yet, after more than sixty years of experience with these two courses, CC and Humanities, and with successive changes in their conduct, it can still be said that the basic aim of the core remains to satisfy the two interrelated needs cited earlier: first for students to gain an understanding of Western civilization and its values in their historical development (though not necessarily seen as exclusive to the West), and second, drawing on this understanding, to confront the problems of contemporary society. More particularly CC has sought to address contemporary problems in historical perspective and in the light of what leading thinkers in the West have said about the central problems of human society. The Humanities courses provide students with an opportunity personally to encounter certain great works of literature, thought, art, and music that can speak to the human condition and enrich the inner life of the individual. Clearly there is, and should be, some overlap between the two.

Each of these courses has changed over the years but together they have retained the following characteristics in common as core courses:

1. They provide students and faculty, regardless of their particular academic and professional interests, with an opportunity to study and reflect upon the major ideas, values, and institutions of Western civilization that have shaped contemporary society.

2. The core courses are text- and problem-oriented, emphasizing the exploration of alternative views and approaches to major topics, rather than initiation into specific disciplines.

3. A common body of required texts and source readings is used to encourage the individual's confrontation with challenging questions and ideas, as well as to facilitate discussion of key issues with

one's fellows. In other words, reading requirements are designed to help the individual student both think for himself and express himself in group discussion, instead of simply remaining a passive recipient or observer.

4. Through such common readings and the exchange of ideas, the core courses promote a shared, nontechnical discourse that, in an age of inescapable specialization, bridges the disciplines and sustains the ability of educated persons to communicate with one another.

5. If group discussion depends for its focus on a common set of readings, the works themselves offer an uncommon combination of accessibility to readers (readily making sense to them) as well as a capacity to perplex and provoke. In this respect the true greatness of "great books" lies not in their perfection as final statements but in their pivotal quality, their ability to focus on key issues and expose the mind to crucial alternatives. Far from settling things, they are unsettling, always open to reinterpretation. They invite and reward rereading.

6. A condition of successful group discussion in core courses is the limitation of class size. Typically at Columbia this has meant groups of twenty to thirty students, allowing for close classroom contact—long considered one of the most distinctive features of a Columbia College education. Yet such a pattern does not exclude the presentation also of special lectures by scholars of high competency as an adjunct to and enhancement of the regular class discussions. This has been done successfully in the past without compromising the basic enterprise.

7. Core courses make use of "classics," "great books," and major historical documents, not just to learn from the past but to put before students models that challenge them personally, stretching the intellect and exercising the moral imagination. In the Humanities courses the inclusion of such works in the syllabus and their reinstatement year after year has come about through election and reelection by the staff, ratification by students, and later confirmation by alumni, who testify that the encounter with such chal-

lenging works has remained the most memorable and meaningful part of their college experience.

8. A "canon" so established in practice serves not so much to enshrine a hundred books or a set of fixed values as to help students become conscious of the values embodied in "classic" works, and thus learn to develop their own standards of evaluation. As a process it encourages reflective thinking, critical analysis, and the formulation of grounds for positive commitment. The canon (if such it be) and the questioning of it go together. There must be questioning, and something of value that has stood the test of time, worth questioning.

9. As the core curriculum addresses age-old human problems, and also finds perennial wisdom or enduring beauty in monuments of the past, it recognizes too that active repossession of the past involves constant re-evaluation in the light of new knowledge and present needs. Thus the sustaining of the core requires some built-in mechanism for review and reformulation.

10. The core courses are to be distinguished from those satisfying other College requirements such as language or physical education requirements, or courses meeting distribution requirements—i.e., courses defined as different from or remote from one's major. Core courses are meant to address questions central to human life and civilization; they are not to be thought of in terms of remoteness, otherness or "non-Western"ness, which suggest a negative or peripheral quality incompatible with the concept of "core."

"Core," then, refers not just to content or canon, but to process and method—to a well-tested body of challenging material, cultivated habits of reflective, critical discourse, and procedures for reexamination and redefinition. A viable core will neither be slave to the past nor captive to the preoccupations, pressures, or fashions of the moment. It will serve rather to advance the intellectual growth and self-awareness of the student, cultivate his powers of thought and expression, and prepare him to take a responsible part in society.

EXTENDING THE CORE

Although CC and Humanities have, for fifty years now, represented the core of the core, in keeping with the original premise that these were to be foundation courses, others were to follow answering to the same concerns and methods of discourse. Thus a variety of secondary offerings, in sequence with CC and Humanities, have dealt with contemporary problems, new methods of study or interpretation, and other aspects of the humanities—especially music and fine arts. Some of these have been part of the College requirements, others optional. All have recognized the need for additional interdisciplinary courses, often team-taught, to sustain the inquiry and dialogue already begun.

A prime example is the so-called "Colloquium," an upper-level seminar traditionally conducted by two instructors which has taken up additional major works of the Western tradition beyond the limited number that could be handled in the required Humanities course. At its inception one needed no special rationale for the Colloquium; it was simply a continuation of the enormously successful Honors course initiated by John Erskine. But since the number of important works to be considered was far greater than one could include in Humanities A without strain or superficiality of treatment, and since no one imagined that the Humanities reading list represented a fixed or closed canon, it was natural for some students to want to continue the process through the Colloquium, on an optional and selective basis, into the junior and senior years.

Most important here is the sense of the core as a sustained process—starting from an adequate foundation experience, in which one is exposed to challenging ideas and develops certain habits of critical discourse, and then, through expanding horizons of intellect, imagination, and aesthetic sensibility, moving on to fresh encounters with other works, old or new. From this naturally emerges the concept and practice of the "Extended Core": a further outreach from the required core to a limited number of defined options, each of them organic outgrowths of what has gone before in terms of central concerns and discussion methods.

In this educational context and climate was born the Oriental Humanities, featuring the "great books of the East," as a natural extension of the earlier Honors, Humanities, and Colloquium programs. The manner in which this happened is described in chapter 2, but a salient fact, and a point worth sharpening here, is that the thought of including Asia in the core curriculum arose in the 1930s, well before either World War II, the postwar boom in Asian studies, or the rise of third-world politics in the sixties. In Columbia's case the matter of Asia assuming its place in the Core was not and is not contaminated by any suspicion of the faculty's bowing to political or ethnic pressures. The real radicals, in the sense of being both rooted in fundamental human concerns and visionary as to future trends, were members of the Columbia faculty in the 1920s and '30s whose breadth of educational outlook and extraordinary foresight made them anticipate the need to bring Asia within the scope of the core curriculum (as further discussed in chapter 2).

Efforts to remedy this lack, not just by the adding of so-called language and area studies (which were already offered at Columbia in the form of Chinese, Japanese, and Arabic studies), but by the organization of courses meeting the same criteria as CC and Humanities, were delayed by the distractions of World War II rather than hastened by America's increasing involvement in the Pacific area. But under the postwar leadership of Dean Harry Carman, courses were established first in an Oriental Colloquium, then in Oriental Humanities, and finally in Oriental Civilizations. There followed a period of the intensive development of teaching materials, source readings, translations of major texts, study guides, syllabi, etc. Though this effort continues even now, already by the late sixties it was possible to say that the materials on Asia for use in general education were fully equivalent to those used in the parent core courses. It could no longer be argued, as some did justifiably at mid-century, that, though the need to bring Asia into the core was clear, materials were simply not available to do the job properly. Suitable translations, texts, and guides have since been developed for use on almost any level of education. These materials are not only widely used in the United States and Canada, but have been reprinted, translated, and even pirated for use in Asia as well.

These facts belie certain claims made by protagonists on both sides in the recent debate. Certainly there is no warrant here for thinking that the inclusion of Asia in the core curriculum has to be seen as a betrayal of the West, a surrender of academic integrity, or a capitulation to the political pressures of disaffected minorities—or indeed, as anything but a natural follow-through on the intentions of those who originally saw the need for a core curriculum and also foresaw that it would be incomplete if it did not make room for other major world traditions. The real issue here is not whether to include Asia, but whether it is wise or necessary to do this at the substantial expense of the West in the core curriculum.

What may well provoke suspicion or arouse alarm among conservatives is the more radical claim that today East and West should be treated on a par, with no privileged status reserved for traditional values or Western civilization. This latter claim gains some plausibility, and undoubted momentum, from current trends toward the globalization of economic, technical, and cultural life. In the space age, with almost instant communication around the world, everyone lives in everyone else's backyard. Hence, anything that resists the inevitable breaking down of cultural barriers seems pointless and, in the longer run, fruitless. It is anachronistic—so this line goes—to try to preserve, much less erect, fences that would protect any cultural sanctuary or privileged curricular position for the Western tradition.

To Allan Bloom this view might well seem the final surrender of the open mind to cultural relativism. I would suggest, however, that there is a sound educational middle way to be found here which is not simply a wishy-washy compromise between hard-line right and left. I would, on the one hand, take seriously the question raised by John Van Doren as to whether the Asian classics, for all their importance on a global scale, are "necessary" in the same sense that the "Great Books" of the West are necessary to students in the West. That "necessity," he says, derives from the fact that such works "already inhabit the minds of students when they come to college," and that "they have to be duly recognized if these minds are to develop properly—that is, with adequate command of their mental furniture." He says further:

> I do not mean, of course, that the students have literally read such works before they come to college. I mean that the works exist within them in the sense that the kind of language they speak, the terms they use, and the ideas they have about themselves and the world around them are derived from such writings. Of course the language is not spoken very well, nor are the terms used with much precision, nor are the ideas sufficiently understood. That is why it is necessary for students to undertake this reading in their college years, and preferably, I should think, at the beginning of their course of study. They have to discover what it is that they think they know, and perhaps how little they really know it, before they can move on to other things.

This strikes me as a serious claim, and I would agree with it in the sense that what Van Doren says is equally true of students the world around. One's own cultural tradition should have priority in undergraduate education anywhere. The globalization of culture may well produce what people like to think of as a "global village," but that it will be global in character as the outcome of irresistible forces seems far more likely than that it will produce anything resembling a village. There are grounds for doubt whether our future habitation will retain any real local color, distinctive culture, or sense of intimate association. Indeed one wonders whether it can be assumed that anything at all will survive of local culture or indigenous tradition in the face of the homogenization of all culture that clearly attends the process of "globalization." May not universities everywhere be doomed, if not to an imposed conformity, then at least to a uniformity as anonymous, dull, and graceless as the shopping malls proliferating around the globe? These are questions that must disturb anyone contemplating the future of our universities.

If globalization of a mindless sort is not to occur, if anything of intellectual diversity and cultural pluralism is to survive in colleges and universities, they must tend the roots of their own cultures and nurture whatever there still is of distinctive excellence in their own traditions. Which is to say, in the matter of core curricula, giving some priority to the study, and understanding in some depth, of those ideas, institutions, or cultural traditions that make each of us —in East or West—what we are and can be at our best.

Yet this is not something that will just happen. Only an active effort of the collective educational will and a conscious structuring of the curriculum will avert this very real threat and salvage a constructive result.

It is a simple fact that learning proceeds from the known to the unknown, and that understanding another culture draws upon what we understand of our own. In important respects we are unready to appreciate, in other than a romantic and superficial way, the depths and excellences of another culture if we are handicapped by an insufficient knowledge of our own.

At the same time, no matter how well our translators do their work, studying another culture is going to be much like learning another language. There are always linguistic or cultural barriers to be overcome. This means that the further removed from our own another culture is—and this applies also to classical civilization as compared to modern—the greater the effort that will be needed to penetrate the barrier and enter deeply into that culture. In other words, the stranger the culture the less accessible it will be, and the greater the risks of misunderstanding and superficiality.

In the early stages of education this factor of accessibility and commensurate difficulty of penetration must be taken into account.

In chapter 2 I argue the point in relation to proposals for bringing all major traditions together in a single "great books" or world civilization course. Here everything depends, as always, on how it is done, on what comparative terms, and on how much time is given to it. In the present context, certainly, a crucial question would be whether adequate justice can be done to the distinctive features of each tradition—especially their inner complexity and rich diversities—in a one-year survey. One can have something like "globality" in the academic equivalent to a one-stop shopping mall, but nothing like the intimate personal experience of life in a village, or the sense of identification with a community for which one takes some personal responsibility.

Even after forty years' experience in dealing with the problem, for me the most essential considerations have never been better stated than they were in 1943, by one of the founding fathers of the Great Books movement, Mark Van Doren, in his *Liberal Education:*

> Imagination always has work to do, whether in single minds or in the general will. It is the guardian angel of desire and decision, accounting for more right action, and for more wrong action, than anybody computes. Without it, for instance, the West can come to no conclusions about the East which war and fate are rapidly making a necessary object of its knowledge. Statistics and surveys of the East will not produce what an image can produce: an image of difference, so that no gross offenses are committed against the human fact of strangeness, and an image of similarity, even of identity, so that nothing homely is forgotten. The capacity for such images comes finally with intellectual and moral virtue; it is not the matter of luck that some suppose it, though single imaginations of great power are pieces of luck that civilization sometimes is favored with. It is a matter of training, of the tempered and prepared character which all educated persons can share. This character is a condition for the solution of any huge problem, either in the relations of peoples—and such rela-

tions, beginning at home, call first for knowledge of self, so that in the centuries to come it will be as important for the West to know itself as it knows the East, which means to know itself better than education now encourages it to do—or in the ranges of pure speculation.[1]

ENDNOTE

1. Mark Van Doren, *Liberal Education* (New York: Holt, 1943), p. 127.

2 ASIAN CLASSICS AS "THE GREAT BOOKS OF THE EAST"

Wm. Theodore de Bary

The "Great Books" may not be one of the "Hundred Great Ideas,"[1] but the idea of books so challenging to the mind, so close to the human heart, and of such impressive depth or stature as to command the attention of generation after generation, is certainly not confined to the Western world. Each of the major Asian civilizations has had its canonical texts and literary classics. Significant differences appear, however, in the way the classic canon is defined —by whom, for what audience, for what purposes, and in what form. To Muḥammad "the people of the book" was an important concept for locating the spiritual roots of Islam in an earlier prophetic tradition, and for affirming a common religious ground in the Bible among Jews, Christians, and Muslims.[2] Yet it is by no means clear that the books of the Old Testament, or such of the New as he in any way recognized, were thought to be essential reading for his own followers, let alone for the other "people of the book." Anyone who today reads the great Muslim philosophers and theologians would know that they, no less than St. Augustine and St. Thomas, engaged in significant dialogue with the Greek philosophers, and were long ago party to the "Great Conversation" which Mark Van Doren, Lyman Bryson, and Jacques Barzun used to talk about at Columbia and on CBS radio. Though the contributions of Islamic philosophers were rarely acknowledged in the discussion Bryson held on CBS' Sunday morning "Invitation to Learning," a recent published series on Western Spirituality recognizes that they do indeed belong in this company.[3] Here too, however, it is doubtful that in the Muslim world itself the writings of Plato and Aristotle would have been thought essential reading for any but the scholarly few who studied Al-Ghazālī, Avicenna, Averroes, or Ibn Khaldūn.

Hindus had their own sacred scriptures, some lines of which would be on the lips of pious Indians, but for the most part these texts were considered the sacred preserve of learned pundits, not to be read—much less discussed—by the faithful. Among the latter oral texts had far more currency than written. In China too there were the classics of the Confucian tradition, again the property principally of a learned elite, though Taoist works like the *Lao Tzu* and *Chuang Tzu* also figured in cultivated discourse among the literati, and thus in a sense qualified as great books even if not as canonical literature.

In Japan eminent Buddhist monks like Saichō and Kūkai in the ninth century advanced the idea that, for those who would occupy positions of social as well as clerical importance, a proper training should include the reading of at least some Confucian classics together with the major scriptures of Mahāyāna Buddhism. So assiduously cultivated in Heian Japan was this classical study that even court ladies like Murasaki Shikibu and Sei Shōnagon, great writers in the vernacular Japanese literature of the eleventh century, had themselves read the major Confucian classics along with the monumental Chinese histories and leading T'ang poets, and would have disdained as uncouth and illiterate anyone who had not done the same. Important later writers in Japan, as diverse as the monk-essayist Kenkō in the fourteenth century, the teacher of military science Yamaga Sokō in the seventeenth century, and the great nativist scholar Motoori Norinaga in the eighteenth, all had read the classic Confucian and Taoist texts as part of their mixed cultural inheritance, whether or not they identified themselves with either of the traditions from which these works derived. Thus the latter were read by non-Chinese too as great books commanding attention even when not compelling assent.

In this respect the Japanese (along with the Koreans and Vietnamese, who shared the same Confucian, Taoist, and Buddhist literature) may have been more accustomed to multi-cultural learning than some other Asian peoples who rarely recognized as classics the major works of traditions other than their own. As a general rule, certainly, the traditions transmitting these texts were apt to be socially circumscribed and more or less culture-bound within the limits of a common "classical" literature. As religions their appeal might be more universal, but in the transmission of texts they stood out as high classical traditions—"great traditions" for the few, rather than little traditions shared in by the many. Their "great books" were most often scriptures preserved and read by particular religious communities or classics cherished by the bearers of high culture. A main reason for this lay in the fact that most classics and scriptures were preserved in difficult classical or sacred languages, and even popular works in the vernacular tended in time to become inaccessible, because spoken tongues, more subject to change (i.e., less fixed and disciplined than classical languages), tend toward their own kind of obsolescence. The recognized "classics" of popular fiction too, as well as philosophical and religious dialogues in the vernacular (such as Zen dialogues or Neo-Confucian "recorded conversations"), could be so studded with colloquialisms as to present special difficulties for readers of a later age.

One can hardly exaggerate the persistence and pervasiveness of this problem in communication. Modern writers sometimes assume that the restricted readership of classical literature in Asian societies is mainly attributable to an exclusivity or possessiveness on the part of the custodians of the high tradition. Their monopoly of learning, it is supposed, gave them a vested interest in preserving sacred knowledge as something precious and recondite, out of the ordinary man's reach. The Confucian literati, one is told, both jealously guarded the purity and reveled in the complexity of a written language the masses were not supposed to touch. Buddhist monks of Heian Japan, historians often say or imply, deliberately mystified religious learning so as to insure their own dominance over credulous masses.

Such imputations are not without some basis, as for instance in the case of the Confucian literati in fifteenth-century Korea who resisted the development and use of a new alphabet for their native language because it would compete for attention with Chinese language and literature—an argument not unmixed with the concern of some to maintain their own privileged position as dispensers of the Chinese classical tradition. Yet there are contrary cases, e.g., the leading Japanese monk Kūkai, himself a spokesman for the so-called Esoteric School of Buddhism, advocated public schooling in the ninth century, and Chu Hsi, the great Neo-Confucian philosopher of the twelfth century, was a strong advocate of universal education through public schools. Chu devoted himself to editing and simplifying the classics with a view to making them more understandable for ordinary persons. Since other leading Neo-Confucians after Chu Hsi took up this cause in their writings, the limited success of their efforts must have been due to factors other than the lack of good intentions. Chief among these were probably 1) the perception of peasants in a predominantly agrarian society that learning yielded few economic benefits unless one could convert it into official position or status, and 2) the government's lack of interest in the matter beyond the needs of bureaucratic recruitment. In such circumstances for those with little leisure to dispose of, the difficulties of mastering the great books in classical languages might not seem worth the costs.

In some ways Chu Hsi, as an educator trying to reach beyond

his immediate scholarly audience, was the Mortimer Adler of his time, but he would probably have thought a reading list of One Hundred Great Books too ambitious. His goal was to reach the aspiring youth of every village and hamlet in China, for which he recommended a shorter list: a program based on the Confucian Four Books and his own compact anthology of Sung dynasty thought, the *Reflections on Things at Hand (Chin-ssu-lu).* Chu's competition in those days, the Ch'an (Zen) masters, were offering enlightenment at no cost in terms of reading, and Zen painters even portrayed sages tearing up the scriptures. Too much book-learning was already seen as injurious to the health, and Chu Hsi himself, as well as his Neo-Confucian predecessors, favored careful reading of a few books, as well as reflection over them and discussion with others, instead of a superficial acquaintance with many. Hence he was modest in his initial demands, trying to keep his reading program simple and within people's means and capabilities.

In his efforts along this line, Chu very early reached the Aspen phase of his great books movement, when snippets and selections would often have to serve in place of whole books if the reading was to be done by other than scholars. Two of his Four Books, in fact, were selected short chapters from the classic *Record of Rites:* "The Great Learning" and "The Mean." These he further revised and edited in order to make them more coherent, systematic, and integral texts—shaping them according to what, in his mind, the classic form must have been.

Chu Hsi also had his rough equivalent of Aspen in sylvan retreats such as the historic White Deer Grotto near Mount Lu, at the deep bend in the Yangtse River, where he conducted colloquia on the Confucian classics for his students and other literati of the day. But so concerned was he with the larger educational needs of his society and with developing a cradle-to-the grave approach for the individual that he even directed the compilation of a preparatory text called the *Elementary Learning (Hsiao hsüeh),* as a guide to the training of the young before they took up the Four Books and Five Classics.

For all of these efforts at providing a Reader's Digest of the Confucian classics, Chu never attempted to translate his scriptures into a Vulgate. Even the *Elementary Learning* was composed of so many excerpts in classical Chinese that it would serve better as a teacher's manual than as a student's primer. Followed or accompanied by the Four Books, and then by the Five Classics, it became part of the standard classical curriculum throughout East Asia and had a remarkable diffusion in pre-modern times, yet always within the severe limits which the classical Chinese language imposed on its adaptability to popular audiences and changing times. In China this sytem lasted down to 1905, when the pressure to adopt Western scientific learning brought the scrapping of Chu's humanistic core curriculum based on the Chinese classics.

Half a world away and by a curious historical coincidence, at about the same time that Chinese classical learning was being abandoned, American college education was being cut loose from its old moorings in classical studies. At what was sometimes called the new "Acropolis on the Hudson," which Columbia presidents Seth Low and Nicholas Murray Butler were erecting on Morningside Heights in the early decades of this century, the old language requirements in Greek and Latin, along with the reading of the classics in the original, were giving way to a new educational approach. John Erskine, following George Woodberry, championed the idea that all the benefits of a liberal education in the classics need not be lost, even if Greek and Latin were no longer obligatory, provided that undergraduates could read and discuss the classics in translation. This was the germ of Erskine's Honors course, first offered just after World War I, out of which grew the later Great Books movement.

When purists objected that something of these classics would be lost by reading them in translation, Erskine countered by asking how many readers of the Bible in his day felt able, or found it necessary, to read the Good Book in the original languages. If that rhetorical question answered itself in Erskine's favor, it was at least partly because his largely WASP audience (a convenient example, by the way, of a colloquialism that may well, a century or so from now, require a footnote to make it understood) was so accustomed to reading and appreciating the Bible in the King James' version that they would no doubt have thought something would be lost reading it in the original.

What Erskine at least implied, if he did not actually say as much, was that great books could be read like the Good Book—that the principal measure of a great book was its having something to say so universal, so perennial, and so personal that it could speak to the human individual even through the medium of translation. Strict logic or hermeneutic method might resist an argument so circular, considering how readily one could be persuaded of a book's greatness if what one most wished to believe could be read into it through translation. As a practical matter, however, and for public purposes, some process of consensus among translators and readers has decided what would be thought sufficiently meaningful and of lasting value to be worth everybody's effort. In this way enough such books have been made available in translation so that there are plenty for the individual to choose from on his or her own terms.

If great books were to be read for something of the deep meaning found in the Good Book, something too of a missionary zeal went into the propagating of the Great Books idea. Its advocates brought to the new movement a depth of conviction and evangelical zeal rarely seen in academic enterprises. The original locale may have been the classroom, but the spread of the Great Books program well beyond the halls of academe had something of the old-time religion about it, as if the religious roots of the early Ivy League foundations had taken on new life in the liberal, cosmopolitan atmosphere of New York, later to be transplanted to Chicago, Annapolis, Aspen, or wherever the populist spirit and new technology—rather than a stuffy traditionalism—might carry it.

An essential feature of the new movement was its insistence on the discussion method. The Honors course, as a colloquium, reasserted not only the primacy of the classics, but also the importance of reading the classics for what they had to say about life as a whole, combining ideas and value judgments that were increasingly, in Erskine's day, becoming pigeon-holed in one or another academic compartment. The discussion method rejected the idea that all learning should be presented in lectures, as specialized subjects taught by authoritative scholars to receptive—but largely passive—students. This latter method had become almost universal with the eclipse of classical education, but Erskine and his followers led a counter-revolution in American education to reassert the kind of intimate, personal engagement of teachers and students which has become increasingly recognized as a necessary antidote to the impersonality and passive ingestion so typical of large lecture classes.

Lionel Trilling once observed that the transition at Columbia from the old-style classical education for gentlemen of the Hudson Valley to the new liberal education was accompanied by a demographic shift toward the assimilation of bright young members of New York's immigrant populations—especially Jewish, Irish, and Italian—into the educated class. Trilling did not himself mention it, so far as I know, but the recently published memoirs of Diana Trilling suggest to me that there was in this process a strong admixture of New York Jewish intellectuality with its legacy of Talmudic discourse from the ghettoes of Europe. In any case that intense speculative and probing mode of discourse could well, it seems to me, have entered into the Great Conversation over the Great Books at this particular time in our cultural history. Subject to Dr. Adler's correction, I shall continue in this belief for more anecdotal reasons than it is appropriate to recite here, where one is supposed to deal with the Great Books of the East rather than with the good news of the Great Books as carried by the apostles to the midwest.

What was then newly depicted as a great conversation over the ages, among the great minds and in the great writings of all time, was not the less real for having been discovered in the twentieth century by teachers and students who converted it into something quite timely and immediate. It was a learning method appropriate to the discussion of classics now no longer read as classical language texts for well-bred gentlemen, but as the new "Great Books." Later these were to be defined and literally packaged by Robert Hutchins and Mortimer Adler as the "Hundred Great Books" in fulfillment of their modern function in democratic education.

When the distinguished British classicist Gilbert Murray wrote in 1938 about liberalism in the modern world, he chose to term it "liberality" in order not to identify it solely with the "liberalism" of contemporary Whig politics but to associate it with a broader, more long-standing tradition of liberal humanism coming down from Greece and Rome. The latter he saw as having a universal mission, taking a particular form in modern times as the bearers of this honored tradition sought to share it with a larger world. In this sense they were conservatives as well as liberals, and of this combination Murray said: "The object of conservatism is to save the social order. The object of liberality is to bring that order a little nearer to what . . . the judgment of a free man—free from selfishness, free from passion, free from prejudice—would require, and by that very change to save it more effectively."[4] The classically educated gentleman and humanist was seen by Murray as the product of a leisured and in some ways privileged class, working "to extend its own privileges to wider and wider circles," aiming at "freedom of thought and discussion, and equally pursuing the free exercise of individual conscience and promotion of the common good."[5]

One could compare it perhaps, in everyday experience, to the way in which the handclasp or handshake as a form of greeting has evolved from the gesture of gentlemen in a more courtly Western age. Originally it signified openness and a meeting on equal terms of persons who shared the same aristocratic traditions of personal honor and good breeding; now it has become a nearly universal gesture of friendship and greeting shared equally among persons of almost every class, culture, social system, or ideology.

Something of that spirit, it seems to me, is to be found in the Great Books movement which arose at the same time in America, aiming to conserve as well as to extend the same humanistic tradition through new forms of liberal education. As Murray's book was being written, the faculty of Columbia College, under the leadership of distinguished teachers who had already converted Erskine's Honors course into a two-year upper college "colloquium," was transforming this program into a required general education course for freshmen, instituted under the title of Humanities A in 1937. It was an extension of the same process ten years later which led to the inauguration of a course in Oriental Humanities, dealing with what is here called the Great Books of the East.

Erskine's original idea, as he explained the Honors Course, was nothing very grand:

> The ideas underlying the course were simple. It was thought that any fairly intelligent person could read with profit any book (except, of course, highly specialized science) which had once made its way to fame among general readers. Even without the introductory study which usually precedes our acquaintance with classics in these various fields, any reader, it was thought, can discover, and enjoy the substance which has made such books remembered. It was thought, also, that a weekly discussion of the reading, such an exchange of ideas as might occur in any group which had read an interesting book, would be more illuminating than a lecture. It was thought, also, that the result of such reading and discussion over a period of two years would be a rich mass of literary information, ideas and principles, even emotions.[6]

Erskine was well aware that such a procedure challenged prevalent scholarly conceptions concerning proper methods of serious study. In the same essay quoted above, written as a preface to a reading list for the Colloquium, he argued:

> Many scholars might object to certain implications in such a reading list as this. They might think that if we read, without assistance, Homer and the Greeks, Virgil and the other Romans, Dante and the other men of the Middle Ages, we shall probably

> get a false idea of each period, and we may even misunderstand the individual book. To a certain extent this is true. Undoubtedly we get a better historical approach to anything that is old if we have the time to study its environment and its associations. But in art it is not the history of a masterpiece which makes it famous so much as qualities of permanent interest. It is precisely those qualities which we recognize first when we take up an old book without prejudice, and read it as intelligently as we can, looking for what seems to concern our times. I personally would go rather far in protest against the exclusively historical approach to literature, or any other art. . . . As a matter of fact, the literature which grows up around a famous book is often composed less because the book needs the aid of interpretation than because it has inspired admiration, and man likes to express his affection. We all write essays about our favorite authors. It is well, however, if the world reads the favorite author, and mercifully forgets the baggage with which our approval has burdened his reputation. (pp. 12–13)

Erskine's claims bespoke his confidence in the intrinsic value of the works themselves and their ability to speak directly to the individual about human life in the broadest terms. An artist and musician himself, as well as a critic, he distinguished this kind of reading from anything which would serve as an introduction to "different fields of knowledge." ". . . it is the critic," he said, "not the artist, who invents distinct fields of knowledge. In life, these fields all overlap. . . . Great books read simply and sensibly are an introduction to the whole of life; it is the completeness of their outlook which makes them great" (p. 18).

When I said above that this meant reading a great book as if it were, in a way, the Good Book, that connection was suggested by the manner in which these "Classics of the Western World" were recommended for a larger audience by the American Library Association, which published Erskine's Honors list for general use in 1927. A second edition in 1934 carried an introductory essay on

"Sharing in the Good Books" by Everett Dean Martin of the People's Institute of New York, who went so far as to distinguish this kind of reading from any kind of "popularization," "uplift enterprise," or even "education," which aimed only at utilitarian goals or social advancement. "Self-improvement is a praiseworthy aim. The pursuit of knowledge is the noblest of quests. But all depends upon the spirit with which one enters upon this adventure." These were books "to be enjoyed for their own sake," he said, part of the temple of learning of which the reader might judge for himself, on reading them, whether "when the temple is done there is 'never a door to get in to the God' " (pp. 17–18).

Yet Martin, though representing the so-called "People's Institute of New York" (at Cooper Union, where promising scholars like Adler and Barzun got their first experience of teaching to general audiences), also spoke for the old amateur ideal of gentlemanly learning against the increasing specialization of scholarship and its technical, analytic method which tended to make the "good books" less naturally enjoyable and meaningful.

> Doubtless the average reader does not turn to the masterpieces of literature because he imagines that such books were written by professionals for professional students and are not for such as he. Critics and commentators and pedantic instructors commonly give this impression of literature. They have sought to appropriate it to themselves. They have placed about it their own barricades of interpretation and have obscured it with historical and biographical irrelevancies. They have sought to reduce reading to a technique and have thus taken the joy out of it.
>
> The literature which human experience has found to be most valuable is not the output of professional educators. It is amateur and was written as a labor of love. This fact cannot be too strongly emphasized. Most of the great books of the world were written by laymen for laymen. It is important that one read such books and not be content with books about books. . . . [This] often comes as something of a revelation to people when they

> first discover that they may read the originals and form their independent judgments. The original is always more interesting. It is better reading. If one has time for only a few books, let him confine his reading to the greatest. There are many commentaries: but the book itself, the original, is something that has happened only once in human history and he who lives through the experience of reading it will never afterwards be quite the same. (pp. 19–20)

Today, more than fifty years later, one can marvel at the ease with which Martin separates the layman from the professional, while deploring the substitution of vulgar popularization by second-rate scholars for direct access to the great minds of the past. He does not equate "lay" with "popular" but conceives of the layman rather as the true spiritual heir of the great humanists. Striking too is the ease with which he speaks of reading his "good books" in the "original," though this could only have been in translation. He is hardly mindful, it seems, of what "original" had meant a few decades earlier to the defenders of reading the classics in the original language. That battle was now over, and the "good books" in translation had emerged victorious. Martin, no less than the apostles of the "great books," could testify himself to a vital truth of his own and others' experience as readers and teachers—the natural stimulation and exhilaration of mind that came from making contact with the great minds of the past and being powerfully challenged by them—even in translation.

Parenthetically, if I may return momentarily to the Confucian tradition, this view was shared by the great Neo-Confucian teachers, like Chu Hsi and Wang Yang-ming, who kept insisting on the importance of the individual's making his first reading a direct contact with the classics in the original text. For this to be done, of course, required that some kind of gloss accompany it, and Chu Hsi, digesting and refining earlier commentaries, provided a concise new one for this purpose. Yet it is significant that he too, while recognizing the need for this kind of "translation" into the current idiom, insisted on everyone's confronting the original by himself. No doubt this reflected the persistence of an earlier oral tradition, which almost everywhere in Asia saw memorization and recitation of the text as the way to achieve a personal appropriation of the classics or scriptures. Ironically, in modern times it was this traditional practice of memorization and recitation, this making of the classic a part of oneself, which struck uninformed Western observers as mere rote-learning—a meaningless process that could not but be stultifying for the individual.

Meanwhile as this traditional reading practice was being attacked in China, a modernized version of Chu Hsi's approach to personal appropriation of the classics was being recreated in New York. No doubt, in Everett Dean Martin's case, this phenomenon exhibited the perennial truth that "each generation chooses its own ancestors," asserting its own independence by reaching back to the classics over the heads of its immediate predecessors. Yet, at Columbia there proved to be more to it than that. A generation later, when the Humanities A course was subjected to reexamination, its position remained secure. A blue-ribbon committee chaired by the historian Fritz Stern was asked to undertake a thoroughgoing critique of the "great books" course, simply as a matter of curriculum review. This was 1967–68, a time when endemic student protest might well have been thought a spur to change. In fact, however, the Stern Committee could find no signs of dissatisfaction with the course among either students or staff, and even when it proposed the most modest revisions, the committee's suggestions were met with almost total rejection. No other required course in living memory has enjoyed such powerful, perennial support from students, faculty, and alumni. Obviously the experience spoken of by Erskine and Martin was not a momentary enthusiasm.

In Erskine's day, and for some time thereafter, the term "great books" was not well-established at Columbia, and the further idea of a "Hundred Great Books" must have been a special revelation from on high to Drs. Adler or Hutchins later. Erskine himself disavowed any claim to having defined, in his list, any fixed number of such classics. In the direct successor to the Honors course, known in the thirties as "The Colloquium on Important Books," the works read were referred to as classics, important books, or major works, but only occasionally as "great books." Even Mark Van Doren made sparing reference to the term in his *Liberal Education*, published in 1943, and not often enough for it to gain entry in the index to the book.

The terminological issue is not itself important, but a syllabus for the Colloquium prepared in 1934 by J. B. Brebner (representing a stellar staff that included Mortimer Adler, Jacques Barzun, Irwin Edman, Moses Hadas, Richard McKeon, Lionel Trilling, Rexford Guy Tugwell, Mark Van Doren, and Raymond Weaver, among other distinguished scholars and teachers) was entitled "Classics of the Western World." More significant than the word "classics" is the fact that even prior to the establishment of the required Humanities A, its advocates and collaborators were conscious of the parochial limits of the Columbia program at that time. I can testify myself to the feeling among prominent leaders of the College faculty in the late thirties that something needed to be done about expanding the horizons of the general education program, including both the older Contemporary Civilization course and Humanities A, so as to bring Asia into the picture. Perhaps the most significant aspect of this progressive ferment was that it arose among scholars and teachers who had no professional interest in Orientalism, but only the kind of intellectual breadth and educational zeal that Gilbert Murray would have appreciated as liberal.

It is true that what Murray saw as the world mission of liberal humanism could appear to others as only cultural imperialism in Sunday dress. In this view classical Orientalism too would be seen, not as progressive scholarship, but only as the intellectual vanguard of the Western assault on other cultures. Yet in actual fact, as matters stood at Columbia in those times, classical Orientalism was in serious decline, if not almost defunct. It had no articulate spokesmen among the College faculty, and since its fortunes had been closely tied to biblical studies, Semitic languages, and the old language requirements, it had few vested interests left to defend or assert once the new liberal education had taken over.

The advocates of the new Oriental Studies program were amateur types, liberal-minded gentlemen who took education, and not just their own scholarly research, seriously. Typical of them were Van Doren himself, his colleague Raymond Weaver, an authority on Herman Melville with a deep appreciation also of Japanese literature; Burdette Kinne, an instructor in French with a passion for everything Chinese; Harry J. Carman, a professor of American History and New York State dirt farmer who wanted to see Asian civilizations brought into the Contemporary Civilization program.

When the first Oriental Humanities course was set up in 1947, about as soon after World War II as one could have mounted such a venture, the lead was taken in this experimental course by such scholars as Moses Hadas, the Greek classicist; Herbert Deane, a political scientist specializing in Harold Laski and St. Augustine; James Gutmann in German philosophy; and Charles Frankel, the philosopher of Western liberalism. Naturally enough, on putting together the reading list for their first Oriental Colloquium (as it was initially called) Deane and Hadas consulted specialists on the Columbia faculty more learned than themselves in the several traditions to be included within the scope of the course. From the start, however, the reading and discussion of the Oriental classics were to be guided by the principles of the earlier Honors course, as stated by Erskine above, and not by the kind of textual study which had long dominated the classical Orientalism of the nineteenth and early twentieth centuries.

The course's distinctive character arose in large measure from the fact that it was conceived as part of a liberal education (later to be called by some "general education"), and was designed to supplement a core curriculum already set in place for the first two undergraduate years. In this program priority had already been given to the study of Western Civilization and the "classics of the Western World" (as the Erskine/Brebner syllabus put it). This is a fact I cite, not to raise the issue of cultural bounds or to question the established educational priorities—which would take us beyond our purpose here—but simply as a historical given in this case (and obviously a given also for the Great Books program). In practice our experience has shown this sequence to entail no disadvantage, since students have come to the new course as a natural next stage in their general education—already familiar with the ground rules of the reading-discussion method, and prepared to take an active part in a discourse well underway. It did mean, however, that the choice of Oriental classics would, in turn, be governed by the same high degree of selectivity as in the Western case and yet further still, by the need to exercise this selectivity in respect to several major Asian traditions at once—indeed all that might be included in the so-called "non-Western" world. In other words, it demanded a rare combination of both breadth and selectivity, much in contrast to the kind of specialized study traditional Orientalism had favored; it went beyond even what advocates of the Hundred Great Books—for all their high standards of selectivity—would have suspected was necessary.

Exercising this selectivity in the multi-cultural East was far more difficult than it had been within the bounds of the more unified Western tradition. There was an added complication in that, though the "East" had something like "great books," it had nothing like the Great Books of the East. The latter is a Western idea, both in seeing the East as one, and in imagining that there had been a common tradition shared by the peoples of this "East." Each of the major Asian traditions tended to see itself as the center of the civilized world and to look inward—spiritually and culturally—toward that center rather than outward on the world or on each other. The famous "Sacred Books of the East," as published at Oxford, was a Western invention. It sprang from the minds of nineteenth-century scholars in Europe as their intellectual horizons reached out with the West's expansion into Asia. "Asia," a geographical designation, represented no common culture or moral bond among the peoples of that continent until, in modern times, a new unity was found in their common reaction to that same expansionism.

There being no common tradition in Asia to define the Great Books of the East, a reading list had to be constructed synthetically out of largely separate and discreet traditions—a construction made all the more difficult and delicate, in the absence of any Eastern canon, by the risk that the very process of its devising might be contaminated by Western preconceptions. Instead therefore of searching for "Eastern" equivalents of Western classics, we were looking for what each of the several Asian traditions honored themselves as an essential part of their own heritage.

Seemingly the least problematical way of doing this was to identify the scriptures or classics already well-known within the distinct ethico-religious traditions of Islam, Hinduism, Buddhism, Confucianism, Taoism, etc. Similarly one could find recognized classics of the literary and intellectual traditions, though these might or might not run parallel to the religious traditions. This method, proceeding inductively from the testimony of Asians themselves rather than deductively from some Western definition of a classic norm or form, has produced what might appear to be an odd assortment of genres. Great poetry exists in each of the major traditions, though it varies considerably in form. Epics can be found in Iran and India that bear comparison to the *Odyssey, Iliad,* and *Aeneid,* but there is nothing like them in China and Japan. The same is true in reverse of the haiku or Nō drama, classic forms in Japan, but found nowhere else. Histories as monumental in their own way as Herodotus and Thucydides have been produced in the Islamic world by Ibn Khaldūn and in China by Ssu-ma Ch'ien but by no one in traditional India or Japan. Perhaps the greatest diversity, however, is exhibited among the religious scriptures, some of which can barely be regarded as "texts" in any ordinary sense of the term (for instance, although the Platform Sutra of the Sixth Ch'an Patriarch is presented in one sense as authoritative scripture, in another sense it points to an abjuration of all scripture). For the purposes of our reading program, however, all this variety has had to be taken in, and more than that, welcomed, as a healthy challenge to Western conventions of discursive and literary form, if there were to be any real dialogue with the multiform East.

Other problems of selection arise from the choice of four major traditions to represent the "East." The four we have identified—the Islamic world, India, China, and Japan—betray a lack of geographic and cultural congruence among themselves. The Islamic world, which covers almost half of Asia and North Africa as well, includes Iran, with its own language, civilization, and indigenous religious traditions (Zoroastrianism and Manichaeism). Our "coverage" of India includes Buddhism as well as Brahmanism and Hinduism, and in China and Japan, Buddhism as well as Confucianism and Taoism. Thus religion cuts across cultures, while it may also provide the underlying continuity in a given culture. For the most part, however, it is in literature that each tradition best reveals its distinguishing features and basic continuity. Hence each has had to be represented by enough classic examples to show both the unity and diversity of the traditions, and to demonstrate how the great religions have assumed a different coloration in each historical and cultural setting, while also revealing the distinctive aesthetic and intellectual qualities of the tradition.

If for instance the case for Islam, and our understanding of the Qur'ān, depend heavily on how one views the distinctive claims made for it as prophecy and for Muhammad as the "seal of the prophets," the significance of that claim cannot be judged from a reading of the Qur'ān alone, without seeing how the matter is dealt with later by Al-Ghazālī in relation to Greek philosophy and Sufi mysticism, or by Ibn Khaldūn in relation to the patterns of human history. The contrasting claim of Hinduism that it transcends any such particular revelation and can accommodate all other religions, may be difficult to evaluate except in some relation to Islam or to the Mahāyāna Buddhist philosophy that Śankara is variously said to have refuted and assimilated into the Vedānta.

These religions or teachings, as represented by the texts we read, may not always have acknowledged each other openly, but if we know or even suspect that there was indeed an unspoken encounter among them, some reconnaissance of the alternative positions is requisite to an understanding of any one of them. By this I mean, to be more specific, that one cannot enter into any serious encounter with the early Buddhist sutras unless one has read the Upanishads, nor can one later come to grips with Śankara if one knows nothing of the major Mahāyāna texts. Likewise, in China, while it is obviously unthinkable that one would take up such major Confucian thinkers as Mencius and Hsün Tzu without first having read the *Analects* of Confucius, it would be no less an error to do so without reference to Lao Tzu and Chuang Tzu.

In China, though the inception of the Confucian tradition is most directly accessible through the *Analects,* if one stopped there and went no further into any of the later Confucian thinkers, one would get only an archaic, fossilized view of Confucianism. Only by going on to the Neo-Confucians Chu Hsi and Wang Yang-ming can one begin to appreciate how the classic teachings underwent further development in response to the challenge of Buddhism and Taoism. In the West it would be like reading the Old Testament without the New, or the latter without St. Augustine, St. Thomas, or Dante. Yet it can equally well be argued that the encounter among the so-called "Three Teachings" in China is even more vividly brought to life in such great Chinese novels as the *Journey to the West* and the *Dream of the Red Chamber* (or, in C. T. Hsia's rendering, *A Dream of Red Mansions*). Thus reading classic fiction can give access to the dialogue in China on levels not reachable through the classical and neo-classical philosophers.

The same—and more—can be said for Japanese literature as a revelation of Buddhism's encounter with the native tradition. Often that tradition is identified with Shinto, but as there were no written texts or scriptures antedating the introduction of the Chinese script, the best one can do is look to the earliest literature in Japanese—such works as the *Manyōshū*, the *Tale of Genji,* and the *Pillow Book,* to name only a few of the finest examples—if one wishes to get, in the absence of open doctrinal debate, a more intimate glimpse of what is going on in the Japanese mind and heart behind the outward show of polite professions. This indeed is where the real struggle has taken place among the deep-seated aesthetic preferences and emotional inclinations of the Japanese as they strove to assimilate the more ascetic or moralistic doctrines imported from the continent. There too one may get a sense of the cultural situation into which Zen Buddhism was later introduced, and judge from the outcome how much of contemporary Zen is actually Japanese or Chinese rather than Buddhist.

Thus unless other guests are invited, there will be no party for us to join—no way to renew the conversation with any of the great works or thinkers of the past without having others present who had engaged in the original dialogue. How long the list of participants may become is always a matter for local discretion, but in no case can just one or two works generate a real conversation. In the silence of Zen there may be such a thing as one hand clapping, but in the discourse we are entering into there is no book that speaks just to itself.

In this way, working through the natural, original associations among the recognized classics of the Asian traditions, one arrives, by the inductive process I referred to above, at a provisional set of the Asian classics or Great Books of the East. Admittedly a modern creation, it is put together from materials quite authentic to one or another of the Asian traditions. The linkages so identified within and among these traditions, though often obscured or suppressed in the past by cultural isolationism and national or religious chauvinisms, are nonetheless real and meaningful. According to this understanding, "The East" is no mere fabrication, made to serve as a foil for the West. Rather it is an East that has emerged in its true reflected colors only since it came to be observed in a modern light.

Rabindranath Tagore, the charismatic cosmopolitan from Calcutta who thought of himself above all as a citizen of the world, was perhaps the first to appreciate this. In his new perception of the "East," brilliantly articulated in an essay on "The Eastern University" but only incompletely realized in his Visva Bharati University at Santiniketan, he saw the need for a multi-cultural curriculum in which the several Asian traditions would complement one another, high-lighting each other's distinctive features in a way no solitary exposure could do.

Regrettably the direction of modern education, whether in India or elsewhere in Asia, has taken a different turn, emphasizing technical learning and specialized training at the expense of any kind of humanistic education, Eastern or Western. In this situation, as in our own, the humanities are taught as discrete disciplines and each national tradition is a separate subject of specialization, a field in which to practice the new humanities technologies. The usual result of this process is that nothing can be seen whole and every great work is subjected by analysis to unmitigated trivialization. In most Asian universities today it is only the student majoring, say, in Sanskrit, Chinese, or Japanese studies, who learns anything of the classics of his own tradition beyond the high school level, and even then it will most likely be to specialize in a single text.

Against this pessimistic estimate of the present situation, a more positive view may be offered that microscopic studies of this kind are the necessary building blocks for the construction tomorrow of a macroscopic, global edifice of human civilization. Yet this conclusion itself leads to the further question, why if nothing less than a total world view is envisaged, should one be trying to establish an intermediate position through the Oriental Humanities, as if to promote a regionalized view of the Asian traditions? Given the present trend toward world history or world literature courses, it might seem perverse—and probably unavailing—to resist the piecemeal incorporation into them of Asian materials. Recognizing too the impacted state of the college curriculum, and the difficulty of finding any time at all in it for Asia, can one afford to pass up whatever opportunities do present themselves for the inclusion of Asia in the core, even though on less than ideal terms? Depending on local circumstances, the answer may well be, perhaps not.

Yet even while conceding this much to present realities, I would still argue the need to make a place, at some point in the curriculum, for a course which includes the Asian classics in something of their traditional setting, rather than, as above, completely out of context. My ground for so arguing is the same need to face squarely the implications of the global view already projected. To me this requires, not necessarily that an equal priority be given to Asia and the West, but only that there should be some parity of treatment for them in the overall program. To understand why I make this distinction between priority and parity, however, it may be well to step back a bit and look at some basic premises.

In the study of other cultures or civilizations some degree of self-understanding is prerequisite to an understanding of others, and similarly an understanding of one's own situation or one's own past, may be accepted as a precondition for understanding another's. Our experience with the Oriental Humanities at Columbia, shows how much deeper and more meaningful the new learning experience can be for those who have first come to an appreciation —or even just a keener awareness—of their own tradition. The same principle, I would readily concede, applies in reverse to the Asians' understanding of the West, which may be just as advantaged or handicapped, depending upon how well they have come to know their own culture. Those who have been deprived by an almost total uprooting from their own cultural traditions, as in China during the long blight of the Maoist era and especially during the Cultural Revolution, may be no less disadvantaged in understanding the West for all the hunger to learn from it which they now show. Not to come to terms with one's past, or in some degree to master one's own tradition, is to remain a hostage to it, even though unconsciously so, and thus not to become fully master of oneself. In such a condition, being unable to take responsibility for oneself and one's own past, one is in a poor position to become truly responsive to others'.

All this may verge on rhetorical overkill, but to me such considerations are bound to enter into what I have referred to above as "parity of treatment." If one can appreciate what it would mean for the Great Books of the Western World to be represented only by Plato's *Republic* or the Book of Job—a meaningless question for anyone who had not read considerably more of the Great Books than that—one can begin to appreciate why a reading of the *Analects* alone might not do sufficient justice to the Confucian tradition; why the *Dhammapada* by itself would be inadequate to represent Buddhism; and why one would face an impossible dilemma if one had to choose between the *Dream of the Red Chamber* and the *Tale of Genji*, Śakuntalā or the Nō drama, the *Rāmāyaṇa* or Tu Fu, as candidates for infiltration into a humanities sequence or world literature course otherwise based on the Western tradition. If the selectivity which is always a prime factor in the design of core curricula or general education programs should be taken to rule out more than token representation for the East, and if to include the *Analects* (or as some generous souls even proposed twenty years ago, Mao Tse-tung) would mean dropping Aristotle, Thomas Aquinas, Dante, John Locke, or Immanuel Kant from the list, one must wonder whether the result would do justice to either East or West.

Even while putting the question this way, I do not rule out the possibility of accepting such unpalatable choices if only to serve the educational purpose of getting an East-West dialogue started. It all depends on knowing where you want to go and how, by what stages and means, you hope to get there. For this it is important to recognize that the risks of distortion or misrepresentation are great. If one knows how painfully abbreviated is even the usual one- or two-year sequence in the Western humanities, or how deficient the student's familiarity often is with the great works of his own tradition, one will not rush to a solution that only compounds the difficulty.

Whatever is to be done, it seems to me, should be governed by two considerations. The first is that the reading and understanding of a text should work, as much as possible, from the inside out rather than from the outside in. Granted that we are indeed outsiders looking in, we must make the effort to put ourselves in the position or situation of the author and his audience. This means that no reading of an Eastern text should be undertaken which is so removed from its original context as to be discussable only in direct juxtaposition to something Western. Such a reading leads almost inevitably to one-sided comparisons, and does not serve genuine dialogue. Party to this new dialogue must be enough of the original discourse (i.e., writings presenting alternative or contrasting views) so that the issues can be defined in their own terms and not simply in opposition to, or agreement with, the West. If a world literature course or humanities program can include enough works of the original tradition to meet this test, the risks run may be worth taking.

Since the inclusion of more than a few such works will put a strain on any reading program that is part of an already-crowded core curriculum, a second set of considerations will likely come into play: how can a total learning process be conceived which makes the best use of scarce resources (deployment of instructional staff, provision of texts and teaching materials), and above all of the student's time, to provide a properly balanced and truly global program?

Most persons who face this question will be teachers and administrators in colleges and universities, but I do not mean to limit the discussion to academics. The need for global education is widely felt and cannot be met simply within the framework of the college curriculum. Granted that the undergraduate years are where the process should start, it is neither reasonable nor realistic to suppose that an adequate liberal or general education can be compressed simply within the typical four-year college program. I have long believed that there is a need for core curricula even in graduate schools, and this for more reasons than just to provide remedial instruction in matters neglected by many colleges (including the Asian humanities, and much else that is antecedent to civilization). But this is not the place to argue the point, and whatever might be undertaken in graduate schools would still not do the whole job.

The Great Books program, however—or some version of it—does seem to me a possible vehicle for introducing the Asian humanities to the West, preferably a program starting in college but in any case extending into adult or continuing education. To my knowledge, the Great Books program was the first to recognize that the gaining of a liberal education would need to be a life-long learning process, and it was also the first to develop a practical format and procedure for its realization, including the three most essential components: appropriate texts, a discussion method, and a suitable guide. From my own experience in conducting seminars and colloquia for many different age and occupational groups, I can also say that, for the Great Books of the East too, this is a well-tested, workable method.

Two qualifications and some amendments may be called for. The first is that the Hundred Great Ideas should be reexamined in the course of incorporating Asian materials into the Great Books program. Reviewing the list now I note some so-called "great ideas" that would seem strange to the Asian traditions. This is not to deny that they pose valid *questions* for us to ask of any body of literature, since even the failure to mention them can be significant. It is to suggest, rather, that reading the great books of Asia, one would not necessarily come upon some of the ideas so listed as of perennial, universal human concern, or as issues one would inescapably encounter in the traditional discourse. Examples of this type are "Constitution," "Evolution," "Liberty," and "Progress"—obviously fairly recent ideas even in the West.

On the other hand—and this is the second qualification—one does encounter ideas of great prominence or issues of deep concern in more than one of the Asian traditions that fail to appear in the present list. A few of them are: Action, Enlightenment, Emptiness, Heart (as well as Mind), Intuition, Mysticism, Nothingness, Public and Private, Revelation, Ritual, Sacrifice, the Sage, the Self or Person, Spirituality, Structure and Process, etc.—not to mention Great Books-Classics-Scriptures again. I realize that these are all arguable points. Most of them could be taken up under the heading of one or another of the existing Great Ideas. "Revelation" or "Spirituality," for instance, might well be discussed in connection with either "Religion" or "Theology." I would suggest however that in Asian traditions not necessarily theistic or theological in character, the nature of Revelation or Spirituality might prove to be a question of broader significance than, say, Theology. "Prophecy" does appear on the list of One Hundred Great Ideas, and it is a question which may usefully be raised even in such non- or only quasi-theistic traditions as Confucianism, but it by no means exhausts the possibilities for Revelation. "Mysticism" could also be discussed under the heading of "Experience" (already on the list), but it is a category so important in Oriental religions generally as to warrant separate consideration. Meanwhile "Experience" itself remains a viable subject of discussion, especially in East Asia, even apart from mysticism.

"Self" or "Person" is another in the category of ideas that could be discussed under one of the existing headings (in this case the Individual), but the centrality of the question of the Self in South and East Asia—in Hinduism, Buddhism, and Confucianism—and the depth to which it was pursued, go beyond the concept of the Individual, important though that has been, in the modern West. Indeed, from an Oriental perspective, the individual would probably be viewed only as one aspect or subheading of Self.

"Authority" is still another arguable case. The nature of authority becomes an almost inescapable issue when one is considering alternative traditions, sources of values, revelation, etc., let alone the specifically political aspects of the matter. It is not included here in my supplementary list because, in formulating the latter, I have tried to keep for the most part to terms for which one can find an equivalent explicitly discussed in the several traditions themselves. This, however, does not seem to have been the case with "Authority," which is often simply taken for granted in the East, no less than in the West.

However these may be, my supplementary list of Great Ideas is meant only to be suggestive, not exhaustive or definitive. In proposing it, I have in mind that if the Hundred Great Ideas be thought a useful device for focusing discussion of the Hundred Great Books, then when one comes to the point of expanding that list to include the Great Books of the East, one should consider reviewing and expanding somewhat the list of Great Ideas. The result of such a reconsideration I am willing to predict, would generally be to confirm the applicability or universality of most of the terms already identified, but the educational benefits of reopening the question and exploring it in new contexts would seem to me to be substantial.

Having come to this point it may be in order for me to suggest what are the Great Books I would consider essential to a basic reading program—a list that could be defined as what might be appropriate for an introductory, one-year course. A more generous selection is found in *A Guide to Oriental Classics*,[7] which gives the teacher or discussion leader more to choose from in meeting the needs of particular groups or to draw upon for a somewhat more leisurely reading and less pressured learning situation. In this light what I propose here is not necessarily ideal, nor on the other hand does it represent the bare minimum, but rather something more like a Mean. As an introduction to the major Asian traditions, one could hope that it would not misrepresent them, but rather provide enough pleasure in the reading and enough stimulus for discussion that most participants would emerge from the experience with an appetite for more, as well as the wherewithal to pursue its satisfaction.

Here then is my list, with a brief comment on each work for the benefit of those to whom the titles alone might be meaningless: (The titles in the original language of those translated here may be found in the corresponding section of the *Guide* referred to in note 7.)

THE ISLAMIC TRADITION

The Qur'ān: a book of revelation that, because of the unique claims made for it, almost defies reading as a "great book," but is nonetheless indispensable to all reading in the later tradition.

The *Assemblies* of Al Ḥarīrī (1054–1122): a major work of classical Arabic literature which illustrates in an engaging way some of the tensions between piety and civilization, the desert and the city in Islamic culture.

The *Deliverance from Error* of Al-Ghazālī (1058–1111): a very personal statement, by perhaps the greatest of the Islamic theologians, concerning the relation of mystical experience to theology and the rational sciences.

The poems of Rūmī (1207–1273): chosen as the most representative of the Sufi poets.

The *Conference of the Birds* by ʿAṭṭār (c. 1141–1220): a symposium on the stages of religious experience in the contemplative ascent to union with God.

The *Prolegomena [to World History]* of Ibn Khaldūn (1332–1406): often called the world's first "social scientist" (a subject of useful discussion in itself). Ibn Khaldūn's encyclopedic discourse on the historical factors in the rise and fall of civilizations is already a classic among modern world historians.

(Options not selected above but obvious candidates for inclusion in a more ample listing: The seven Odes of pre-Islamic poetry; the *Thousand and One Nights;* other Arab philosophers like Averroes and Ibn Arabi; other Sufi poets like Ḥāfiẓ, etc.)

THE INDIAN TRADITION

Hymns from the *Ṛg Veda*—bedrock of the Hindu tradition.

The *Upanishads:* classic discourses which laid the foundation for Hindu religious and philosophical speculation.

The Bhagavad Gītā: major work of religious and philosophical synthesis and basic scripture of Hindu devotionalism.

The Rāmāyaṇa of Vālmīki (c. 200 B.C.): The earlier of the two great Indian epics and the best known in Indian art and legendry. Exemplifies the fundamental values and tensions in the classical Indian tradition.

Basic texts of Theravāda Buddhism: No one text represents a complete statement of Buddhism, but the Dhammapada, Mahāsatipaṭṭhana Sutta, Milindapañha, and Mahāparinibbana Suttānta come closest perhaps to "basic discourses."

Scriptures of Indian Mahāyāna Buddhism: Again no one work suffices, but the Prajñapāramitā texts (especially the Heart Sutra), the works of Nāgārjuna and Śāntideva and the Vimalakīrti Sutra all represent basic statements.

The *Śakuntalā:* Major work of Kālidāsa (c. A.D. 400), the greatest of Indian dramatists and arguably the greatest in Asia.

The Vedānta Sūtra with Commentary of Śaṅkarācārya (c. 780–820): generally regarded as the leading Indian philosopher, representing the dominant non-dualistic school of the Vedānta.

The *Gītagovinda* of Jayadeva (c. A.D. 12th c.): great religious poem in Sanskrit and major work of medieval devotionalism.

Rabindranath Tagore and Mohandas Gandhi: two contrasting views of the Indian tradition in its encounter with the West. (These are the only modern writers on our list, but Tagore's poems and plays and Gandhi's so-called *Autobiography,* though admittedly not "classics," have been perennial favorites for the way they juxtapose aspects of Indian tradition in response to the challenges of the West.)

(Major options not availed of above: the epic Mahābhārata; the Yoga sutras of Patañjali; Kautilya's *Artha Śāstra,* a guide to politics; the *Little Clay Cart* of King Śudraka (c. A.D. 400), a most entertaining domestic drama; the famous collection of fables in the *Pañcatantra;* Bhartrihari's verses on worldly life, passion, and renunciation; Rāmānuja, a rival to Śankara in religious philosophy, etc., as described in the *Guide,* n. 7.)

THE CHINESE TRADITION

The Analects of Confucius (551–479 B.C.): the best single source for the ideas of Confucius.

Mo Tzu or Mo Ti: A sharp critic of Confucianism in the 5th c. B.C. and a major alternative voice in politics and religion.

Lao Tzu: a basic text of Taoism which has become a world classic because of its radical challenge to the underlying assumptions of both traditional and modern civilizations.

Chuang Tzu: delightful speculative ramblings and philosophical parodies by a Taoist writer of the late 4th, early 3d c. B.C.

Mencius (372–289 B.C.): a thinker second in importance only to Confucius in that school, who addressed a broad range of practical and philosophical problems.

Hsün Tzu (3d c. B.C.): the third great statement of the Confucian teaching, with special attention to the basis of learning and rites.

Han Fei Tzu (3d c. B.C.): the fullest theoretical statement and synthesis of the ancient Legalist school, a major influence on the Chinese political tradition.

Records of the Historian by Ssu-ma Ch'ien (c. 145–90 B.C.): a monumental history of early China, notable for its combination of chronicles, topical treatises, and biographical accounts.

The Lotus Sutra: by far the most important text of Chinese Mahāyāna Buddhism, influential throughout East Asia.

The Platform Sutra: an original Chinese work and early statement of Ch'an (Zen) thought, which assumed the status of both classic and scripture because of its unique claim to religious enlightenment.

T'ang poetry: selections from the great poets of the T'ang dynasty, generally viewed as the classic age of Chinese verse.

Chu Hsi (1130–1200): leading exponent and synthesizer of Neo-Confucianism, which became the dominant teaching in later centuries and spread throughout East Asia.

Wang Yang-ming (1472–1529): principal Neo-Confucian thinker of the Ming period, who modified Chu Hsi's philosophy most particularly in respect to the nature and importance of learning (especially the role of moral intuition vs. cognitive learning).

The Journey to the West attributed to Wu Ch'eng-en (c. 1506–1581): a fantastic fictional account of the historic pilgrimage to India of the Buddhist monk Hsüan-tsang.

The Dream of the Red Chamber (or *The Dream of Red Mansions*) by Ts'ao Hsüeh-ch'in (d. 1763): An 18th c. realistic-allegorical novel of the decline of a great family and its young heir's involvement in the world of passion and depravity.

(Other options within the Chinese tradition are such Buddhist texts as *The Awakening of Faith*, the *Śurangama Sutra*, and if it has not been read as a work of the Indian tradition, the Vimilakīrti Sutra; and other major novels like the *Water Margin (All Men are Brothers); Golden Lotus*, and the *Scholars (Ju-lin wai-shih.)*

THE JAPANESE TRADITION

Here it is worthy of special note that women are prominent as authors of the earlier classic works and as dominant figures in many of the later works of drama and fiction.

Manyōshū: the earliest anthology of Japanese poetry (8th century and before).

The Tale of Genji by Murasaki Shikibu (978–1015?): the world's first great novel, about court life in Heian period Japan and the loves of Prince Genji.

The Pillow Book of Sei Shōnagon (A.D. late 10th-early 11 c.): Observations on life, religion, aesthetic sensibility, and taste in Heian Japan.

"An Account of My Hut" by Kamo no Chōmei (1153–1236): a kind of Japanese Thoreau, meditating on the vicissitudes of the world, the beauties of nature, and the satisfactions of the simple life—but at the farthest remove from Thoreau's civil disobedience.

Essays in Idleness by Yoshida no Kenkō (1283–1350): observations on life, society, nature, and art by a worldly monk and classic literary stylist, in journal form.

Nō plays: the classic drama, distinctive to Japan, but now much admired in the West as well. Preferably to be seen and heard as well as read.

The novels of Ihara Saikaku (1642–93): fictional writings in a poetic style, expressive of the new culture of the townspeople in 17th c. Japan.

The poetry of Matsuo Bashō (1644–94): Poetry and prose by the master of the *haiku* and one of the greatest of all Japanese poets.

The plays of Chikamatsu (1653–1725): works written for the puppet theater by Japan's leading dramatist, focusing on conflicts between love and duty.

(Alternative selections: Religious writings of the eminent Japanese monks Kūkai, Dōgen, and Hakuin, while important in the history of Japanese religion, were difficult even for the Japanese to understand and, though respected, did not have a wide readership. The more widely read literary and dramatic works were probably also more expressive of the actual religious sentiments of the Japanese, as well as of their literary preferences. These might include, in addition to the above, the major poetry anthologies *Kokinshū* and *Shinkokinshū*, the war tale *The Tale of the Heike*, and the eighteenth century drama Chūshingura.)

The foregoing lists give, I hope, a fair representation of the different preferences and shared values among the great traditions of Asia. They include works that have withstood the tests of time not only in their own traditions but in nearly forty years of reading and discussion with American students of all ages. The optional or alternative readings have been tried from time to time but, for a variety of reasons, have not always worked well. It should be pointed out that not everything on the list has been assigned in its entirety. This is especially true of the long epics and novels. We make concessions to what works in practice and accept compromises for the sake of getting the best overall mix.

The availability of adequate translations has also been a factor in our decisions, especially in the early days of the program, but it has become less of a problem as more good translations have been produced in recent years of a kind suited to our need, i.e., in a form accessible to students. If earlier it was said that one test of a great book is how well it survives translation, now the test might well be restated as the great book's ability not only to survive one translation but also to attract, withstand, and outlast several others.

Today, with more than one translation available of a given work, the layman naturally wants the scholar's recommendation as to which is best. Not only laymen but even some scholars still have a touching faith in the idea that there is one "authoritative" or "definitive" translation of a work. In truth it is possible for scholars of equal technical competence to produce translations of almost equal merit, each bringing out different meanings and nuances of the original. Burton Watson and A. C. Graham have each written excellent translations of the *Chuang Tzu;* neither, I suspect, would claim his own was perfect, but Watson's may appeal more to those whose interests and tastes are literary, and Graham's to the more philosophical. Interpretations like Thomas Merton's of the *Chuang Tzu* also have their place, but should be understood for what they are and not regarded as translations. It is also possible for non-professionals like Ezra Pound, Witter Bynner, or Lin Yutang sometimes to capture the meaning of certain passages in Chinese works and render them in vivid English that is less literal than the sinologue would like but more meaningful or moving to the reader.

Our practice is to recommend at least one preferred translation (if only for the sake of having a common basis for discussion), but to urge students, wherever possible, to read more than one rendering and arrive at their own sense of where the common denominator among them may lie. In this process of triangulation—getting a bearing or fix on a text from several translators' different angles of vision—the reader has his own proper judgmental part to play, bringing his or her own learning and experience to bear on the assessment of what the original might mean. If so used, translations need not stand in the way of the reader having some active, personal encounter with the text, which the great thinkers and teachers have so often called for.

Further to assist the reader in knowing what to look for in these books, I have asked colleagues knowledgeable in the several traditions to write brief essays on what they perceive to be the most essential values in the works they know well or most enjoy. Among these guest essayists are several distinguished scholars who have themselves contributed substantially to making the great books available in translation. In responding to this opportunity they have, in several cases, chosen to write about works somewhat less well known in the West than those already highly acclaimed.

In conclusion I should like to make one further point concerning the importance of reading the "Great Books of the East." The basic criterion for recognizing them as classics has been that they were first so admired in their own tradition. In quite a few cases this admiration spread to other countries and these works came to be regarded as either scriptures or great books outside their own homeland. Further, after substantial contact was made by the West with Asia in the sixteenth and seventeenth centuries, many of these works came to be translated and admired in the West as well. Some of the exotic appeal of the unknown and "mysterious" East may still attach to them and they can still be called "Great Books of the East" in the sense of their being "from" the East, but for at least two centuries they have been essential reading for many of the best minds in the West—philosophers, historians, poets, playwrights, and indeed major writers in almost every field of thought and scholarship. Thus one whose education does not include a reading of the Asian classics or Great Books of the East today is a stranger not only to Asia but to much of the best that has been thought and written in the modern West. While not perhaps to be called "Great Books of the West," many of these works and their authors have already entered the mainstream of the conversation that is going on in the West today. As that conversation is broadened to include a fairer representation of the Asian traditions, bringing out the implicit dialogue within and among them, it could indeed become a Great Conversation for all the world.

ENDNOTES

I wish to express my indebtedness to Jacques Barzun and the late Lionel Trilling for background information contained in the introductory portions of this essay, based on earlier conversations with them.

1. Listed in the fly-leaf of *The Great Ideas Today*, in the 1987 issue of which portions of this essay originally appeared.

2. The Islamic tradition is no less a great tradition in much of Asia for also sharing this common ground with major religious traditions of the West. Since in practice the major works of the Islamic tradition are rarely included among the "great books" of the West, it is appropriate to recognize them here.

3. See Richard Payne, (ed., *Classics of Western Spirituality*, 60 vols. (New York: Paulist Press, 1978–); and Ewart Cousins, gen. ed., *World Spirituality: An Encyclopedic History of the Religious Quest*, 25 vols. (New York: Crossroads, 1985–).

4. Gilbert Murray, *Liberality and Civilization* (London: Allen and Unwin, 1938), pp. 46–47.

5. Ibid. pp. 30–31.

6. J. Bartlett Brebner et al., *Classics of the Western World* (Chicago: American Library Association, 1934), pp. 11–12.

7. *A Guide to Oriental Classics*, ed. Wm. Theodore de Bary and Ainslie Embree, 3d ed., Amy Heinrich, ed. (New York: Columbia University Press, 1989).

3 CLASSICS OF THE ISLAMIC TRADITION

The Qur'ān

Peter J. Awn

The Qur'ān, the sacred scripture of the estimated 900 million Muslims in the world, is one of the most influential religious documents of human history. Islamic tradition does not question the authenticity of God's earlier revelations to Moses and Jesus, enshrined in the Torah and New Testament. But Muslims believe that, in the seventh century of the common era, God chose to complete the revelatory process by communicating his final word to humanity through the Prophet Muḥammad.

Fascination with the power of sacred word pervades the great semitic traditions of Judaism, Christianity, and Islam. In the Torah, God's creative power manifests itself through word ("And God *said*, 'Let there be light'; and there was light" [Genesis 1:3]); in Christianity the creative word of God actually takes on human form in the person of Jesus Christ ("And the *Word became flesh* and dwelt among us. . . ." [John 1:14]). In the final and last of the revelations, God's word becomes book in the Qur'ān.

The world of pre-Islamic Arabia, in which Muḥammad was born around 570 C.E., located the power of sacred word primarily in the speech of poets and soothsayers, who claimed unique access to the realm of spirits and divine power. Their rhymed and cadenced utterances were believed actually to effect what they said. One can understand, therefore, the great respect, even fear, experienced by the Arabs of pre-Islamic Arabia when confronted by a satirical poet who had the power to dishonor great heroes because of the inherent power of his words. In the same way, poems of praise were said to insure immortality to warriors and tribes by preserving their exploits in the minds and hearts of future generations.

When Muḥammad began to receive revelations from God (Allāh) in the year 610 C.E., he was accused by many in the city of Mecca of being yet another poet-soothsayer. Muḥammad denied this charge vehemently, although the revelations he proclaimed were in a rhymed prose style similar to that of traditional religious practitioners. Muḥammad understood himself to be a messenger *(rasūl)* and prophet *(nabī)*, who had been chosen to be the intermediary through whom God would reveal His final word. Nevertheless, like the works of pre-Islamic poets, Muḥammad's revelations, which he received continuously from 610 C.E. until his death in 632 C.E., were preserved primarily through memorization, although some were written down. Muslim historians record that the text of the Qur'ān was not collected and codified in written form until more than twenty years after Muḥammad's death, under the caliph ʿUthmān (d. 656 C.E.). And even after this codification, because the Arabic writing system was defective and in the process of evolution, great reliance continued to be placed on the oral tradition to guarantee the accuracy of the written text and insure its proper interpretation. Even today, to have memorized the entire Qur'ān, especially at a young age, is considered exceptionally meritorious. Moreover, it has traditionally been a prerequisite for acceptance by certain religious schools that prospective students know the Qur'ān by heart.

The fact that the Qur'ān is believed to be the record of God's actual words has had far-reaching consequences for determining the form and structure of the text as we have it. First and foremost, Muslims are adamant that Muḥammad did not in any way participate in the actual creation of the text. The only speaker in the Qur'ān is God Himself. Muḥammad was neither author nor editor, only the instrument through whom God's words were transmitted.

Muslim tradition asserts that, before creation, God's Pen had inscribed on the Preserved Tablet all that would ever occur in cosmic history, including His revelations to prophets and messengers. It is the Angel Gabriel who communicated God's words from the Tablet to Muḥammad, who then proclaimed them to his followers, who would memorize them, or, as tradition relates, write them on pieces of parchment, bone, or other material. On numerous occasions Muḥammad would be overcome by the revelatory experience, falling into a trance-like state and experiencing physical distress.

The final process of collection and codification of the Qur'ān text was guided by one over-arching principle: God's words must not in any way be distorted or sullied by human intervention. For this reason, no serious attempt, apparently, was made to edit the numerous revelations, organize them into thematic units, or present them in chronological order. The goal was to preserve them as they had actually occurred. This has given rise in the past to a great deal of criticism by European and American scholars of Islam, who find the Qur'ān disorganized, repetitive, and very difficult to read.

For anyone unfamiliar with the Qur'ān, who begins to read it for the first time, a caveat is in order. One must not presume to know what a scripture is, simply because one is familiar with the Hebrew Bible or the New Testament. Both of those earlier texts have undergone substantial editing and revision in order to shape them into what we generally understand to be a book. The Qur'ān is quite different. It remains, in an extraordinary way, a piece of dramatic, oral literature that happens to have been preserved in written form out of fear that the original words would be lost. The lack of chronological order, the repetitions, the absence of a clear thematic or narrative structure—all point to the fact that the Qur'ān should not be dealt with as a book, but as a collection of oral communications that are believed by Muslims to be of divine provenance. The name of the text itself, i.e., "Al-Qur'ān" ("The Recitation"), points to the primacy of orality over literary structure.

Because of the oral nature of the work, the Qur'ān reveals itself most forcefully when recited aloud or chanted. It is during a Qur'ān recital performed by a well-trained cantor that one appreciates fully the rhymed prose style of the text. The act of chanting the Qur'ān has evolved into a sophisticated art form, requiring years of specialized training. At those times when the Qur'ān is read quietly, especially by non-Muslims unfamiliar with the text, it is best to focus on a relatively brief amount of material, either one or more of the shorter *sūra*s at the end of the Qur'ān or a thematically unified section from a longer chapter. This allows the reader to approximate better the original structure of the collected revelations.

The primacy of recitation and chanting over reading the Qur'ān silently as a book cannot be overemphasized. For many Muslims the power of sacred word embodied in the Qur'ān is communicated through the sound patterns. Europeans and Americans do not often realize that most Muslims are not native speakers of Arabic, nor even trained in Arabic at all. Islam is truly an international and multi-ethnic religion; thus the majority of Muslims in the world are not found, as one might suspect, in the Arab world, but in Indonesia, Malaysia, the Indian subcontinent, and in other non-Arabic speaking countries. Muslims may learn to read Arabic script and, thus, to sound out the words of the Qur'ān, but they often require translations in their own languages to understand the meaning of the Qur'ān text. This does not, however, bar them from encountering the power of the words, for they are exposed from their earliest days to Qur'ānic recitations. The Qur'ān comes alive in this dynamic interaction between believer and word, transforming a static written document into an instrument of vibrant religious power.

The text as we have it now is broken down into one hundred and fourteen chapters known as *sūras*, which are subdivided into verses or *āyas*. The versification of certain *sūras* varies, depending on the edition of the Qur'ān being used. This does not indicate, however, a difference in the text itself, only a difference in the way divisions in the text have been marked. The order of the chapters is neither thematic nor chronological, but, generally, according to length, with the longer *sūras* first and shorter *sūras* at the end. The chapters range from a few verses to several hundred, and may comprise one revelation or a collection of several revelations received at different times. The shorter revelations represent thematic wholes; the longer ones are more fluid in structure. The only chapter that represents a single narrative unit is *sūra* 12, *Yūsuf (Joseph)*, which recounts the Muslim reinterpretation of the biblical story of Joseph, his father Jacob, and his brothers, who sold Joseph into slavery in Egypt.

A general chronology of the revelations can be determined from the headings of each *sūra*, which indicate whether the chapter was revealed to Muḥammad while he lived in Mecca or Medina. The shift from Mecca to Medina is critical for the history of Islam. When Muḥammad began to proclaim his revelations in the name of the one God, Allāh, his preaching was rejected by the tribes of Mecca. Allāh was not a new deity in pre-Islamic Arabian religion, but the highest god among many divinities, some of whose images were housed in the sacred cube in Mecca, the Kaʿba. Muḥammad's preaching was aimed at reforming the old religious tradition by returning it to the pure monotheism that he believed to be at the foundation of the great semitic traditions of Judaism and Christianity. Worship was to be offered only to the one God, Allāh, and all other deities were condemned as false. The Kaʿba, he insisted, must be cleansed of idols and revered once again as the house of the one

God. The radical monotheism of Islam is captured best in the Muslim confession of faith: *Lā ilāha ill' allāh, wa muḥammad rasūl allāh* ("There is absolutely no deity but God, and Muḥammad is His messenger").

Since the Meccans refused to submit to Allāh, but continued to worship the various deities housed in the Kaᶜba, and persecuted Muḥammad and his early followers, Muḥammad was obliged in 622 C.E. to move from Mecca to the neighboring city of Yathrib, where he was accepted by the population. Yathrib was later renamed Medinat an-nabī (City of the Prophet), now known simply as Medina. The emigration, known as the *hijra*, marks a turning point in Muslim history, for it is in 622 C.E. that Islam is transformed into a viable community embodying the religious vision articulated in the revelations. Consequently, it is from this year that Muslims begin their dating system, since 622 C.E. represents for them the true birth of Islam.

Each *sūra* of the Qur'ān contains in its heading the word Mecca or Medina to indicate whether the chapter was revealed before or after the *hijra*. In addition, the number of verses or *āyas* in the *sūra* is recorded. And finally, the heading gives the name of the *sūra*. Once again the modern European or American reader must be on guard, for it is usually presumed that chapter titles capture in some way the central theme of the particular chapter to be read. This is not the case in the Qur'ān; the names of the chapters seem to have been a type of filing system by which the *sūras* were organized. While it is true that the title often refers to an important word or idea contained in the *sūra*, it does not necessarily represent the main focus of the entire chapter. There are, in addition, multiple titles for some *sūras* of the Qur'ān. Scholars suggest that the titles were not original with the Qur'ān but added later as the various revelations were being organized for codification.

Each *sūra* of the Qur'ān, except *sūra* 9, begins with the invocation: "In the name of God, the Compassionate, the Merciful." It is this emphasis on the mercy and compassion of God that embraces the whole of the Qur'ān. In addition to the *basmala*, as the above invocation is called, a number of *sūras* have as their first verse one or more letters whose meaning remains a mystery, despite speculation by both Muslim and non-Muslim scholars as to their possible significance. These letters constitute an integral element of the *sūras* in which they appear, and are chanted as part of the text. This fact once again illustrates that the Qur'ān possesses the ability, not only to convey ideas, but also to communicate power through the very letters themselves. The believer may not know the meaning of these mysterious letters, but he or she does not disregard their potency as part of the revelation.

The centrality of the actual words and letters of the Qur'ān in the religious consciousness of Muslims acts as the catalyst for the development of calligraphy as a highly sophisticated art form in Islam. Moreover, the conviction that the Qur'ān represents God's speech, i.e., that God communicated his words to Muḥammad in the Arabic language, raises Arabic, in the minds of Muslims, to a level of perfection achieved by no other language in human history. The style of this miraculous document is considered inimitable, and its grammar, many believe, should be the model for all Arabic literary expression. Muslim tradition insists, in addition, that it is impossible to translate the Qur'ān, because any translation would be but a dim reflection, if not distortion, of the perfection of the original divine language, Arabic.

It should be noted that, out of reverence for the Arabic language and its script, many non-Arab groups who converted to Islam abandoned their own writing systems and began to write their languages in Arabic script, e.g., Persian, Urdu, and Ottoman Turkish. The pervasive impact of the Qur'ān on Islamic society has resulted, moreover, in the absorption of numerous Arabic words into these non-Arabic languages. It is not an exaggeration to say that the most important influence on Islamic literature, in whichever Islamic language, is the spirit and actual text of the Qur'ān.

A non-Muslim reader of the Qur'ān is often struck by the many resonances between the Qur'ān and the scriptures of the Jews and Christians. Familiar figures, like Abraham, Noah, Moses, Jesus, and Mary, and familiar themes of faith, repentance, covenant, judgment, heaven, and hell appear throughout the text. Islam is not a radically new religion that nullifies Judaism and Christianity, but rather constitutes for Muslims the fulfillment of the revelatory process that began with Adam at the creation of the world, and continued through the work of great messenger-prophets, especially Moses and Jesus. Islam, therefore, understands itself to be in continuity with, not opposition to, the great traditions that preceded the revelations accorded Muḥammad. In the Qur'ān itself, special reverence and protection is shown to the *Ahl al-kitāb*, "The People of the Book," those communities who are the recipients of earlier revelations.

Why, then, was it necessary for God, once again, to break into the historical process to reveal an Arabic Qur'ān? Islamic tradition insists that, whereas the previous revelations were authentic, their meaning, and perhaps the texts themselves, had been distorted by the communities to whom they had been entrusted. The Qur'ān, therefore, becomes the lens through which the previous scriptures must be read, and the criterion by which they must be judged. When conflicts in interpretation among the three great scriptures occur, one must rely, insist Muslim scholars, on the Qur'ān as the final arbiter of truth.

The similarities between the Qur'ān and the previous scriptures of the great semitic traditions have, in the past, given rise to criticisms by European and American scholars that the Qur'ān is a derivative document, an amalgam of materials culled from Christian and Jewish oral and written sources available in seventh-century Arabia.

Nothing is farther from the truth. What is striking about the Qur'ān is not the resonances with Judaism and Christianity, but the distinctive Muslim stamp placed on the traditional material. A fine illustration of this fact is the Qur'ānic treatment of the notion of prophet *(nabī)*, a central theme in the text. What the non-Muslim reader notices on closer reading is that individuals are called prophets who would never have been thus honored in the

Hebrew Bible or New Testament, e.g., Solomon, Joseph, and John the Baptist. The title of prophet is much more broadly conceived in the Qur'ān, and accorded to those individuals who have been granted some unique form of divine inspiration.

Much more important than the role of prophet in the Qur'ān is that of apostle or messenger *(rasūl)*. It is the *rasūl* who is chosen both to be the intermediary for the communication of divine revelation, which is eventually codified into book form, and to preach this truth publicly to a community. Most important among the great *rasūls* are Moses and Jesus, whose books, the Torah *(Tawrā)* and New Testament *(Injīl)*, are the foundations of the Jewish and Christian communities. Some great figures of religious history are both prophets and messengers, but the central point is that the number of messengers is considerably smaller than the number of prophets, and the messengers are of much greater significance.

Another misperception about the Qur'ān, in addition to considering it a document derived from Jewish and Christian sources, is the notion that it is, primarily, a legal document. There is no doubt that one discovers important legal material in the Qur'ān relating to a number of issues, e.g., the regulation of marriage, divorce, and inheritance, but these sections do not in any way represent the core of the text.

The Qur'ān, more accurately, is a compendium of the general religious and ethical principles that are to be the foundation of the Islamic community *(Umma)*. The ideal vision of community in Islam is that of a seamless fabric of society that is imbued on all levels with the principles of Islam. Much more important than the Qur'ān for the articulation of the specifics of Islamic Law *(sharīᶜa)* are the vast collections of recorded traditions, known as *ḥadīth*, believed by Muslims to preserve the actual words of Muḥammad on topics ranging from particular details of home life to broad theological and ethical issues.

Among the fundamental principles articulated in the Qur'ān text are the God-man relationship, predestination, eschatology, i.e., the belief that, after death, God will judge the believer for his or her actions, and assign the soul reward or punishment in Paradise or Hell, and the five pillars of Islam, which constitute the heart of Islamic religious practice.

The Qur'ān reiterates the perspective of the great semitic religions that the cosmos was created by an omnipotent and omniscient power who is God. In the Qur'ān, man takes precedence over all other created realities because God breathed into Adam part of His own spirit *(rūḥ)*. While the possession of the divine spirit does raise humankind above all creation, it does not make men and women equal with God. The basic relationship described in the Qur'ān is that of Lord *(rabb)* and Servant *(ʿabd)*, bound together by a covenant relationship.

There is a radical difference between slavery and servanthood. The slave is chattel, often deprived of human dignity, and at the mercy of his master's whims. The servant, on the other hand, while not equal to his Lord, is granted rights and dignity because of the binding covenant entered into freely by the Lord. No Muslim whose religious life has been imbued with the Qur'ān can lose sight of the overwhelming transcendence and power of Allāh. Nevertheless, verse after verse of the Qur'ān points to the intimacy between God and humankind, an intimacy based on the original gift of divine spirit, and on men and women's complete reliance on the Almighty for life, protection, and, ultimately, mercy and forgiveness.

There is no doubt, however, that, despite the emphasis on the essential dignity of humans in the Qur'ān, one is struck, time and again, by the reiteration of predestinarian themes that seem to reduce men and women to pawns in the divine chess game. The Qur'ān will insist that Allāh performs whatever He wills; consequently, human freedom, if it exists at all, cannot be allowed to challenge Allāh's preeminence. The radical monotheism of Islam leads Muslims to be very wary, lest somehow they accord any power—be it human, natural, or from the spirit world—an independence of action apart from God. This smacks of polytheism and is known as the cardinal sin of *shirk*, associationism.

On the other hand, why would God reveal His word to men and women if they were incapable of participating, by either accepting or rejecting the revelation? The Qur'ān confronts the believing Muslim with a paradox: men and women must possess some modicum of freedom and yet nothing occurs that is not Allāh's will. The solution to the dilemma is quintessentially Islamic, for the believer is encouraged to affirm both poles of the paradox, namely, responsibility for personal actions and the fact that all is determined by God's will. Respect for the word of Allāh is so central to Islam that, what to fallible human reason appears to be a paradox must, nevertheless, be affirmed as true because God has spoken it in the Qur'ān.

The eternal consequences of human action for each and every man and woman are described in the Qur'ān in perhaps the most vivid sections of the text. Allāh is the just judge whose punishment of hypocrites and evildoers is unrelenting. The torments of hellfire are meant to shock every man or women who is tempted to succumb to the wiles of Satan and his devilish cohorts.

Just as concrete are the descriptions of Paradise in the Qur'ān, where flowing waters, abundance of food, wine, and sensual pleasures epitomize an idealized human existence. Non-Muslim commentators, in the past, have expressed disdain, if not shock, at such a human view of Paradise. Doubtless such negative attitudes toward physicality reflect as much the social and religious bias of the critics as the limitations of the Islamic world view.

Equally prominent in the Qur'ān are concerns with religious practice, especially with what have become known as the five pillars of Islam. All the pillars have their roots in the Qur'ān text, although their present form has been determined by later Islamic Law *(sharīʿa)*. The first, the *shahāda* or confession of faith, affirms the two essential elements required for conversion to Islam, namely, acceptance of radical monotheism and the role of Muḥammad as God's final messenger ("There is absolutely no deity but God and Muḥammad is His messenger"). The second is prayer *(ṣalāt)*, now performed five times a day, which infuses all the daily events of

Muslim life, both public and private, with religious ritual. A Muslim may pray anywhere—at home, work, in the street, or in a mosque. It is traditional, however, for members of the community to assemble in the mosque for the more formal noon prayers on Friday.

The third pillar, *ṣawm* or fasting, requires all Muslim men and women to fast from dawn until sunset during the thirty days of the Muslim lunar month of Ramaḍān. The rigor of the Muslim fast derives from the fact that the faithful are required to abstain not only from solid food, but from liquids as well, an especially arduous discipline when Ramaḍān falls during the summer season.

Throughout the Qur'ān Muslims are urged to take special care of the weaker and more vulnerable members of the community, especially widows and orphans. The fourth pillar of Islam, almsgiving or *zakāt,* responds in a formal way to these Qur'ānic injunctions. All are expected to contribute a percentage of their earnings to the support of pious institutions in order to foster the egalitarian values that are reiterated so frequently in the Qur'ān.

The fifth and final pillar requires that all Muslim men and women, at least one time in their lives, perform the pilgrimage to Mecca *(ḥajj)* during the specified pilgrimage season. If, however, the performance of the pilgrimage would place too much of a financial burden on one's family, or if one suffers from ill health, Islamic Law excuses the individual from this obligation. The yearly pilgrimage to Mecca is, without doubt, the most extraordinary religious assembly in the world. Upwards of two million people participate at present, requiring a level of sophisticated organization and financial subsidy unimaginable in the early days of Islam.

While not officially considered a pillar of Islam by all Muslims, *jihād,* often badly translated as "Holy War," serves an equally important function within the community, and is a pivotal concept in the Qur'ān. *Jihād* literally means the act of struggling or striving, i.e., striving on the path of Allāh. It has two prime areas of focus, the individual and the community. The private *jihād* of every Muslim man or woman is the struggle against the devilish forces that attempt to lure the believer from the straight path. It is, thus, primarily a principle of personal religious renewal.

Jihād also possesses a public dimension and is described in the Qur'ān as a defensive mechanism by which the community, when threatened, protects itself. One should not, however, reduce *jihād* to a political tactic. The central point expressed throughout the Qur'ān is that the most serious threat to the *Umma,* the Islamic community, will come from those men and women who have consciously rejected the truth of God's revelation. They are, therefore, not enemies solely in a political sense, but moral enemies whose community of evil has determined to destroy the community of truth. The defense of the truth becomes, therefore, not solely a political choice, but a moral obligation that falls on all believers.

It is in this context that discussions of martyrdom become understandable. Throughout the Qur'ān the focus is on the primacy of community over the individual, for, were the community not to exist, Islam would not exist. When Muslim men and women are called upon to strive on the path of Allāh against the forces of evil, even to die in the struggle, they perform the greatest act of altruism by offering themselves for the welfare and continued survival of the Islamic community. This heroic act, according to Islamic tradition, deserves a hero's reward, namely, immediate acceptance into Paradise.

All religious texts, be they the scriptures of Jews, Christians, Hindus, Buddhists, Muslims, or other religious communities, have been catalysts both for extraordinary human creativity and grotesque inhuman violence perpetrated in the name of religious ideals. One can only hope that, through the exploration of one another's religious traditions and cultural history, we will come to appreciate more the complexity of elements that comprise different religious world views. And perhaps in this common exploration of the profoundest levels of one another's understanding of humanity and ultimate reality, we will learn how better to elicit from ourselves, and from each other, those positive aspects of religiousness that lead to the enhancement of quality of life. To appreciate the Islamic vision of society and human existence, one must first and foremost encounter the Qur'ān. Equally as important is to appreciate how the Qur'ān has shaped the history, society, literature, and art of the extraordinarily diverse communities that call themselves Muslim. And, finally, we must acknowledge that the Qur'ān will continue to mold modern Islamic societies, hopefully in a way that will highlight those human and transcendent values that epitomize the best of the Islamic vision of the world.

Reading *The Conference of the Birds*

James Winston Morris

Farīd al-Dīn ʿAṭṭār's *Conference of the Birds* is not just a literary masterpiece: its wider popular influence throughout the Eastern Islamic world, both directly and through centuries of retelling of its stories by subsequent writers in Persian, Turkish, Urdu, and other vernacular languages, can only be compared, for example, to the place of Milton, Bunyan, or even the King James Bible in pre-twentieth-century Anglo-Saxon culture. ʿAṭṭār's primary aim, in this and all his other writings was to bring the spiritual teachings and insights of the Qur'ān and ḥadīth (the sayings of the Prophet Muḥammad), as they had been understood by earlier generations of saints and Sufis, vividly alive for the majority of his compatriots unfamiliar with the learned Arabic forms of those traditions. As with the other monuments of Persian mystical literature, such as the poetry of Ḥāfiẓ or Rūmī, the very success of ʿAṭṭār's effort makes it almost impossible for the modern translator to do equal justice to (a) the universality of the author's ideas and intentions; (b) the poetic qualities and general readability of the original; and (c) the complex web of historical allusions, including scriptural themes and symbols, common Islamic practices and assumptions, specifically Sufi terminology and activities, and local social customs and attitudes, that is almost always presupposed. (In fact, virtually every story is meant to paraphrase or illuminate specific Qur'ānic themes or canonical sayings attributed to Muḥammad, and ʿAṭṭār's treatment often presupposes many earlier literary or practical Sufi applications of those scriptural sources.) So it is a measure of the remarkable success of Darbandi and Davis' recent translation on the first two scores—and of the true universality of ʿAṭṭār's artistry—that the uninitiated student can still read through *The Conference of the Birds* with both enjoyment and edification, without referring to explanatory notes or any further Islamic background.

The central—indeed the unique—subject of ʿAṭṭār's poem is the intimate relation of God and the human soul, a relation that he describes most often in terms of the mystery or "secret" of divine Love. The actual Arabic words of his title, *Manṭiq al-Ṭayr* ("the language of the birds"), refer in the Qur'ān (27:17) to Solomon's God-given ability to understand that secret as it is revealed in the inner states of all beings. Starting from the same Qur'ānic chapter, ʿAṭṭār takes Solomon (and the many other monarchs in his poem) to represent God, the hoopoe (and various messengers or ministers) to represent the prophets and other spiritual guides and intermediaries, and the birds to typify all the manifold human spiritual states and attitudes. For the love that concerns him throughout this work is not simply a particular human emotion, or even the deeper goal of man's striving, but rather the ultimate Ground of all existence: the birds'/soul's pilgrimage itself turns out to be the unending self-discovery of that creative Love. Thus the entire poem is in fact an extended commentary on the famous divine saying "I (God) was a hidden treasure, and I *loved* to be known, so I created the world that I might be known"—and on another, even more celebrated ḥadīth restating that reality from the human point of view: "he who knows his soul/self, knows his Lord."

The poem as a whole moves from the outward statement to the full inner realization of that Love, to the true, ever-recurrent revelation. It begins with a dense summary of the underlying metaphysical doctrine and its Islamic symbols; proceeds through the more familiar manifestations of that reality in the universal human experiences of "separation," of absence, longing, suffering, and incompleteness; and gradually ascends through that awareness to the highest spiritual states of union and rapture. ʿAṭṭār's long Introduction, woven together from key scriptural passages, echoes the Qur'ānic insistence on God's paradoxical transcendence *and* immanence, and on Adam's theomorphic reality (and responsibility) as the divine vice-regent, the unique "talisman" through which that mystery becomes known. Its omission in this translation certainly does increase the dramatic power of his narrative for modern readers unfamiliar with (or even initially allergic to) his religious presuppositions, inasmuch as it creates heightened suspense about the goal of the birds' pilgrimage and the nature of the divine "Simorgh" that is largely missing in the original. But the dramatic weight in the original poem is more evenly distributed over the individual episodes and the spiritual lessons potentially contained in each story, which each reader must rediscover for himself.

For the stage of ʿAṭṭār's drama is not the outer world of history or of nature (as in many of Rūmī's ecstatic lyrics), but the human Heart—echoing the celebrated ḥadīth identifying the heart of the man of faith as "the throne of the Merciful" which "encompasses" God, or mirrors Him. His birds are not "out there"; they are not just so many social or psychological types, but rather a sort of catalogue of all possible spiritual states, mirroring each individual's own outlook and condition. The reader objectifies them at his own risk. That is even more true of the figures (messengers, ministers, the hoopoe, etc.) he uses to symbolize the spiritual mediation of the prophets, angels, saints, and other guides: his constant shifting of those symbols eventually forces the reader to see that their reality can likewise only be truly perceived in light of their divine Source—again as mirrored in his own soul and personal experience. The drama ʿAṭṭār celebrates is always within: his central protagonists are not so visibly God and man—although ultimately that is always the case—but rather the inner tension within each person between his uncreated Spirit *(rūḥ)*, the vehicle of divine Grace, and the endless illusions perpetrated by the carnal soul, the egocentric "self commanding evil" (*nafs-i ammāra*, or "the Self" in this translation).

ʿAṭṭār's drama—like its archetype in the Qur'ānic account of Adam's creation and temptation—is a story of loss and rediscovery. As in the Qur'ān (or the Bible), that story is recounted and meant to be reenacted from two complementary—and practically inseparable—perspectives: man's own efforts (of worship, ethical purification, and spiritual awareness and realization), and God's grace, compassion, and guidance. And here one crucial caution is in order, at least for modern readers, concerning ʿAṭṭār's *rhetoric*, a warning that should not have been necessary for his original audience. His poetic language in this and other works involves a rhetoric of extremes, of hyperbole, violence, and almost Kierkegaardian paradox or contradiction designed to awaken each reader's personal awareness of God's grace and living presence, beyond the routine social observance of "religious" forms which was probably the norm in his own society (and the even wider tendency to separate and reify "God"). Clearly, such renewed spiritual awareness was only intended as a first step toward the types of appropriate effort and activity that are alluded to throughout the spiritual progression depicted in the later parts of the poem. But *The Conference of the Birds* itself was not written as a practical spiritual guidebook, and its frequently "antinomian" tales and "superhuman" counsels were not meant to be taken literally, certainly not as practical advice for all comers.

• • •

The structure of ʿAṭṭār's poem resembles a spiraling ascension around a central core. That core, with which he begins and ends, and to which he constantly returns, is the ineffable "mystery" or "secret" of God's presence within man—a mystery which cannot really be told (despite all the scriptural symbols and the poet's own recurrent attempts), but only lived and directly realized—as ʿAṭṭār stresses in his own concluding remarks (p. 229). The stories and symbols referring to this reality typically involve the paired figures of a ruler (prophet, etc.) and his subject (son, slave, etc.), and often a more enigmatic connecting figure representing the Spirit, or the various manifestations or "emissaries" of God's Grace: if the identification of one of these persons as "God" and the other as the "soul" is often obvious in the earlier passages, by the end of the birds' journey ʿAṭṭār has made it almost impossible to say which is which.

The gradual approach to that inner secret—which is of course only subjectively a voyage, since ʿAṭṭār constantly reminds his reader that our momentary feelings of God's "absence" are like a child's stubbornly closing his eyes to the sun's light—focuses on all the temptations and manifestations of the carnal Self *(nafs)*, and on the activities and spiritual virtues needed to overcome that opponent. Both those aspects of the Way of perfection are depicted and analyzed at increasingly subtle and profound spiritual stages, beginning with obvious ethical and social allegories, but moving inward until in the final section their portrayal is often inseparable from the central spiritual realization itself. That dramatic structure can be outlined as follows, with ʿAṭṭār's puzzling reminders of the divine Mystery in the left-hand paragraphs and the more accessible stages of spiritual progression in the numbered ones.

Scriptural Introduction (omitted here): The omnipresence (and paradoxical "invisibility") of God, and man's spirit/soul as the secret key to that mystery.

I. Dramatic introduction (pp. 29–35): The "Simorgh's feather" of God's Love in each heart, and the need to overcome the carnal "Self" *(nafs)*—through God's Grace—in order to rediscover Him.

II. The Birds' Excuses (pp. 35–51): The shortsightedness of our ordinary loves and attachments, the suffering and fears that flow from them, and the first step toward enlightenment: disciplining the Self.

The Mystery of God and man (pp. 52–56): Men as the Simorgh's "shadows" (and veils); God's mirror in the Heart; the secret gateway of repentance and forgiveness.

III. Shaykh Samʿan (pp. 57–75): The transforming direct experience of God's Love as the indispensable starting point on the Path; true surrender to His will—beyond outward piety and religious learning—as the corresponding attitude and goal.

The Mystery of Grace and prayer (pp. 76–82): Tales of providential transformation (the hoopoe's "lot"; Bayazid's "luck"; Solomon's glance . . .), and mankind's one duty: "Pray always." The saving intercession of the prophets and saints, and three key stories on the central mystery of religious practice and divine compassion (the king and the fisherboy; the king and the old woodgatherer; the murderer redeemed by the glance of a true saint).

IV. The birds' fears, and the proper response (pp. 83–124): ʿAṭṭār begins to explore deeper signs of attachment to the Self and the corresponding spiritual virtues (as distinguished from the more conventional ethical and social ones): repentance, renunciation, praise, devotion, and surrender to God.

The Mystery of loving submission (pp. 125–128): true obedience and submission—to God, and to one's spiritual master—as the condition for receiving divine guidance. It is no accident that this point, where the conscious awareness of the Way and the personal commitment to follow it come into play, is also where

ʿAṭṭār necessarily begins to leave some readers behind. From now on the birds' questions (and their master's replies) refer less and less to outward, familiar attitudes and experiences, and increasingly deal with deeper spiritual temptations and discoveries.

V. The basic virtues of the Way (pp. 128–166): purity of intention, spiritual aspiration, and justice and loyalty (perseverance); the recurrent pitfalls of pride and self-satisfaction. This section (on "true dignity and servitude" in the spiritual path) deals entirely with what Islamic mystics called *adab:* the spiritually appropriate behavior and attitude of the disciple toward both God and his master, something which cannot be defined by outward, formal rules.

Recapitulation—the Seven Valleys of the Way (pp. 166–213): Here, as ʿAṭṭār artfully summarizes the wisdom of generations of earlier Sufis, each "station" is in itself a window on the goal. The particular stages mentioned here (of spiritual Quest, Love, Insight, Detachment, Union, Bewilderment, and Poverty) should not be taken as a rigid or standard schema, either with regard to their order or their number. ʿAṭṭār's Sufi predecessors (and later imitators) used the same terms to refer to other spiritual stations, or ranked them differently, often adding dozens of other stages, depending on their own context and intentions. But what is typical here—and perhaps even autobiographical—is not so much the specific order of these stages as it is ʿAṭṭār's persistent emphasis on the revelatory, purifying value of suffering, and on the necessary painful emptying of one's self (spiritual "nothingness") in order for God's will to be done.

Journey's End (pp. 214–229): The decisive point here is not the "thirty birds' " silent contemplation of the Simorgh's image in their soul, since that mystery has already been mentioned dozens of times. Rather it is what happens afterward (220 ff.), when "their Selves had been restored": the further, endless journey *within* God symbolized here in Hallāj's exemplary martyrdom and the last, bewildering story of temptation, redemptive suffering, and self-sacrifice. Quite intentionally, that tale is a koan, an insoluble allegory whose only "interpretation" is transformation.

We began by emphasizing the explicitly popular and universal intentions of ʿAṭṭār's poem. The "divine comedy" of his birds, especially as they set out on their journey, mixes the romantic, the tragic, and the ridiculous aspects of everyday life in ways often more reminiscent of Woody Allen than of Dante—although, like Dante, it also points insistently to the ultimate context, the potentially transforming reality underlying those same experiences. What ʿAṭṭār asks of his reader to begin with, though, is not any particular religious belief or piety (his favorite targets!), but simply a willingness to look. More and more deeply. His poem, like Dante's, is a marvelous portrayal of his own, now far-away world, but his subject is the deeper world that never changes. It succeeds to the extent that it can create a mirror for each reader's own life, here and now.

BIBLIOGRAPHIC NOTE

References throughout this article are to the recent translation by A. Darbandi and D. Davis, *The Conference of the Birds* (London: Penguin Classics, 1984). An earlier English prose version by C. S. Nott, based on the nineteenth-century French translation by G. DeTassy (Berkeley: University of California Press, 1971), is quite readable, but generally less accurate and complete, although it does briefly summarize (pp. 3–7) the opening 615 lines omitted in the newer translation. The translation by A. J. Arberry of ʿAṭṭār's *Muslim Saints and Mystics: Episodes from the Tadhkirat al-Auliyā'* (London: Routledge and Kegan Paul, 1966, reprint 1976) contains an illuminating account of his motives for writing in Persian, and is also a fascinating introduction to earlier Sufi tradition.

Readers curious to know more about unexplained characters, symbols, and technical terminology will usually find at least a preliminary explanation somewhere in Annemarie Schimmel's *Mystical Dimensions of Islam* (Chapel Hill: University of North Carolina Press, 1975). (The presence of so many of ʿAṭṭār's themes and characters throughout Schimmel's survey is another indicator of the massive influence of his writing on later Eastern

Islamic spirituality, both learned and popular.) A more detailed historical study of ʿAṭṭār's specifically Islamic background can be found in Helmutt Ritter's classic study, *Das Meer der Seele: Gott, Welt und Mensch in den Geschichten Farīduddīn ʿAṭṭārs* (Leiden: E. J. Brill, 1955).

The length of this article did not allow a discussion of the peculiar features of ʿAṭṭār's own rhetorical style in relation to the Persian language and literary norms of his time. However, one can begin to appreciate something of the distinctiveness of his language and style simply by comparing *The Conference of the Birds* with any of the many English translations from Rūmī or Khayyām, for example.

Al-Ghazālī, Abū Ḥāmid Muḥammad ibn Muḥammad: *(Munqidh min aḍ-ḍalāl)* *Deliverance from Error*

Peter J. Awn

Muslim tradition records a saying attributed to the Prophet Muḥammad that, over the centuries, has become proverbial in Islamic religious literature: "He who knows his inner self knows his Lord" *(man ʿarafa nafsahu faqad ʿarafa rabbahu)*. The Holy Book of Islam, the Qur'ān, emphasizes both the utter dependence of the self upon God (Allāh), encapsulated in the oft-repeated image of Lord *(rabb)*—servant *(ʿabd)*, and his immanence, for Allāh is more intimately united to the believer than his own jugular vein (Qur'ān 50:16). Consequently the Muslim's quest for wisdom, while revealing hidden facets of the self, is, at the same time, an exploration of the nature of God, to whom the self is irrevocably bound by a covenant relationship sealed before the creation of time (see Qur'ān 7:172).

The ideal sage in Islam, therefore, is one who combines two unique gifts, intellectual virtuosity with profound spiritual development. These qualities, rarely associated with religious lawyers and dogmatists, seem more often to be the domain of poets, mystics, and creative artists. One exception in Islamic history is Abū Ḥāmid Muḥammad ibn Muḥammad Al-Ghazālī (1058–1111 C.E.), even today one of the most influential religious thinkers in the Muslim world. His writings, especially his magnum opus *Iḥyā' ʿulūm ad-dīn (The Revivification of the Religious Sciences)*, constitute an essential part of the training of any religious scholar, be he Arab, Iranian, or Malaysian; Indonesian, African, American, or from the Indian subcontinent.

Al-Ghazālī was born in 1058 C.E. at Ṭūs, near the present-day city of Mashhad in Eastern Iran. His early education led to a specialization in both law and theology, at which he excelled. In 1091 C.E. the vizier Niẓām Al-Mulk, with whom Al-Ghazālī had been associated since 1085 C.E., appointed him professor at the prestigious Niẓāmiyya in Baghdād.

It is not, however, in the bare outline of Al-Ghazālī's life that one discovers the man, but in the vivid self-portrait that he himself has left us, namely, his *Munqidh min aḍ-ḍalāl (Deliverance from Error)*. The *Munqidh*, in Al-Ghazālī's own words, is "an account of my travail in disengaging the truth." Far from being a dry philosophical treatise about the quest for wisdom, this autobiography is first and foremost a personal testament to the power of the human spirit.

In addition to recounting the crucial personal and political events that shaped Al-Ghazālī's career, the *Munqidh* lays bare the traumas that threatened his mental equilibrium. Al-Ghazālī's life illustrates in sobering fashion that relentless self-scrutiny, while perhaps opening the way to higher states of gnosis, risks provoking psychological disintegration. The personal stakes are high; ultimate success depends, as Al-Ghazālī insists, not solely on the individual, whose potential is finite, but on the merciful intervention of the divine.

The *Munqidh*, written toward the end of Al-Ghazālī's life, should not be mistaken for a modern autobiography. Doubtless it contains more factual data about Al-Ghazālī than any of his other works.

Nevertheless he weaves together his personal crises and successes in a self-consciously contrived manner in order to create a multileveled thematic structure whose purpose is unabashedly didactic. This text is meant to teach what Al-Ghazālī has himself discovered to be the means to actualize fully human potential, both intellectual and spiritual, within the context of Islam.

In Al-Ghazālī's time there was no dearth of influential personalities who claimed already to have marked out the path to the attainment of wisdom. Two groups possessed particularly influential spokesmen: the rationalists who insisted that science and philosophy—the products of human intellection—were the sole roads to truth, and the staunch religious dogmatists who relied unquestioningly on a literalist interpretation of the revelation. Neither the atheistic wisdom of science and philosophy nor the blind faith of the committed believer was, for Al-Ghazālī, a convincing intellectual or religious stance.

The apparently irreconcilable conflict between reason and revelation, Al-Ghazālī explains, is due to a lack of critical understanding. The power of the intellect to discover truth with God's help cannot be denied; yet one must not fall into the trap of relying solely on the power of finite, human reason. Balance, coupled with a sharp critical eye, provides the key. Cede to revelation its primacy of place, insists Al-Ghazālī, but do not at the same time abandon the God-given gift of critical thinking. Seek knowledge wherever it may be found but always submit one's insights to the final arbiter, God's revealed Word.

Al-Ghazālī initiates his critique of reason by juxtaposing, at the outset of the *Munqidh*, his instinctive "thirst for grasping the real meaning of things" with what he describes as a major crisis of skepticism. It is unclear whether his bout with skepticism, which lasted for two months, occurred in his mature years or in young adulthood. Regardless, Al-Ghazālī is unambiguous in asserting that his skepticism did not lead him to reject the faith of Islam but called into question only the power of human reason.

His critique of men and women's ability to know begins with a thoroughgoing examination of the power of the senses to lead to sure and certain knowledge. All the senses, Al-Ghazālī demonstrates, are proved by reason to be unreliable, e.g., sight which perceives the sun to be a tiny object when in reality it is far larger than the earth. If the higher power of reason proves sense data false, Al-Ghazālī speculates, might there not exist an even higher power able to prove reason false? Consider, for example, the dream state. Reason distinguishes for us the difference between dreaming and waking states, but can we prove that what we consider the waking state is not but another form of the dream state?

Al-Ghazālī's conclusion that certain apparently self-evident truths are suspect led him to question the veracity of all supposedly self-evident truths, even those of mathematics. In Al-Ghazālī's solution to this initial crisis of skepticism one discovers a central principle in his theory of knowledge. For it was not through the construction of an intellectual proof that Al-Ghazālī was able to recover his faith in self-evident truths, since reason alone is fallible. "On the contrary," he affirms, "it was the effect of a light which God Most High cast into my breast. And that light is the key to most knowledge." The didactic purpose of Al-Ghazālī's bout with skepticism is, therefore, to demonstrate that the experience of truth is both cognitive and noncognitive. To ignore one or the other aspect of truth is to limit drastically one's potential to attain the fullness of wisdom.

If reliance solely on reason is fraught with danger in dealing with supposedly self-evident truths, how much more careful must a seeker after truth be when evaluating the speculative claims of philosophers, theologians, and religious zealots, each of whom purports to be the sole guardian of unimpeachable truth. It is a tribute to Al-Ghazālī's breadth of vision and intellectual integrity that he directs his scathing critique first at the religious establishment, i.e., the practitioners of the science of Islamic theology *(kalām)*. Al-Ghazālī's aim is not to undermine the belief system of Islam, for he remains throughout the *Munqidh* a man of unshakable faith. The object of his analysis is more narrowly focused. While the truth of revelation is certain, its interpreters leave much to be desired. The defenders of orthodoxy are, in brief, uncritical thinkers who rely too heavily on accepted premises derived from the Qur'ān, the tradition literature *(ḥadīth)*, or even from the works of their adversaries.

To find men who think critically, Al-Ghazālī readily admits, one must turn to the philosophers. Philosophy, for Al-Ghazālī and the intellectuals of his day, comprised a number of disciplines: mathematics (arithmetic, geometry, astronomy), logic, the physical sciences, the metaphysical sciences, political science, and moral philosophy. The sciences of mathematics and logic, especially, represented for Al-Ghazālī the genius of human reason. To reject them on pseudo-religious grounds, because some mathematicians and logicians reject basic truths of Islam, is to reduce religion to a farce.

Al-Ghazālī speaks to modern men and women as well as to the people of his own age when he counsels, quoting a saying attributed to ʿAlī, Muḥammad's cousin and son-in-law: "Do not know the truth by men, but rather, know the truth and you will know its adherents." If mathematics is true, accept it, even if some of its proponents err in their religious views. In the same way, do not blindly adhere to the words of religious men simply because they claim the authority of God and his revelation. Truth must stand on its own and should survive the most relentless of intellectual critiques, otherwise it is not worthy of the name. Neither the truths of science nor of religion depend on the men who proclaim them, no matter how misguided or charismatic they may appear.

Not all the sub-fields of philosophy, however, were without problems. Mathematics, logic, the physical, political, and moral sciences were considered by Al-Ghazālī the least open to criticism. Metaphysics, however, is considerably more problematic for it is here that many philosophers have gone astray. Some rationalists, for example, insist that matter is eternal and deny, consequently, that God has created the universe out of nothing *(creatio ex nihilo)*. Other scientists have concluded from their study of anatomy and nature that the life force dies with the body. The existence of the soul, therefore, is questioned as well as the existence of a realm of reward or punishment for the soul after death. Many other metaphysical hypotheses relating to the nature of God proposed by Plato and Aristotle, and elaborated by their Arab interpreters, must be evaluated with great care, warns Al-Ghazālī, for many run counter to the truths expounded clearly in the revelation.

A secondary theme closely related to Al-Ghazālī's critique of rationalist philosophers is his fervent opposition to Shīʿism, especially the Shīʿī reliance on the infallible guidance of a living or hidden teacher known as the Imām. In the same way that he condemns blind devotion to the rationalist philosopher who portrays himself as the sole arbiter of reason and truth, so too, Al-Ghazālī warns, must one be wary of his religious counterpart, the authoritative teacher who claims infallible inspiration and who presents himself as the sole avenue of true guidance. Both the diehard rationalist and the infallible Imām represent to Al-Ghazālī extremist positions that refuse to admit the complexity and variety of human experiences of truth. Guidance comes through the creative blending of both the cognitive and noncognitive, not the blind acceptance of a position articulated from one or another extreme.

Al-Ghazālī introduces the second constellation of complex themes in a manner similar to his initial discussion, with a personal crisis whose significance is underscored by providing an exact time and place: Baghdād, July 1095 C.E. The catalyst for this new conflict is Al-Ghazālī's realization that the truth which he has thus far discovered is incapable of fully nourishing the human spirit. The trauma is not simply intellectual but physical as well. The symptoms are dramatic: loss of speech, depression, and progressive debilitation.

Al-Ghazālī turns for help in this crisis, not to philosophers, theologians, or sectarian religious leaders, but to the mystics of Islam, the Sufis. (The name Sufi is derived most probably from the Arabic *ṣūf*, wool, referring to the coarse woolen garments worn by the early ascetics of Islam.) The writings of Sufis date as far back as the eighth century. Important manuals of the spiritual life eventually began to appear, analyzing with subtlety the psychology of mysticism and exploring in detail the stages and states of the mystic path. By the time of Al-Ghazālī the corpus of Sufi mystical literature was rich and varied, comprising poetry, aphorisms, didactic fables, manuals for initiates, and elaborate treatises for the skilled practitioners.

Al-Ghazālī dedicated himself to the study of Sufism, as he had before to the study of science, philosophy, theology, and law. But he soon discovered that mastering the writings of the Sufis was insufficient. For the very essence of Sufism is not reliance on reason *(ʿaql)* but personal experience (*dhawq*, lit. "taste"). The attainment of Sufi gnosis is possible only through immersion in the Sufi life and total commitment to the goals of Sufi practice, viz., purification of the heart and absorption in God.

The resolution of Al-Ghazālī's personal dilemma demanded, in addition to study, concrete action. After six months of personal anguish and vacillation, he resolved to abandon his academic career and to dedicate himself fully to the mystic path. In order to cut himself off completely from his past, he informed the Caliph and his friends that he was leaving for Mecca, when in reality he departed for Damascus. Al-Ghazālī's spiritual quest, which lasted ten years, was to take him to many parts of the Islamic world, including Syria, Arabia, Iran, and Iraq.

The modern reader, when confronted with Al-Ghazālī's dramatic rejection of his past successes and with his turn to Sufism, might easily become suspicious. What has happened to the champion of critical thinking and to the seeker after unassailable truth? Has he not abandoned his stated goal by opting for a form of esoteric piety accessible only to the chosen few? Doubtless many of the great Sufi teachers of the classical period considered themselves and their disciples, because of their unique spiritual achievements, to be superior to the mass of Muslims whose lives revolve primarily around the observance of the religious law *(sharīʿa)*.

Al-Ghazālī's contribution in the *Munqidh*, however, is to take a firm stand against the elitist current that threatened to isolate Sufism from mainstream Islam. A number of important Sufis had incurred the wrath of the religious establishment by preaching a kind of union with God that sounded, at least to the ears of the uninitiated, like self-divinization. Al-Ghazālī was acutely aware of the potential for divisiveness that Sufism represented to the Islamic community. He insisted that debates over the nature of mystical union should be reserved for those who understood clearly the implications of the arguments. Rather than scandalize the community with shocking claims of intimacy with the Divine, it was better, Al-Ghazālī felt, to follow the advice given by the poet Ibn Al-Muʿtazz and keep silent:

> There was what was of what I do not mention:
> So think well of it, and ask for no account!

Rather than embrace the position of those elitists who vaunted before the masses their unique religious experience, Al-Ghazālī sought to convince Muslims that all men and women have the potential to experience some degree of the gnostic vision. The argument he offers focuses on the pivotal concept of "the light of prophecy" and its ability to lead to fruitional experience. Men and women possess sense faculties and the faculty of intellect through which they attain different levels of knowledge. In the same way, however, that the power of reason is superior to that of the senses, so too there is a realm of knowledge and experience inaccessible to reason, a suprarational realm. To attain this level of insight, only the spiritual eye illumined by the light of prophecy is efficacious. By giving himself fully to the Sufi path the initiate learns to tap the potential of this prophetic light.

Al-Ghazālī does not intend to drown the reader in a tidal wave of esoteric jargon. His aim is more concrete. Every man and woman, he insists, has the natural capacity for a level of religious experience that cannot be encompassed by logic and philosophical categories. An analogy with aesthetics would not be off the mark. In the same way that one's aesthetic sense must be nourished through involvement in the arts, so too one's innate religious potential must be assiduously cultivated, otherwise it will remain stunted.

Al-Ghazālī presents the reader with a provocative challenge. If you wish to share the most profound levels of human experience, you must move beyond the limited potential of rational discourse to a noncognitive, experiential plane illumined by the light of prophecy. The proof he offers is his own life; it is in living the truth that one comes fully to know the truth.

The fact that all men and women share in the light of prophecy which opens the way to suprarational knowledge and experience does not imply that all are potential prophets. The prophetic power is far more complex, the gnostic vision being only one of its characteristics. But Al-Ghazālī's linkage of mystical insight and prophecy is not accidental, for he wishes thereby to forge an even stronger link between Sufism and mainstream Islam.

Whereas some Sufis claimed that the perfected mystic is superior to the prophet, Al-Ghazālī insists that prophecy by its very nature includes the spiritual attainments of Sufism. The life of Muḥammad is the prime example. The Prophet's intimacy with the divine was fostered through meditation on Mt. Ḥīra; only after his spiritual progress did the revelations come. The last stages of the mystic path, therefore, are but the earliest stages of the prophetic office. Most men and women will do well to achieve some level of mystic insight; few have ever been blessed with the fullness of prophecy. Nor is that any longer a possibility since, for Muslims, Muḥammad is the final messenger, the seal of the prophets.

Mysticism in the popular mind is often associated with flight from the world and the abandonment of temporal concerns. While it is undeniable that detachment from the preoccupations of family and career are essential aspects of Sufism, it is wrong to presume that mysticism requires a permanent exile from the life of the *polis*. On the contrary, a strong current in Sufi thought advises the adept to return to the community in order to witness to the new-found experience of divine intimacy and to minister to Muslim men and women as a "physician of the heart." It is the heart that is the essence of man's spirit and the seat of knowledge of God.

In Al-Ghazālī's case, the call came in 1106 C.E. from the vizier Fakhr Al-Mulk, the son of his former patron Niẓām Al-Mulk, who appointed him to a professorship at the Niẓāmiyya in Nīshāpūr. Al-Ghazālī takes pains to make clear that his return is not a simple recapitulation of his former career, for he has undergone a dramatic spiritual transformation which brings to his teaching the freshness of spiritual rebirth.

The "light of prophecy," as Al-Ghazālī describes it, leads not only to the gnostic vision but also to concrete action. Once again Muḥammad is the model, for the Prophet labored assiduously to mold the social and political life of the nascent Muslim community. So too his later followers should be encouraged to engage in the pursuit of spiritual wisdom as well as to embrace fully the public life of the community.

The wedding of religion and politics is more the rule than the exception in Islamic history; Al-Ghazālī represents one of the more enlightened offspring of such a union. He was an intimate of the powerful and spokesman for a state-sponsored Sunnī orthodoxy. The Niẓāmiyya university system, with which he was so closely associated, was put into place to combat the Shīʿī propagandists whose influence, both intellectual and political, was deeply felt in many parts of the Muslim world.

Al-Ghazālī's departure from Baghdād in 1095 C.E., while motivated primarily by his spiritual crisis, may have been hastened by an unfavorable political climate and by fear of reprisals from his Shīʿī adversaries who, in 1092 C.E., had assassinated his patron, Niẓām Al-Mulk. Al-Ghazālī's political involvements in no way tarnish his reputation in the eyes of Muslims. On the contrary, his public prominence and political influence represent the community's recognition of his extraordinary worth.

There remains a far more serious objection of the modern reader to Al-Ghazālī's *Munqidh,* other than his mixing of religion with politics. Must one be a religious man or woman to appreciate both the work and the man? Undeniably Al-Ghazālī is writing as a committed Muslim for an audience of fellow believers. Nevertheless, this work is far more than a sectarian religious polemic. It is the diary of a human spirit who refuses to conform blindly to the conventional wisdom of his age, be that wisdom scientific or religious.

Al-Ghazālī counsels us to scrutinize relentlessly those self-styled masters who purport to teach truths of ultimate significance. The *Munqidh* challenges us to move beyond the limits of our comfortable world in which there is little room for criticism or concern with self-reflection. Self-scrutiny of necessity creates anxiety, fear, and lack of certainty. Yet this very crisis may be catalytic, initiating a breakthrough to greater insight and to a more intense experience of human life.

Above all Al-Ghazālī invites us to explore dimensions of human existence that move beyond the scope of reason's ability to comprehend. He does not suggest that we abandon ourselves to the irrational, but that we take seriously the fact that there are levels of noncognitive, suprarational experience unexplored by the majority of men and women. An unswerving commitment to self-reflection and the single-minded pursuit of more profoundly enriching human experience—these are the ideals at the heart of the *Munqidh,* ideals which are by no means the sole property of traditional religious communities but which are intimately bound to the search for quality of life.

ENDNOTES

The best translation of Al-Ghazālī's autobiography is Richard J. McCarthy's *Freedom and Fulfillment* (Boston: Twayne, 1980). The most available translation is William Montgomery Watt's *The Faith and Practice of Al-Ghazālī* (London: Allen and Unwin, 1953; reprint ed., Chicago: Kazi, 1982).

All citations from the *Munqidh min aḍ-ḍalāl* are taken from the McCarthy translation, *Freedom and Fulfillment*.

Ibn Khaldūn

Muhsin Mahdi

Ibn Khaldūn's "History" (especially the Introduction and book 1, which treat the general problem of history and the "science of culture" respectively and which are known together as the *Muqaddimah* or "Introduction") is presented to the reader with the following claims made for it by its author: 1) It speaks directly to him concerning problems lying at the foundation of his thought and views about the nature of history and society; it attempts a critical and scientific investigation of the opinions commonly held, and the axioms consciously or unconsciously accepted or rejected, by previous writers on these subjects. Since the generally admitted desirability for a correct historical account and for correcting existing historical accounts requires, among other things, an understanding of the nature and causes of human association or culture, it becomes necessary and useful that these opinions and axioms be brought to light and those of them that prove valid be made the premises of a comprehensive science useful for writing a correct historical account and for correcting existing historical accounts. 2) Such a science of culture had not been attempted or constructed before; Ibn Khaldūn's work is saying something that had not been said before, except for incomplete beginnings and primitive efforts in the same direction. 3) This science is deeply rooted in philosophy or wisdom and deserves to be considered one of the philosophic sciences. It fills a gap in the established philosophic sciences through the application of their general principles and methods to a new field.

These claims were in substance accepted in the subsequent history of Islamic civilization. Since Ibn Khaldūn's time, his work has continued to have a unique and permanent place in Islamic thought on history and society, in Arabic literature as well as in the newly emerging literature in Turkish and Urdu. The role of the "History" in the history of Islamic civilization, not only substantiated Ibn Khaldūn's claim, but supplied further evidence of its importance: 1) Most of the important works on the nature of history and society had to face the challenge of Ibn Khaldūn's work irrespective of whether they admitted or rejected it; 2) In a number of cases, Ibn Khaldūn's work had great impact on the writing and interpretation of history by Muslim authors, especially, though not exclusively, in Turkey; 3) To all appearances, Ibn Khaldūn's work seems to be there to stay, and its value seems to increase with the greater attention given to the problems of history and society in the Islamic world; 4) Finally, and for reasons that will be discussed in detail, the value of Ibn Khaldūn's work seems to transcend the boundaries of Islamic civilization. More specifically, it has been translated and studied in the West, not merely as representative of Islamic thought or the Islamic world view, but as saying something directly relevant to modern scientific thought, a thought which aims at transcending all previous world views. This seems to indicate that Ibn Khaldūn's work may have something to contribute to the understanding of the nature of history and society as such.

This paper will attempt to indicate some of the didactic problems faced in teaching this work on the undergraduate level, both in general courses on Islamic civilization and as a great book of a non-Western civilization. It will attempt to anticipate the probable reactions of students to a first reading of Ibn Khaldūn's text, and to indicate the direction in which the discussion is to be led in order to elicit Ibn Khaldūn's intention, make possible a more thorough understanding of the fundamental principles underlying his thought, and arouse in the student the incentive for reexamining his own opinions on the issues brought to light by a more genuine confrontation with Ibn Khaldūn's position.

It will be found in general that the peculiar obstacle in the way of understanding Ibn Khaldūn's thought is not its alien or singular character, but an assumed similarity, if not identity, between it and modern thought. This has invariably been the reaction of his modern readers, and there is no reason to suppose that it could be avoided except through a more critical effort on the part of the instructor to understand the reasons for such a reaction, and to devise effective methods for challenging it and leading the student to realize the significant difference between the foundations of Ibn Khaldūn's science of culture and those of modern social science.

It is perhaps trite to say that Ibn Khaldūn addressed himself to the educated Muslims of the fourteenth century. But his art of addressing the educated Muslims of his time, when intelligently studied, can raise problems which transcend the particular cultural and historical context of his time. The contemporary tendency toward cultural relativism needs to be counterbalanced by asking where and in what manner Ibn Khaldūn, while writing for the educated Muslims of his time, has something to say to the educated non-Muslim of our time.

The central problem of Islamic thought, which is ever present throughout Ibn Khaldūn's work, is the conflicting claims of the religious-legal sciences and the philosophic-rational sciences that each offers the only proper set of principles and methods for the study and understanding of history and society. Ibn Khaldūn made the most massive and comprehensive attempt in Islamic thought to steal away the study of history and society from the religious-legal sciences and to incorporate it within the sphere of the philosophic-rational sciences in general and of the natural sciences in particular. This required, not only a theoretical, scientific effort to apply the principles and methods of the philosophic-rational sciences to a new field, but also an extremely subtle art of communication through which he sought to convince the educated Muslim, trained in the religious-legal sciences, that the principles and methods of these sciences are insufficient and inadequate for the proper understanding of the nature of society and of the real meaning and use of history, to show him the need to turn to philosophy, and to suggest to him the superiority of the explanations offered by the latter.

Yet the general run of educated Muslims, and the learned upholders of the religious-legal sciences, were suspicious of the philosophic-rational sciences and openly antagonistic to the protagonists of Greek philosophy, especially when these sought, as in this case, to challenge them in a field most intimately related to the way of life of the Islamic community. They also had effective ways of persecuting, silencing, and eliminating them. In such a context, it would have been, of course, disastrous for Ibn Khaldūn to make a frontal attack, both for his own person and for the success of his enterprise. Therefore, he chose the more effective method of openly aligning himself with the religious-legal sciences, while gradually undermining their authority in the specific field he chose as the object of his investigation. In this, he followed a well-established and well-known art of communication which Muslim philosophers had inherited from their Greek and Hellenistic masters, and which they elaborated to meet the particular exigencies they faced in their own religious community.

In a liberal society in which rationalism and science have triumphed, and in which religion seems to have been for a considerable time suspected and persecuted, and at a time when religion, rather than reason and science, seems to be struggling to lay claims to domains for long monopolized by science, the student is not likely to become excited over such problems as hiding one's intention to gain an initial hearing or to escape the censure and wrath of the religious community—problems which could not escape the trained mind of an educated Muslim of Ibn Khaldūn's time. In addition, the modern educated man suffers from an almost complete forgetfulness of even the existence of what were once commonplace ways of writing, especially among great authors of the past. Consequently, he is not at all equipped properly to read their works. He seems to think that only a confused author would not say exactly what is in his mind; and he is more likely to admire an author's rashness than his prudence.

These are the most formidable obstacles in the way of the appreciation and understanding of many of the important Islamic classics, including Ibn Khaldūn's work. Because of them, these classics remain mute and helpless to communicate their message to the educated modern man. The most notable contribution that an instructor can make is to remind his students of these issues by pointing them out whenever encountered in the reading of these classics, and thus aid their authors by establishing a wider channel of communication between them and their modern readers.

Perhaps the simplest approach would be for the instructor to appeal to the student's desire for historical understanding, which demands the appreciation of the particular context within which an author like Ibn Khaldūn wrote, the specific problems he intended to solve, and the alternative methods which were open to him in pursuing his aim. But once these issues are reopened, he could enhance the interest of the student in them by directing his attention to what he could learn from an author like Ibn Khaldūn concerning the character of public dogmas in all societies, including his own, of the restraints and limits they impose on public expression, and of the ways and means followed in suppressing or persecuting those who challenge them in societies most dedicated to the free expression of thought. The student will thus be brought to face the theoretical and practical considerations which make prudence rather than rashness the more desirable virtue in a writer.

• • •

In its positive teachings relative to history and society, experience has shown that, unlike many other Islamic classics, Ibn Khaldūn's work is able for the most part to command immediate acceptance, if not admiration, by the modern educated man. Its modern reader is drawn to its subject matter and to its scientific approach. It reminds him of a science, and of a critical approach, which he had thought to be specifically modern and to which he is usually already committed. Thus he begins to trust its author's scientific intentions, and to accept his analysis and interpretation of Islamic history and the Islamic society. Ibn Khaldūn has thus been able to escape the fate of many Muslim authors who aroused only the interest of the antiquarian, or were subjected to a historicist interpretation, i.e., were placed in a particular historical context and explained accordingly as representatives of a particular world view. He is admitted to the company of modern scientists as a fellow investigator in a common endeavor for objective knowledge.

This, however, is a mixed blessing. It certainly lightens the work of the instructor who is freed from the burden of attempting to arouse, at the outset, sufficient interest in, and respect for, the author, both of which are necessary conditions for a sustained dialogue between such an author and his reader. Therefore, this initial acceptance and trust should at first be encouraged. But in fairness to Ibn Khaldūn's text, the instructor must sooner or later turn this surprising rapport into a problem, and raise the question as to its reasons and the degree of its validity. He will soon discover that it is based on a conception of science and its method which, though at certain points coinciding with that of Ibn Khaldūn, differs from it on fundamental issues. The most important of these is the deep gulf that separates the modern conception of natural science and its relation to the science of society from that of Ibn Khaldūn.

Both Ibn Khaldūn and modern social science have attempted to develop a natural science, or a physics, of society. There are, of course, important differences in the reasons for following such a course and in the uses contemplated from the results, and in general in the place of the resulting science of society within the totality of human knowledge. Nevertheless, it could be said that in both cases it was thought that a science of society drawing its principles and methods from the wider study of nature, of which man is but a part, would be more exact and more explanatory, and would do less violence to the data which are being investigated, than a science of society based on principles whose only justification is tradition, faith, or common opinion.

But as soon as we stop to inquire into the precise character of Ibn Khaldūn's natural science, the similarity ends. For we find that, for Ibn Khaldūn, natural science meant traditional Aristotelian natural science as found in that part of Aristotle's corpus which begins with the *Physics* and ends with the *De Anima*, together with the commentaries of Muslim philosophers in general and of Avicenna in particular. Our modern social science, on the other hand, was patterned after modern classical and post-classical physics with its radical departure from, and rejection of, traditional natural science or natural philosophy. How then could a science of society based on traditional natural philosophy be as scientific, and its conclusions as worthy of our consent, as a science of society based on modern physics? Is it that it makes no difference what kind of natural science one starts with? Does this mean that our modern physics has no higher claim to validity, at least insofar as its implications for social science are concerned, than traditional natural philosophy?

The central importance of Ibn Khaldūn's work is that it forces us to raise such questions and that it may be of use in seeking answers for them; for it is the only comprehensive attempt to develop a science of society on the basis of traditional natural philosophy. As one pursues such questions through his text, the real differences between his science of society and our modern social science begin to emerge. It will be found for instance that, in spite of the fact that he lays special emphasis on material and efficient causes, his conception of the "nature" of man and society is wider than that of modern social science: it includes their purpose and end, the good, and happiness.

It is, of course, not to be expected that when this fact is pointed out to the modern reader, he will continue to admire or trust Ibn Khaldūn's conclusions and judgments. What would be didactically useful and significant is that the shock resulting from the loss of initial and naive admiration and trust be taken as an opportunity to raise the important question of the status of modern physics, to question the naive acceptance of its presuppositions, to question the uncritical faith in its principles and methods as the only ones which can lay claim to being unquestionably scientific, and to question the character and the degree of explanation offered by a social science patterned after this physics.

Ibn Khaldūn certainly did not know of our modern physics in its specific details. But he knew of physical theories that had something in common with it, e.g., ancient materialism, and Islamic atomism and occasionalism. Yet, for the purpose of explaining the nature of society, he decided in favor of Aristotelian natural philosophy because he believed in its superiority as natural philosophy and in the superiority of a science of society that could be based upon it. He did not seem to be of the opinion that, so far as the science of society is concerned, it makes no difference what science of nature one chooses; and he seemed to place more confidence in Aristotelian natural philosophy and in the usefulness of its principles and methods for the science of society. Thus he seems to challenge rather seriously the superiority of our modern physics as well as of our modern social science.

At a time when both modern physics and modern social science have begun to entertain doubts about their presuppositions and to be concerned with problems of a more philosophic nature, such a challenge should be made to command more attention, and to offer an additional reason for a more serious examination of the claims of traditional natural philosophy and of the science of society based upon it.

One of the aspects of traditional natural philosophy that needs special attention in this respect is its place within traditional philosophy or science as a whole. For the fact that it was an integral part of general philosophy made the understanding of the relationship between nature, soul, and intellect more accessible. Consequently, Ibn Khaldūn's study of the nature of man and society, though based upon the principles and methods of natural philosophy, could still take into account such human and social phenomena as the sciences, inspiration, and prophecy, and in general things that are specifically human and superhuman, and for whose understanding natural philosophy alone is not sufficient.

It was this belief in the accessibility to reason of the principles of all things natural and beyond nature, and in the possibility of knowing what is best for man as man, that made it possible for Ibn Khaldūn to arrive at the necessary detachment from, and to pass judgment upon, the opinions and actions of his community. Modern students uniformly admire his objectivity, his intellectual honesty, and his severity in judging the shortcomings of his community. On the other hand, they see that he is definitely committed to the proposition that the principles upon which the religious Law of his community was based made it superior to other communities. Their initial reaction to this seemingly contradictory position is usually that his toughness is the result of his positive scientific attitude, while his belief in the superiority of his own community is socially conditioned. This is the characteristically modern conception of the universal character of positive science, of which Ibn Khaldūn is supposed to have been a precursor, and the relative and socially conditioned character of cultural values, from which he is thought not to have been able to free himself.

It will no doubt prove extremely difficult to convince the modern reader of the dogmatic character of this position. But it should at least be pointed out that the attempt to understand Ibn Khaldūn on this basis is liable to prejudice the issue and close the mind of the reader to what Ibn Khaldūn could teach him concerning the relation between science and cultural values. Here again, and at the risk of another shock and additional loss of confidence in the scientific character of Ibn Khaldūn's thought, the instructor will have to point out, perhaps with the aid of suggesting the need for an objective understanding of his thought, that Ibn Khaldūn's attachment to science or philosophy, as he understood it, made tough and polite judgments equally possible; and that for him praise and blame, and the recognition of superiority and inferiority, are both equally grounded in the understanding, or at least in a dim vision, of what is best for man and society.

In this respect, the understanding of Ibn Khaldūn's text requires an approach which substitutes for the modern distinction between facts and values the distinction between events, commonly known and generally accepted opinions and beliefs, and the pursuit of knowledge, the results of which, when fulfilling the requirements of logical reasoning, constitute science. Opinions and beliefs may agree or disagree with, may be identical with or contradictory to, or may come close to or may be remote from, scientifically demonstrated conclusions. All existing communities are based on opinions and beliefs; and differences among the opinions and beliefs of different communities, and among their ways of life which are based on such opinions and beliefs, are not only possible but to a certain extent natural. But such plurality does not exclude the possibility of scientific knowledge on the basis of which one could transcend the opinions and beliefs of his own community. Therefore, all men are not fated to accept blindly the opinions and beliefs of their community as being identical with truth or the good. Yet men of science are not those who simply dismiss opinions and beliefs as mere opinions and beliefs, but those who, on the basis of their scientific knowledge, and experience and prudence, can correctly judge the degree of truth contained in, and the practical use of, different opinions and beliefs, including those of their own community.

The reader must first be made to see how Ibn Khaldūn was able to do this with respect to the communities with which he was acquainted, and particularly how this approach enabled him to understand and judge his own community, its opinions and beliefs, and its way of life. This becomes rather delicate when he studies matters such as revelation, prophecy, and religious law. But when the reader becomes acquainted with his art of writing, he will begin to see that the general approach outlined above holds even in the study of such matters.

Since Ibn Khaldūn's work was on the whole concerned with the Islamic society, it will be easier for the educated Westerner to accept his critique of that society, as his own opinions, beliefs, and way of life, and those of his own community, are not immediately at stake. Indeed, it would be useful to reveal the various facets of Ibn Khaldūn's critique of the Islamic community as thoroughly as possible, yet insist throughout upon the theoretical foundation on the basis of which such a critique was possible. The instructor will find that, because the student's own preferences and those of his own community are not directly involved, he is more likely to be open-minded and more willing to be tough. If sufficient control is exercised to prevent this from becoming a free indulgence in common prejudices against other communities, it will prove an excellent training ground for developing his power of critical judgment, the exercise of which can and must eventually be transferred to the critical study of his own community, its opinions and beliefs, and its way of life.

For ultimately, Ibn Khaldūn's study of the nature of man and society will prove of little value for general education if it fails to arouse in the modern reader a genuine concern for understanding himself and the character of his own community. A necessary prerequisite for such an understanding is the readiness to question the generally known opinions and the commonly accepted beliefs of his own community. The general tendency has been to see in Ibn Khaldūn a confirmation of established opinions and beliefs. The continued use of his work for this purpose will mean the perpetuation of a misunderstanding of Ibn Khaldūn's thought and intention. Further, since it will encourage opinionated complacency, it will prove harmful to general education. The task of the instructor is to initiate a dialectical process in which the reading of Ibn Khaldūn serves to help the student to question his own opinions and beliefs, and then use this critical attitude for a more thorough and a more critical understanding of Ibn Khaldūn's text.

It is to be hoped that the preceding remarks have shown that the problems confronting the teaching and the study of Ibn Khaldūn's text are not primarily philological or historical in character, at least not in the narrow sense of philological and historical criticism. The text has been preserved in numerous copies, many of which were excellently transcribed under the supervision of an author who also prided himself on writing in a clear and free manner, upon which modern philology need not presume that it can improve. Ibn Khaldūn himself also supplies in the same text all the historical background relevant for understanding it. He was, after all, a great authority on the history of his time.

There are, it is true, difficulties related to the appreciation of his art of writing, the understanding of the precise character of his scientific investigation of society, and the recapturing of his conception of the nature of scientific knowledge in general and its place within the social order in particular. But these difficulties are for the most part not faced, but only sidetracked, by modern philological and historical criticism. These latter are the scientific offspring of a modern philosophic attitude which has invariably supplied the premises (sometimes accepted dogmatically by these specialized disciplines) in the light of which Ibn Khaldūn's text has been interpreted. Since the proper understanding of the text seems to require, and to lead to, the questioning of the dogmatic character of this attitude, it is evident that the reader, if he is to profit intellectually from his reading, must regain a certain innocence and be willing to think, to doubt, and to question both his own ideas as well as those presented to him by the author.

If the reader is an undergraduate student, he will need an adequate translation of the text prepared for him with the assumption that he is a serious reader, and an instructor trained to arouse his curiosity about important issues in general and direct his attention to the specific issues raised by Ibn Khaldūn's text in particular.

There are a host of summaries, paraphrases, and selections in the various Western languages, but very few of them are executed with proper care. They subscribe (at least the most popular among them) to the notion of the modern character of Ibn Khaldūn's thought. Thus they omit or mistranslate the sections that do not harmonize with this notion; they rearrange the text, modernize its expressions, and in general try to present it in a perspective intended to prove or suggest the modern, scientific character of the thought of its author.

The student should be encouraged to turn to the two complete translations of the "Introduction," that of Baron de Slane in French and that of Franz Rosenthal in English. He will find them of much greater use in learning about the scope of the work and of its internal structure. Of the two, the English translation is the more recent and the superior one. However, under the influence of previous summaries, selections, and monographs, it accepts the notion that the text is "modern in thought yet alien in language and style," and a great effort is made throughout to make the text comprehensible to the general reader through an extensive use of the modernizing type of rendering. Therefore, the careful reader, willing to spend the time and effort required by a more exact (even if less literary and more dry) rendering of the Arabic style and of the technical terms, with the hope of a sounder understanding of the text, will still find himself severely handicapped. Thus the burden is shifted to the instructor, who will have to control the translation.

This, of course, is the most elementary task that will be faced by the instructor, and one which is by no means the most difficult to overcome. The teaching of Ibn Khaldūn's text as a great book and for the purposes of general education makes demands on the instructor which very few specialists in Arabic and Islamic studies are at present prepared to meet. This is not an accident. It is intimately linked with the past and present status of these studies. Arabic and Islamic studies as scientific academic disciplines are relatively recent ventures. They developed in the nineteenth century as special branches of philology and history; were influenced by the current trends in these two disciplines; and continued to remain loyal to them in the critical editions of texts and in textual criticism, and in the critical study of Islamic history. It would be sheer folly at this juncture in the development of these studies to detract from the value of the type of specialized training they offer, to say nothing of disrupting a tradition built with great dedication and effort. Yet it must in all honesty be recognized that such a training does not by itself supply the required background for the critical reading, understanding, and interpreting, of the great Islamic classics. If one had enough courage, he might even dare to say that they are not, strictly speaking, an indispensable requirement for such a work. (Averroes and Aquinas were able, without them, to understand the text of Aristotle better than most, if not all, modern philologists and historians.) The normal trend within these studies has been to have recourse to the theories that happen to be popular at the time (historicism, sociologism, psychologism, etc.), or other commonly accepted beliefs and opinions, and to adopt them in interpreting these classics, thus enjoying the advantage of following the latest scientific style.

Such scientific interpretations are usually harmless exercises, and they can, on rare occasions, be useful in providing certain insights into the Islamic classics. But they tend also to become substitutes for the direct critical reading of these classics with the intention of finding what one can learn from them. And they even get incorporated into the texts of these classics through the modernized type of rendering. Perhaps no great Muslim author has suffered from this tendency as much as Ibn Khaldūn. Thus when the innocent student proceeds to read and understand his text with an open mind, he is likely to have before him a not-so-innocent version of it, and to have as his guide an instructor who seems to know all about Ibn Khaldūn's background, his psychology, the social forces that determined his thought, the reasons for his belief in God and superstition and religion, etc.—in short everything except how to critically read the text before him, analyze it, closely follow the steps of Ibn Khaldūn's argument, enjoy his "doubletalk," appreciate his hints and allusions, and arouse and encourage in the student a passion for reading the text, appreciating it, and criticizing it as a great work of the mind. He seems often to have been trained to explain the text away, and to lack the readiness for allowing the text to explain away his own notions, to form his mind, and to train it in dealing with the great issues of life and of the world.

The grafting of this latter attitude upon the existing structure of Arabic and Islamic studies requires a concerted effort on the part of educators and Arabists and Islamists alike. Nor should the latter be thought of as immune or insufficiently responsive to new demands, especially if coupled with the expectation of more solid rewards. Many Arabists and Islamists have, for instance, proved obligingly willing in recent times to meet the demand for popular versions of Islamic history and civilization—sometimes even at the expense of their own scientific conscience, and in spite of the reproachful and censorious attitude of their colleagues. The teaching of the Islamic classics as great books, however, is of a completely different order.

There is already in existence an established academic, and even para-academic, tradition with respect to the introduction of the classics of the Western world into programs of general education. By now, educators have a rather clear idea of what the problems and prospects of this enterprise are, and the training required of a successful instructor in this field. This experience must be made available to specialists in Arabic and Islamic studies so that they would gain a precise notion of the nature of the new needs. It should, in particular, be impressed upon them that the critical reading, analysis, understanding, and interpretation of an important text requires a special skill and training that cannot be acquired in one's spare time, that need not be subjective, nor the work of an undisciplined amateur.

If Arabists and Islamists find that the history and character of their discipline make it difficult for them at present to offer such a training, then the best practical arrangement will be for them to encourage the student to acquire such training through interdepartmental committees, in fields where such a training is offered, such as in philosophy, and in classical and modern literatures, i.e., in fields where the classics are made the backbone of the program of study. This is certainly a second-best arrangement, since it involves the task of subsequently transferring the skills thus acquired to texts of somewhat different character. But in addition to substantially meeting the present need for qualified instructors to teach the Islamic classics, the result will no doubt prove a significant gain to Arabic and Islamic studies themselves. For no matter how necessary or useful philological and historical criticism may be, they should never be separated from the study of Islamic classics as classics.

4 CLASSICS OF THE INDIAN TRADITION

The Upanishads

Joel Brereton

The Upanishads are early texts of the Hindu tradition which set forth the foundations of the world and the true nature of the self. They are formally quite diverse, for they include narratives, dialogues, verses, and the teachings of ancient sages. The principal Upanishads, which were composed probably between 600 and 300 B.C.E., constitute the concluding portion of the Veda, the most ancient and conventionally the most fundamental scripture of Hinduism. According to most reckonings, there are fourteen Vedic Upanishads, and these can be assigned a relative chronology on the basis of their literary form and language. The oldest are in prose. Among them are the *Bṛhad Āraṇyaka, Chāndogya, Kauṣītakī, Taittirīya,* and *Aitareya Upaniṣads*. A second, generally later group of Upanishads were written in verse. These include the *Kaṭha, Īśā, Muṇḍaka,* and *Śvetāśvatara Upaniṣads*. Finally, the youngest are also in prose, but in a style which is closer to classical Sanskrit than to the more archaic language of the oldest Upanishads. These include the *Maitrī* and *Māṇḍūkya Upaniṣads.* This division is only approximate, for individual Upanishads may contain material from different periods.

It is not quite accurate to say that the Upanishadic period ended with these texts. The term "Upanishad" became the designation of a genre rather than of specific texts, for works called Upanishads continued to be written through the Middle Ages and even into the early modern period. Tradition holds that there are 108 Upanishads —108 is a sacred number—but even more texts claim the status of Upanishads. These later Upanishads fall into different types which reflect the major developments in Hindu religious thought and practice. Some discuss topics and ideas introduced in the earlier Upanishads, others teach yoga and the renunciation of the world, and still others reflect sectarian worship of the classical Hindu deities. These Upanishads are significant, but none of them has had the enduring influence on Indic thought that the Vedic Upanishads have had. This essay, therefore, will be concerned entirely with the latter.

The Vedic Upanishads play a critical role in the history of Indic religion. Literarily, they are the last sections of the Brāhmanas, which are commentaries on the great public rites of the Vedic tradition. This literary position also reflects their historical place, for they are later than most of the Brāhmanas, and their thought developed out of the Brāhmanas. Historically, their period was one of transition, when the foundations of classical Hindu religion were established and archaic forms of Vedic religion were superseded. Therefore, many basic elements of Hindu religion were first clearly articulated in the Vedic Upanishads. These include the ideas of *karma* and rebirth; instructions concerning yoga, meditation, and asceticism; the concept of a self beyond the individual self; and the view that there is a single reality hidden by the multiple forms of the world.

The Upanishads are significant also because they continued to exercise a decisive role in Hindu religious history long after their composition. In fact, unlike the rest of the Veda, they still remain a major source of inspiration and authority within Hinduism. The most influential schools of Hindu religious thought are the schools of the Vedānta, a term that means "the end of the Veda." They have that name because they understand the Upanishads, which are the last part of the Veda, to be the essence of Vedic teaching and the ultimate authority regarding the true nature of things. Of these schools, one has dominated both Indic and Western interpretation of the Upanishads. This school is the Advaita Vedānta, the "Nondualist Vedānta," which was established by a teacher named Śaṅkara, who lived around 700 C.E. According to Śaṅkara, the Upanishads teach that ultimately there exists one, and only one, indivisible reality. Hence the world and all its distinctions are less than fully real, and whatever reality they do possess derives from that one reality. Śankara must occasionally struggle hard to ground this view in the Upanishads, for although much of Upanishadic thought does stress the coherence and final unity of all things, it is not easily reduced to his or any other simple formula.

Other schools of the Vedānta differed profoundly with Śaṅkara and with one another in their interpretations of the Upanishads. And these differences point to an important characteristic of the Upanishads. Like Western scriptures, they are not catechisms of direct answers to religious questions, which obviate the need for any further reflection. Rather, they stimulate thought and challenge interpretation. They have this character for several reasons. First, even individual Upanishads are far from systematic. They were composed by different people, living at different times and in different areas of northern India. Moreover, those who put the Upanishads into their final shape combined and even interwove various teachings. As a result, an argument may move in different directions even within one section of one Upanishad. Second, especially the older Upanishads used the language of symbols and concrete images rather than that of abstraction. Some symbols were traditional, but the Upanishadic sages also created new images and refashioned old ones, especially the symbols of the Vedic ritual.

Such language gives Upanishadic diction the appeal of concrete narrative and the resonance of images, but it also opens them to very different interpretations. Thus, though the Upanishads are often understood philosophically, they call for not so much a systemization and specification of meaning as a reading which permits the associations and expansions of poetic discourse.

While the complexity of Upanishadic language and literary history precludes any easy summary of their teaching, there is a broad theme that encompasses much of their thought. In general, each Upanishadic teaching creates an integrative vision, a view of the whole which draws together the separate elements of the world and of human experience and compresses them into a single form. To one who has this larger vision of things, the world is not a set of diverse and disorganized objects and living beings, but rather forms a totality with a distinct shape and character.

The Upanishads often create such an integrative vision by identifying a single, comprehensive and fundamental principle which shapes the world. One term by which the Upanishads designate that fundamental principle is "*brahman.*" For later followers of the Vedānta, the *brahman* has a particular definition and a specific character, but for the Upanishads, the *brahman* remains an open concept. It is simply the designation given to whatever principle or power a sage believes to lie behind the world and to make the world explicable. It is the reality sought by the householder who asks a sage: "Through knowing what, sir, does this whole world become known?" (*Muṇḍaka Upaniṣad* 1.13).

Such an aspiration for a total vision of things is not unique to the Upanishads or to India. One distinctive turn which the Upanishads give to this vision is their understanding that the fundamental principle of everything is also the core of each individual. The typical designation for that core is the *ātman*, the "self." Thus, in Upanishadic terms, the *brahman* is discovered within the *ātman*, or conversely, the secret of one's self lies in the root of all existence.

Within this common approach, however, the Upanishads differ among themselves in the shape they give to that vision of totality and the means by which they create it. To clarify this vision of the Upanishads and to show their diversity, I will present five paradigms that these teachings follow. Each paradigm is a method or pattern through which the Upanishads construct a totality out of the multiplicity of the world. These five Upanishadic paradigms are: (1) the correlation of different aspects of reality to one another; (2) the emergence of the world from a single reality and its resolution back into it; (3) a hierarchy which leads ultimately to the foundation of all things; (4) a paradoxical coincidence of things which are ordinarily understood to exclude or oppose one another; and (5) a cycle which encompasses the processes of life and the world. These paradigms do not exhaust the variety of Upanishadic teachings, but collectively they suggest their range.

CORRELATION

One means of demonstrating unity behind apparent diversity is by displaying correspondences among things belonging to different domains. This was not a new technique in Indic thought, since already the Brāhmanas had made extensive use of the same paradigm. But while the Brāhmanas sought such correlations within the domain of the ritual and between the domains of the ritual and the outside world, the Upanishads search primarily for those that exist within and among the human and natural domains.

The Upanishads have several ways of identifying these correspondences. One is to link various parts of the world to a single, structured entity. That is, they take a symbol or set of symbols which is comprehensible and ordered, and then relate items from different domains to it. In this way, the symbol becomes a map. Just as one understands an unfamiliar territory by comparing various places and objects to areas on a map, so one comprehends the world by associating its parts to a known object. In the Upanishads, the ordering object or domain is normally something concrete. Thus in the opening of the *Bṛhad Āraṇyaka Upaniṣad,* the sacrificial horse is the image of the world. The passage begins: "Now, the head of the sacrificial horse is dawn; his eye, the sun; his breath, the wind; his open mouth, the fire which is common to all" (*Bṛhad Āraṇyaka Upaniṣad* 1.1.1). The passage thus identifies the head of the horse with the symbols of the main divisions of space. The sun represents the heaven; wind, the midspace between earth and heaven; and fire, the earth. It then goes on to equate other parts of the land and air with the body of the horse, the seas with the sacrificial vessels which stand on either side of the horse, and various living beings, from gods to humans, with the different names by which the horse is addressed in the ritual. The passage thus reduces the whole world to the form of the horse, and by doing so, it makes the world a single, comprehensible object. Therefore, those who reflect on the horse understand and embrace everything in their contemplation.

The use of a ritual object like the sacrificial horse in such a system of correlations is more typical of Brāhmanas than of Upanishads. For the latter, the most frequent correlation is between the macrocosm and the human body. That is, they equate the parts of the body to the constituents of the visible world, so that the whole world becomes the image of the human form. In this way, instead of appearing external and alien, the world becomes a familiar place and a place in which humans occupy a central position.

The *Aitareya Upaniṣad,* for example, opens with a narrative which tells how the world and the body became the twin images of one another. Although this narrative has the form of a creation story, it is better read not as describing the actual process of creation, but as establishing the connections that now exist within the world.

In the beginning, there was only the self, the *ātman.* This self resolves to create. It first produces the basic form of the world, and then from the waters, it draws forth a being that the text calls the "person." This person is egg-like, for it is without faculties of sense or action. Therefore the self next creates these faculties by bringing them forth from the person one by one. Then from these faculties, it extracts the characteristic product or activity of each one, and from these in turn, it brings forth a corresponding aspect of the world. Thus, from the mouth of the person comes speech and then fire; from its nostrils, breath and wind; from its eyes, sight and sun; from its ears, hearing and the four directions; from its skin, hair and plants; from its heart, thought and the moon; from its navel, inhalation and death; and from its penis, semen and water.

The associations which provide the basis for most of these correlations are not difficult. The one exception is the odd correlation of the navel, inhalation and death. On the one hand, the inhalation is drawn toward the navel, which connotes birth and life. But on the other, inhalation is linked with eating, which implies human physicality and therefore human mortality. Hence, inhalation also signifies death.

The creation of the human being follows in the next part of the narrative. The macrocosmic realities just created fall into the sea once again, back to their place of origins. This descent into the sea figuratively expresses the disorganization of these powers. They need an order, and to find it, they enter into the human form once again. Fire becomes speech and enters the mouth; wind becomes breath and enters the nostrils; the sun becomes sight and enters the eyes, and so on. The sequence exactly reverses the order of their creation. Thus, the elements of the world are created from the cosmic person, and then they return again to the human form in which all people share. Hence, the world mirrors the human body, and its parts correspond to human faculties.

Finally, at the end of the process, the self itself enters into the newly created human form. In this way, the self, which is the origin of all, becomes the self of each human being. Thus, as the body corresponds to the visible world, the self of the world coincides with the self of the individual. Both physically and spiritually, therefore, the human being is a perfect microcosm.

The correspondence between the microcosm and the macrocosm illustrates how the Upanishads fashion a vision of totality through correlation. This correspondence unifies the world in the form of the person, and therefore makes the world comprehensible as a whole. Furthermore, it also implies that the world and the power that controls it are not outside, bearing down upon and threatening the individual. Rather, because the parts of the world are equivalent to the parts of a person, humans include everything within themselves.

EMERGENCE AND RESOLUTION

The Upanishads also create a sense of the unity of all things through viewing creation as an emergence from a single reality and destruction as a return to that reality. The *Muṇḍaka Upaniṣad* provides some striking images of this process: "As a spider spins and gathers (its web), as plants grow upon the earth, as head and body hair (grow) from a living person, so everything here arises from the imperishable" (*Muṇḍaka Upaniṣad* 1.1.7). The image of the spider and its web is especially strong. The spider stands alone at the beginning, spins its web out of itself, and finally draws it back into itself. In the same way, the "imperishable" *brahman* emits the world from itself and ultimately reabsorbs it back into itself. Thus, the world is only the outward projection of the *brahman*.

One of the most influential realizations of this paradigm occurs in *Chāndogya Upaniṣad* 6. The chapter takes the form of a dialogue between a sage named Uddālaka and his arrogant son Śvetaketu. After studying the Vedas for twelve years, Śvetaketu comes home very proud of his achievement. His father then asks him if during his education, his teachers taught him that "by which what has been unheard becomes heard, what has been unthought becomes thought, what has been unknown becomes known" (*Chāndogya Upaniṣad* 6.1.3). To understand clay or copper, for example, means that one also knows the character of all clay and copper utensils, because their qualities will reflect the substance of their composition. In the same way, he asks, has Śvetaketu been taught the basic reality which comprises all things and through which the character of all things is known? Śvetaketu admits that he knows nothing of this, and Uddālaka begins his explanation of that reality.

In the beginning there was only being. From being then follows an evolution toward increasing materiality. Being, which is imperceptible, first gives rise to heat, which can be felt. Then heat gives rise to water, which can be felt and seen, and finally water gives rise to food, which can be felt, seen, and tasted. Food connotes full materiality. Uddālaka then confirms these relations by seeing their reflection in natural processes. Heat does produce water in humans, for when they are hot, they sweat, and rainwater does produce food. Similarly, human experience corroborates the reverse process, the resolution of each factor into the previous one. According to Uddālaka, people become thirsty when heat absorbs water and hungry when water absorbs food.

Once he has established the fundamental evolution from being, Uddālaka then shows how everything, and especially human beings, are the products of the intermingling and segmentation of the three evolutes. In the body, for example, each of the evolutes divides into three: food becomes mind, flesh, and excrement; water becomes breath, blood, and urine; heat becomes speech, marrow, and bone. Thus, the human being is nothing but a composite of the three basic factors. Likewise, the continuous process of the emergence and resolution of the three evolutes is reflected in the process of dying. When people die, they first lose consciousness, but they still breathe. This is the reabsorption of food by water, for mind and consciousness derive from food, but breath comes from water. Then, when water returns to heat, the breath ceases, for water corresponds to breath. Even without the breath, however, the body remains warm, for heat still remains. Finally, as the heat and the life of the person dissipate into being, the body becomes cold and death becomes complete. In Uddālaka's vision, therefore, being is the ultimate, pervasive source of mind, body, and the world, and life continues through a constant process of movement out of and into being.

In the second half of his teaching, Uddālaka drives home its significance for Śvetaketu's self-understanding. In one section, he asks his son to bring him a fruit from the *nyagrodha* tree, one of the sacred fig trees of India. He tells him to cut it open to find the seed, and then to cut the seed open. When he does so, Śvetaketu finds the seeds in the fruit, but then he cannot find anything in the seed. Yet within that seed is an essence, says Uddālaka, and that invisible essence is the source of the life of the huge *nyagrodha* tree. "Believe me, my child," he concludes, "that which is this finest essence—this whole world has that as its self. That is the real. That is the self. Thus are you, Śvetaketu" (*Chāndogya Upaniṣad* 6.12.3). Being is that essence, for being is the imperceptible source of all creation. This being is therefore the self of the *nyagrodha*, the self of the world, and the self of Śvetaketu.

Here again, as in the *Aitareya Upaniṣad*, the true self is not the individual self, but rather the identity that one shares with everything else. There is no true distinction among living beings, for they all emerge from being and retreat to it. All things, both animate and inanimate, are unified in being, because they are all the transformations of being. To understand the nature of being, therefore, is to have the knowledge that Uddālaka promised Śvetaketu, the knowledge that accounts for everything, the knowledge of the totality of things.

HIERARCHY

A third method of organizing experience is through constructing a hierarchy. That is to say, the Upanishadic sages set up a system of levels that shows which powers include other powers or which are dependent on which others. Ultimately, by moving toward progressively deeper levels, the sage identifies the fundamental principle on which everything else is established.

In one sense, this is the most characteristic technique of Upanishads, for it is from it that the Upanishads have their name. The word "*upaniṣad*," though usually translated "secret teaching" or the like, originally meant the subordination of one thing to another. The purpose of arranging things in such a progression is finally to identify the dominant reality behind an object. In *Chāndogya Upaniṣad* 8.7–12, for example, the god Indra and the antigod Virocana approach the creator deity, Prajāpati. They ask him the true nature of the self. Rather than giving them the real answer straightaway, Prajāpati first tells them that the true self is nothing but the self that one sees in a reflection. This answer satisfies Virocana: "So then, with tranquil heart Virocana went to the antigods. To them he declared this *upaniṣad:* 'Oneself *(ātman)* is to be satisfied here. Oneself is to be served. He who satisfies his own self here, who serves himself—he gains both worlds, this one here and yonder (heavenly world)' " (*Chāndogya Upaniṣad* 8.8.4). Virocana's *upaniṣad* holds that the physical self is subordinate to no other self but is the true and fundamental self. However, to revere the physical self as ultimate is a very dangerous *upaniṣad.* As Indra and Virocana depart with this teaching, Prajāpati observes that whoever "will follow this *upaniṣad,* whether they be gods or antigods, will pass away" (*Chāndogya Upaniṣad* 8.8.4). They will perish, for they do not identify themselves with an immortal self but with a self that dies. This truth is finally recognized by Indra, who returns to Prajāpati for further instruction. Gradually, Prajāpati leads Indra into more profound definitions of the self until at last, after Indra has studied with him for 101 years, Prajāpati reveals to him the reality behind the physical self and the true foundation of the self.

The definition of the self which Indra and Virocana seek is one of the dominant concerns of Upanishads. And of all the Upanishadic teachers, the one most closely associated with the quest for the self is a sage named Yājnavalkya. Yājnavalkya appears in *Bṛhad Āraṇyaka Upaniṣad* 3–4, first in a verbal contest with other brahmins and then in dialogue with King Janaka of Videha. According to Yājnavalkya, the foundation of the self is the subject upon which all consciousness depends and all action is established. Because that true self is always the perceiving subject, it itself can never become an object of thought or perception: "You could not see the seer of seeing. You could not hear the hearer of hearing. You could not think the thinker of thinking. You could not know the knower of knowing" (*Bṛhad Āraṇyaka Upaniṣad* 3.4.2).

That same self, however, is also the self of the world. Yājnavalkya calls it the "inner controller," which sustains both the body and the world, but which neither the person nor the world knows (*Bṛhad Āraṇyaka Upaniṣad* 3.7). It is the "imperishable," at whose command "the sun and the moon," "heaven and earth," and "moments, hours, days and nights, fortnights, months, seasons and years remain distinct," and at whose command, "some rivers flow eastward, others westward" (*Bṛhad Āraṇyaka Upaniṣad* 3.8.9). The only way to understand this self is to strip it of any positive content: "This is described as 'not this, not that' *(neti, neti)*. It is ungraspable, for it is never grasped. It is indestructible, for it is never destroyed. Without attachment, for it is not attached. Unbound, (yet) it is never unstable, never injured" (*Bṛhad Āraṇyaka Upaniṣad* 4.4.22). The end of this passage suggests the personal significance of this view of the self. To identify oneself with a self which stands above any recognizable object is to become invulnerable. Mind, body, emotions—all these are susceptible to pain and suffering. But all these can be made objects of knowing, and therefore there must be a knowing subject that is deeper and more fundamental than they. It is that unknowable, knowing subject which is the true self. Why then fear sickness, suffering, or death? These affect what the self perceives; they do not affect what the self is.

Even if the self cannot become an object of thought, it can still be experienced. To investigate the experience of the self, Yājnavalkya examines dreamless sleep, which for him is a state in which everything other than the self is forgotten. In this state, the self emerges alone and as it truly is. This state of the self in itself is one of complete fulfillment: "Now, this is that form of his which is beyond pleasure, in which evil is removed, which is free of fear" (*Bṛhad Āraṇyaka Upaniṣad* 4.3.21). For one who experiences the true self, there is nothing wanted and nothing lacking, and therefore neither yearning nor grief can trouble that person.

In this state, the self never loses consciousness, "for there is no complete loss of knowing for the knower, because (the knower) is indestructible" (*Bṛhad Āraṇyaka Upaniṣad* 4.3.30). However, because there is nothing to be perceived, that consciousness has no object. Yājnavalkya captures this aspect of the experience of the self through an analogy: "Just as a man, when embraced by his dear wife, knows nothing within or without, even so this embodied self, when embraced by the conscious self, knows nothing within or without" (*Bṛhad Āraṇyaka Upaniṣad* 4.3.21). As the moment of sexual climax attenuates the awareness of any object and the distinction between oneself and the other, so the self knows nothing outside of itself. One's own self (the "embodied self") experiences only itself as the "conscious self," the ultimate subject of all knowing.

However there is a problem in all of this. Yājnavalkya's analogies of deep sleep and sexual intercourse apparently contradict one another, since people normally experience deep sleep as a state of unconsciousness, not one of objectless consciousness. For this reason, other Upanishadic teachers followed Yājnavalkya in identifying the true self as the ultimate subject, but rejected his identification of the state of the self and the state of deep sleep. Recall that in the dialogue between Prajāpati and Indra (*Chāndogya Upaniṣad* 8), Indra rejected Prajāpati's first explanation of the true self as the bodily self. After further definitions of the self and after 96 years of study, Prajāpati tells Indra that the self is experienced in deep sleep. "Then with tranquil heart, (Indra) went forth. But even before reaching the gods, he saw this danger: 'Obviously, now this (self) does not know itself, (does not know that) "This am I," neither does it know (other) beings here. It becomes one gone to destruction. I see nothing useful in this' " (*Chāndogya Upaniṣad* 8.11.1). Indra finds the teaching inadequate because it suggests that when everything is removed from the self, only unconsciousness remains. So once more, Indra returns to Prajāpati, and after another five years, Prajāpati reveals to him the true self. Similarly, the *Māṇḍūkya Upaniṣad* teaches that the self is experienced in a fourth state beyond waking, dreaming, and dreamless sleep. According to this text, that fourth state is not unconsciousness, but neither is it consciousness, at least not consciousness as it is normally understood. The state of the imperceptible self is unique and not identifiable with any other state.

These discussions of the self and of the experience of it are a reminder that the Upanishadic search for a definition of totality is not only an intellectual one. To be sure, the Upanishads seek the satisfaction of a comprehensive understanding of the world and the psychologically fulfilling identification with a deathless self beyond the individual self. But in addition, the Upanishadic views of self and the world also shape experiences in which the unknown self is directly realized. Some Upanishads make clear that the self is not something that can be taught, and that successful realization of self is not in the conscious control of the one seeking it: "This self cannot be attained by instruction, nor by intellect, nor by much learning. It can be attained only by the one whom it chooses. To him that self reveals its own form" (*Kaṭha Upaniṣad* 2.23, *Muṇḍaka Upaniṣad* 3.2.3). According to these texts, the knowledge of the self comes as if it were a revelation that breaks in upon the mind, and not as something intellectually achieved.

Yet within the Upanishads, there are attempts to devise methods of reaching the self. The *Śvetāśvatara Upaniṣad,* one of the latest Upanishads, comes close to classical yogic methods of finding the self. According to *Śvetāśvatara Upaniṣad* 2.8ff., a yogi should sit with the body erect and steady, checking bodily movements and restraining the breath. Thus quieting the senses and the mind, the yogi begins to move inward toward the core of the self and the world: "Fog, smoke, sun, wind, fire, fireflies, lightning, crystal, the moon—these are the preliminary appearances" (*Śvetāśvatara Upaniṣad* 2.11). Deprived of external distraction, the mind experiences these forms of light, which emerge from the inner light of the self. Eventually, the yogi moves through the layers of the self to its innermost core: "Just as a mirror stained by dust shines brilliantly when it is well cleansed, so the embodied (self), seeing the nature of the self, becomes single, its goal attained, free from sorrow" (*Śvetāśvatara Upaniṣad* 2.14). The true self is the end of the journey, for it is the foundation on which are built all the other states of mind and self.

Comparing the approach of Yājnavalkya and his successors and that of Uddālaka shows both the range and the common direction of the Upanishads. The two approaches begin with different paradigms for defining totality. Uddālaka's method is to describe the principle from which the world evolves and into which it devolves. In contrast, Prajāpati, Yājnavalkya, and the yoga teacher of the *Śvetāśvatara Upaniṣad* distinguish different levels of existence and experience and then move through these levels until they uncover the final, fundamental level. Thus, according to Yājnavalkya, to shift from the world experienced while awake to that of dreamless sleep is to advance to the deepest level of the self. Similarly, in the *Śvetāśvatara Upaniṣad,* different meditative states mark the progress toward the true self. Their approach is based on a hierarchical ordering of reality.

Not only do Yājnavalkya and Uddālaka operate with different paradigms, but also they begin from opposite directions. Yājnavalkya's is essentially an internal approach, which seeks the fundamental principle by turning back the layers of the self. Uddālaka, on the other hand, begins externally, with the world outside the self. Yājnavalkya investigates the self psychologically by observing its different states of consciousness, while Uddālaka analyzes the physical world and reduces its constituents and processes to a simple system. But both try to confirm their teachings by observation, either of internal states or of external realities. And both, whether they move from inside to outside or outside to inside, finally locate a principle which is simultaneously at the core of both the self and the world. For Yājnavalkya, the self that is the unknowable subject of all knowing is also the self of the whole world. For Uddālaka, being gives rise to the world, but it is also the self to which all living things return at death and from which they come forth at birth. Thus both teachers create visions of totality, even though they construct them differently.

PARADOX

Oddly, and perhaps even paradoxically, paradoxes can also create a unified vision. In a paradox, normally distinct objects are unexpectedly related or even equated to one another. If we encountered a very poor but happy couple, we could say that "paradoxically, they are rich in their poverty." Normally, wealth and poverty exclude one another, but in these people, material want and emotional richness coincide. In the same way, the Upanishads can use paradox to bring together things that appear to be separate in order to create a larger whole.

The best known Upanishadic paradox is the teaching of the sage Śāṇḍilya. Actually, this teaching occurs for the first time in a late portion of the *Śatapatha Brāhmana,* but it is repeated almost verbatim in *Chāndogya Upaniṣad* 3.14. Śāṇḍilya's teaching fuses the extremes of reality in a paradox. It concludes: "that self of mine in the heart is smaller than a grain of rice or of barley or a mustard seed or a grain of millet or the kernel of a grain of millet; that self of mine in the heart is greater than the earth, greater than the midspace, greater than the sky, greater than these worlds" (*Chāndogya Upaniṣad* 3.14.3). The self is the most intimate part of a person, the very center of one's being, and therefore it is the smallest of the small. Yet, at the same time, it surpasses everything. The paradox thus undercuts any exclusion or any separation of an individual from the rest of the world, for there is nothing beyond the self. If the self is the very smallest and the very largest, what is not encompassed by it?

For one Upanishad, the *Īśā Upaniṣad,* paradox is a central strategy. This entire poem consists of sets of paradoxes and antinomies. In v. 4, for example, the poet says that the One, the fundamental principle of things, is "unmoving" and yet it is swift, "swifter than the mind." It is unmoving because it is eternal; it is swifter than the mind because it is inconceivable. Therefore the paradox, like that of the couple's wealth and poverty, does not express a real contradiction, only a rhetorical one. But this rhetorical paradox lays the basis for a real paradox in the next verse. There the Upaniṣad says that the One "moves and does not move. It is far away and it is near. It is within everything and outside of everthing" (*Īśā Upaniṣad* 5). Here the running-standing model from the previous verse is restated as a moving-not moving opposition. The rest of the verse then develops this opposition. The consequence of moving is that the One is far; the consequence of not moving is that it remains near. The limit of distance is to be outside everything; the limit of nearness is to be inside. The paradoxical claim is that the One is both. In some way, the One is beyond time and space, and yet it is also within the world as the source of everything. Timelessness and time, perfection and movement—these only appear to be opposites, for in actuality, the One is all of them.

Both the teaching of Śāṇḍilya and that of the *Īśā Upaniṣad,* therefore, connect a single principle to opposite and apparently exclusive extremes. By so linking the extremes, they imply that this principle comprehends everything else as well. There is nothing that the principle does not include, nothing that remains separate from it and from everything else within it. In that way, the self of Śāṇḍilya and the One of the *Īśā Upaniṣad* become symbols of the totality of things.

CYCLES

A final strategy for creating an integrative vision is to represent world processes as a cycle. Of the various constructions of a vision of totality, this has the clearest foundation in the earlier Veda. The Vedic rituals followed the repeating sequences of natural events: the alternation of day and night, the phases of the moon, the seasons of rain and no rain, and the succession of years. Through the rituals, therefore, people understood and regulated their lives according to the course of nature. Even more explicitly than this ritual tradition, the Upanishads consolidate life and death, the succession of natural events and the divisions of time into recurring cycles.

One such cycle follows the movement of water, which represents the essence of life. This pattern appears in the parallel texts, *Chāndogya Upaniṣad* 5.3.7ff. and *Bṛhad Āraṇyaka Upaniṣad* 6.2.9ff. According to them, the gods fill the moon with *soma*, which is the holiest of all ritual offerings and which represents the elixir of life. As the moon wanes, *soma* is poured out as rain, which falls to earth where it nourishes the plants and becomes their sap and juice. Men ingest it with their food and pass that life essence to women through their semen. Within a woman, semen gives birth to a new human being. When that person dies and the body is cremated, the life essence rises once again with the smoke. For some, the life essence then returns to the moon and the cycle begins again. This vision thus integrates the birth and death of humans into the natural movement of water down to earth and up again to the sky. But that cycle does not continue for everyone. For those who understand this process and do not allow themselves to be entangled in the world controlled by this pattern, the cycle is broken at death. They go on to realms from which there is no further birth.

These passages, therefore, contain two concepts which were to become central to the Indic tradition: the idea that time moves in cycles and the idea of rebirth. The earliest Upanishads present rebirth as a concept which few know. In *Bṛhad Āraṇyaka Upaniṣad* 3.2, for example, a brahmin named Ārtabhāga quizzes Yājnavalkya again and again about a person's destiny after death. Finally, Yājnavalkya says, " 'Ārtabhāga, my friend, take my hand. We two alone will know of this. This matter of ours is not (to be discussed) in public.' So the two went away and deliberated. What they spoke of was action *(karma)*. What they proclaimed was action. Now, by good action one becomes good, by bad action bad" (*Bṛhad Āraṇyaka Upaniṣad* 3.2.13). This passage points toward the classical concept of *karma*, which comes to mean not only action but also the effect of action on one's own destiny. According to the developed tradition, by the accumulation of good *karma,* one secures a good rebirth, by bad *karma,* a bad one.

Later Upanishads take the reality of rebirth and *karma* for granted, and frame their goals in terms of them. The constant cycle of rebirths comes to express entrapment by death and suffering, and therefore release from that cycle becomes the critical achievement. Thus, the *Kaṭha Upaniṣad* starkly opposes the two possible fates: "On the one hand, he who is without understanding, who is unmindful and ever impure, does not attain the goal and goes into the cycle of rebirths. But he who understands, who is mindful and ever pure, attains the goal from which he is not born again" (*Kaṭha Upaniṣad* 3.7f.).

This negative turn gives the cyclical paradigm an equivocal status. In the Brāhmanas and early Upanishads, the natural cycles provided models for making sense of the world and human life, and even in later texts, they never completely lost that significance. However, these cycles could also be seen not just as embracing life but also as imprisoning it. For this reason, in order to break out of the cycle of constant death and rebirth, this paradigm had to be rejected as the final truth about human life.

THE INTEGRATIVE VISION

An integrative vision of things was not the only concern of the Upanishads, but it was a central one. This survey suggests some of the reasons for its significance. First and fundamental was the aesthetic and intellectual satisfaction in the ability to see things as a whole. The vision comprehends the world, and by it, people know who they are and where they are. People understand that they are a part of everything, in fact, that they are at the very center of everything, and they know that everything is a part of them. Second, this vision was a powerful knowledge. From early in the Vedic tradition, to know the truth of something was to have control over it. To know the world is therefore also to master the world and to direct one's fate. Especially the later Upanishads insist that insight into the true nature of things effects the highest attainment of all, the attainment of a final release from all temporal and spatial limitation. Third, the vision of totality was a transforming vision. Above all, it required a reevaluation of what one truly is and therefore what is truly consequential. In their various ways, the Upanishads argue that people are really not what they appear to be. They seem to be individuals, vulnerable to suffering and death, subject to their private destinies. That individual self, however, is not the true self. Death cannot affect the true self, nor can anything else, for the self precedes and embraces everything. The person who truly sees the self in this way, therefore, should have neither desire nor fear, for that person knows that no harm can come to the self. Fourth, this vision was a compelling experience. The Upanishads are not first-person records of religious or mystical experiences but rather the intellectual forms which molded and reflected such experiences. As a result, they do not give direct access to the experience of knowing the *ātman* or the *brahman*. Nevertheless, they do suggest the drama of that experience. The vision is only fully known when one becomes the true self or when one directly perceives the world in its singleness.

Why did this vision develop at this time and in this place? One reason was that its basis was firmly established in the Brāhmanas, which anticipate the Upanishadic aspiration to see the world as a totality. Moreover, the search for an integrative vision and the ability to experience this vision are not unique to India. Other cultures have also created paradigms for consolidating the diverse elements of experience, and other societies have given rise to mystical movements. The reason for the crystallization of Upanishadic thought may lie partly in the social and political changes occurring at the end of the Vedic period. This was not only a time of intellectual change, but one which saw the creation of cities and the consolidation of tribes into states. The stress on personal more than corporate identity, which can accompany these developments, may have provoked a nostalgia for a sense of the whole and for a definition of the self which did not isolate the individual.

At the same time, the Upanishads are a result of the very individuality they seem to compromise. They are the compositions of creative individuals, and they address themselves to individuals. Some Upanishads imply that the realization of the truth can occur only by a supremely individualistic act: breaking away from society and retreating to the forest for a life of study and meditation. Thus, the Upanishads may be the product of a contradiction, but if so, it is one of the creative contradictions which have driven the development of Indic culture and its complexity.

SUGGESTED TRANSLATIONS

Paul Deussen, *Sixty Upaniṣads of the Veda*, 2 vols. (Delhi: Motilal Banarsidass, 1980). This is an English version of a German translation of the Upanishads, originally published in 1897. Despite the age of the original and the problems of a double translation, this collection is still useful, especially because it includes a large number of the later Upanishads.

Franklin Edgerton, *The Beginnings of Indian Philosophy* (Cambridge: Harvard University Press, 1965). This work contains good translations of the central chapters of the *Bṛhad Āraṇyaka Upaniṣad, Chāndogya Upaniṣad* 6, and the *Kaṭha Upaniṣad*. These selections provide an excellent introduction to Upaniṣadic thought.

Swami Gambhirananda, *Eight Upaniṣads*, 2 vols. (Calcutta: Advaita Ashrama, 1957–58). These translations of the shorter Vedic Upanishads include Śankara's commentary, for those who wish to see how the Upanishads' most influential interpreter understood them.

Robert Ernest Hume, *The Thirteen Principal Upanishads* 2d ed. (London: Oxford University Press, 1931). This remains the best translation of the Upanishads. But the translation is literal, so much so that at times it can be difficult to read.

The *Mahābhārata* as Theater

Barbara Stoler Miller

The drama of moral chaos and war that lies at the heart of the *Mahābhārata* is intensified in the visual poetry of Peter Brook's version through techniques that derive from ancient Indian theater. The work of Brook, writer Jean-Claude Carrière, and the international company of actors belongs to a tradition of Indian poets and performers who have exploited the theatrical possibilities of the *Mahābhārata* by elaborating the epic stories through dramatic enactment. Ancient Indian theorists call drama "visual poetry," as opposed to "aural poetry," because it presents us with a world to see. The word for acting in Sanskrit is *abhinaya,* the language of gesture that has been a distinctive feature of the Indian stage from the earliest times. Particular importance is given to the use of hands and eyes for translating ideas, objects, and emotions into aesthetic statements. Arduous training is necessary to perfect *abhinaya.* Acting in Indian theater is considered a discipline *(yoga)* whereby the actor and acted become one. Gestures, however carefully learned and conventionalized, must not be mechanical; they must appear ceremonious, graceful, and spontaneous. An actor or actress, like a *yogī*, must cultivate a spontaneity that transcends learned conventions, artificiality, and limitations of the stage. It is intense concentration that allows the performer to become absorbed in creating scenes that put the audience in intimate touch with vital aspects of nature and human psychology. According to ancient Indian myth, the origin of drama was a holy presentation that the gods offered to give ethical instruction through diversion when people were no longer listening to the scriptures. Ancient texts stress the reward a king will gain if he presents dramatic performances as a gift to his subjects and an offering to the gods. For centuries Indian dramas have been commissioned and presented on the occasion of a seasonal festival, the birth of a son, a marriage, a royal consecration, a political victory, or any other climactic event.

Most scholars would agree that the *Mahābhārata* has its roots in events that took place in the period following the entry of the Indo-Aryan speaking nomadic tribes into northwestern India around 1200 B.C. The composition of the epic began as these tribes settled in the river valleys of the Indus and the Ganges during the first millennium B.C., when their nomadic sacrificial cults began to develop into the religious traditions of Hinduism. The work has stylistic and mythological roots in the ancient ritual hymns of the *Ṛg Veda* and narrative sources in oral tales of a tribal war fought in the Punjab early in the first millennium B.C. As the tradition was taken over by professional storytellers and intellectuals, many sorts of legend, myth, and speculative thought were absorbed, including the *Bhagavad Gītā*, which belongs to the layer of the epic that took form around the first century A.D. In its present form the *Mahābhārata*, consists of over one hundred thousand verses divided into eighteen books. The martial saga has been expanded into an encyclopedic repository of ancient Indian myths, ideals, and concepts. Indians say of it: "What is not here is not found anywhere else."

Just as Greek culture has drawn on the Homeric epics to represent its values, so Hindu culture has drawn upon the *Mahābhārata*, as well as the *Rāmāyaṇa*, to represent its values, dominant among which is the idea of order and sacred duty *(dharma)*. Appropriate to the authority of their social position as warrior-kings, the epic heroes embody order and sacred duty *(dharma)*, while their foes, whether human or demonic, embody chaos *(adharma)*. The ritualization of warrior life and the demands of sacred duty define the religious and moral meaning of heroism throughout the *Mahābhārata*. Acts of heroism are characterized less by physical prowess than by *dharma*, often involving extraordinary forms of sacrifice, penance, devotion to a divine authority, and spiritual victory over evil.

In *The Shifting Point* (Harper and Row, 1987), Peter Brook speaks of *dharma* in the theater:

> The *Mahābhārata* as a whole acquires its concrete meaning from the fact that *dharma* cannot be defined. What can be said about something that can't be defined, if one wants to avoid philosophical abstractions? For no one can be helped in life by abstractions.
>
> The *Mahābhārata* does not attempt to explain the secret of *dharma*, but lets it become a living presence. It does this through dramatic situations which force *dharma* into the open.
>
> When one enters into the drama of the *Mahābhārata*, one is living with *dharma*. And when one has passed through the work, one has a feeling for what *dharma* is and what is the opposite, *adharma*. Here lies the responsibility of the theatre: what a book cannot convey, what no philosopher can truly explain, can be brought into our understanding by the theatre. Translating the untranslatable is one of its roles.

In Indian terms, the success of a drama is the resolution of emotional disharmonies in the microcosm of the theater by exploring deeper relations that bind apparent conflicts of existence. The manifestation of these relations produces in the audience the intense aesthetic experience called *rasa*. Though usually translated by "sentiment" or "mood," *rasa* more literally means the "flavor" or "taste" of something. *Rasa* is the flavor that the dramatist and performers distill from ordinary emotional situations in order to present them for aesthetic appreciation. Human emotion, the basic material of *rasa,* is divided by theorists into nine categories: the erotic, the heroic, the comic, the pathetic, the furious, the horrible, the disgusting, the marvelous, and the calm. The intricate relationships among these underlie all Indian literature, beginning with the Sanskrit epics.

Consonant with ancient Indian oral and dramatic traditions, the Brook/Carrière version of the *Mahābhārata* begins with a prologue on the creation of the epic itself. The first character to speak is Vyāsa, the author to whom the epic is traditionally attributed. Formally, he plays the role that the director, or *sutradhāra,* plays in the prologue of traditional Indian theater. Vyāsa's role penetrates deep into the epic; he is coexistent with it and intimately involved with the actors. He is both the epic's author and the sage grandfather of the epic heroes. He is a figure whose presence defines and animates the drama he inhabits. The story of Vyāsa's ancestry allows the audience to enter the imaginative universe of the *Mahābhārata* from its origin.

Within the epic text, the story is narrated by the priest Vaisampāyana, a disciple of Vyāsa, at an assembly of warriors come together for the snake sacrifice being held by Janamejaya, a descendant of the Pāṇḍavas. The birth of Vyāsa is narrated in response to Janamejaya's request to hear the *whole* epic text. In the Brook/Carrière version, Vyāsa relates his own story at the suggestion of his scribe, Ganeṣa. Vyāsa recites for his companion, a young boy who is a descendant of the Pāṇḍavas. The narrator begins by telling of King Vasu, through whose city a river flowed. A mountain fell in love with the river, waylaid her, and begot twins of her. The king freed her by kicking the mountain with his foot. In gratitude, when her children were born she gave them to the king. He made the boy chief of his army and married the girl, whose beauty was so great that thought of her made him spill his seed, which eventually fell into the river Yamunā, where it impregnated a nymph who had been cursed by Brahmā to become a fish. When she was in her tenth month she was caught by fishermen who pulled human twins from her belly and presented the marvelous pair to their king. He raised the boy as his son, but the girl, who smelled like a fish, he gave to a fisherman. She plied a ferry on the river Yamunā, and so Parāśara came to see her when he was traveling on a pilgrimage. The "bull among hermits" was instantly smitten by her beauty and began making love to her. She protested that there were holy men standing on both sides of the river watching. Then he created a fog that "seemed to cover the entire region in darkness." Again she protested, pleading her virginity and filial piety. The great sage was pleased by her virtue and promised that his love would not ruin her virginity; then he granted her a boon. She chose as her boon that her body would always smell delicious. On the same day that she lay with Parāśara, she gave birth to Vyāsa on an island in the river Yamunā. He stood before his mother and set his mind on asceticism. "When you think of me, I shall appear to you if any task needs to be done."

The mating of the hermit with the fish-girl and the birth of Vyāsa is an epic play-within-a-play that echoes the obscure origins and kinship relations governing the entire *Mahābhārata*. The epic poet's birth and descent, like the birth and history of the epic heroes, is a story of seduction, restored virginity, and substitute fathers (human and divine). Vyāsa, like Karṇa, the first-born of the Pāṇḍavas, is born outside and before his mother's marriage. Just as Karṇa's mother, Kuntī, is the hub of a multivalent set of relations that constitute the epic story, so Vyāsa's mother, Satyavatī, is the hub of a set of relations that constitute the formal prologue of the poem. Later, when the continuity of the Bhārata lineage is threatened, Satyavatī calls on Vyāsa to sire sons. Not only does he carry on the Bhārata line, but he teaches the *Mahābhārata* to the bards so that the story will be passed down through the ages.

The story of Vyāsa's birth is not an isolated epic event. The births of the epic's main characters occur in equally dramatic episodes in which powerful desire initiates action. King Śantanu's passion for an irresistable woman, who is in reality the river goddess Gangā, results in the birth of Bhīṣma, who later renounces his claim to the throne and takes a terrible vow of celibacy to allow Śantanu to marry Satyavatī, so sweet-smelling now that she seduces the king with her fragrance. These episodes, like the scenes of the births of Paṇḍu and Dhṛtarāṣṭra and their sons, the Pāṇḍavas and the Kauravas, achieve their aesthetic and moral impact through the perennial human conflict between sacred duty *(dharma)* and desire *(kāma)*. Though the Pāṇḍava and Kaurava cousins should be united by common blood and ambitions, instead they are deadly enemies. The unbridled desire that dominates the Kali Yuga causes the Kauravas to frustrate their cousins' exercise of their rights and eventually usurp their patrimony. Base desires motivate the Kauravas to engage Yudhiṣṭhira in a crooked dice game that he plays with ritual obsessiveness, losing. Although the participants in the dice game are often warned about the danger of their course, once they begin the end is inevitable—noble heroes become trapped in a degenerating world over which they have no control. Even *dharma* cannot escape the demands of the age, and it too falls victim to Kali Yuga. The slow degeneration of Śantanu's clan culminates in its final disaster—the scions of Vyāsa become engaged in a mutually destructive war, whose drama their ancestor himself is directing.

The actual war, which ends with the destruction of both armies, is represented in a series of dramatic confrontations and moral crises. Exemplary among these is the mystical dialogue between the mighty Pāṇḍava warrior Arjuna and Kṛṣṇa in the *Bhagavad Gītā*, a dialogue that informs the entire epic and underlies the Brook/Carrière version. Before the war begins, Duryodhana and Arjuna approach Kṛṣṇa to seek his alliance—he refuses to take arms, but allows them to chose between himself and his troops. Arjuna chooses Kṛṣṇa as his charioteer, and Duryodhana is delighted to have Kṛṣṇa's troops for the Kaurava army. In the face of doing battle against his own relatives, Arjuna's nerve fails. Kṛṣṇa's arguments on why Arjuna must overcome his uncertainty and fear of the battle contain ideas that resonate throughout the entire epic. We can sympathize with the warrior's impulse to shrink from the violence of the human condition and can also learn from what Kṛṣṇa teaches him about his own and others' mortality. Kṛṣṇa's exposition of the relationship between death, sacrifice, and devotion explores the idea that one must heroically confront death in order to transcend the limits of ordinary existence.

For Arjuna, the epic warriors and the audience of the *Mahābhārata,* Kṛṣṇa is a perplexing figure. He is a companion and teacher, as well as a potent god who commands devotion. Kṛṣṇa's mythology suggests that he was originally a tribal hero who was transformed into a cult divinity, becoming an incarnation of cosmic power who periodically descends to earth to accomplish the restoration of order in times of chaos. The interweaving of mundane and cosmic levels of his activity throughout the epic makes his role as divine charioteer to Arjuna more comprehensible. From the start, Arjuna and the epic audience know that Kṛṣṇa is no common mortal. Despite his human foibles, he speaks with the authority of omniscience as his divinity unfolds in the terrible spectacle of destruction. In the Brook/Carrière version, the dramatization of Kṛṣṇa's enigmatic presence reveals basic contradictions inherent in the epic universe.

Arjuna's only real rival in the *Mahābhārata* is his brother Karṇa, whom he is sworn to kill. In his solitary power and heroism, Karṇa is the epic's most tragic figure. Among the many dramas based on the *Mahābhārata* one of the most moving is the *Karṇabhāra,* attributed to the ancient South Indian dramatist Bhāsa. The short drama is based on episodes related in the first, third, fifth, eighth, and twelfth books of the *Mahābhārata.* The story of Karṇa forms the basis of some of the most poignant epic scenes. Karṇa is the son of the sun-god, Sūrya, and the Pāṇḍava queen Kuntī. Kuntī, daughter of King Śūrasena, was raised in childhood by King Kuntibhoja; it was in his house that she served the divine sage Durvāsas with extraordinary hospitality and was rewarded with a mantra by which she could invoke any god she named. She used this magic power to invoke the sun while she was still a virgin living in her father's house; the sun embraced her and promised that in bearing his son her virginity would remain pure. The child was born wearing divine solar ornaments: earrings of immortality that made his ears splendid (thus he was called Karṇa) and protective armor. From the sun he also inherited a character of natural generosity that finally cost him his immortality. Afraid to expose her affair with the sun-god, Kuntī placed Karṇa in a box at birth and abandoned him to the river, where he was found by the charioteer Adhiratha, who brought the infant home to his childless wife. Karṇa, brought up by a humble charioteer, earned royal rank by his skill at arms, learned from the Pāṇḍavas' teacher Droṇa and from Paraśurāma, Jamadagni's son, who cursed him for pretending to be a brahman. He was made King of Aṅga by his cousin, the Kuru chief Duryodhana, and unknowingly became the sworn rival of his own brother Arjuna. Only as the war was about to begin did he learn from Kuntī about his true origins. She petitioned him to join his brothers, a plea that was approved by the sun, but he remained loyal to Duryodhana, who had conferred kingship on him.

In response to Kuntī's words he promised not to kill any of his brothers but Arjuna. Karṇa's character is throughout the epic challenged by the storm-god Indra, chief of the gods and adversary of the sun-god. Indra's son by Kuntī is Arjuna, the warrior whom Karṇa had to face at the time of his death, when the curse of Paraśurāma rendered his divine weapons useless and the curse of another brahman made the wheel of his chariot sink into the mire of the battlefield.

These epic incidents are reordered in the play to reveal, through the figure of Karṇa, the heightened mood of heroism *(vīrarasa)*, developed through exposition of subordinate moods of fear *(bhayānakarasa)* and compassion *(karuṇarasa)*. By transferring to the battlefield the scene of Karṇa's gift of his earrings and armor of immortality, which occurs in the epic at the beginning of the thirteenth year of the Pāṇḍavas' exile, the encounter with Indra intensifies the drama of Karṇa's vision of his own death. In the play, his charioteer Śalya is a foil for Karṇa's dramatic monologue and a sympathetic observer, unlike his haughty role in the epic.

At the beginning of the play, Karṇa is overcome by an uncanny fear in the face of battle:

In great battles
where avenging weapons severed
the limbs of warriors,
horses, elephants, and chariots,
my power was equal
to cruel death—
but this time war strikes
desperate fear in my heart. (6)

He is obsessed by what he has learned of his birth from Kuntī and by his memory of Paraśurāma's curse he finds omens of death in the stumbling of his horses and in the putrid smell of the elephants' ichor, as well as in the dread silence of the war drums and conches. It is at this point in the drama that Karṇa recites a verse (verse 12) that is a variant of Kṛṣṇa's crucial words to Arjuna in the second section of the *Bhagavad Gītā* (2.37):

If you are killed, you will win heaven,
if you triumph, you will enjoy earth—
so stand up, son of Kuntī,
and resolve to fight the war.
Karṇa says to Śalya:

If a man is killed, he wins heaven,
if he triumphs, he wins fame—
both ends are prized in the world,
so war is not without reward.

The report of the battlefield and Karṇa's depression also recall the opening of the *Gītā*. The vocabulary of duty, action, and sacrifice that is central to the *Gītā* permeates the play and is relevant to understanding Karṇa's response to the realization of his own imminent death. But in a significant variation of the *Gītā* verse, Karṇa sets the contrast not between heaven and earth, but between heaven and heroic fame, which are the rewards of war. This is consonant with Karṇa's character in the epic, where he tells Sūrya that he will win fame as a hero by giving the earrings and armor of his immortality to Indra (15).

The play's exposition of the relationship between sacrifice, mortality, and heroism dramatizes the Indian idea that one must heroically confront death in order to enjoy the freedom that comes by transcending the barrier between mortality and immortality. The immortality conferred by Karṇa's divine paternity is for him less important than his act of heroic sacrifice and generosity, even when he suspects that the demanding brahman has come to deceive him. Karṇa's identity is defined by his earrings and armor, but his nature is determined by his great generosity, which sets up an inevitable conflict between his immortality and ability for self-sacrifice. It is these very ornaments and armor of immortality that are, ironically, his burden—an irony implied in the title of the play, which may also mean "the burden to the ears [of Karṇa]."

The mythology of the sun is at the basis of this conflict: in ancient Vedic mythology the sun, called Mārtaṇḍa, is the first born of Aditi and is considered the first mortal. There is an intentional parallelism between the sons of Aditi and the sons of Kuntī. Karṇa, being the first-born son of Kuntī, must also be the first to die, despite his divine birth. The play thus brings to the fore the epic hero who epitomizes the paradox of Indian epic heroism, which is expressed as extraordinary personal integrity and effort limited by the inevitabilities of destiny, duty, karma, curses, and divine intervention. The magical weapon that Indra grants to Karṇa out of guilt for taking his immortality, a spear that can be used once to kill one of the Pāṇḍavas, is symbolic of the heroic sacrifice. Upon being granted the weapon, Karṇa mounts his chariot and again hears the sounds of the war conches that his fear had silenced; he directs

Śalya to drive him to meet Arjuna. The scene of brother battling brother unto death that follows is a paradigm of the *Mahābhārata*'s cosmic drama of destruction.

SUGGESTED READING

Jean Claude Carrière, *The Mahabharata*, trans. from French by Peter Brook (New York: Harper and Row, 1987).
Barbara Stoler Miller, *The Bhagavad Gita: Krishna's Counsel in Time of War* (New York: Bantam Books, 1986).

Indian and Greek Epics

Robert Antoine

One who undertakes a comparative study between two cultures is usually guided by a half-conscious bias which can assume either of the two following forms. He may so handle the material at his disposal as to concentrate almost exclusively on the similarities, real or apparent, of the terms of the comparison. Or his mind may react more spontaneously to the differences and unconsciously exaggerate them.

The first attitude—which we could conveniently call "cultural syncretism"—is often the characteristic of a generous yet shallow mind. Generous, because it is anxious to bring about harmony and unity and naturally refrains from extolling one culture at the expense of another. Shallow, because, in order to achieve its ideal of harmony, it rests satisfied with a superficial view of things and avoids the labor of deeper analysis for fear of seeing its conclusions challenged.

The second attitude—to which we give the name of "cultural chauvinism"—is that of a mind whose natural sharpness is placed at the service of partisan spirit. It seeks to establish the superiority and uniqueness of one culture and, in pursuing its end, exercises its ingenuity either to undermine any attempt at comparison or to prove that all similarities are the result of dependence or plagiarism.

Is it at all possible to combine the syncretist's generosity and the partisan's acuity while avoiding the former's simplicity and the latter's parochialism? A perfectly unbiased mind, if it could at all exist, would probably remain inactive, for the human mind never acts as a passive mirror, but rather as an actively selective organ. Facts, and especially human facts, never speak for themselves. They are made to say what the human observer prompts them to express.

Should we, therefore, give up all comparative studies on the plea that perfect impartiality is impossible? I do not think so. It is enough to know, and to guard oneself against, the dangers which such studies entail. If we keep in mind that, within the general pattern according to which human societies arise and evolve, there remains ample room for individuality and originality, we can safely undertake the fascinating task of comparing cultures.

THE GENERAL PATTERN OF HEROIC SOCIETY

All the great heroic traditions owe their existence to tribal culture. The basis on which tribal society rests is the principle of kinship and its social unit is the family group. Whereas the higher culture of the territorial state is founded on the idea of individual citizenship and gives rise to urban civilization, the tribal organization ignores national feeling and finds its social expression in feudalism. Feudalism is essentially an exchange of services between defenseless peasants and the military lord. In return for the protection which the lord gives them, the peasants offer him their land and promise to man his armies. When, to the economic necessity of finding a protector is added the element of personal devotion to the leader, the cult of the hero is born.

On the other hand, epic poetry is usually retrospective. It develops at a time when tribal society enters into contact with a higher civilization and tends to project into the past certain elements of urban culture which give to the old capitals an anachronic aspect of modernity. It is this marginal character of epic poetry which explains how tribal heroes can gradually be transformed into national heroes.

It is interesting to note how epic poetry, in three different historical contexts, blossomed at an intermediary period, a kind of "Middle Ages" between two urban civilizations. In India, after the disappearance of the Indus civilization and before the rise of the Mauryas; in Greece, after the decline of Aegean culture and before the emergence of Athenian dominance; in Europe, after the fall of the Roman Empire and of the short-lived Carolingian renaissance and before the urban civilization of the fourteenth century.

The Aristocrats at War

Heroic society is an aristocratic society. In the Greek epic, the heroes are called the *"aristoi,"* i.e., the best among men. Stereotyped adjectives are used, referring probably to some well-known quality of some ancestor, and the name of the father or a patronymic *"taddhitānta"* continually reminds us that nobility is hereditary. The feuds which result in bloody battles have never the character of national wars in which the common people play the prominent part. In fact, the common people do not appear at all except as a necessary background against which the valor and prowess of the heroes stand out in greater splendor. Most of the fights are single fights, extraordinary duels witnessed by a crowd of spellbound soldiers and retainers.

The origin of the great battles is, in all cases, the personal offense of a hero's honor. And it is generally a woman who supplies the occasion. In the *Iliad,* it is self-evident. The Greek tribes, personified in their leaders, agree to avenge the honor of Menelaus whose wanton wife has eloped with the Trojan Paris. There is not the slightest hint of a national campaign, and the leadership of Agamemnon has no other reason than the necessity of a concerted attack. Again, it is the wounded pride of Achilles which proves fatal to the Greek armies and brings the Trojans within an ace of victory. The young lady whom Achilles had received as a prize for his bravery is arbitrarily taken away from him by Agamemnon. Finally, if Achilles decided to enter the fray, it is not out of a sense of solidarity with the routed Greeks, but of the purely personal desire to avenge his friend's death. National feeling, if it exists at all in the *Iliad,* is to be found among the Trojans. For them, everything is at stake, as it will be for the Greeks at the time of Marathon and Salamis. Yet, in spite of the simple solution of returning to her lawful husband the woman who is the cause of their extreme misfortune, they choose to fight because the Greeks have challenged them. It is a question of panache and it overrides the security of the city.

The tragedy of the *Rāmāyaṇa* begins with the foolish claim of a vain woman, Kaikeyī. King Daśaratha who knows her claim to be unreasonable considers himself bound by the sacred duty of keeping his word. The welfare of his subjects and their undisguised disapproval count for nothing before his misconceived obligation toward Bharata's mother. And thus Rāma, Sītā, and Lakṣmaṇa leave for the forest. Bharata is the only one whose attitude must have made sense to the more enlightened. But his efforts are all in vain. The capture of Sītā by Rāvana constitutes a lesser national problem than Helen's elopement, for the people of Ayodhyā have nothing to do in rescuing her. It is a personal injury to Rāma who, instead of calling on his own people to fight with him for their beloved princess, gets involved in the family dispute of a monkey tribe and gains the allegiance of the winning side. After Rāvana's defeat and the recovery of Sītā, it may be argued that Rāma gives up the arbitrary rule of a feudal lord and rates very high the feelings and opinions of his subjects. The fire ordeal and the second banishment of Sītā are undeniable proofs of his new policy. Yet, one wonders if that new policy heralds the dawn of a new era. It is so much in keeping with Rāma's submissiveness at the time of his banishment. Rightly has Rāma been given as the ideal of the "śānta" hero and one aspect of his love for peace seems to be that trouble should be avoided at any cost: neither his right to the throne nor his absolute conviction that Sītā is innocent can arouse in him the passion necessary to resist the troublemakers.

The destinies of the Pāṇḍavas and the Kauravas are decided in a game of dice. This is typical of a feudal setting where the rulers dispose of their kingdoms as they would of their private fortunes. The overbearing pride of the winners and the spiteful humiliation of the losers reaches its climax in the Draupadī incident. It is around the ill-used Draupadī that the personal antagonism of the feudal lords crystallizes. The terrible imprecation of Bhīma against Duḥśāsana, "I shall split his breast and drink his blood" (*Mahābhārata*, Sabhā-parvan, 90.57), is the real declaration of war and the long exile will be unable to delete its memory. Its gruesome realization can easily bear comparison with the savage profanation of Hector's body at the hands of Achilles.

After the exile, when the Pāṇḍavas delegate Kṛṣṇa to Duryodhana in order to reach a compromise, it is Draupadī, with her untied hair as a perpetual reminder of her humiliation, who passionately opposes all kinds of peaceful settlement. The way in which Kṛṣṇa conducts the interview with the leader of the Kauravas is strongly influenced by the bellicose attitude of Pāñcālī.

The Aristocrats in Peace Time

Success in war being at the same time the condition of survival and the highest glory to which the heroes aspire, it is quite natural to see the young aristocrats apply themselves enthusiastically to their military training. Under the wise guidance of Droṇa, the young Pāṇḍavas and Kauravas vie with one another in the display of their skill, while the elders and a crowd of simple admirers look on with immense delight. Their loud acclamation fills the air (*Mahābhārata*, Ādi-parvan, 144.39).

In the *Rāmāyaṇa,* young Rāma receives his training from Viśvāmitra. The expedition against the demons is not just a game but is meant to give Rāma an idea of the evil forces with which he will have to grapple in his maturity. Homer has not depicted the early training of his heroes. Old Phoenix, however, gives us a glimpse of Achilles' education. Pleading with the sulking hero, Phoenix tells him: "My noble Lord Achilles, if you really think of sailing home and are so obsessed by anger that you refuse to save the gallant ships from going up in flames, what is to become of me without you, my dear child? How could I possibly stay there alone? Did not the old charioteer Peleus make me your guardian when he sent you off from Phthia to join Agamemnon? You were a mere lad, with no experience of the hazards of war, nor of debate, where people make their mark. It was to teach you all these things, to make a speaker of you, and a man of action, that he sent me with you; and I could not bring myself to let you go, dear child, and to stay behind, not if God himself undertook to strip me of my years and turn me into the sturdy youngster I was when I first left Hellas, the land of lovely women" (*Iliad,* Rieu trans. [Penguin], book 10, p. 172).

Skill and strength are the necessary qualities of warriors. But these qualities have also a social importance which cannot be ignored. They are rated so high that a king is ready to give his daughter in marriage to the strongest, irrespective of the caste to which he belongs. Dṛṣṭadyumna, brother of Draupadī solemnly declares: "Be he a brahmin or a king or a merchant or a śūdra, he who will string this excellent bow will get my sister in marriage" (*Mahābhārata,* Ādi-parvan, 203.19–20).

Sītā is won by Rāma because he alone can bend the bow. Draupadī is won by Arjuna for the same reason. Arjuna, to avoid detection, had come in the guise of a brahmin. The amusing scene describing the misgivings of the brahmins as one of them rises to perform a feat which the well-trained princes were unable to accomplish makes us guess the pride and joy they felt when Arjuna defeated the kings at their own game. At the end of the *Odyssey,* Ulysses, having reached Ithaca after his long peregrinations, finds his place occupied by the suitors. Penelope, prompted by Athena, decides to put them to the test: "Listen, my lords, you have fastened on this house in the long absence of its master, as the scene of your perpetual feasts, and you could offer no better pretext for your conduct than your wish to win my hand in marriage. That being the prize, come forward now, my gallant lords; for I challenge you to try your skill on the great bow of King Ulysses. And whichever man among you proves the handiest at stringing the bow and shoots an arrow through every one of these twelve axes, with that man I will go, bidding goodbye to this house which welcomed me as a bride." The suitors fail. No doubt, they are grieved at the loss of Penelope, but, as Eurymachus puts it, "What does grieve me more is the thought that our failure with his bow proves us such weaklings compared with the godlike Ulysses. The disgrace will stick to our names for ever." Like Arjuna, Ulysses appears unrecognized and humbly asks to be allowed to test the strength of his hands. The suitors are annoyed: "We don't want the common folk to be saying things like this, 'A poor lot, these; not up to the fine gentleman whose wife they want to marry! *They* can't string his bow. But in comes some casual tramp, strings the bow with the greatest ease and shoots through all the marks!' That is the kind of thing they will say; and our reputation might suffer" (*Odyssey*, Rieu trans. [Penguin], book 22, pp. 317–18, 324). We live here in the same world and breathe the same atmosphere as in Drupada's palace and Janaka's capital.

The Aristocrats Facing the Mystery of Life

Life in the Epic Age was essentially active. Games, gambling, conquests, and military campaigns kept the heroes occupied, while the recital by bards of the glorious deeds of their ancestors gave an ever new luster to the flame of chivalry. Before the compilation of the main epic narratives as we have them today, there must have existed a great number of independent lays celebrating different families or dynasties. The *Mahābhārata* contains a great wealth of such stories quoted as examples to the heroes. The *Iliad* and the *Odyssey,* though less rich than the *Mahābhārata,* use the same device and the Greek tragedy testifies to the existence of numerous epic cycles not incorporated in the works of Homer. The teaching which appealed to the knights of old was a concrete teaching which left out abstruse speculations. It may be reasonably surmised that Arjuna and the Kṛṣṇa of the *Bhagavad Gītā* belong to a later age when speculation had taken precedence over action.

In fact, a life of action has its own problems. Man realizes that his plans are often thwarted and that he is not the sovereign master of his destiny. There are mysterious forces at work which must be reckoned with. Above all, the great mystery of death is ever present in the precarious life of warriors. The heroic mentality acknowledges the presence of the mystery, is deeply impressed by it, but does not attempt to give it an abstract solution.

In the face of the mystery of life with its passions, its failures, its cruelty, the hero, while feeling responsible for his actions, knows that the divine power ordains and guides everything. To our rationalistic minds, his position may seem to be illogical: either one is a fatalist and denies human freedom and responsibility, or one believes in freedom and denies the supreme power of fate. But our argument would not disturb the hero's belief. It is reality which interests him and reality is complex. The human and divine worlds are not juxtaposed, they intermingle so intimately that to consider one apart from the other destroys the very texture of reality. It is the divine world which gives to human existence its third dimension and makes of it a living and full-blooded tragedy. Who would be so devoid of sensitivity as to affirm that the epic heroes are mere marionettes activated by the mechanical device of a hidden magician?

Naturalism which has cut off human life from its mysterious roots and claims to explain everything by an analysis of superficial psychology would have made our heroes smile. They knew better and the modern tendency to reaffirm the mystery is much closer to the heroic mentality than the so-called realism of the last century.

It is not without significance that depth psychology borrows from the epic some of its most important symbolism. The inner mystery it tries to penetrate may not be without connection with the transcendent mystery which the heroes of old acknowledged with awe and trembling.

Death, the lurking and inevitable menace, is a constant reminder of life's precarious stability. Sadly recalling the forebodings of defeat in a long and beautiful threnody, old King Dhṛtarāṣṭra, in a crescendo of despair punctuated by the recurring refrain *"tadā nāśamse vijayāya Sanjaya,"* concludes by expressing his desire to leave this fruitless existence: "O Sanjaya, since life is such my desire is to die without delay, for I do not see the slightest advantage in keeping alive" (*Mahābhārata*, Ādi-parvan, i. 245).

In true epic fashion, Sanjaya replies by quoting the examples of hundreds of kings and warriors, far superior to the Kaurava princes, who have lived, fought, and died. Their death takes nothing away from their fame and valor, and life is worth living as long as fate does not snatch it away. Sanjaya does not speculate about future life or rebirth, he states the mystery of life and death and accepts it as a matter of fact: "There is no reason to lament over what is to be. Who can, through endeavor, change the course of fate? Time is the root of everything, of life and death, of happiness and adversity" (*Mahābhārata*, Ādi-parvan, i. 271–72).

In the *Iliad*, the scene between Hector and Andromache has the same message to convey. Andromache is frightened by the bellicose enthusiasm of her husband: "Hector, you are possessed. This bravery of yours will be your end. You do not think of your little boy and of your unhappy wife, whom you will make a widow soon. Some day the Achaeans are bound to kill you in a massed attack. And when I lose you I might as well be dead. There will be no comfort left, when you have met your doom—nothing but grief." Hector is not indifferent to his wife's appeal. He loves his son and his wife dearly. Yet, he is a warrior and fate calls him to battle. "My dear, I beg you not to be too much distressed. No one is going to send me down to Hades before my proper time. But Fate is a thing that no man born of woman, coward or hero, can escape. Go home now, and attend to your own work, the loom and the spindle, and see that the maidservants go on with theirs. War is men's business; and this war is the business of every man in Ilium, myself above all" (*Iliad,* book 6, pp. 128–29).

INDIAN AND GREEK PERSPECTIVES

Although much more might be said about the similarity between the Indian and the Greek epic, we must now turn our attention to what makes them different. For they are different. There is an atmosphere, a spiritual climate proper to the Indian epic, as there is an outlook and a perspective which characterize the Homeric world. Why is it, for instance, that not a single Greek hero decides, after a life full of activity, to end his days in the peaceful retirement of the forest? Or how is it that the *Rāmāyaṇa* and the *Mahābhārata* have been and still are religious books from which millions draw spiritual comfort and guidance, whereas the *Iliad* and the *Odyssey,* which have shaped the Greek temperament, have never been sacred books?

The mystery of death is ever present in the life of epic heroes. But the Indian temperament, so well depicted in the boy Nachiketas of the *Kaṭha-Upaniṣad,* seeks to penetrate the mystery which the Greek temperament is rather inclined to accept. Hence, a fundamental difference between the two outlooks. The more deeply the Indian soul meditates and reflects on the transitoriness of life, the less importance it gives to purely human achievement. The more forcibly death appears as inevitable to the Greek hero, the more urgent also the necessity to live fully the short time which destiny allots to man. The similarity which we have pointed out in the first part of this essay is the similarity of a spontaneous and prospective tendency which precedes all metaphysical reflection. The Greek epic remains all through spontaneous and prospective. The Indian epic shows a gradual evolution toward a more reflexive and meditative attitude. In Greece, epic poetry and the metaphysical quest have remained two separate achievements. In India, both have met and blended, and that blending has conferred on the epic itself a character of its own. It has been the work of long centuries, especially for the *Mahābhārata*. Each generation had its contribution to make, and the whole work was not written under guidance of a logical mind anxious to safeguard the logical consistency of the various portions, but under the inspiration of the vital unity of a living people whose growth and development are reflected in its numerous verses as the changing landscape in the waters of a powerful river. What we are looking for in our study of the epic is not an abstract system which could be neatly summarized in a few clear and definite propositions, but human and concrete attitudes which reveal not the vision of a few philosophers but the temperament of living peoples. Our aim is not to pass a verdict or to decide that one temperament is better than the other, but to vibrate in unison with both temperaments since both are able to reveal to us hidden depths of the human soul.

Temperament, Indian and Greek

When we read the Greek epic, we are forced to concentrate on the story and on the heroes. Without preamble, the *Iliad* begins with the narrative of Achilles' wrath. In spite of lengthy speeches and inconsistencies in the narrative, the story of the Achaeans' gradual discomfiture proceeds apace, and we are never allowed to forget the central theme. The sulking Achilles remains ever present, and we are anxiously waiting for the relenting of his stubborn resentment. The death of Patroclus arouses Achilles from his inaction and the doom of Ilium is sealed. The *Odyssey* is perhaps the first novel ever written. Ulysses drifting on the high seas, among unspeakable dangers, pursued by the vindictiveness of the god Poseidon, relates his adventures and finally reaches his dear Ithaca, while his son Telemachus, unable to solve the difficulties which he faces at home, undertakes a long and vain quest for his father. Both finally meet at Ithaca and defeat the suitors.

The *Mahābhārata* has been called "a vast repository of Hindu traditional lore, philosophy and legend." Its bulk is eight times as great as that of the *Iliad* and *Odyssey* put together. It would be ridiculous to look for a well-focused narrative without digressions. It is not meant to be a simple story, and its greatness lies in the fact that, around the main story which occupies about one fifth of the whole work, the folklore, the wisdom, and the religious aspirations of long centuries have clustered into an immense florilegium of Indian life. The Ādi-parvan, after announcing the great tale, keeps us waiting for sixty chapters (i.e., over 2,000 verses) before beginning the story of the Pāṇḍavas and Kauravas. Then, like a majestic river, the story follows its slow development, with many interruptions. The Sabhā-parvan with its 2,500 verses brings us to the exile of the Pāṇḍavas. The Vana-parvan is a real storehouse of legends and beautiful tales and spreads over more than 17,000 verses. It is a real forest of myths, legends, and instructions of all kinds. The Virāṭa-parvan is like a short interlude of more than 2,000 verses. After the failure of a peaceful solution and the preparation of the armies (Udyoga-parvan with nearly 8,000 verses), Sanjaya's account of the great battle begins. The Bhīṣma-parvan (close to 6,000 verses) ends with the pathetic sight of Bhīṣma dying on a bed of arrows. The Droṇa-parvan (about 9,500 verses) relates the fall of Jayadratha and the end of Droṇa. Bhīma's revenge over Duḥśāsana and Karṇa's death at the hands of Arjuna are related in the Karṇa-parvan (about 5,000 verses). After a long interruption devoted to the relation of Balarāma's pilgrimage to the Sarasvatī, the battle comes to an end with the unfair victory of Bhīma over Duryodhana. That is the Śalya-parvan (about 4,000 verses). The remaining Kauravas attack the Pāṇḍavas at night and massacre their armies. The five brothers and Kṛṣṇa escape death (Sauptika-parvan with 800 verses). In the Strī-parvan (800 verses), the Kaurava ladies, headed by Gāndhārī, visit the battlefield. The story is ended. But the great poem goes on with the Śānti-parvan (14,000 verses) and the Anuśāsana-parvan (8,000 verses) embodying the teachings of Bhīṣma. They are the richest portions of the *Mahābhārata* as a treasure house of Indian tradition: artha-śāstra, dharma-śāstra, civil law, strategy, popular wisdom, cosmogony, theology, yoga, psychology—all the branches of knowledge are represented in that immense discourse which must have taken centuries to be written. The story is resumed with Yudishthira's *aśvamedha*. Dhṛtarāṣṭra, accompanied by Gāndhārī, Kuntī, and Vidura, retires to the forest and is granted a vision of the deceased warriors. After the death of Balarāma and Kṛṣṇa, the Pāṇḍavas renounce the world.

Although the *Rāmāyaṇa* is much more similar to the Greek epic than the *Mahābhārata*, there are elements in its composition which differentiate it sharply from Homer's poems. Like Homer, Vālmīki is a historical poet who has composed a great epic of startling literary qualities. There is even a great similarity between the general theme of the poems: the great war brought about by the abduction of a princess, the siege of the abductor's capital, the victory of the lawful husband, and the return of the princess to her conjugal home. There is little doubt that the origin of the *Rāmāyaṇa*, like that of the *Iliad* and the *Odyssey*, is to be found in the heroic traditions of warring tribes. Yet, like the *Mahābhārata*, although to a lesser extent, the *Rāmāyaṇa* incorporates an imposing collection of interpolated legends and myths which have no direct connection with the central theme. More explicitly than in the *Mahābhārata*, the hero of the *Rāmāyaṇa* has become a divine incarnation, and the human interest of the story, without being destroyed, is sublimated into a divine episode.

Humanism, Greek and Indian

From a purely literary point of view, we might be tempted to conclude that the Greek epic avoids many of the defects of the Indian epic by a greater fidelity to the objective it has in view. Yet, we may wonder if the lengthy digressions of the Indian epic and the tendency to divinize its heroes have nothing else to reveal than bad literary workmanship. Is there not a fundamental difference between the Greek and the Indian conception of humanism? "Conception" is perhaps the wrong word, for we are not comparing two systems of philosophy, but two literary testimonies. It would be better, perhaps, to speak of two tendencies, two innate visions which try to find an expression without ever succeeding in reducing it to a clear-cut system. Have you ever heard the same story told by two persons of different temperaments? An extrovert will tell the story with passion, but a passion for the story itself, and he will leave out his personal reflections and subjective impressions, because he obscurely knows that the story can speak for itself. An introvert will allow his mind to wander and try to find in the incidents of the story props for his personal considerations regarding life and destiny. His passion is more interior, and the story itself will gradually lose something of its importance, without, however, disappearing completely. The thread of the narrative will be loose yet continuous. Am I far off the mark when I qualify the Greek epic temperament as extrovert, and the Indian as introvert?

The Extrovert Humanism of Greece

Spengler's remark that the soul of European antiquity is "pure present" is certainly very true of the Greek epic. We have already remarked on the hero's attitude toward death and what follows. It is a mystery which he recoils from investigating and which he accepts without question. Similarly, the mystery of human suffering and human wickedness is solved summarily. "Are not the gods responsible for that, weaving catastrophe into the pattern of events to make a song for future generations?" That is how King Alcinous consoles Ulysses for the loss of many of his dear friends. What the king is interested in is the story which Ulysses has to tell: "Explain to us what secret sorrow makes you weep as you listen to the tragic story of the Argives and the fall of Troy" (*Odyssey*, book 8, p. 138).

What matters for the Greek hero is to make the most of the time allotted to him. Too much speculation is of no avail; it will not postpone the fatal day foreseen by the gods. To fight, to enjoy the pleasures of love and of congenial company, to make a name for himself, "to listen to a minstrel, while the tables are laden with bread and meat, and a steward carries round the wine and fills the cups," that is life, and the rest does not count. The transitoriness of human existence never prompts the Greek hero to give up the world to retire to the forest. Death is the great retirement and it will come in its appointed time.

There are no demons in the Greek epic. The Cyclops himself is just a savage of immense physical strength who does not represent in any way the dark power which resists the ruling of the gods. Both evil and good in human behavior have a divine origin. They remain human and we witness in them that strange blending of fatalism and responsibility which are the two facets of all human activities. Listen to Helen after her return to her husband's palace. She is fully conscious of her sin when she declares: "The Achaeans boldly declared war and took the field against Troy for my sake, shameless creature that I was." Yet, she also knows that it was not her independent doing: "Aphrodite blinded me when she lured me to Troy from my own dear country and made me forsake my daughter, my bridal chamber, and a husband who had all one could wish in the way of brains and good looks" (*Odyssey*, book 4, pp. 68, 71).

But the gods themselves are so very close to man. Except for the blind submission which they command regarding their arbitrary decisions and partialities, they behave exactly like the heroes of the poem, more recklessly even, for they have nobody to fear. Those humanized gods of the Homeric pantheon will remain "a fit inspiration for an athletic contest, a statue, or an ode, but [they are] of little use to the philosopher, and entirely unsympathetic to the simple everyday sorrows of mankind."[1] Although they rule everything, they never rob the heroes of their humanity. Their quarrels are reflected in the conflicts that oppose man to man, they positively help their protégés and are personally engaged in the battles of men. But the human warriors do not rise above their human status. We may compare, in this connection, the decisive fight between Achilles and Hector, and the final struggle between Rāma and Rāvana. We are in two different worlds, the Greek world in which man would be what he is without divine interference, the Indian world in which man, a mere instrument raised to a divine efficiency, breaks his human limits. The Greek heroes are so human that they make one forget the divine operation which sustains them. The Indian gods are so prominent that they blur the human outlines of the heroes.

The Introvert Humanism of India

This last remark of mine should not lead one to conclude that I have failed to respond to the deep human appeal of innumerable passages of the Indian epic. I shall try to explain my meaning by a concrete example. I, who am not a Vedāntin, have great friends who are Vedāntins. In our usual human relations I fully appreciate their humane qualities. But I know that, deep down in their soul, they have a vision which is incompatible with that human distinction between "I" and "Thou" which is the very foundation of friendship. And that makes me feel uneasy. My attitude towards the Indian epic is something of that kind. I love Rāma and Sītā. Yudhiṣṭhira arouses my admiration. The Strī-parvan brings tears to my eyes. Arjuna's grief at the news of his son's death moves me deeply. As long as I forget the pattern to which they belong I feel one with them. But there is a pattern. Before trying to describe it, let us first understand how the Indian epic completes and deepens the Greek vision of life.

The simple fact that the *Mahābhārata* and the *Rāmāyaṇa* are accepted, even today, as the divine answer to the religious aspirations of millions is a clear indication of the depth of their message. They have given an answer to the eternal questions of the "why," the "whence," and the "whither" of human existence. The epic story has become an occasion to reflect on the instability of things mundane and to seek for stability. The great heroes who survive the heroic struggle for power realize that power is an empty shell which must be discarded. Evil is a reality which is at work in the world, and the demons are bent on checking the divine control of the universe. They represent a terrible force, both external and internal to man, against which it is the duty of all, according to each one's situation, to fight. Human destiny is not to find its fulfillment in this world. Wisdom more than bravery has the key to the mystery of life. The heroes are continually invited to make the decisive struggle an internal struggle towards final emancipation, while the external struggle is nothing but a passing phase of the world of appearances. With the Indian epic, we enter into a vast pattern in which human life, human emotions, human values are assumed and transformed.

In the *Rāmāyaṇa,* that pattern is outlined in the first book which is certainly a later addition revealing to a nicety the Indian temperament. The gods are much troubled by the demon Rāvaṇa who cannot be destroyed except by man. But, in order to kill him, one would need divine power. Hence, Viṣṇu agrees to be born as a man. The divine struggle weaves itself into a human fabric. Daśaratha begets four sons. Rāma is the full incarnation of Viṣṇu, his three brothers are partial incarnations. We may forget about that divine prelude when we read the story of the exile, of the siege of Lankā, and of Rāvaṇa's defeat. But what we discuss here is not whether or not the addition of the first book fulfills its purpose, but the fact that the first book has been added. In the perspective of that first book, the whole human story of Rāma and Sītā, the abduction of Sītā by Rāvaṇa, and the battle between Rāma and Rāvaṇa, become a kind of camouflage of the real story. A camouflage, as we have pointed out, which is not always successful, since the heroes often lose their human dimensions.

For the *Mahābhārata,* the pattern is much more complex. Toward the end, we come to know that all the heroes are divine incarnations. But let us consider one instance, the *Bhagavad Gītā.* There is Arjuna, deeply moved at the prospect that he has to fight against his relatives, and his gurus. Kṛṣṇa encourages him to do his duty as a worthy Kṣatriya, and that remains within the boundaries of the Greek epic. But when Kṛṣṇa teaches Arjuna about the eternity of the Self and the illusion of the bodily individuality, the whole struggle, viewed from that perspective, vanishes into something unreal. The whole thing is a big puppet show in which the actors are moved by supernatural agencies.

The Indian pattern, as distinguished from the Greek outlook, is characterized by the fact that there is no strict division between the divine, the demonic, and the human. The Law of Rebirth allows the spirit to move across the three worlds in its pilgrimage toward liberation. How many demons do we not see released from their bondage once the heroes, under divine guidance, act as the unconscious instruments of a superior power? That fluidity of the Indian universe dissolves, as it were, all that is specifically divine, demonic, or human, into an immense current of mysterious and predetermined events which follow their course under the appearance of spontaneity.

Appearance or reality? That is the question which the confrontation of the Greek and the Indian epic brings to our minds, but which it does not solve. Both the Indian and the Greek heroes have a keen perception of "that void, that nothingness at the bottom of things," but are inclined to react differently to it. While the Greek hero feels that human existence is a gift which must be enjoyed, the Indian hero tends to see in it a bondage from which one should escape. The greatest passages of both epics are those where the gift-aspect and the bondage-aspect are blended into that energizing humility which is man's closest realization of what he is.

ENDNOTE

Reprinted and revised, with the permission of the Editors, from *Quest* (Calcutta), April–June 1958, pp. 37–49.

1. A. R. Burn, *Minoans, Philistines and Greeks* (New York: Knopf, 1930), p. 256.

Kālidāsa's *Śakuntalā*

Barbara Stoler Miller

If you want the bloom of youth and fruit of later years,
If you want what enchants, fulfills, and nourishes,
If you want heaven and earth contained in one name—
I say Śakuntalā and all is spoken.
—*J. W. von Goethe, "Willst du die Blüte . . ."*

Kālidāsa's drama the *Śakuntalā* has had many enthusiastic admirers in the West as well as in India, where from the time of its composition in the early fifth century A.D., it has been considered the masterpiece of classical Indian literature. The *Śakuntalā,* first known to Goethe through the English translation of William Jones that was published in 1789, appealed to him for the beauty of its nature imagery, the complexity of its structure, and the unity of art and religion on which it was based.

With its semidivine characters, rich mythological layers, and vast cosmic landscape drawn from an episode in the epic *Mahābhārata,* the *Śakuntalā* is the model of the most elevated Indian dramatic form, which may be classed as "heroic romance." Dramatic romances in Western literature, such as Aeschylus' *Oresteia,* Euripides' *Alcestis,* or Shakespeare's *The Tempest,* are comparable. The *Śakuntalā* can be appreciated today for the ways in which it explores the human spirit's potential for harmony with nature in a chaotic world where desire comes into conflict with duty.

Kālidāsa is the greatest poet of Sanskrit, the classical Indo-European language of India. His literary reputation is based on six surviving works that are generally attributed to him by Indian critics and commentators. The coherent language, poetic technique, style, and sentiment that these works express seem to be the product of a single mind. The poems include a lyric monologue of nature, "Meghadūta" (The Cloud Messenger"), and two long lyric narratives, *Raghuvaṁśa* ("The Dynasty of Raghu") and *Kumārasambhava* ("The Birth of Śiva's Son"). There are three dramas, all of which begin with prologues that refer to Kālidāsa as the author: *Mālavikāgnimitra* ("Mālavikā and Agnimitra"), *Vikramorvaśī* ("Urvaśī Won by Valor"), and *Abhijñānaśākuntala* ("Śakuntalā and the Ring of Recollection"), often referred to in critical literature simply as the *Śakuntalā*.

While we have no way of establishing Kālidāsa's exact dates, an upper limit is provided by an inscription on the shrine of Aihoḷe, dated A.D. 634, in which he is praised as a great poet. The sense of the world that one gets from Kālidāsa's work is consonant with historical, geographic, and linguistic factors supporting the Indian tradition that associates the poet with the Gupta monarch Candra Gupta II, who ruled most of northern India from Pāṭaliputra, the ancient capital of the Gangetic valley, between A.D. 380 and 415. The central role played by the figure of the king in his dramas and in his epic *Raghuvaṁśa* suggests that Kālidāsa enjoyed royal patronage.

That Kālidāsa was a devotee of Śiva and his consort, the goddess Kālī, is evident in his work, as well as in legends that recount his transformation from a fool into a poet through the grace of Kālī. The powerful images of nature that dominate his poetry and drama are ultimately determined by his conception of Śiva's creative mystery. This is implicit in the doctrine of Śiva as the god of eight manifest forms *(aṣṭamūrti)*, who is Kālidāsa's poetic icon. The most compressed expression of it is in the benediction of the *Śakuntalā:*

The water that was first created,
the sacrifice-bearing fire, the priest,
the time-setting sun and moon,
audible space that fills the universe,
what men call nature, the source of all seeds,
the air that living creatures breathe—
through his eight embodied forms,
may Lord Śiva come to bless you!

The natural world of Kālidāsa's poetry is never a static landscape; it reverberates with Śiva's presence. Nature functions, not as a setting or allegorical landscape, but as a dynamic surface on which the unmanifest cosmic unity plays. This unity is Śiva; his creative nature is expressed through the eight essential constituents of empirical existence: the elements (water, fire, ether, earth, air), the sun, and the moon, and the ritual sacrificer, who is integrated into this cosmic system. In their sustained interplay, creation and destruction of life occur.

The conception of Śiva's eight manifest forms also has inherent in it the identification of Śiva himself with Nature *(prakṛti)*, the female half of his cosmic totality. Śiva is also called "The God Who is Half Female" *(ardhanarīśvara)*. The male and female aspects of existence *(puruṣa* and *prakṛti)*, separately personified as Śiva and his consort, are bound into a single androgynous figure. These ideas are fundamental to the meaning of Kālidāsa's poetry; in the *Śakuntalā*, as in his other dramas, they set the romantic relationship between the hero and heroine in a specific religious context.

The mythic origin of drama was a holy presentation that the gods offered to give ethical instruction through diversion when people were no longer listening to the scriptures. Ancient texts stress the reward a king will gain if he presents dramatic performances as a gift to his subjects and an offering to the gods. For centuries, Indian dramas have been commissioned and presented on the occasion of a seasonal festival, a birth of a son, a marriage, a royal consecration, a political victory, or any other auspicious event.

Indian heroic romances represent human emotions in a theatrical universe of symbolically charged characters and events in order to lead the audience into a state of extraordinary pleasure and insight. The goal of a Sanskrit drama is to establish emotional harmony in the microcosm of the theater by exploring the deeper relations that bind apparent conflicts of experience. The manifestation of these relations produces the intense aesthetic experience called *rasa.*

Kālidāsa's dramas focus on the critical tension between desire *(kāma)* and duty *(dharma)* that is aesthetically manifest in the relation of the erotic sentiment *(śṛṅgāra-rasa)* to the heroic *(vīra-rasa)*. His dramas achieve their aesthetic and moral impact not through conflicts of individuals but through the perennial human conflict between desire and duty. His dramatic expositions are rooted in an ancient Indian scheme for reconciling life's multiple possibilities. The scheme is called the "four human pursuits" *(puruṣārtha)* and is divided into a worldly triad of duty, material gain, and pleasure, plus a supermundane concern for liberation from worldly existence. The conflict is transformed into aesthetic experience by the poet's skillful presentation of his characters' emotional reactions to various situations. These characters are not unique individuals with personal destinies, like Shakespeare's Hamlet or Lear, but generic types defined within stylized social contexts that reflect the hierarchical nature of traditional Indian society.

In the *Śakuntalā,* the hero and heroine are the main dramatic vehicles for exposing the states of mind of the poet and his audience. They are supported by clusters of characters who, like them, appear as symbolic personalities defined by social position, gender, and language. Besides the king, the male characters are the buffoon, sages, ministers, priests, students, policemen, and a fisherman. The female characters are nymphs, queens, ascetics, doorkeepers, bow-bearers, and serving maids. With the exception of the buffoon and other comic characters like the policemen, the male characters speak Sanskrit. The female characters speak Prākrit, a stylized version of a "natural" language, in contrast to more artificial Sanskrit. It is as if the high-ranking male characters spoke Latin while the others spoke Italian.

The hero of the play is King Duṣyanta, whose character is expressed according to the norms of classical social and dramatic theory. The high qualities of kingship he possesses qualify him to be called a "royal sage." This epithet signifies that the king's spiritual power is equal to his martial strength and moral superiority. The ideal royal sage is a figure of enormous physical strength who also has the power to control his senses. He is a sage by virtue of his discipline, austerity, and knowledge of sacred law. It is his religious duty to keep order in the cosmos by guarding his kingdom; in this he is like a sage guarding the realm of holy sacrifice. His responsibility to guide and protect those beneath him involves him in acts of austerity that place him in the highest position of the temporal and spiritual hierarchy.

The heroine of the play, Śakuntalā, is the daughter born of a union between the nymph Menakā and the royal sage Viśvāmitra. Menakā, a paradigmatic figure of feminine beauty, is sent to seduce Viśvāmitra when his ascetic powers threaten the gods. She succeeds and becomes pregnant with a daughter whom she bears and abandons to birds of prey near a river. The birds worship and protect the child until another great sage, the ascetic Kaṇva, finds her and brings her to live in his forest hermitage as his daughter. Having found her among the śakunta birds, he names her Śakuntalā.

Śakuntalā is a beautiful nymph whose spontaneous love embraces the hero and leads him beyond the world of everyday experience into the imaginative universe where dichotomies of sensual desire and sacred duty are reintegrated. Her presence reassures the audience that the energy of nature is always available to reintegrate conflicting aspects of life. Her body is an object of worship—poetic ornaments are like the auspicious ornaments placed on an image in religious ritual or on a bride for her marriage ritual. The wearer is put in a sacred state in which she is transformed from a nubile creature—whose sexual power invites violence and threatens to produce chaos—into a fecund vessel for the production of offspring. As the heroine of a drama, she is the vehicle for transforming erotic passion into the aesthetic experience of love, which incorporates the erotic and transcends its limitations.

In the realm of passionate desire, the king's general, minister, and chamberlain are replaced as advisers by a Brahman buffoon who is his "minister of amorous affairs." The buffoon's proverbial gluttony, carelessness, and cowardice give a broad caricature of the normally sacred Brahman priest. His words and actions often remind one of Shakespearean clowns like Touchstone and Feste. He speaks a comic Prākrit, in contrast with the king's heroic Sanskrit, and is as obsessed with satisfying his hunger for sweets as the king is with satisfying his erotic desires. His literal interpretation of *rasa* as a feast of flavors makes the king's passion absurdly concrete. His humor provides the comic sentiment *(hāsya-rasa)* that gives the *Śakuntalā* a special liveliness.

Kālidāsa reshapes the ancient epic story through these characters. The epic story begins with the scene of a tumultuous hunt in which Duṣyanta kills numerous forest animals. The play begins with the benediction to Śiva and a prologue. The prologue is a play-within-a-play that initiates a conventional pattern of structural oppositions. They include contrasts between verse and prose, Sanskrit and Prākrit, authority (in the person of the director) and spontaneity (in the person of the actress).

DIRECTOR *(looking backstage)*: If you are in costume now, madam, please come on stage!

ACTRESS: I'm here, sir.

DIRECTOR: Our audience is learned. We shall play Kālidāsa's new drama called *Śakuntalā and the Ring of Recollection.* Let the players take their parts to heart!

ACTRESS: With you directing, sir, nothing will be lost.

DIRECTOR: Madam, the truth is:

I find no performance perfect
until the critics are pleased;

the better trained we are
the more we doubt ourselves.

ACTRESS: So true . . . now tell me what to do first!

DIRECTOR: What captures an audience better than a song? Sing about the new summer season and its pleasures:

To plunge in fresh waters
swept by scented forest winds
and dream in soft shadows
of the day's ripened charms.

ACTRESS: *(singing)*:

Sensuous women
in summer love
weave
flower earrings
from fragile petals
of mimosa
while wild bees
kiss them gently.

DIRECTOR: Well sung, madam! Your melody enchants the audience. The silent theater is like a painting. What drama should we play to please it?

ACTRESS: But didn't you just direct us to perform a new play called *Śakuntalā and the Ring of Recollection?*

DIRECTOR: Madam, I'm conscious again! For a moment I forgot.

The mood of your song's melody
carried me off by force,
just as the swift dark antelope
enchanted King Duṣyanta.

The actress' singing, like the beautiful movements of the magical antelope, or the art of poetry, makes the audience "forget" the everyday world and enter the fantastic realm of imagination that is latent within them. The mind of the poet, the hero, and the audience is symbolized here by the director, who holds together the various strands of the theater so that the aesthetic experience *(rasa)* of the play can be realized and savored. The end of the prologue marks a transition to the action of the drama itself.

The king enters with his charioteer, armed with a bow and arrow, like "the wild bowman Śiva, hunting the dark antelope." We witness the king hunting a fleeing antelope in the sacred forest where Śakuntalā dwells. The movement of the chase creates a sense of uncertainty and excitement for the mind's eye as it is drawn deeper into a mythical world. The poet's intention to pierce the boundaries of ordinary time and space is explicit in the king's description of his perspective as he enters the forest:

> What is small suddenly looms large,
> split forms seem to reunite,
> bent shapes straighten before my eyes—
> from the chariot's speed
> nothing ever stays distant or near.

The intensity of the hunt is interrupted by two ascetics, who identify the antelope as a creature of sage Kaṇva's hermitage.

The mood of the drama is set with great economy and magical speed by the black buck as he penetrates the forest and charges the atmosphere with danger. Kālidāsa portrays the elegant animal altered by the violence of the hunt:

> The graceful turn of his neck
> as he glances back at our speeding car,
> the haunches folded into his chest
> in fear of my speeding arrow,
> the open mouth dropping
> half-chewed grass on our path—
> watch how he leaps, bounding on air,
> barely touching the earth.

The antelope is Śakuntalā's "son," adopted by her when it was orphaned as a fawn. This scene shows the king captivated by the graceful creature of nature he is bent on killing. His passion threatens the calm of the forest. This is the prelude to Duṣyanta's discovery of Śakuntalā. As the buffoon aptly jests to the king, "you've turned that ascetics' grove into a pleasure garden."

It is summertime. Śakuntalā is a nubile virgin. Kaṇva is away on a pilgrimage to avert some danger that threatens her. The king's presence arouses the world of nature. When he enters the hermitage, he hides behind a tree to watch Śakuntalā and her friends watering the trees of the ascetics' grove. While they are watering the trees and plants, the friends notice that the spring vine Śakuntalā loves like a sister is blossoming unseasonably, clinging to the male mango tree. A bee in the grove lustily attacks Śakuntalā, giving the king a chance to reveal himself as her protector. As her apparent inaccessibility to him vanishes with the revelation that she is not the child of a Brahman hermit but of a warrior sage, he pursues her insistently, controlled only by her weak resistance. Finally passion overwhelms them both and they consummate their love in a secret marriage of mutual consent. Śakuntalā transfers her creative energy from the forest animals and plants she nurtured by her touch to her human lover, she herself becoming pregnant in the process. Soon after their union, the king is recalled to his capital and leaves Śakuntalā behind. He gives her his signet ring as a sign of their marriage and promises to send for her.

Śakuntalā is distracted by her lover's parting and neglects her religious duties in the hermitage. She ignores the approach of the irascible sage Durvāsas, arouses his wrath, and incurs his curse that the king will forget her, until he sees the ring again. Kaṇva learns from the voice of the forest that Śakuntalā is pregnant. He presides over the ceremonies that sanctify her marriage and poignantly arranges for her departure from the hermitage. The ascetic women come to worship her, and two hermit boys who had been sent to gather flowers from the trees in the woods enter with offerings of jewels and garments produced by the forest trees. The scene of her last moments in the hermitage represents a ritual of breaking her bonds with the world of her childhood. Indian critics consider it to be the emotional core of the drama. On the way to the king's capital, Śakuntalā and her escorts stop to worship at the river shrine of the consort of Indra, king of the gods. There Śakuntalā loses the ring and with it the power to make the king remember her.

Despite his forgetfulness, the king experiences vague traces of their love. While he and the buffoon are listening to the singing of a lady whom the king once loved, he muses to himself: "Why did hearing the song's words fill me with such strong desire? I'm not parted from anyone I love. . . ."

> Seeing rare beauty,
> hearing lovely sounds,
> even a happy man
> becomes strangely uneasy . . .
> perhaps he remembers,
> without knowing why,
> loves of another life
> buried deep in his being.

When Śakuntalā is brought before him in his palace, the king's clouded memory struggles to clarify what he feels intuitively, increasing the intensity of the lover's "separation" for the audience. When she is rejected by the king and abandoned by the ascetics, Śakuntalā rises to anger and invokes the earth to open and receive her. Before the eyes of the king's astonished priest, a light in the shape of a woman appears and carries her off. Eventually the ring is retrieved by a fisherman, and when the king sees it, the curse is broken.

But Duṣyanta transgressed his duty in the hermitage and he too has to undergo a trial of separation before he is ready to be reunited with Śakuntalā. When his vivid memory is restored by seeing the ring, the image of the bee in the song becomes visible in the picture he paints of Śakuntalā and her friends as he first saw them in the hermitage. He uses the painting to represent his experience, but love makes him create a picture of such perfection that he rises in anger to chastise the painted bee who attacks Śakuntalā. When the buffoon reminds him that he is raving at a picture, he awakens from tasting the joy of love and returns to the painful reality of separation:

> My heart's affection made me feel
> the joy of seeing her—
> but you reminded me again
> that my love is only a picture.

This episode evokes for the audience the first meeting of the king and Śakuntalā, that unique moment of sensory and emotional awareness in which their mutual passion sowed the seed of separation and reunion. The fire of parted love that the king experiences as he worships her in his memory consecrates him for the sacred work of destroying cosmic demons that threaten the gods. Afterward, he is transported by Indra's charioteer to the hermitage of a divine sage on the celestial mountain called Golden Peak. The scene of their descent in Indra's aerial chariot recalls and parallels the earlier entry of Duṣyanta and his earthly charioteer into the forest near Kaṇva's hermitage, where he first encountered Śakuntalā.

In this enchanted grove of coral trees, the king observes a child. As he analyzes his attraction to the boy, the king's Sanskrit is set in contrast with the Prākrit speeches of two female ascetics and the hermit boy whom Duṣyanta begins to suspect is his own son. The boy is portrayed as a natural warrior despite his birth in a hermitage and his education in religious practice. This scene also recalls the beginning of the play, when Duṣyanta discovered Śakuntalā in the company of her two friends in the hermitage of Kaṇva. Here the dialogue culminates in a Prākrit pun on Śakuntalā's name, followed by her appearance before the contrite king. The fugue-like interplay of fluid Prākrit prose with more formal Sanskrit prose and verse emphasizes the tension between emotional responses and socially ordained behavior, which is Kālidāsa's major theme. He is not advocating unrestrained passion, but desire tempered by duty and duty brought alive by desire. Once the balance of these vital forces is restored, the king can recognize his son and his wife Śakuntalā.

Duṣyanta's victory over the demons, unlike his wanton pursuit of the antelope, is an act of heroism that entitles him to the love of his virtuous wife and the joy of knowing that his son is destined to be a universal emperor endowed with a great spiritual and temporal power. The richly developed counterpoint of the final act is built from latent impressions of images and events that accumulate throughout the play. By sharing these with Duṣyanta as he moves through the enchanted celestial grove to find his son and Śakuntalā, the audience participates in the celebration of their reunion.

In terms of Kālidāsa's aesthetics, creativity is regenerated by the power of the goddess, whom Śakuntalā embodies. She is endowed with a magical revelation of nature that makes beauty come to life in the dramatic process. Duṣyanta is bound to Śakuntalā by shared experience and by a child who symbolizes the integration of religious discipline and royal power. The play ends with the hero's recitation of a benediction. It marks the resolution of dramatic conflicts and the nature of the play's success:

> May the king serve nature's good!
> May priests honor the goddess of speech!
> And may Śiva's dazzling power
> destroy my cycle of rebirths!

ENDNOTE

There have been many translations of the *Śakuntalā* into European languages since Jones first translated it into English in the late eighteenth century. The most recent is a translation of the so-called Devanagari Recension of the text in *Theater of Memory: The Plays of Kālidāsa*, edited by Barbara Stoler Miller (New York: Columbia University Press, 1984). The slightly different Bengali Recension is best read in a translation by Michael Coulson, *Three Sanskrit Plays* (Harmondsworth: Penguin Books, 1981).

Gandhi's *Autobiography*

Ainslie T. Embree

As Mahatma Gandhi began to write his autobiography in the early 1920s, he was conscious that he was engaged in a literary activity that was foreign to the Indian cultural tradition. "A God-fearing friend" had chided him when he heard what he was doing, reminding him that autobiographies were only written by Westerners or people who had accepted Western cultural values. The friend's argument against autobiographical writing is revealing. Suppose, he said, you reject or revise your opinions at a later period: the people who base their conduct on the authority of your words will be misled (p. x). As a person who was greatly revered by his fellow Indians, Gandhi had a special responsibility to present only an authoritative understanding of truth; personal confession and introspection, baring one's soul to the world, had no social value.

Gandhi's friend was correct: in all the immense corpus of Indian classical literature, there is no real equivalent to the autobiography of the European tradition; there are no confessions of an Augustine or a Rousseau. Only in the second half of the nineteenth century do we begin to get Indian autobiographies, and while many of them are of considerable value for social and political history, they move on the surface of life, describing events and influential people, only rarely speculating on the psychological roots of action. In the twentieth century in India, as elsewhere, public figures have been anxious to provide a record of their lives, but it is probably fair to say that only two are of any great distinction. One is Jawaharlal Nehru's *Towards Freedom,* an elegant political apologia that carefully avoids personal revelation; the other is Nirad Chaudhari's *Autobiography of an Unknown Indian,* a mordant evocation of a society in transition. But Gandhi's book came first, and it is very different in its purpose and approach from either of these. His intention, stated in its simplest form, is to use his life to illustrate how Truth may be sought. The passion to show how he attempted to make all his actions congruent with truth is one reason for the book's importance and appeal. Another is that in the book Gandhi very deliberately and self-consciously places his life in the Indian matrix. Here he is in sharp contrast with most previous writers of Indian autobiographies who, as Judith Walsh has argued in her insightful study, *Growing Up in British India* (New York, 1981), tend to obscure, rather than emphasize, the regional and cultural backgrounds from which they came (p. x). For Gandhi, it is important that his cultural origins were deeply rooted in the devotional piety of his mother's religious practices, those of the Vaishnav cult of Gujarat. But, as he is at pains to emphasize, he knew very little in a formal, academic sense of the Hindu tradition, and he had learned much about it through English books. In the *Autobiography,* he stresses the importance of the Western tradition for him, especially where it provided linkages with his own. Thus he first read the *Gītā* in Sir Edwin Arnold's mellifluous, but not very accurate translation; his vegetarianism found its intellectual foundation from his reading of obscure English tracts; he acknowledged Ruskin and Tolstoy as his mentors. This catholicity of taste is an important aspect of Gandhi's personality and thought, for as will be noted below, his ability to transform and mold divergent, even contradictory, ideas into a consistent pattern is one of the keys to the *Autobiography*.

The form and context of Gandhi's autobiography was determined to a large extent by its appearance as a series of weekly articles, beginning in 1925, in *Navajivan*, the Gujarati weekly newspaper he edited to popularize his social and political views. Friends had urged him to write an autobiographical account of his years in South Africa where he had fought for the rights of Indian settlers, and since he had to contribute something every week to *Navajivan*, he asked himself, "Why should it not be the autobiography?" So each week he wrote a brief article of about one thousand words, a total of 179 in all, centering on some specific incident of his life from his childhood through 1921, the year in which he became a dominant force in Indian politics. The period from 1921 to his death in 1948, the crowded years of political and social activity in India, thus are not touched upon, but the *Autobiography* is, nonetheless, fundamental for an understanding of his extraordinary role in Indian life.

But while the book has special meaning for those who know Indian history, those who know little of its details will respond to it as an authentic document of the human spirit. Some of Gandhi's actions may seem repellent and wrong-headed, but it is not easy to escape the implications of the inner logic that impelled his life.

The original newspaper articles were written in Gujarati, Gandhi's mother tongue, as one of his firm convictions was that Indians must speak to each other in Indian languages, but they were translated into English for *Young India*, the English language version of *Navajivan*. They were translated by his secretary, Mahadev Desai, and then collected and published in two volumes, the first in 1925 and the second in 1927. The title of the work as first published is not, as it later became, "An Autobiography," but *The Story of My Experiments with Truth*. Desai's English version was carefully revised by Gandhi, who had a masterly command of nervous, simple

English, so one can be sure that the text as it stands gives the meaning Gandhi intended. Erik Erikson, who used the *Autobiography* extensively in his study *Gandhi's Truth,* suggests that the translation subdues "the passion, the significant poignancy, and the gentle humor" of Gandhi's own English, but these qualities are more common in his personal letters than in his public writings.

Gandhi's reply to his friend's objection to his writing an autobiography was that he had no intention of writing one in the Western style: all he intended to do was to record "the story of my experiments with truth" (p. 3). His life, he insisted, was made up of experiments, that is, attempts to act out, or to perform, the truth. "Acts of truth" are a characteristic feature of the Indian tradition, with truth not stated in a verbal definition but validated in an act of truth, with faith demonstrated, not in a confession, but in a ritual act of truth. For Gandhi, each action of daily life was to be such a ritual act. The *Autobiography,* he wrote, would show the goal he had been striving to achieve for thirty years: "Self-realization, to see God face to face, to attain *moksha*" (pp. 4, 5).

For an understanding of the *Autobiography* it is important to recognize that these three terms—self-realization, seeing God, and *moksha*—were, for Gandhi, synonyms, not separate categories. A reader familiar with both Western and Indian religious thought may object that the three terms stand for quite different, even contradictory, understandings of spiritual reality, but Gandhi's use of them as synonyms reveals the complexity of his thought behind its seeming simplicity. To look at the terms in reverse order, *moksha* is one of the most common words in the Hindu religious vocabulary. The translator's footnote is instructive: he says it literally refers to the ending of the cycle of birth and death, and suggests "salvation" as a translation. But that term comes weighted with too heavy a meaning from Christian theology, distorting Gandhi's intention. His usage gives him at once a familiar linkage with his Hindu readers' world view, but, as he did continually, he transfused a familiar term with his own meaning. In the *Autobiography,* *moksha* means many things: action dedicated to God, freedom from attachment; the path of nonviolence; the service of one's country; love; and, quite simply, Truth. This leads to the recurring theme of the *Autobiography:* "Truth is God," not, it should be noted, "God is Truth." In insisting that "Truth is God," Gandhi is aligning his thought with philosophic concepts deeply embedded in the Hindu tradition.

The second of the phrases he uses to define his goal is "to see God face to face." It can be argued that this, too, can find its counterpart in the *bhakti* tradition of devotional Hinduism, but Gandhi's usage was almost certainly derived from Christian imagery, especially as found in nineteenth-century British hymnology and religious verse, of which he had an intimate knowledge. It is difficult not to hear an echo of Tennyson's line from *Crossing the Bar:* "And I shall see my Pilot face to face." This use of the imagery made an enormous appeal to Western Christians, such as the American missionary E. Stanley Jones and the New York clergyman John Haynes Holmes, who identified Gandhi's terminology with its customary Christian meanings. But Gandhi was using it as a synonym for *moksha,* whose meaning he had transformed, and he now equated all those reinterpretations with Christian imagery. Gandhi's "God" was not the "God" of the Western biblical tradition, and he was probably aware of this. He willingly departed from what he realized was the accepted view, even from what we might call "the historical" actuality. This was also his attitude toward the Hindu tradition. In his revealing introduction to the Hindu religious classic *The Bhagavad Gītā,* he argues very persuasively that, while the plain sense of some of the verses seems to be to encourage war and violence, this cannot now be accepted as the teaching of a holy book since it is contrary to Truth. It is the text, not Gandhi's vision, that must yield. In prison, before he wrote the *Autobiography,* he had said, "That which is permanent and, therefore, necessary, eludes the historian of events. Truth transcends history." This does not mean, of course, that Gandhi distorts history in the *Autobiography,* but rather that, as he put it, "names and forms" are at best the shadow of Truth, not its essence. This is an idea that reverberates through the Indian metaphysical tradition, whether in its Brahmanic, Buddhist, or Jain versions.

This emphasis on the search for reality leads back to the first of Gandhi's three synonyms to describe his goal—self-realization. Seeing God face to face and *moksha* are convertible terms. Self-realization, to know what one truly is, will lead to freedom, to *moksha*, to the vision of God, call it what one will. The "Experiments with Truth" are ways of finding out what one truly is, what is one's essence. His striking summation of his quest comes on the last page of the autobiography: "I must reduce myself to zero." One must get rid of the extraneous, the unnecessary: when that is gone, Truth remains.

Gandhi's diverse and sometimes bizarre experiments with diet, sexual behavior, and the education of children, as well as his economic theories and his political decisions, above all, the way of nonviolence, are all integrated in his thinking under the rubric of the search for the self. To realize the self is to see God, to find *moksha*. To put it in a nonreligious vocabulary, he struggled to be a totally integrated personality, one for whom any action he performed must be the right action, since self-realization would mean perfect purity, and any act would then of necessity be pure. But "to attain to perfect purity," he wrote, "one has to become absolutely passion-free in thought, speech and action; to arise above the opposing currents of love and hatred, attachment and repulsion." This is a virtual paraphrase of the verses of the *Bhagavad Gītā* that Gandhi considered to be the essence of Hinduism. He insisted that while he himself was far from such a state, he knew where he wanted to go, and each experiment, even if it failed, was leading him there. He once commented that he had never said or written anything he later regretted; an astonishing statement from someone whose collected works run to over ninety large volumes. What he meant, presumably, was that if the motivation was the search for truth and an expression of the self, then what was said was always the "truth" at that moment. This is not an easy concept to accept, but it helps to explain what seems inconsistent and arbitrary in Gandhi's actions.

The *Autobiography* makes clear that Gandhi was well aware that his emphasis on the centrality of the self, on the autonomous being free from passion and attachment, seemed to be in conflict with his own complete commitment to involvement in politics and schemes for transforming society. In traditional Indian society the good man, the holy man, demonstrated his spiritual achievements by withdrawal from the world: the great symbols of sanctity are the rishis lost in contemplation in their Himalayan retreats. But such a life was not a psychological possibility for Gandhi. The conclusion he reaches at the end of the *Autobiography* is that those who say that religion has nothing to do with politics do not know what religion means.

While he drew upon Ruskin, Tolstoy, and the Gospels to support his arguments, he was able to show that *dharma,* the great over-arching concept of the Indian world view, insisted that self-realization meant involvement in the social order. *Dharma* has no exact English equivalent, but Gandhi uses it to mean duty, obligation, ethics, social conscience, religion. Here again Gandhi was giving new meaning to familiar Hindu religious vocabulary. In traditional Hindu society, following one's *dharma* meant, for example, engaging in the occupation of one's father and ancestors, but for Gandhi it meant ethical behavior in economic and political life. Precisely the same norms were to govern the conduct of a great business corporation or a government and the individual in the most private aspects of life. The famous distinction that the American theologian Reinhold Niebuhr made between moral man and immoral society would have been repugnant to Gandhi. In the *Autobiography,* as he looked back over his long career in South Africa, and forward to the beginning of his involvement in Indian politics, he insisted that economics, politics, and personal morality were identical. The great figure available to him from the Indian tradition to symbolize this assertion was Rāma, the god-hero of Hindu mythology. *Rāmrājya,* the kingdom of virtue, became his common way of describing the good society that he sought. That it was a profoundly Hindu symbol was not important, since Truth was one.

Self and society are, therefore, indissolubly united in Gandhi's thought, and both are equally important. This means, of course, that he has to define what the good society is and it is this that leads him to his fierce and unrelenting criticism of modern industrial society, whether in the West or in India. The peril he saw for India was that it would ape the West, that it would seek to become "modern," which meant a turning away from the search for the self. He saw the characteristics of modern industrial society, whether in the West itself or in India, as competition, greed, dehumanization, the replacement of the human hand and mind by the machine, by multiplication of unnecessary desires for material things. His vision of India was that it should be an agrarian society, made up of self-contained village units, with people producing their own food and clothing, not because they were forced to do so, but because they knew this was truly the good society in which they could be truly human. Gandhi must have known, even when he was writing the *Autobiography*, that few of those who supported him—the Nehru family, the great industrialists of Ahmedabad, the university students—really shared his vision of the good society, but this did not alter his own conviction that it was the logical economic and political pathway for India—and the world.

The key to the relationship between the self and society was found in *ahimsa*, the spirit of nonviolence, which Gandhi insisted was the only basis for the search for Truth. *Ahimsa* is another term from classical Indian thought, meaning not taking life because violence would recoil upon one, adding to the burden of one's sins. It was essentially a negative concept, but Gandhi transformed it into an active force, which he equated with love. The methodology for expressing *ahimsa* is *satyāgraha*, and Gandhi tells in the *Autobiography* how he and his friends coined the word to express the way of truth. "Passive resistance" was rejected because that could be a weapon of the weak, and the weak can be filled with hatred as they allow the strong to triumph. *Ahimsa* is a way for the strong and loving, not for the weak and resentful. All of this was summed up for Gandhi in one of his favorite Gujarati hymns; "The way of the Lord is for heroes, it is not for cowards" (C. F. Andrews, *Mahatma Gandhi's Ideas,* p. 309). For Gandhi, the good man is a hero, and the word has, of course, deep resonance in the nineteenth-century Western thought with which he was familiar. It was from Carlyle, for example, that he came to understand the greatness of Muḥammad. Gandhi's "hero" is, however, not the same as that of Carlyle or Nietzsche, for his hero's way to freedom and autonomy is through loving service of mankind. The hero will suffer, not because he is weak, but because he is strong.

Both self and society for Gandhi are part of nature. Gandhi's concept of "nature" is not clearly explicated in the *Autobiography,* but he is drawing upon the classical Indian idea that there is a harmony relating the self, society, and the cosmic order. All are of one piece; there is a continuum of being in the universe, linking not only sentient beings but the insentient as well. To find what is "natural" is an essential element in all the experiments with truth recorded in the *Autobiography,* and for Gandhi to find what was natural, one must find what is necessary. Thus celibacy is natural because sexual pleasure is not necessary, it detracts from the single-mindedness that is required for the pursuit of truth. Thus the only permitted form of birth control is abstinence, since the only justification for sex is the procreation of children, and then only when one's particular role in society permits the inevitable distraction that family responsibilities bring. Diet is also of overriding importance, because it relates to simplicity, to finding out what is essential to health. Gandhi's view of nature also explains his opposition to Western medicine and modern medical practice. He relied on earth and cold water, for example, to cure his son's broken arm. In the same way, it was against nature to drink milk, which was meant for calves, not humans. All of this sounds freakish, but it arises from the conviction of the continuum of life. He is using the same basic ideas when he is experimenting with diet and sex as when he is working out the details of a constitution for the Indian National Congress, the arrangement for great nonviolent movements, or negotiation with the viceroy. Gandhi's thought is often said to be unsystematic, inconsistent, contradictory; what the *Autobiography* reveals is a man of almost maddening consistency. One of the most morally puzzling passages in the *Autobiography* describes how he made his wife clean the chamber pot of an untouchable, an act that was not only aesthetically repugnant but, to a pious Hindu woman, spiritually polluting. For him, however, there was no place in his household for someone who did not understand that the lowliest service was a ritual act of love. Self, society, and nature come into harmony, even if, from the point of view that gives primacy to the individual, the scene speaks of disharmony and inequality.

The *Autobiography* does not yield its charm and greatness to random sampling, for despite its origins as a series of newspaper articles, it is a coherently, even very artfully, constructed work. One can make judicious selections to get its flavor, but there is hardly a chapter that does not add something to its total argument. And Gandhi's intention is plain enough: to explain the way of nonviolence, to justify his life, and to demonstrate his experiment with truth. These experiments at the time seem trivial—diet, sex, clothing—but, as he insists over and over again in the *Autobiography*, the battle for one's soul is a battle for the world. That is surely the point of a note he wrote as he broke his Delhi fast in 1924. "Presently," he said, "from the world of peace I shall enter the world of strife." What he had in mind were the demands that would be made on him to end Muslim-Hindu conflicts and to unite the factions within the Congress Party. He knew there was little he could do, so he prayed, "Lord! make me thy fit instrument and use me as thou wilt." The imagery is conventional to Christian piety; but the examples that he gives are startling: Napoleon and Kaiser Wilhelm. They had aimed high and lost; so Gandhi said, "Let us contemplate such examples and be humble." Erikson, in commenting on this, remarks that it can only impress us as a conflict between power and spirit (*Gandhi's Truth*, p. 59). *The Autobiography* is a witness to that conflict, ending with Gandhi's calm assurance that the Hero would emerge victorious.

ENDNOTE

The text used here is the first edition: M. K. Gandhi: *The Story of My Experiments with Truth,* translated from the Gujarati by Mahadev Desai, 2 vols. (Ahmedabad: Navajivan Press, 1927 and 1929). There are many other editions, including the one published by Beacon Press, Boston.

5
CLASSICS OF THE CHINESE TRADITION AND BUDDHISM

On the *Mencius* as a Chinese Classic

Irene Bloom

The *Mencius* has had a long career as a classic in China and in East Asia as a whole. Probably a compilation prepared by Mencius' disciples, and dating from the third century B.C.E., the text has been studied, memorized, absorbed, quoted, reflected upon, and argued about in China over the course of some twenty-three centuries. With a possible interlude during the period of the Cultural Revolution in the late 1960s and early 1970s, the text of the *Mencius* has continued its career, despite official hostility toward Confucianism. It is being studied there today. It has also exerted great influence throughout the recorded history of Korea, Japan, and Vietnam. There is probably no text more influential in terms of the way all of the Confucianized people of East Asia have come to think about human nature and what it means to be human.

In its traditional Chinese context the *Mencius* was unambiguously one of the "great books." For many centuries it was counted as one of the Thirteen Classics. These thirteen—a very varied group of texts which evolved between, roughly, the eleventh century B.C.E. and the second century C.E.—were regarded as cultural expressions of timeless value. One might note, however, that, while we use the English term "classic," deriving from the Latin *classicus*, to translate the Chinese word *ching* 經, their connotations are quite different. Unlike the Latin *classicus*, referring to the classes of the Roman people and, by implication, to a production of the first or highest class, the Chinese word *ching* has no association with social class. The Chinese character is composed of two elements: on the left is the radical denoting "silk," which is an artifact, a production of human civilization; on the right is a representation of an underground stream, a phenomenon of nature. "Classics," for the Chinese, have something of that character: they are human products, but they also incorporate something of the natural, as if a classic involved a particularly apt human response to the realities of a larger nature in which human beings participate. Such an idea—the confluence of the human and the natural—is above all manifest in the *Classic of Change* (or the *Book of Changes*) and discernible in a different way in the *Mencius*. But whereas the *Book of Changes* has an oracular tone, Mencius' view of what it means to be human, and how human nature figures into Nature as a whole, is communicated in a distinctly personal voice.

Mencius was among the first followers of Confucius to elaborate the original Confucian vision both in the area of political philosophy and in the philosophy of mind and human nature. And so to understand what Mencius was about, we need some perspective on the seminal role of Confucius. Confucius had been active in the late sixth and early fifth centuries B.C.E. The reigning Chou dynasty was in an advanced state of decline. Power had devolved into the hands of a number of feudal rulers who were engaged in elaborate power plays and in constant warfare, heedless of its human consequences. The mission of Confucius, if one can summarize briefly something that in cultural terms was enormous, involved: 1) transfer of attention from a supernatural world largely beyond human control to the human world and to the value and efficacy of an ethical attitude; 2) promotion of a livelier and more egalitarian conception of humanity; 3) advocacy of humane government based on respect for a common humanity; and 4) reliance on ritual or ceremony as against harsh and arbitrary laws. Confucius had been a peripatetic, traveling from state to state, seeking a hearing which might lead to official employment. While he had made no influential converts among the hardened rulers of a violent age, he had attracted an unprecedented following as a teacher. By the time of Mencius, who lived in the late fourth and early third centuries B.C.E., Confucius had also acquired the reputation of a sage.

The career of Mencius was similar. During the Warring States Period (463–222 B.C.E.), when warfare had become even more prevalent and the fate of the Chou dynasty even more problematical, he traveled from state to state, talking with rulers, still pleading the practicality of humaneness. By then the political situation had deteriorated. Mencius' response to it was determined, yet subtle: on the one hand, reaffirmation of a profound Confucian confidence in the efficacy of morality and, at the same time, resignation to the possibility that he himself might not figure into, or even witness, the restoration of a moral order.

A number of recent writers have urged attention to the beginnings and ends of texts. As John Drury observes in his essay on Luke in the *Literary Guide to the Bible*, "It is when books begin and end that their relation to the world is most problematic. In mid-reading we are in the book's world, but starting and finishing we are in transition between world and book. At these exits and entrances the artificiality of texts is troublesome."[1] Though the text of the *Mencius* was not written by Mencius himself, but compiled after his time on the basis of his teachings, the beginning and ending of the text are indeed troublesome.

The tone of the entire text is set in the opening exchange (1A:1). Mencius, braving a journey of some hundreds of miles, has come to visit King Hui of Liang and is greeted by the king.

> "Venerable sir," said the King. "You have come all this distance, thinking nothing of a thousand *li*. You must surely have some way of profiting my kingdom?"
>
> "King," answered Mencius. "What is the point of mentioning the word 'profit'? All that matters is that there should be humaneness and rightness. If the King says, 'How can I profit my state?' and the Counsellors say, 'How can I profit my family?' and the Gentlemen and Commoners say, 'How can I profit my person?' then those above and those below will be trying to profit at the expense of one another and the state will be imperilled. When regicide is committed in a state of ten thousand chariots, it is certain to be by a vassal with a thousand chariots, and when it is committed in a state of a thousand chariots, it is certain to be by a vassal with a hundred chariots. A share of a thousand in ten thousand or a hundred in a thousand is by no means insignificant, yet if profit is put before rightness, there is no satisfaction short of total usurpation. No humane man ever abandons his parents, and no righteous man ever puts his prince last. Perhaps you will now endorse what I have said, 'All that matters is that there should be humaneness and rightness'. What is the point of mentioning the word 'profit'?"

The language Mencius uses here is, by Chinese standards, very strong. He confronts this king with a stunning boldness and a sublime confidence. The king is extremely polite—addressing Mencius as "venerable sir," and leading with a question which conveys a respectful assurance of his attention. Mencius lashes out at him with a stinging rebuke, not only for the question, which to us seems utterly innocent, but for his whole moral stance. He even has the temerity to imply that rulers who put profit ahead of humaneness court regicide. As readers—and this is obviously as true of Chinese readers as of Western readers—we are at this point still in the transition between world and book, and the message we are given in the beginning is that moral commitment is not only of the utmost seriousness but of the most certain efficacy. More than that, a lack of commitment to humaneness must have awful consequences. We shall return to this opening conversation shortly.

For the moment, however, let us skip to the close of the book (7B:38), so that we have the beginning and the end of the book clearly in mind. At the end we find the venerable Mencius revealing some doubt about his own role as a vehicle for the transmission of the moral Way. He must feel intimations of mortality; toward his life's close the efficacy of his teachings is far from clear. Warfare continues. He seems to brood over the possibility that the transmission he believed had passed over the course of centuries, from the ancient sage kings to the Shang dynasty founder, and from him down to the Chou dynasty founders, and from the early Chou rulers down to Confucius, might be broken if there were no one in his own time capable of carrying on the mission of the sage. At the very end, the last thing we hear before the voice fades is, "From Confucius to the present day there have intervened something over a hundred years. We are so little removed from the time of the sage and so close to the place where he dwelled. Is there then no one? Then indeed there is no one" (7B:38).

The mode of expression of classical Chinese is spare and economical. The text does not specify the nature of the absence, yet we feel that, while Mencius longs to be assured of his own capacity for sagehood, he is resigned to the possibility that he may not figure into the tradition as the sages of the past had done. At the same time the unpromising nature of the historical situation makes that much more unambiguous the depth of his aspiration and of his devotion to Confucius as an exemplar of sagehood. And so there is an interplay of doubt and confidence, neither cancelling out the other. In exiting from the text and returning to the world, the reader must be affected by the subtle blend of high moral idealism and thoroughgoing realism. This seems to become part of the Confucian fiber and may be seen later on as quintessentially Confucian.

In mid-reading, while we are still very much in the book's world, Mencius also presents us with a philosophy of human nature, stating it in terms memorable to Chinese readers and to Western readers alike. I will say more about this view of human nature in what follows. What is relevant to our appreciation of the place of Mencius in the Chinese tradition is that this view of human nature —which confirms both our fundamental similarity to one another and our potential for goodness—is rather like a spring which is in turn the source for a stream that runs through the entire Chinese philosophical tradition. With the later development of Neo-Confucianism from the tenth century on, it becomes the mainstream. It even permeates the most distinctive forms of Chinese Buddhism, including Ch'an or Zen, filtering through to the rest of East Asia not only through Confucian channels but through Buddhist channels as well.

In addition to reflecting on human nature in a mode some might call idealistic, Mencius in mid-book is also highly realistic and practical in his awareness that human beings have certain basic needs for food, clothing, shelter, and education—and that these must be met if our very existence as human beings is to be possible. Without these essentials, human life is susceptible to appalling degradation. What he says about the responsibility of the state in meeting basic needs prefigures ongoing Confucian concerns for the material well-being of the people and may figure as significantly as Marxism does in contemporary Chinese "materialism" and the focus on what we in the West call economic and social rights.

Mencius, like Confucius, was concerned both with fundamental human questions, such as the nature of human nature and the functioning of consciousness, and with the matter of government. Nor did he see these issues as in any way separate or distinct. Modern readers are bound to be struck with how continuous the world of Mencius appears to have been, the private and public spheres being experienced as entirely interfused. Apparently the concerns which those grounded in Western thought might see subsumed under the categories of "moral philosophy" and "political philosophy," or pertaining to "private" and "public" spheres, were so continuous for Mencius that he saw no need to argue for or even to explain their relation. It probably would not have occurred to him to propose that the components of individual personality might serve as an analogy for the constituents of the state, as did Plato in the *Republic.* (The very fact of Socrates' proposing this analogy in the great dialogue "on justice" indicates that he is juxtaposing two realities which are ordinarily regarded as distinct in order to challenge Glaucon et al. to discover the relation between the two.) Mencius hardly speaks about individuals apart from society: we see no attempt to consider what human beings might be like prior to society or apart from it or even, as with Aristotle in his *Politics,* what human beings might be like in different kinds of polities.

There are least two factors which might explain why, for Mencius, the private and public worlds are continuous rather than analogous. The first has to do with the Confucian view of the family. Mencius seems to take as a given that the patriarchal family and the monarchical state are constant features of social life. It is not simply that one is the model for the other. The family is the source for the profound sense of relatedness and mutual regard on which civilization as a whole is predicated. The sentiments originally nurtured within the family are the same that guide all of the transactions of human life. The private life of the family is based on an affirmation of human interrelatedness, and such an affirmation is thought to be natural in the public sphere as well. Readers of the *Republic* may be struck with the fact that Plato and Mencius have such different views of the family—in Plato's view, it is a narrow and constricted environment which contrasts with the public world of the *polis;* in Mencius' view, it is the source and matrix for humane attitudes which are to be extended outward in widening circles of concern.

Another factor involved in Mencius' view of the continuity of private and public life is his conviction that human nature is universal and that human beings are essentially alike. The belief that human beings are fundamentally similar and mutually responsive tends to link the private and the public spheres: people are expected to have, on the one hand, the same fundamental needs and wants and, on the other, the same potential for recognizing themselves in others. As Mencius argues in interviews with several rulers, the humaneness of rulers involves the recognition of a shared humanity; the reciprocal of this is that the subjects of a humane ruler can be counted on to recognize and support him as such. The problem of ethical and political life is to encourage individuals and rulers alike to fulfill the potential of their natures by playing their allotted roles as well as possible. This always involves affirming their interrelatedness.

Not only the connection between private and public spheres, but the connection between the lofty idealism and the intense realism of Mencius may be discovered in his commitment to *jen*, variously translated as goodness, benevolence, or humaneness. *Jen* is the term which expresses the notion of interrelatedness in its moral dimension. The Chinese character for *jen* 仁 is made up of a radical element denoting a person or the human on the left 人 and, on the right, the number two 二 , a multiplier, suggesting a person together with others or interaction among human beings.

The term was one that Mencius had inherited from Confucius. But when Confucius spoke about *jen* he had always left its significance open for further reflection, as though he preferred his hearers to ponder it rather than to presume that they could fully grasp it. The term eludes definition—Confucius seemed intent on our appreciating this. Mencius builds on the vision of human relatedness found in the *Analects*, saying so much more about *jen* that it is almost possible to grasp, though certainly not to exhaust, its meaning. It emerges that *jen* involves moral responsiveness, being able to put oneself in the position of the other, being able to recognize oneself in the other. Rather than personal attributes or qualities that we possess as individuals, it involves the quality of the interactions to which we are party. We may glimpse a kind of "golden rule" here, but it becomes clear that it is a matter of empathy more than precept.

In a sense the *Mencius* is a more public text than the *Analects*.

Mencius may have been as complex and multifaceted a personality as the Confucius we encounter in the *Analects,* but we do not observe him, as we do Confucius, in intimate and personal exchanges with his disciples, nor do we seem to discover him in moments of informality or striking personal candor. Mencius usually appears to us, as in the opening chapters of the work, in direct exchanges with rulers of the contending feudal states of the time or at occasions, apparently rather formal in character, when he is engaged in encounters with memorable antagonists over major philosophical questions. His discussions of *jen* come up first in the context of his conversations with rulers of several of the feudal states of the late Chou period. In these conversations Mencius tries to convey to them what constitutes humane government, how the ruler may recognize in himself the impulse to humaneness, and why a humane government is bound to be effective.

To return now to the conversation between Mencius and the aged and besieged King Hui of Liang with which the text opens: Recall that the king has suggested hopefully that Mencius, who has just arrived in Liang, must have journeyed there prepared with strategies for profiting the state. Mencius dismisses this question as inappropriate, contending with the utmost conviction that "profit," as a motive, must prove divisive and destructive. Once the ruler begins to think in terms of "profit," everyone in the state, from the ministers to the common people, will do the same. When everyone thinks in terms of profit, the common good will have been forgotten, and there can be no greater loss than this. The conclusion is that, "All that matters is that there should be humaneness and rightness. What is the point of mentioning the word 'profit'?"

We may note that, in advancing such an argument, Mencius articulated a view with as much moral resonance as any in Confucian teaching. Echoing and reechoing in virtually all later Confucian discourse is the idea that what ultimately matters in human interactions is the motivation of the actors and their capacity for mutual respect and regard based on recognition of a common humanity. This common humanity is understood to be variously expressed by individuals performing distinct roles and confronting the different circumstances of life according to the complementary principle of *i* or rightness, a complex idea of what is right in particular situations, coupled with a sense of the judgment required to ensure appropriate behavior.

The depth of Mencius' interest in human motivation and commitment to the ethical complementarity of *jen* and *i,* becomes clear when his central concerns are set over against the most compelling alternative views of the time. One of these was Legalism. Though Mencius lived before the time of Han Fei, who produced the classic distillation of Legalist thought in the late third century B.C.E., the hardbitten approach to the problems of government which came to be labeled "the school of laws" had already been current for several centuries. Mencius, when conversing with various rulers of the time, does not allude to Legalist philosophy per se, but it is clear that he is arguing, at least indirectly, against the kind of toughminded *Realpolitik* which appealed to many who were dedicated to advancing the interests of their states in an age of bitter contention and brutal warfare. The Legalists, in their pragmatism, their exaltation of military might, their reliance on the coercive force of laws and punishments, their contempt for culture, and their almost exclusive concern with the advantage or "profit" of rulers, show little concern for the capacity for moral responsiveness which, for Mencius, is the very essence of being human.

Many of Mencius' pronouncements about humaneness and rightness are targeted at rulers who seem not only skeptical of what he has to say, but steeped in an alternative, and much less generous, set of values. It is no doubt a measure of his absolute confidence in the rightness and cogency of his own moral standpoint that he is direct to the point of acerbity in making his case with several rulers against the squandering of life and resources in warfare and belligerence. Nor has he any compunction about informing King Hsüan of Ch'i, who may well have had some sensitivity on this score, that there is no moral principle which precludes the ousting of a ruler who "mutilates humaneness and cripples rightness." Mencius insists that, historically, it was an extreme of corruption that led to the overthrow of the last ruler of the Hsia dynasty by the Shang founder and, in turn, of the last ruler of the Shang by the Chou founders. These acts, having been morally justified, were not regicide but merely the "punishment" of rulers who had done violence against others and against their own humanity (1B:8). This judgment, often understood as representing a defense by Mencius of a "right of revolution," was no doubt intended to apply to only the most extreme circumstances, though, given the high moral standards proposed by Mencius for any ruler, it is hardly surprising that many throughout the centuries have been made decidedly uneasy by it.

Philosophically speaking, Mencius identifies his primary antagonists as the adherents of the schools of Yang Chu and Mo Tzu (3B:9). Yang Chu, sometimes characterized as an individualist, evidently defended the individual's withdrawal from public life or from official service in the interests of self-preservation. As Mencius understood him, Yang saw the individual as appropriately self-regarding, a view which Confucians would consistently condemn as morally vacant. Mo Tzu, often described as a utilitarian, espoused a morality predicated on the idea that a purely rational calculation of personal advantage should prompt everyone to adopt the imperative of universal love, or love without discrimination. Such love, which was to be extended to everyone equally, and correspondingly to be received from everyone equally, without regard to the primacy of familial bonds, put morality at a remove from the familial context which Confucians believed was its natural source and matrix.

For Mencius, Yang Chu's view involved the denial of one's ruler, Mo Tzu's, denial of one's parents. Because his own morality was based on a conception of the subtlety and richness of the human moral sense, with its roots in the deepest dimensions of biological and psychic life and its ramifications in the whole of human experience, both of these represented a denial of what he took to be truly human:

> If the way of Yang and the way of Mo are not stopped and the Way of Confucius is not made manifest, the people will be deluded by perverse views and humaneness and rightness will be blocked. When humaneness and rightness are blocked, then we lead animals to devour humans, and humans to devour one another. I am alarmed about this and am determined to defend the way of the former sages by opposing Yang and Mo.

Profit, whether it is understood to entail the advantage of an individual, a ruler, or the state as a whole, is rejected by Mencius as an appropriate motive for action. But the fact that profit is rejected as a motive does not mean that any concession is made in regard to the potential efficacy of humane government. It is clear from conversations which Mencius has with King Hui, his successor King Hsiang, King Hsüan of Ch'i, and others that he is convinced that it is the complementarity of humaneness and rightness that finally "works." Any narrower calculation of what might be advantageous to a ruler or even to a state as a whole is bound ultimately to be self-defeating because such calculation fails to encourage mutual regard and fellow feeling, impulses which lead in the direction of *jen* and are conducive to that most enduringly important of all political phenomena, human unity.

Jen, for Mencius, involves more than a disposition of the mind and heart. It is that, but it also necessarily carries over into action and, in the case of a ruler, into policy. Mencius' awareness that people share basic needs for food, clothing, shelter, and education is reflected in an active interest in the ruler's policies in the areas of landholding, taxation, famine relief, the establishment of schools, hunting, arboriculture, and sericulture (1A:3, 2A:5, 3A:3). In the measures he advocates Mencius seems considerably more specific than the Mohists in projecting what must be done by a ruler in order to provide on a long-term basis for these needs. And whereas the Mohists are concerned, almost as much as the Legalists, with the mobilization and control of the people in order to stave off disorder, always underlying Mencius' philosophy of government there is the concern with motivation and with moral authority. Such authority depends above all on the ruler's ability to empathize with his people and to exercise "the transforming influence of morality" (2A:3).

The ability to exercise a "transforming influence" is the mark of a sage. What makes it possible for a sage to perform such a function is that human beings are highly responsive to one another, and they are responsive because they are both alike by nature and aware of this likeness. They differ, according to Mencius, primarily owing to the environment in which they are nurtured. In one of the many passages in the *Mencius* which employ agricultural analogies of plants and growing things (6A:7), the human condition is likened to that of seeds which grow more or less well depending on the richness of the soil, the regularity of the rain and dew, and the amount of human effort invested in cultivation. "Now things of the same kind are all alike. Why should we have doubts when it comes to man? The sage and I are of the same kind." Not only are human beings similar by nature, they are also capable of growing to the kind of perfection exemplified by the sages Yao and Shun of antiquity.

When we survey the history of Confucian thought, Mencius was unquestionably the single most influential contributor to a view of human nature which ultimately became dominant, not only in China but in the rest of Confucianized East Asia as well, and not only in the thought of an intellectual and social elite, but in the value system of an entire culture. It is a view quite different from that of the Biblical religions, which share a conception of human beings as inherently flawed and having to struggle to reverse the distance between themselves and God, a defect which entered the definition of humanness almost at the beginning of human history. Mencius, for his part, does not delve into the creation of the universe and of man. By the time he begins his reflections, both are understood to be in place, human history to be well underway, the patterns of human behavior and relationship already set. Mencius begins with the here and now and with the actual lives of his contemporaries, all of whom, he finds, have within themselves the potential for goodness.

The evidence he adduces, in perhaps the most celebrated passage in the work (2A:6), rests on a single powerful example. "All men," he says, "have a mind (or heart) which cannot bear to see the sufferings of others."

> I say that all men have a mind which cannot bear to see the sufferings of others knowing that any of our contemporaries, seeing a child about to fall into a well, will without exception experience a feeling of alarm and distress. They will feel so, not so as to gain the favor of the child's parents, nor so as to seek the praise of their neighbors and friends, nor from dislike of the reputation of having been unmoved by such a thing . . .

Mencius does not need to tell us what the person who sees the child teetering on the edge of a well will do. We ourselves fill this in out of our own humanity. We recognize that all human beings can be counted on, insofar as they retain their humanity, to act on the spontaneous impulse to save the child by pulling it from danger.

According to Mencius, the human mind or heart which cannot bear to see the sufferings of others is, in a positive sense, compassion. "Whoever is devoid of the mind of compassion is not human," he says. Then he extends the argument considerably by adding, "Whoever is devoid of the mind of shame is not human, whoever is devoid of the mind of courtesy and modesty is not human, and whoever is devoid of the mind of right and wrong is not human." These four—compassion, shame, courtesy and modesty, and the sense of right and wrong—he calls the "four beginnings" or the "four seeds" of virtue. These he believes are present in every human being.

As promptings of the mind or heart, as sentiments, these inclinations are not confirmed or complete at any given point in a person's life. Developing them is a matter of experience, effort, and cultivation, but they are always there as a potential. The sense of compassion Mencius recognizes as the beginning of humaneness;

the sense of shame, the beginning of rightness; the sense of modesty, the beginning of propriety; and the sense of right and wrong, the beginning of wisdom. These promptings are present in every person, without exception. As Mencius puts it,

> Human beings have these four beginnings just as they have their four limbs. When one who has these four beginnings, says of himself that he cannot develop them, he acts as a thief to himself, and one who says of his prince that he cannot develop them, acts as a thief to his prince. We have these four beginnings within us, and if we know how to develop and complete them, it will be like a fire starting to burn or a spring beginning to come through. By bringing them to completion, we are able to protect all within the four seas. In failing to bring them to completion, we have not even the wherewithal to serve our parents.

One may cultivate the "four beginnings" in oneself, or one may not. If one does not, one injures oneself and one's intimates quite as much as others. By even expressing skepticism about the moral capacity of another, one injures that person—one literally steals from him something that is his and that is precious.

Some may notice that when Mencius speaks of the "beginnings" of virtue—compassion, for example—he is referring to affective or emotional responses. He believes "thinking" or "reflection" to be distinctively human, but nowhere does he speak of a distinct faculty of reason, nor does he separate "thinking" from the emotions, desires, and appetites. In fact, the terms "mind" and "heart" are not distinguished in Chinese. There is just one word—*hsin*. There is also no mind-body dualism here, suggesting that Mencius stands at the beginning of a philosophical tradition which was to be quite different from the one which evolved in the West from Plato to Spinoza. Nor does Mencius make any mention of a soul, which, of course, again separates him from Plato, for whom the essential person is, finally, the soul.

As we get further into it, we realize that Mencius' conception of the human is different from that found in the Biblical or Platonic traditions. Mencius does not analyze human beings in terms of distinct components—body, mind, soul. The human moral capacity derives, in this view, not from some still, small voice within us that guides us toward the right and away from the wrong, but from a kind of energy that is built up within ourselves in the course of our entire experience and education. When he speaks about his personal strengths he understands them to be 1) an insight into language—in other words, a capacity for communication; and 2) skill in cultivating his "flood-like *ch'i*," (or, as one translator aptly put it, his "overwhelming energy"). This energy belongs to every living thing. In humans, it is, as he says,

> in the highest degree, vast and unyielding. Nourish it with integrity and place no obstacle in its path and it will fill the space between Heaven and Earth. It is *ch'i* which unites rightness and the Way. Deprive it of these and it will collapse. It is born of accumulated rightness and cannot be appropriated by anyone through a sporadic show of rightness. Whenever one acts in a way that falls below the standard in one's heart, it will collapse. (2A:2)

Mencius is arguing in this case against his principal antagonist, Kao Tzu, who maintains (6A:4) that, whereas humaneness is internal, rightness is external, something assimilated through learning or conditioning, but not inherently in us as part of our nature. Mencius for his part sees that rightness—doing what is right in given circumstances—is related to our psychophysical energy, to our feelings of vitality and well-being, and to our positive sense of identity as persons. Doing right, and doing so consistently, not sporadically, bears on our stamina and affects the energy with which we lead our lives. It is associated with a sense of human dignity, which prompts us to do certain things and to refrain from doing others. It suggests certain priorities that on grounds of simple self-interest might be unintelligible. This *ch'i*, or psychophysical energy, which Mencius would have us carefully and actively cultivate, is powerful and yet fragile, dependent on and sensitive to the quality and rightness of our moral lives.

Later Chinese philosophy owes an enormous debt to Mencius. No small part of this debt is for enlarging and clarifying the very sense of what it means to be human—a sense which is quite definite and particular and yet also consciously open and rich with possibilities. "Humaneness is what it means to be human," he says. "When these two are conjoined, the result is "the Way' " (7B:16). "Humaneness is the mind of man, and rightness his road" (6A:11). However the concepts of humaneness and rightness were interpreted and reinterpreted following Mencius, they would always imply the primary value of the dignity of persons and, particularly, the connectedness among them and the directedness in their moral lives. It is as if the work of Confucius—which involved drawing attention to the natural equality of human beings, their fundamental relatedness, and their ability to control their own lives through learning and effort—was confirmed by Mencius.

It was also furthered by him through his remarkable psychological insight and his secure sense for the scope of the human enterprise. There is in Mencius a deepened confidence concerning the place of human beings in the universe. Near the end of the text that bears his name he speaks about the relation of human beings to nature or to the universe as a whole:

> One who gives full realization to his mind (or heart) understands his own nature, and by knowing his own nature, knows Heaven. Preserving one's mind and nourishing one's nature is the way to serve Heaven. (7A:1)

Here the word which has been translated as "Heaven" may also be understood as Nature or the natural process as a whole. Following on his affirmation of the connectedness among persons, past and present, such an affirmation of the connectedness between human beings and the universe is rich with possibilities. Is this a kind of mysticism, we wonder? Idealism? Possibly even realism? The categories themselves begin to seem arbitrary, perhaps a little hollow.

What is clear is that Mencius' conception of the human is essentially biological; his conception of Nature, a biosphere in which everything is mutually interreactive. His affirmation of the connectedness among persons and between human beings and the universe as a whole has had a long and fruitful career in East Asia. It may have much to say to the modern West as well.

ENDNOTE

1. Robert Alter and Frank Kermode, eds., *A Literary Guide to the Bible* (Cambridge: Belknap Press of Harvard University Press, 1987), p. 422.

The Place of the *Lao Tzu* in Early Chinese Thought

Franciscus Verellen

The *Lao Tzu* is a short collection of aphorisms which probably took shape around the middle of the third century B.C. The first commentaries on the *Lao Tzu*, found in the book of Han Fei Tzu (d. 233 B.C.), appear also to date from that period, but their authorship is contested. The oldest extant version of the *Lao Tzu* itself, however, two silk manuscripts from the beginning of the second century B.C., trace the textual transmission of the work back to within decades of the presumed date of compilation.

The commentary by Wang Pi (226–249), some five centuries after the *Han Fei Tzu*, is in fact the earliest to which both a date and an author may be confidently assigned. By the end of the T'ang, in a preface dated A.D. 901, a scholiastic editor of the official commentary promulgated by Emperor Hsüan-tsung (r. 712–756) listed no fewer than sixty-one commentators preceding him. Today, the number of commentaries is said to exceed two hundred.

For all its brevity and mystery, the *Lao Tzu* constitutes one of the most challenging, intriguing, and influential sets of propositions put forward in the history of both Chinese philosophy and religion. Over the last century, several probing translations and many popular renditions have secured for it a permanent place in the literature of the West as well. One reason for this abiding interest, and the perennial supply of reinterpretations, is suggested in the *Lao Tzu* itself: "My words are very easy to understand and very easy to practice. In the whole world nobody is able to understand them and nobody is able to practice them" (chapter 70).

Interpretations are indeed apt to differ between any two individuals, let alone readers widely separated by intellectual background and historical period. The quotations from the *Lao Tzu* in the present brief introduction reflect my own interpretations while also drawing on translations of the relevant passages by Wing-tsit Chan, J. J. L. Duyvendak, Max Kaltenmark, Bernhard Karlgren, D. C. Lau, and Arthur Waley.

THE LAO TZU LEGEND IN ANTIQUITY

Despite the remarkable discovery of the two ancient manuscripts at Ma wang tui (Hunan) in 1973, the history of Lao Tzu's teaching prior to the compilation of the work bearing his name remains difficult to ascertain. Already by Former Han times (206 B.C.–A.D. 8), the most circumstantial biographical account of the sage consisted of a composite legend incorporating episodes from the lives of several distinct figures. These early traditions about Lao Tzu's career and reluctant bequest of his teaching to the world serve at any rate as indications of the views held by an early school of followers concerning their founder and the transmission of his teaching during the Warring States period (475–221 B.C.).

The main elements of the ancient legend are as follows: the real name of Lao Tzu, to whom several early texts also refer as Lao Tan, was Li Erh or Li Tan. He was a native of Hu-hsien in the state of Ch'u, not far from modern Po-hsien (Anhwei), the site which has been officially revered as Lao Tzu's birthplace since Han times. He is said to have served as curator of archives under the Eastern Chou (770–256) in Loyang.

An alleged visit by Confucius (551–479), and Lao Tzu's lofty rebuke of his interlocutor, afforded an opportunity for polemics between the rival schools not unlike the later controversy concerning Lao Tzu's "conversion of the [Western] barbarians," intended to challenge the independent status of Buddhism in China, to which the following episode of the legend gave rise:

Eventually, Lao Tzu departed from the court of the declining Chou to journey to K'un-lun, the mythical sacred mountain of the Western regions. On the point of leaving the Middle Kingdoms, however, Lao Tzu was detained by the guardian of the Han-ku Pass, a hundred miles west of Loyang. This discerning officer, named Yin Hsi, persuaded the sage to impart his teaching, which he then committed to writing. The result, the Book of Five Thousand [Characters] *(Wu-ch'ien wen)*, as the *Lao Tzu* also came to be known, was thus procured and transmitted by Yin Hsi.

THE WAY AND VIRTUE

The third traditional title for the work is *Tao-te ching*, or Classic of Tao and Te. The two manuscripts mentioned above confirm the division of the ancient text into two sections, though arranged in the reverse order—"Te" followed by "Tao." One of the two copies actually features those terms as headings.

Bibliographic considerations aside, the concepts "Way" *(tao)* and "Virtue," the latter in the sense of "inherent power" or "operative influence" *(te)*, are indeed central to the philosophy of the *Lao Tzu*. A direct relationship between the two is often implied by translating the pair as "the Way and its Virtue (or power)." The opening lines of the *Lao Tzu* read:

> The Way that can be defined is not the unchanging Way. The name that can be named is not the unchanging name. Nameless,

[the Way] is at the origin of Heaven and Earth. Having a name, it is the mother of all things. (chapter 1)

The ineffable eternal Tao, which existed before the universe, also has a particular, manifest aspect which is inherent in all things constituting the phenomenal world. As such, it is endowed with qualities. Hence it is capable of being conceptualized; and it is subject to change:

There was something formless but complete which existed prior to Heaven and Earth. Soundless and indistinct, it stands alone, unchanging; it pervades all, unfailing. It can be regarded as the mother of all things. We do not know its name but style it "Tao." If I were compelled to name it, I would say "Ta" (the Great). (chapter 25)

Because the eternal Tao is devoid of the qualities of phenomenal existence, termed *yu* (literally "to have"), the *Lao Tzu* attributes to it the quality of nothingness *wu* (literally "not to have"). Nothingness, in contrast to "non-being," harbors the potential of every thing: "The Tao is empty, yet it can be used without ever being filled. How deep it is: the ancestor of all things!" (chapter 4).

The terms "valley," "mother," and "womb" stand in *Lao Tzu* for the receptivity and potential productivity of emptiness *(hsü)*, as do also various hollow implements:

The space between Heaven and Earth is like a bellows or a flute: though empty, it is inexhaustible. In operation, it produces ever more. (chapter 5)

Thirty spokes make a wheel, yet the use of the cart depends on that which does not contain anything [i.e., the hub]. We shape clay to make a vessel, yet the use of the vessel depends on that which does not contain anything. (chapter 11)

If, as we have said, the Tao in its aspect of nothingness harbors the potential of all things, then Virtue, Te, is the aspect of Tao which lends specific potency to each particular thing or being. In man, Te is, for example, the skill necessary to perform a specific task.

> Skillful action leaves no trace, skillful speech is unblemished, a skilled reckoner uses no tallies, a well-closed [door] needs neither bolts nor bars yet cannot be opened, a well-tied knot needs neither rope nor twine yet cannot be loosened. (chapter 27)

It is also the moral influence which causes him to hold sway over fellow men. The true possessor of Te is unaware of Virtue and never strives to use it to advantage:

> Superior Virtue does not [pretend to] Virtue; thereby Virtue is possessed. Inferior Virtue does not disregard Virtue; thereby Virtue is not possessed. Superior Virtue does not act, but has no reason to act. Inferior Virtue acts, but has its [ulterior] reasons for acting. (chapter 38)

In the examples of Te as skill quoted above from chapter 27, the practitioner refrains from imposing himself or any extraneous means on his work. In fact, his ability to recognize the operative principle inherent in a thing or situation allows him to utilize its natural, spontaneous *(tzu-jan)* efficacy, unhampered by his interference. This is the mode of efficacious action of the Tao itself, which the *Lao Tzu* literally calls "absence of [purposive] action" *(wu-wei),* and which might usefully be rendered as "non-intervention": "The Tao never acts, yet nothing is left undone. If lords and princes adhered to this [principle], all things would evolve spontaneously" (chapter 37).

Before examining some topical aspects of Lao Tzu's application of *wu-wei* to political theory, we shall consider for a moment another approach to his philosophy of Tao, Te, and *wu-wei* which suggests a rather different dimension to the work.

LAO TZU AS MYSTIC

In the last phrase of the opening section of the *Lao Tzu,* in its present arrangement, the chapter's cryptic pronouncements concerning the eternal Tao and the different existential modes decidedly adopt the language of mystical contemplation: "Together, [*wu* and *yu*] are called mysterious *(hsüan)*, the mystery of mysteries, the gate to all wonders" (chapter 1).

The notion of the ineffable eternal Tao ("The Way that can be defined is not the unchanging Way" etc.), itself evokes the familiar theme in mystical literature of the unchanging and undifferentiated first principle in which everything coexists simultaneously, as One: "I find only an undifferentiated Unity . . . Indiscernible, it cannot be named" (chapter 14). From the One proceed all of creation, and the One proceeds from the Tao: "Tao produced the One. The One produced the two. Two produced the three. And three produced the ten thousand things" (chapter 42).

For many mystics the postulate of unity, the idea that everything is ultimately one, has given rise to the expectation of *gnosis*, the possibility of an esoteric knowledge of spiritual mysteries, if not of union with the Absolute. The *Lao Tzu* is a case in point:

> Attain complete emptiness and hold fast to quiescence. All things arise together. I thereby witness their return. Creatures flourish profusely, but each returns to its root. To return to one's root means quiescence, quiescence is the return to one's destiny, the return to one's destiny is called the Eternal. To know the Eternal is called illumination. Not to know the Eternal is to act in vain and invite misfortune. (chapter 16)

Lao Tzu's law of the return to the origin appears to be universal. There is no conclusive evidence that the work reflects the cult of immortality which was to flourish under the Han. It does, however, emphasize the ideal of longevity attainable through a regime of spiritual and physical discipline, in particular quiescence and *yoga*-like techniques of breath control (chapter 10).

Paradoxical discourse, a feature of prophetic and mystical writings in many traditions, is another way in which the *Lao Tzu* draws the reader into a mystical mode of enquiry and apprehension:

strong is weak and vice versa; female, soft, and passive prevail over male, hard, and active; water, the most pliant of elements, endures; single drops in time penetrate the hardest rock; the dark valley is where the waters gather; the low and submissive are exalted, the proud and exalted will be brought low; the infant, the "uncarved block" are symbols of the power to become; the obscure "spirit of the valley" is the mystical matrix of the creative and productive forces of the Tao.

In this context, *wu-wei* becomes mystical quiescence: not absolute stillness but nonresistance to the Way, as water runs its course, passively but inexorably, in compliance with the law of gravity and the lay of the land.

CLASSICAL TAOISM

The term "Taoist" *(tao-chia)* originated as a category of ancient books in the imperial library of the Former Han dynasty. In the catalogue *Ch'i-lüeh* (6 B.C.), it designated the branch of philosophical learning which included the *Lao Tzu*. Han sources also mention the doctrine of Huang-Lao (named after the mythical Yellow Emperor Huang-ti and Lao Tzu), which enjoyed considerable influence up to the reign of Emperor Wu-ti (140–87 B.C.). The textual traditions associated with the terms Tao-chia and Huang-Lao constitute the classical corpus of Taoist literature.

Though it is an open question to what extent Han bibliographical classifications reflected historical movements as well as sets of texts, it is useful to consider the teaching of the *Lao Tzu* against the background of some of the rival schools of political philosophy which flourished in the Warring States period.

Philosophical debate in the mid-third century B.C. was characterized by intense competition for the implementation of theories of statecraft addressing such topics as military tactics, economic policy, and law and administration. In 221 B.C., both the practical and the theoretical aspects of this contention came to a head with the foundation of the Ch'in empire, the first to unite all of China under one rule.

The strategy of the successful state of Ch'in was based on policies proposed by the "Legalists" *(fa-chia)*, a school which advocated the administration of a rigorous system of penal law to control every aspect of society and the state. While the nature and extent of the interaction between Taoist and Legalist thought remain to be fully explored, the *Lao Tzu*'s policy of government by non-intervention was plainly in conflict with the major tenet of Legalism: "The more laws and ordinances are promulgated, the more thieves and robbers there will be" (chapter 57).

Half of the occurrences of the term *wu-wei* in the *Lao Tzu* refer explicitly to laissez-faire governmental policies. Many additional passages convey the same advice. The famous line "governing a large kingdom is like cooking small fish" (i.e., don't overdo it) from chapter 60 was appropriately adduced by a recent U.S. President advocating "small government."

In a passage which parallels the examples of skillful work cited above from chapter 27, the *Lao Tzu* requires a successful leader to refrain from coercion:

> A skillful commander does not seem martial, a skillful warrior does not display anger, a skillful victor does not contend, a skillful user of men humbles himself. This is called the Virtue of not contending. (chapter 68)

The *Lao Tzu* regretfully admits the necessity of certain military operations (chapter 69). Despite its visions of a utopian society living in peace, harmony, self-sufficiency, and simple contentment (chapter 47), its political attitudes are on the whole pragmatic, and its mystical insights, rather than denying worldly reality, claim a "truer" grasp of the sources and exercise of power.

Although Legalism briefly won the day in 221 B.C., the only ancient indigenous school of thought with which Taoism was to contend beyond the Han period was Confucianism. It would appear that already the compilers of the *Lao Tzu* were taking issue with some of the positions of the older school, e.g., in rejecting the importance which Confucians attached to humaneness *(jen)* and morality, and to learning and education:

> When the great Way fell into disuse, humaneness and a sense of duty *(i)* arose. When intellect and cleverness appeared, great falsehood came into being. When the six relations of kinship were in disharmony, filial piety and parental love came into being. When the state fell into anarchy, loyal subjects came into being. (chapter 18)

Consistent with the above, and in striking contrast to Confucian thinking, is the *Lao Tzu*'s insistence on the indifference of both the cosmic powers and the sage *(sheng-jen)* to human affairs: "Heaven and Earth are not humane. They treat the ten thousand creatures as [sacrificial] straw dogs. Sages are not humane. They treat the people as straw dogs," (chapter 5).

In a similar vein, the *Lao Tzu* seemed to condemn the Confucian ideals of government through moral influence, by means of education (chapter 65) and the performance of rites (chapter 38). Perhaps on a more fundamental level, however, the *Lao Tzu* raised the question of the comparative values of the active and the contemplative roles of the sage *(sheng)* in human society, an issue eventually incorporated and reexamined over the centuries within the Confucian tradition itself.

LAO TZU IN MEDIEVAL THOUGHT AND RELIGION

Favored by the Huang-Lao tradition and by association with messianic movements devoted to the fall of the Later Han dynasty (A.D. 25–220), the Lao Tzu legend took a dramatic turn in the second century with the apotheosis of the founder as a cosmic deity titled Most High Lord Lao (T'ai-shang Lao-chün). By the end of the century, the *Lao Tzu* had accordingly attained the status of a revealed scripture and was the object of fervent recitations by followers of Celestial Master Taoism in western China.

The third century saw the celebrated syncretic revival of Taoist and Confucian philosophy under the Hsüan-hsüeh school led by Wang Pi. The name of this movement, Study of Mysteries, was inspired by the passage in chapter 1 of the *Lao Tzu* quoted above ("Together, [*wu* and *yu*] are called mysterious . . ."). Wang Pi's principal contribution consisted in a refinement of Lao Tzu's theory of the existential modes *wu* and *yu*, coupled with the complementary concepts of "substantiality" *(t'i)* and "functionality" *(yung)*.

Following its encounter with Confucian thought in Hsüan-hsüeh, Taoist philosophy entered in the fourth century into an ongoing intellectual exchange with Mahāyāna Buddhism, both on the subject of existential and ontological issues on which Chinese Buddhists could bring a rich Indian legacy to bear and in the area of mystical *gnosis* and meditation techniques. The resulting interpenetration of Buddhist and Taoist ideas in the latter domain was to become instrumental to the development of Ch'an (Zen) Buddhism under the T'ang (618–907).

The ruling Li clan of the T'ang dynasty declared Lao Tzu their ancestor. Emperor Hsüan-tsung, promulgator of the official commentary mentioned above, canonized the *Lao Tzu* as the most important scripture recognized by the state, to be revered throughout the empire. Under the T'ang, the *Lao Tzu* also became a civil service examination text.

In medieval China, and to the present day, the *Lao Tzu* continued to be regarded as the fundamental religious scripture of Taoism. The ancient category of *tao-chia* philosophers had since Han times assumed the new meaning of "Taoist clergy." In the fifth century, the religious tradition based on the early Celestial Master movement in Szechwan, and incorporating subsequent scriptural and liturgical developments, codified its teaching into a structured Taoist Canon, with a division consecrated to the *Lao Tzu*.

By T'ang times, a uniform ordination system had evolved which linked the initiation into each grade of the hierarchy to the transmission of a set body of sacred texts, including the *Tao-te ching*. The transmission of the *Lao Tzu* thus became institutionalized as part of an esoteric instruction passed on from Taoist master to disciple.

The Lotus Sutra

Wing-tsit Chan

No one can understand the Far East without some knowledge of the teachings of the *Lotus Sutra,* because it is the most important scripture of Mahāyāna Buddhism, which cuts across the entire Far East. In a narrow sense it is a scripture of the T'ien-t'ai School in China and Tendai in Japan and the chief sutra of the Nichiren School in Japan. But in a broad sense it is the most basic sutra for all Mahāyāna, shared by practically all the different schools. It was the first to preach revolutionary Mahāyāna doctrines, is still the most comprehensive statement of them; and most important of all, has been the source of inspiration for Buddhist practice in the Far East for the last 1,500 years. If out of several hundred Mahāyāna sutras one were to choose only one as the most representative and most meaningful, most students would select the *Lotus*. No wonder that when Chang Jung, an ardent advocate of the harmony of Confucianism, Buddhism, and Taoism, died in A.D. 497, he held in his left hand a copy of the *Classic of Filial Piety* and the *Tao-te ching* and in his right hand the *Lotus*.

Ever since its appearance in China in the third century, and especially after the fifth, the study of the *Lotus* has been pursued most vigorously and extensively. According to the *Biographies of Eminent Monks (Kao-seng chuan)*, of twenty-one monks famous for reciting sutras, sixteen recited the *Lotus*. More lectures have been given, more research conducted into its subject matter and terminology, and more commentaries written on it than on any other Buddhist scripture.

This scripture is written in the form of a drama in the loose sense of the word. It is a drama on the greatest scale ever conceived by man. Its stage is many Buddha-worlds. Its time is eternity. And its actors are the Lord Buddha Śākyamuni and innumerable beings. The scene opens with Śākyamuni sitting in a trance. Gathered before him are 12,000 arhats, 6,000 nuns headed by his mother and including his wife, 8,000 bodhisattvas, 60,000 gods, Brahma with his 12,000 dragon kings, and hundreds of thousands of heavenly beings, demons, and other beings. As the congregation fold their hands in homage to him, a ray of light issues forth from his forehead which illuminates the 18,000 Buddha-worlds in the East, in each of which a Buddha is preaching. The entire universe is shaking. Flowers rain all over and perfume fills all space. It is announced that the Lord is now going to give a discourse (ch. 1).

Out of trance, the Buddha begins to speak and says that only Buddhas have perfect knowledge and are qualified to preach and they are now preaching to all beings. At this the proud arhats, saints of Hīnayāna or Small Vehicle Buddhism, or rather Theravāda Buddhism, who consider themselves already perfectly enlightened, leave in silent protest. Śākyamuni teaches not the Three Vehicles —those of the Śrāvakas who attain their salvation by hearing the Buddha's teaching, the Pratyeka-buddhas who attain to their personal enlightenment by their own exertions, and the bodhisattvas who postpone their own Buddhahood for the sake of helping all beings to be saved. Instead he teaches only the One Vehicle. He has taught the other vehicles merely as an expediency or as a convenient means to those who were not yet ready for the highest truth, the One Vehicle. In this vehicle, Nirvāna is not extinction of existence, as taught in Hīnayāna, but extinction of illusions and ignorance. Everyone will be saved. Anyone who practices charity, is patient, observes discipline, is diligent in spiritual cultivation, makes offerings to the Buddha, builds a stupa with gold, silver, crystal, amber, sandalwood, clay, or in the case of a child at play, sand, who carves a Buddha figure in copper, pewter, or lacquered cloth, or paints a Buddha figure with a brush or even a fingernail, makes music, recites a verse, offers a sound or a flower to the Buddha, or merely raises his head or folds his hands or utters a simple word of admiration, *namo*, will attain salvation (ch. 2).

The disciple Śāriputra is now full of joy and in ecstasy. He realizes that he is really a son of the Buddha, produced from the Buddha Law or Dharma and born out of the Buddha's mouth. He is assured by the Lord that he will be the Flower-light Buddha in the Buddha-world whose ground is crystal with eight broad walks lined with golden ropes, and where a jewel flower will spring up wherever the feet of his disciples will tread. Anyone with devotion and faith will become a Buddha. He applies expedient and convenient means to save them all in accordance with the requirements of the circumstances, just as a father, whose house is on fire and whose sons still think of play, offers them a goat cart, a deer cart, and an ox cart to lure them out. Thus saved, they are given only the ox cart, the best of all carts; that is, not the Three Vehicles but the One Vehicle (ch. 3). Or like the father of the wandering son, who comes to work for hire without knowing their relationship, and who receives from the loving father not only wages but all his wealth (ch. 4).

Speaking to Mahākāśyapa and other disciples, the Lord tells the parable of rain. It falls on all plants, though they are ignorant of the fact that because their natures differ they respond to the rain in different ways. Only the Buddha knows the true character and reality of existence. He will care for all beings and enable them to become Buddhas provided they have faith, however simple (ch. 5).

Then Śākyamuni foretells many future Buddhas. So-and-so will become Buddha Radiance, in the Buddha-world of Brilliant Virtue, whose period will last for thirty-two kalpas or billions of years and will be called Great Splendor. So-and-so will become the Buddha of Sandalwood Fragrance in the Buddha-world called Happy Feeling, whose period, called Perfect Joy, will be 104 kalpas. And so on (ch. 6).

Interrupting his predictions, he tells of an Ancient Buddha who, he remembers, has a life of 5,400,000 myriads of ten million cycles. After attaining enlightenment, he recited the *Lotus* for 8,000 cycles. All his sixteen sons have become Buddhas and continue to recite the sutra. His last son, Śākyamuni, is the one repeating it now (ch. 7). Then he continues to foretell the future of all disciples, monks, and the multitude, that they will all be Buddhas and live in Buddha-worlds where there will be no evil ways or women (ch. 8). The surest way to become a Buddha is reverence for the *Lotus Sutra*, whether by obeying its teachings, studying it, expounding it, copying it, distributing it, or offering it in temples. Reciting even one verse will lead to salvation. On the other hand, a single word of blasphemy is a great sin (chs. 9, 10).

Now a great seven-jeweled stupa arises from the ground and is suspended in midair. As a voice emits from inside, Śākyamuni tells the congregation that inside is the total body of the Buddha, Prabhūtaratna, who has vowed to appear wherever the *Lotus Sutra* is first proclaimed. As Śākyamuni issues a light from his forehead and lights up all Buddha-worlds, Buddhas as innumerable as sand in the Ganges River arrive before the shrine. He opens it with his finger. There the Ancient Buddha sits in a lion throne in meditation. He has come, he says, to hear the gospel as he has vowed to do. He invites Śākyamuni to sit beside him in the shrine (ch. 11). Following this, all present vow to proclaim the *Lotus*. A girl who wants to do the same has to change her sex in order to do so (chs. 12–13).

Now Śākyamuni turns to Mañjuśrī and other bodhisattvas and tells them how to preach the *Lotus*. The preaching, he says, is to be done in four ways, namely, with right actions and intimacy, with a serene, pure, honest, brave, and joyful heart, with uprightness and no depravity, and with great compassion (ch. 14). Some offer to continue to preach the *Lotus* after Śākyamuni departs, but he assures them that it is unnecessary, for the earth will always bring forth an infinite number of bodhisattvas to do the work. Asked how he could have taught so many followers in only forty years of teaching, he replies that in fact he is teaching throughout eternity (ch. 15). For the Buddha is really eternal. His true character knows neither being nor nonbeing, neither life nor death. Before restoring the stupa to its place, the two Buddhas, Śākyamuni and Prabhūtaratna, continue to preach for 100,000 years.

As the eternal preaching goes on, all believers receive immense rewards, such as happiness (ch. 17), freedom from ailments, being born among gods, fulfilling all wishes (ch. 18), and special abilities of the body such as the ability to hear the sound of the universe (ch. 19). The bodhisattvas are always ready to help them and bestow these blessings, and it is very important that bodhisattvas be revered (ch. 20). At this point, the Buddha reveals the miraculous power (ch. 21). Amazed and awed, all beings now come before the shrine (ch. 22). Touching the foreheads of an infinite number of bodhisattvas, he urges them to spread the gospel. All then depart rejoicing (ch. 22), and the drama ends.

The remaining chapters explain that the *Lotus* can heal the sick (ch. 23); tell about Buddha Wonder Sound who manifests himself to preach the sutra and to save people even by transforming himself, if necessary, into a woman (ch. 24); and about bodhisattva Avalokiteśvara (Kuan-yin in Chinese and Kannon in Japanese), who will save people from fire, water, prison, and punishment, whether or not they are guilty, possess evil desires, or suffer from ignorance, delusions, etc; and who will bestow children, boys and girls, upon all (ch. 25). Other chapters describe certain spells (ch. 26), relate the conversion of King Wonderful Splendor (ch. 27), and tell about bodhisattva Universal Virtue's offer to protect the *Lotus* (ch. 28).

This drama is as fascinating as it is fantastic. It is full of light, color, sound, fragrance, and action. It has a great deal of suspense and anticipation. It contains verses and fables. And it is a beautiful blending of fact and imagination. As a literary piece it is too repetitious, for what is said in prose is virtually all repeated in verse form. It lacks unity and balance. The climax comes too early with the appearance of the stupa in chapter eleven. Buddhist scholars have tried their best to argue that the first fourteen chapters deal with manifestations of the "realm of traces" while the last fourteen deal with reality or "the realm of origin,"[1] or that the first half deals with salvation of the world, or figuratively speaking, the lotus flower, while the second half deals with the nature and personality of the buddha, or the lotus seed. This, however, is making the sutra more systematic and more philosophical than it really is. The *Lotus* is neither a theological treatise nor a philosophical essay. There is only a very brief passage in chapter fourteen expressing the idea of the Void: that dharmas are neither born nor annihilated, neither begin nor end, neither rise nor fall. Rather it is a dramatic presentation of fresh and revolutionary ideas offered as a message to enable religious practice and enrich religious experience. As such it is personal, dynamic, warm, and inspiring. It is a message of faith, hope, and love.

These novel and appealing religious ideas are not presented in abstract terms but in concrete images and living symbols. More than any other scripture, the *Lotus* has been the source of motifs of Buddhist art. Its figures dominate such famous caves as Tun-huang and Yün-kang. For several hundred years the twin figures of the two Buddhas in the shrine were the most popular subjects in Buddhist painting and sculpture.[2]

Of all the symbols, the lotus flower itself is the central one. It has penetrated Far Eastern culture, both Buddhist and non-Buddhist. It has been the symbol for Buddhism in general. In a popular sense, it stands for purity, as it rises from mud but remains clean, and it is in this sense that most Chinese and Japanese understand it, especially women, who take it to symbolize their feminine purity. The Neo-Confucian philosopher, Chou Tun-i (1017–1073), in his famous essay on the lotus, saw in it nobility of character. But in its original meaning, the symbol has a far more philosophical import. It means the source of life and the power to continue to give life.[3] When the *Lotus Sutra* says that wherever the Buddha's disciples tread, flowers will spring up, it means that Buddhas will be born out of the lotus. Thus the springing up of a lotus means the beginning of a new life. When Chinese poets secularized the Buddhist symbol and described women's small feet as lotuses, saying that with every step a lotus would spring up, they were thinking only of feminine beauty and did not realize that unwittingly they hit upon the central idea of the lotus symbol, namely, that it is life-giving. This is the idea underlying all Mahāyāna concepts.

What are these concepts as expressed in the *Lotus Sutra*? First and foremost is the new concept of the Buddha. He is no longer just an ascetic who preached for forty years in India. Instead he is an eternal being, omniscient, omnipotent, and omnipresent. He is neither one Buddha nor many, and therefore all Western terms like monotheism are meaningless for Buddhism. He is the father of all Buddhas. He is not only the hero of the drama, but also the organizer and proprietor. He not only acts but also leads all the dramatic personnel, including the most humble, who in time will play a role. In short, he is a living buddha, whose voice of teaching continues for all time and is heard everywhere. The truth preached by him and all the Buddha-sons is living truth, continuously unfolding itself and continuously enlightening people, just as lotuses are continuously springing up. This concept of the Supreme Being makes Mahāyāna radically different from Hīnayāna Buddhism, which insists that the Buddha was but a man in history. It also fulfills a dire need in the Far East which is not met by Confucian humanism or Taoist naturalism.

Equally revolutionary and important is the doctrine of universal salvation. Instead of having each arhat work out his own salvation, as in Hīnayāna, the new message promises that all will be saved by bodhisattvas. No misfortune, ignorance, or even sin will condemn a being to eternal suffering. This is the Great Vehicle, salvation for all.

This Great Vehicle, or rather Great Career, is the career of the bodhisattva, who voluntarily postpones Buddhahood to help save all beings. An infinite number of bodhisattvas go through all sufferings in order to save them. Their whole personality and career can be characterized by one word, compassion. They inspire, console, protect, and lead all beings to ultimate Buddhahood. They have taken vows and dedicated themselves to this end, and they will not become Buddhas until all become so. What a magnificent concept! These buddhas and bodhisattvas are willing to undertake tremendous toil, go anywhere, and use any means to bring about salvation. Like the father saving his sons from the burning house, they are resourceful and resort to many expedient and convenient ways. This is not only a benevolent concept but also a very liberal one, for the very narrow path of rigid discipline to salvation in the Hīnayāna is now widely broadened so that none will be prevented from entering Buddha Land.

This doctrine of convenient means has been misinterpreted in the West as the end justifying any means. Like any other religion, Buddhism has not been free from abuse. But the four ways required for teaching the *Lotus* already mentioned should leave no doubt about the moral and spiritual prerequisites for any action. In reality, the various convenient means are but different phases of the same thing. It is the One Vehicle. The other Vehicles are but expedients to meet the requirements of those who have not seen the highest truth but understand only the common truth. People with an either-or point of view will find this Buddhist doctrine of twofold truth difficult to understand. But there is nothing contradictory in viewing the lotus on the common level as flower, leaves, and stem, and on the higher level as the lotus itself, that is, the seed. Similarly, viewed as common truth, the Buddha is Śākyamuni, a historical being, a Buddha of the "realm of traces"; but viewed on a higher level, he is Tathāgata, the eternal being, or Buddha of the "realm of origin." These two levels are not contradictory. They are harmonious.

The ever-readiness of bodhisattvas to save beings by all means does not suggest that people should be passive. On their part, they must show devotion and faith. Faith, even as expressed in so simple a form as reciting the name of the Buddha, will lead to salvation. This is another aspect of Mahāyāna Buddhism that satisfies a great need in the Far East, where Confucian and Taoist rationalism leave little room for such tender feelings as faith and devotion in religion. Whether or not the element of devotion was derived from Hinduism, it gives the great multitude hope for salvation through simple means.

This hope for salvation is beautifully and affectionately personified in the most popular bodhisattva, Kuan-yin. The embodiment of mercy and compassion, he goes through much suffering and assumes many forms, whether that of a Buddha or an animal, and goes everywhere and anywhere to save all beings. He has four, eight, eighteen, or a thousand hands, to save them in all possible ways under all possible circumstances. In Japan, Kannon retains his transcendental character as a Future Buddha. In China, however, he has been presented in feminine form, perhaps to satisfy the Chinese love of sensuous beauty, perhaps to represent more appropriately the quality of compassion, especially as a protector of women and bestower of children, or perhaps to give Buddhism a loving Mother, much as the Virgin Mary is in Christianity. At any rate, Kuan-yin has been for centuries an inexhaustible source of comfort and inspiration for the Chinese. The twenty-fifth chapter of the *Lotus Sutra* is especially devoted to him and has been singled out as a separate sutra. It has been studied, recited, copied, distributed, and offered in temples, all as expressions of devotion and faith, by millions and millions of followers century after century.

These basic Mahāyāna ideas—the eternal Buddha, universal salvation, the bodhisattva doctrine, the teaching of convenient means, the gospel of the One Vehicle, the message of salvation by faith and devotion, and the compassion of Kuan-yin—are all here presented in a single sutra for the first time in Buddhism. It would be claiming too much for the *Lotus* to say that it contains all the important Mahāyāna doctrines. Those on the Void, Twofold Truth, Instantaneous Transformation, Meditation, etc., are not treated here. But as a single document, it contains more important ideas than any other Buddhist scripture.

All this is contained in a book of twenty-eight chapters totaling about 69,000 Chinese characters. This, of course, refers to the Chinese translation *Miao-fa lien-hua ching*[4] made by Kumārajīva (344–413). This is the version used and revered by the Chinese and Japanese and the one rendered, with deletions, into English by W. E. Soothill, entitled *The Lotus of the Wonderful Law, or the Lotus Gospel.*[5] We have no idea who the author or authors of the sutra were, when it was written, or in what language. All we know is that it must be older than A.D. 255 because the first Chinese translation, a partial one, was done by an unknown missionary in China in 255 or 256.[6] Of the three extant Chinese translations—by Dharmaraksha (Chu Fa-hu), called *Cheng fa-hua ching,* in 286; by Kumārajīva in 406; and jointly by Jñānagupta and Dharmagupta, called *T'ien-p'in miao-fa lien-hua ching,* in 601—that of Kumārajīva has been accepted in the last fifteen centuries as the most authoritative. His original translation contained only twenty-seven chapters. The famous Chinese monk, Fa-hsien (d. 497), in quest of the twenty-eighth chapter, started for India in 475. He found in Khotan the chapter on Devadatta, a cousin of the Buddha (and a traitor). He returned and requested Fa-i to translate it. This chapter has since been added to the Kumārajīva version.

Kumārajīva's version has surpassed others partly because it is the translation of the oldest text. Most probably the original came from Khotan. Jñānagupta said that it agreed with a manuscript in the Kuchean language, which he had seen. Since Mahāyāna Buddhism developed in Northern India or even further north in Central Asia, its early sutras were in local dialects of these areas and only later put into Sanskrit. Kumārajīva's version also agrees with the

Tibetan, and Tibetan translations are generally from the oldest texts. Takakusu believes Kumārajīva's original to be the oldest because it quotes from Nāgārjuna (c. 100–200), etc.[7] On the basis of textual criticism, scholars believe that the original was in twenty-one chapters, dated about A.D. 250, later expanded to twenty-eight.[8]

The more important reason for the supremacy of the Kumārajīva version is Kumārajīva himself. He was the one who opened up new studies in Buddhism in China, inaugurated a new era in translation, and trained as his pupils some of the most prominent Buddhist scholars, including the so-called Ten Philosophers of the Kumārajīva School, in Chinese history. Half Indian and half Kuchean, Kumārajīva became a monk at seven. He had such a great reputation in the Western regions that a Chinese king sent a general to bring him back to China. After the general had kept him in northwestern China for seventeen years, another Chinese king dispatched an army to bring him to the capital in 401. There he enjoyed the highest honors and had the highest title of National Teacher conferred on him. Over a thousand monks sat in his daily lectures. When he translated the *Lotus*, no fewer than 2,000 scholars from all parts of China gathered around him. His scholarship and Chinese literary ability matched the best of the time. All in all, he started a new epoch in Chinese Buddhism, and the *Lotus* is one of the monuments of that achievement.

Since the translation agrees with the Tibetan, its accuracy cannot be questioned. However, Kumārajīva did take liberties. For example, he translated both *tathāgataśarīra*, literally, "bone of the Tathāgata," as *ju-lai ch'üan-shen* or the Total Body of the Buddha (chs. 11 and 19).[9] Evidently he preferred to preserve the spirit of the work rather than translate literally. No wonder the lively Mahāyāna spirit prevails throughout the whole book.

How shall we read it? We should not look in it for arguments or information. Since it was written and has been used for religious practice and experience, it is to be appreciated with good will and understanding. It does not matter whether one reads it in its entirety or in part, whether this or that section first, and whether in great seriousness or with a carefree spirit. One should approach it as he approaches a lotus flower. Look at its color now and then, and smell its fragrance here and there. If one is in the proper spirit, a new lotus may even spring up for him.

ENDNOTES

The Lotus remains a basic scripture for several Japanese Buddhist sects today, active in translating and disseminating it worldwide. A scholarly translation into English of Kumārajīva's Chinese version by Leon Hurwitz was published by Columbia University Press in 1976, under the title *The Scripture of the Lotus Blossom of the Fine Dharma;* a new translation by Burton Watson was published by Columbia in 1993 under the title *The Lotus Sutra.* A partial English translation by W. E. Soothill *The Lotus of the Wonderful Law* (Oxford: Clarendon Press, 1931), omits many repetitious passages, but generally preserves the inspirational qualities of Kumārajīva's version. The translation of H. Kern, *The Saddharma Puṇḍarīka or the Lotus of the True Law* (Oxford: Clarendon Press, 1984), is complete, but it is from a Sanskrit manuscript dated 1039, much later than the Kumārajīva text.

1. Junjirō Takakusu, *The Essentials of Buddhist Philosophy,* edited by Charles Moore and Wing-tsit Chan (Honolulu: University Press of Hawaii, 1947), p. 182.
2. J. Leroy Davidson, *The Lotus Sutra in Chinese Art* (New Haven: Yale University Press, 1954), p. 24ff.
3. A. K. Coomaraswamy, *Elements of Buddhist Iconography* (Cambridge: Harvard University Press, 1935), p. 18.
4. Sanskrit title, *Saddharma-puṇḍarīka Sūtra.* For a good study of the sutra, see Edward J. Thomas, *The History of Buddhistic Thought* (London: Kegan Paul, 1933), ch. 14.
5. Oxford: Clarendon Press, 1930 (275 pp.).
6. Another translation was done in 335 by Chih Tao-ken, now lost.
7. Takakusu, *Essentials of Buddhist Philosophy,* p. 178.
8. Takakusu, *Essentials of Buddhist Philosophy,* p. 177; H. Kern, *The Saddharmapuṇḍarīka or the Lotus of the True Law,* vol. 21 of Sacred Books of the East (Oxford: Clarendon Press, 1884), p. xxii.
9. Fuse Kōgaku, "Hokkekyō no seishin to yakkai no mondai" ("The Spirit of the Lotus and Problems of its Translation and Interpretation"), *Journal of Indian and Buddhist Studies* (Tokyo), (January 1957), 5(1): 73–82.

The Teaching of Vimalakīrti

Robert A. F. Thurman

The Teaching of Vimalakīrti has been one of the most popular of Asian classics for about two thousand years. It was originally written in Sanskrit, based on accounts preserved in colloquial Indic languages, probably in the first century before the common era. It nevertheless presents itself as recording events and conversations that took place in the time of Śākyamuni Buddha, over four hundred years earlier. It was first translated into Chinese in 170 C.E., into Korean, Uighur, and Tibetan in the seventh through ninth centuries, and eventually into Mongolian and Manchu, as well as twice more into Chinese. In modern times, it has been translated into over ten languages, including most European languages, and at least five times into English (chapter numbering and references in this essay are to Robert Thurman, *The Holy Teaching of Vimalakīrti*, Pennsylvania State University Press, 1976).

The *Vimalakīrti* is one of a class of texts called "*Ārya Mahāyāna*

Sūtra," "Holy Scripture of the Universal Vehicle" of Buddhism. These texts form the "Bibles" of Mahāyāna Buddhists, the Buddhists who flourished in first millennium C.E. India and in Central and East Asia. These Scriptures include hundreds of major texts and thousands of minor ones, with thousands more reportedly lost over the millennia. They began to emerge in India of the first century B.C.E. They purported to proclaim a new gospel of the Buddha, adding to the monastic Buddhist concern for individual liberation from suffering a teaching of universal love and compassion for all beings. They claimed that this explicitly messianic teaching had been taught by the same Śākyamuni Buddha, but had been kept esoteric for four hundred years, while Indian civilization developed the need for such a socially progressive doctrine. For, in spite of the fact that many monastic Buddhists did not (and still do not) consider these Mahāyāna Scriptures to be authentic teachings of the Buddha, these texts sparked a messianic movement that reached out from the monastic strongholds the Buddha's earlier teaching had established all over India to inspire lay men and women with the "bodhisattva ideal." This ideal was that each person should assume responsibility for the salvation of all others, not accepting personal liberation in Nirvana until becoming a perfect Buddha, defined as an enlightened savior with the actual ability to save all beings.

Whatever the provenance of the text, the *Vimalakīrti* attained its importance and popularity as much for its readability as for its sanctity. It opens with the Buddha and his company living in the pleasure grove of Āmrapālī, a famous *femme fatale* of the great merchant city of Vaiśālī. It is a slightly unconventional situation, since this elegant lady had won the race to invite the Buddha and company as her guests, beating the delegation of the fathers of the city. And so the dignified society of the city had taken some offense, and were temporarily refraining from visiting the Buddha. As the scene opens, however, a group of five hundred noble youths, cream of the city's younger generation, does come from the city to the grove to visit the Buddha and request his teaching.

They bring five hundred jeweled parasols as offerings, and the Buddha at once performs a miracle and forges them into a jeweled dome over the audience. In its bright surfaces, all behold reflected all parts of the universe, much like a magical planetarium. After their awe has calmed and they have sung his praises, they ask the Buddha not "How do we attain enlightenment?" or "What is the true nature of reality?" but "How does the bodhisattva perfect the Buddha land?" In more modern terms, "How does the messianic idealist make a perfect world for the benefit of all beings?" The Buddha answers with an elaborate description of the perfections of a Buddha-land, and how they evolved from the perfections of the bodhisattva who becomes a Buddha.

At the end of this discourse, the wise and saintly monk Śāriputra, one of the Buddha's closest "apostles," becomes doubtful about this notion of a "perfect world," thinking that it contradicts the "holy truth of suffering," and that the world he sees around him is far from perfect. The Buddha reads his mind, chides him for his lack of faith and insight, and then plants his toe on the ground and miraculously grants the entire audience a second vision, a vision of the universe as a place of utter perfection, with each being exalted in his or her own highest fulfillment and enjoyment. He then lifts his toe, withdraws the fleeting vision. These dramatic events at the opening of the text set up the core tension of the *Vimalakīrti*, perhaps the central problematic of the Universal Vehicle itself. If Buddhahood is the perfection of the world as well as of the self, the saving of all beings as well as the freeing of the individual, then why did not the turbulent history of the planet come to an end with the Buddhahood of Śākyamuni? Why did not the struggle of evolution terminate with the Buddhahood of the first bodhisattva? Or, if this world is perfect to enlightened eyes, why does this perfection appear to the so highly evolved human beings as a faulty mess, an endless, seemingly futile struggle, filled with needless suffering?

Once this problem has been posed, the scene shifts to downtown

Vaiśālī, and Vimalakīrti is introduced as the very embodiment of a Buddha's liberative arts. He is a wealthy householder, respected by all the citizens from highest to lowest, a jack of all trades, a deeply religious man, and an accomplished philosopher known for his inspiring brilliance and matchless eloquence. Indeed, as we soon come to see, he is thought by some to be a little too eloquent. As the plot moves forward, Vimalakīrti becomes sick, and uses the occasion to lecture the citizens of Vaiśālī about the inadequacy of the ordinary body, the unlivability of the unenlightened life, contrasting his miserable state with the blissful perfect health of an enlightened Buddha, with his body of diamond. He also complains that, now that he has become ill, the monks of Buddha's company do not come to call on him, to cheer him and raise his spirits.

The scene then changes back to the Buddha in his grove, where, on cue, the Buddha begins to ask his major disciples, monks and lay supporters, if they would not be so kind as to go to town to pay a sick call on the good Vimalakīrti. To his surprise, no one wants to go. Each of the major apostles among the saintly and learned monks tells a story about the last time he met with Vimalakīrti, how Vimalakīrti challenged the narrowness of some central idea precious to that saint, how he refuted such partiality and powerfully opened up a whole new vista, but overwhelmed the poor fellow and left him speechless. Each of the major lay supporters has a similar tale to tell. All are united in their aversion to another encounter with the whirlwind of Vimalakīrti's adamant eloquence. Fortunately, the bodhisattva Mañjuśrī known as the "crown prince of wisdom," finally volunteers to go, to save the community the embarrassment of failing to pay a call on one of their most respected members during his time of sickness, as well as to enjoy a chat with the householder sage.

As soon as Mañjuśrī decides to go, the entire community decides to follow along, as the conversation between Vimalakīrti and Mañjuśrī promises to be richly entertaining. The scene again shifts to the house of Vimalakīrti, where the central scenes occur. First, the two sages engage in cryptic dialogues, during which the profound side of the Mahāyāna is clearly expounded, the teachings of subjective and objective selflessness and absolute emptiness. For example:

> Mañjuśrī: "Householder, why is your house empty? Why have you no servants?" Vimalakīrti: "Mañjuśrī, all buddha-lands are also empty," M: "What makes them empty?" V: "They are empty because of emptiness." M: "What is empty about emptiness?" V: "Constructions are empty, because of emptiness." M: "Can emptiness be conceptually constructed?" V: "Even that concept is itself empty, and emptiness cannot construct emptiness." M: "Householder, where should emptiness be sought?" V: "Mañjuśrī, emptiness should be sought among the sixty-two false convictions." M: "Where should the sixty-two convictions be sought?" V: "They should be sought in the liberation of the Tathāgatas." M: "Where should the liberation of the Tathāgatas be sought?" V: "It should be sought in the prime mental activity of all beings" (*HTV*, pp. 43–44)

Vimalakīrti here turns an ordinary question into a probe into the ultimate nature of things, declaring it to be total emptiness of all intrinsic reality. Mañjuśrī presses him on this, looking for traces of a nihilistic reification of emptiness into a real nothingness. Vimalakīrti holds his ground, and reaffirms the emptiness of emptiness, which logically necessitates the reality of the world of relativity, which contains both delusions and enlightenment. Enlightenment itself is not something far away from ordinary life, but something perhaps so close to the heart of every being it tends to go unnoticed. This nondualism, based on a critique of the monastic Buddhist reification of Nirvana as a realm of freedom apart from *saṃsāric* life, is the hallmark of the Mahāyāna movement, underlying its ultimate concern for universal compassion.

These dialogues were highly cherished by those Taoist intellectuals devoted to "enlightening conversation" during Buddhism's early years in China, since they used wit and earnest conversation to open up the deep experience of reality. They served as the earliest model for the type of master-disciple exchanges eventually recorded in the *koan*, or "public cases" of the Ch'an/Zen tradition. But they were a little much for Śāriputra, who found himself quite at a loss, with no place to stand or chair to sit on in the realm of ultimate groundlessness.

Once emptiness is opened up for the audience, Vimalakīrti begins to play with the dimensions of relativity as well. He obtains giant lion thrones from another universe and seats everyone upon one, causing each to feel as tall as a mountain. He then teaches the "inconceivable liberation of the bodhisattvas," a teaching of the miraculous reality, how anything is possible for the compassionate activity of the bodhisattva. He declares that to understand that teaching, one must understand the mystery of how a bodhisattva in the inconceivable liberation can place the axial mountain, Sumeru, into a mustard seed, without shrinking the mountain or rupturing the seed. Based on emptiness, he presents the mutual interpenetration and mutual non-obstruction of all things.

He and Mañjuśrī then discuss the problems of the paradoxical mutual indispensability of wisdom and compassion, insight and liberative art. Overjoyed by the inspiring teachings, the goddess of wisdom, *Prajñāpāramitā* herself becomes manifest to bless the audience with flowers. After some deep conversations, she ends up teasing Śāriputra, the typical "male chauvinist" of those times, teaching him the lack of intrinsic reality of maleness and femaleness in the most charming and graphic way imaginable.

Vimalakīrti and Mañjuśrī then turn to the problem of good and evil, as Vimalakīrti expounds the code of bodhisattva deeds called "the reconciliation of dichotomies." The high point of events in the mansion is reached after Vimalakīrti has asked twenty-five of the advanced bodhisattvas present to give their views of the truth of nonduality, the highest expression of ultimate Truth. Each teaches deeply and subtly, though Mañjuśrī expresses some dissatisfaction with their teachings before giving his own idea. Then they all ask Vimalakīrti his idea, and he maintains a thunderous silence. This silence of Vimalakīrti is perhaps the most famous silence in all

Buddhist literature. It is the equivalent of the "Great Statement" of ultimate Truth in the Upanishads, "That Thou Art!" But perhaps Vimalakīrti felt that all his audience were so much That, he needed absolutely not to say so! It had special impact coming from him, of course, as he usually talks so inexhaustibly.

After this "lion's roar" of great silence, Vimalakīrti sends out to another universe for lunch, bringing a few grains of rice from the Buddha Sugandhakūṭa of the Perfume Universe, which he multiplies to feed the great crowd that has magically fit into his empty house by this time. Along with the food comes a group of perfume bodhisattvas from that universe, who are curious to see the "Barely Tolerable" *(Sahā)* universe of Buddha Śākyamuni and the amazing bodhisattva Vimalakīrti who could beam an emanation out across the galaxies to bring back lunch! They are shocked to see how unheavenly our universe is, compared to theirs, and they and Vimalakīrti have an extended dialogue, during which he presents the "answer" to the problem posed in the beginning of the text. He persuades the perfume bodhisattvas that Śākyamuni's "Tolerable" universe is ideal for bodhisattvas, better than a heavenly perfume world, precisely because there is so much struggle and hardship in it. This difficulty of life is just what is needed for the development of compassion. Wisdom can certainly be cultivated in deep contemplation under a perfume tree, perhaps more conveniently than in our busy world. But without struggle, without nearness to suffering and relationship with earthly beings, it is impossible to develop great compassion. And it is only compassion that creates eventually the Body of Buddhahood, as wisdom creates the Mind. This section presents one of the clearest rationalizations of suffering in any Mahāyāna text; a veritable Buddhist "theodicy."

The scene changes again for the final act of the drama, as Vimalakīrti shows his inconceivable liberation yet again. He miniaturizes the entire assembly, picks it up in his hand, and places it gently down outside of town in the grove of Āmrapālī, in the presence of the Buddha. There is a reunion between the monk Buddha and the layman Buddha, as Vimalakīrti has emerged by this point. Vimalakīrti stands directly before the Buddha and gives a penetrating discourse about how only one who does not see any Buddha can actually see the Buddha, as the Buddha is not this body of form, not sensation, not ideation and so forth. The Buddha accepts that he is not there as well as there, and praises his householder colleague.

It is eventually revealed that Vimalakīrti is an Emanation Body of the Akṣobhya Buddha of the Buddha-land known as "Abhirati" ("Intense Delight"). Vimalakīrti performs a last miracle of bringing the entire Abhirati world in miniature form on the palm of his hand into this world to show it to all present. Abhirati is described as a paradise, but a paradise much more like our world, much more earthy than the heavenly Buddha-lands of perfume and jewel lotus palaces. The main difference between Abhirati and our world is that the stairways from its earth to its heavens are always visible and gods and humans mingle equally, all gravitating around the august presence of Akṣobhya Buddha. This is the culminating dramatic symbol of the text, being Vimalakīrti's holding out of a hope for the future of this planet of ours in the Sahā universe.

The *Vimalakīrti* seems to have been designed as a kind of anthology of the major themes of all Mahāyāna Scriptures. The wisdom teachings of especially chapters five and nine are as if drawn from the *Transcendent Wisdom (Prajñāpāramitā)* Scriptures. The miraculous glimpses of various "pure" Buddha-lands are cameos of the *Pure Land of Bliss (Sukhāvatī)* Scriptures. The third and fourth chapters of dialogues between Vimalakīrti and various monks and laymen could have been drawn from any of the early *Jewel Heap (Ratnakūṭa)* Scriptures, which are full of the controversies between those clinging to the strict dualism of the old monastic Buddhism and those inspired with the messianic nonduality of the Mahāyāna. The second chapter on "liberative art" or "technique" as well as the chapters proving to the perfume bodhisattvas the greater perfection of this seemingly imperfect Buddha-land of Śākyamuni give the central message of the *White Lotus of Holy Truth (Saddharma Puṇḍarīkā)* Scriptures. The sixth chapter on "Inconceivable Liberation" actually refers to the *Avataṃsaka (Garland)* Scriptures, presenting the teaching of the chapter as a drop of that ocean, and the first miracle of the jeweled canopy resonates with the famous "Jewel Net of Indra" analogy for the mutually interpenetrative nature of all things that is a central vision of the *Garland.* And finally, the ritual and magical nature of the mansion of Vimalakīrti, the enthronement of all members of the audience, the consecration of all by the Goddess, the teachings of the "Family of the Tathāgatas" and the reconciliation of dichotomies, and finally the magical, spiritual feast which cannot be digested until the participant achieves a higher stage of enlightenment—all these elements unquestionably convey an atmosphere of esoteric Buddhism, the apocalyptic vehicle later codified in the Buddhist Tantras.

The *Vimalakīrti* can be read in a sitting. Its drama and visions and humor can carry a reader past some of the difficult passages. But it can also be repeatedly browsed in, as its mysterious dialogues and paradoxes can stimulate contemplative thinking. For those new to the Buddhist literature, or more generally the wisdom literature of India, it can serve as an excellent introduction. And for those who have read widely, studied deeply, and taken time to contemplate, it seems to endure as a quintessential summary.

ENDNOTE

For a full translation from the Tibetan version, see the aforementioned *Holy Teaching of Vimalakīrti*, translated by Robert Thurman, Pennsylvania State University Press, 1976.

The *Platform Sutra* of the Sixth Patriarch

Philip Yampolsky

The *Platform Sutra* is one of the most celebrated works in the vast literature of Ch'an (Zen) Buddhism, representing the "autobiography" and the recorded sayings of the Sixth Patriarch, Hui-neng, the Chinese master from whom all later Ch'an derives. Compilation is assigned to a monk by the name of Fa-hai, identified in the work itself as a resident monk in charge of Hui-neng's temple. The work has gone through numerous recensions, ranging from the primitive and error-filled manuscript found in the Tun-huang caves, to the greatly enlarged Yüan dynasty versions some five centuries later. Hui-neng is honored as the illiterate firewood gatherer, who by his innate understanding of the principles of Buddhism, became heir to the Ch'an teachings and who in turn handed them down to all future generations.

The *Platform Sutra,* particularly the expanded Yüan dynasty version, has been reprinted numerous times over the centuries and it remains one of the most popular of Ch'an works. Until modern times one can count almost a hundred different printings in China, Korea, and Japan, many of the them ordered by pious believers seeking merit for the virtue of widening the distribution of the text. The work has had enormous popularity, particularly as a text for laymen to read and monks to admire. Surprisingly, the work, although often praised, has been the subject of very few commentaries, and seems not to have been widely used as a source for the study of Ch'an or for the subject of lectures by Ch'an masters.

The *Platform Sutra* is distinctly a Ch'an work; it champions a Ch'an teacher and emphasizes a particular meditative tradition. Yet at the same time it is characteristically Buddhist, very much in the tradition of other works of the time. Elements common to all Buddhism: liturgy, refuges, repentances, vows, acceptance of the precepts, and various standardized formulae are very much in evidence in the *Platform Sutra*. The work shares much with other schools of T'ang Buddhism; its concerns are very much the concerns of all Buddhism. The four vows, intoned today by virtually all Buddhist groups, are here in a form almost identical with contemporary usage, and we may assume that they, along with the refuges and repentances, were in the repertoire of all schools of Buddhism. The giving of the precepts and their acceptance by both monks and laymen were widely practiced throughout the history of Buddhism in China. The appeal of the work and its immense popularity over the centuries stem perhaps from the combination of standard Buddhist concepts shared by Ch'an and all forms of Mahāyāna Buddhism with many of the encounter stories so characteristic of later Ch'an literature.

The Formless Precepts are an important element of the *Platform Sutra*. It has been suggested that one of the particular functions of this text was to assist in giving these precepts. If this suggestion is correct it would aid in solving one of the more puzzling features of the work, its title. The term *sutra* is used exclusively for works said to have been spoken by the Buddha. Only in this one peculiar instance is the term applied to the sayings of a Patriarch. There are, however, several works relating to the precepts that bear in their title the term "platform precept book" *(chieh-t'an t'u ching)* and it is quite likely that the term for *Platform Sutra (t'an-ching)* derives from the contraction of these two words.

While the *Platform Sutra* holds an honored position as an early Ch'an text that champions the teachings of a revered founder, it differs considerably from the various genres of Ch'an writings that follow it. The *Platform Sutra* is obviously composed of various layers: an autobiographical section, the basic sermons attributed to Hui-neng, and a number of miscellaneous independent pieces, verses, stories, the genealogy of the school, admonitions and exhortations to students of Ch'an. The autobiography seems designed to emphasize the humble origins of the Sixth Patriarch, his illiteracy, and the availability of the teaching to laymen. Although we are told that Hui-neng cannot read and later Ch'an makes much of the claim that it is a silent transmission from master to disciple without recourse to words and letters, it is obvious from the frequent quotations from canonical works that the person who delivered the sermons was fully conversant with scriptural literature. We can, however, gain little knowledge of how Ch'an was taught, what methods were used, or what was expected of the student. Obviously, sermons, aimed at both monks and laymen, played an important part in the teaching. Recorded by a disciple, they may well serve as predecessors to the later "Recorded Sayings" *(yü-lu)* genre of Ch'an literature. Individual monks appear to have come virtually at will to question the master, probably in public assemblies, although private meetings were held as well. There is no evidence as yet of the koan interview between master and disciple, in which the student gave his solution to the brief story, or koan, on which he was meditating at the time. The question and answer encounter between Hui-neng and Shen-hui contained in the *Platform Sutra* is representative of the type of story that was later adopted for use in koan meditation. In the early days of Ch'an there was no organized monastic community with the elaborate regulations and rules that developed later. Monks came and went at will;

those for whom the Master's teaching was attractive might stay and eventually become disciples and heirs; others might wander in search of teachers more suitable to their temperaments. We may assume that intensive meditations were practiced, although nowhere are the techniques described nor the role of the teacher specified.

But if we examine the biography of Hui-neng and the work that is attributed to his name from the unclouded vantage of historical plausibility, we are at once confronted with a series of problems. Although there is little doubt that a monk by the name of Hui-neng existed, and the dates assigned to him, 638-713, are in all probability correct, there is little else that we really know about him. His autobiography, as contained in the *Platform Sutra*, and all later biographies are fabrications of later generations. The standard history of early Ch'an, the "official" history that has been handed down over the centuries, is replete with unfounded simplifications; the forgotten history, revealed in the documents discovered at Tun-huang, is a combination of fact and deliberate fabrication; the actual history that can be reconstructed from the above two, despite lacunae and areas of uncertainty, is the story of the struggle of various Ch'an factions to establish themselves during the eighth century and of the eventual emergence of a group that had little connection with the Ch'an of the *Platform Sutra*, but that nevertheless traced its origins to the Sixth Patriarch, Hui-neng.

The work known as the *Platform Sutra* has a curious and in many ways an obscure history. A cursory examination of the earliest version we have, the Tun-huang manuscript, which bears an elaborate title that reads in part: "Southern School Sudden Doctrine, Supreme Mahāyāna Great Perfection of Wisdom: The Platform Sutra preached by the Sixth Patriarch Hui-neng at the Tafan Temple . . ." indicates that it itself is a copy of an earlier, no longer extant, version. Evidence, both external and internal, indicates that an original text dating to around 780 must have existed and that the present Tun-huang manuscript is written in a calligraphic style that would place it around 820. The great popularity that the work has enjoyed in China is attested to by the large number of versions that have appeared over the centuries. In the Sung dynasty there were several editions, some preserved in Japan, and others now lost, that were fairly faithful to the early Tun-huang text; they correct errors, improve on the literary style, and eliminate certain sections that are no longer pertinent. By the Yüan dynasty some ten different versions can be accounted for. The two different Yüan texts, of 1290 and 1291, are largely expanded works, twice the size of the Tun-huang edition. While they treat to a large extent the same teachings that are expounded in the earlier versions, the biographical sections are greatly enlarged and a wealth of new stories of Hui-neng's encounters with other monks is provided.

To understand the significance of the *Platform Sutra*, one must examine briefly the background from which it emerged. Our knowledge of this background derives largely from the documents discovered at Tun-huang, of which the *Platform Sutra* is but one. Numerous works relating to Ch'an Buddhism in the seventh and eighth centuries were discovered in the caves at Tun-huang, and they form the primary source of our knowledge of Ch'an history. Ch'an was, of course, only one of several forms of Buddhism, some esoteric, some scholarly, some popular, that flourished in the T'ang dynasty. In the early eighth century Ch'an was in the process of attempting to establish itself, and several competing groups were striving for recognition. Among them the most prominent was a group descended from the Fifth Patriarch, Hung-jen, which based its teaching on the *Laṅkāvatāra Sutra*, and which devised genealogical histories of its own tradition to strengthen its claim for legitimacy. This group traced its origins to the semi-legendary Bodhidharma, the first patriarch in China, who had brought the teachings from India, and who had handed down, through successive patriarchs, the teachings of the *Laṅkāvatāra Sutra*.

This group and its heirs came to be known as Northern Ch'an, although it did not initially refer to itself as such. Most prominent among this group was a famous monk. Shen-hsiu (606?–706), later to be maligned in the *Platform Sutra,* who was greatly honored by the T'ang court and treated with the utmost pomp and respect. For the first decades of the eighth century, Shen-hsiu and his descendants dominated the Ch'an of the capital cities.

In 732, however, an obscure monk by the name of Shen-hui (684–758; his dates have recently been revised, based on the discovery on the mainland of his stele) mounted a platform at his temple in Hua-t'ai, northeast of Loyang, and launched a virulent attack on P'u-chi (561–739), the heir of Shen-hsiu, before a large audience. In speeches and in written texts Shen-hui, who had studied briefly with Hui-neng, denounced what he called Northern Ch'an and extolled the Southern School of Hui-neng. Hui-neng was the legitimate Sixth Patriarch, he maintained; Shen-hsiu never pretended to that station, but now his heir claims to be the Seventh Patriarch. Shen-hui went on to assign to the leaders of Northern Ch'an a variety of crimes: P'u-chi is accused of sending an emissary to remove the head from Hui-neng's mummified body and of having sent a disciple to efface the inscription on Hui-neng's stele and to substitute one that stated that Shen-hsiu was the Sixth Patriarch. Shen-hui wrote in detail the biography of Hui-neng, either inventing details or repeating legends current at the time. He never quotes from the *Platform Sutra,* although there are numerous instances where his writings and those of the *Sutra* are identical. Shen-hui did not limit his invective to accusations of the misrepresentation of the lineage; he attacked Northern Ch'an for the quality and content of its teaching. The most radical claim was that it was not the *Laṅkāvatāra Sutra* that had been handed down from Bodhidharma, but rather the *Diamond Sutra.* This was a complete fabrication on Shen-hui's part, yet it has been accepted by all later biographers of Hui-neng. Furthermore, perhaps the most damaging accusation was that Northern Ch'an adopted a gradual, step-by-step method of attaining enlightenment, whereas Hui-neng's Southern School called for a sudden method for awakening to the self-nature. Whether this attack was justified is quite debatable—the Northern

School in all probability advocated a more sophisticated process—but it was effective. By the year 780, Shen-hui had won the battle; Hui-neng was accepted by all schools of Ch'an as the legitimate Sixth Patriarch. Shen-hui himself and the line that descended from him did not share in the success. He was never recognized as a legitimate heir to the teachings and his descendants failed to prosper. Shen-hui virtually disappeared from the pages of traditional Ch'an history; it was not until the documents at Tun-huang were discovered that his real role was made clear.

Up to now it has been assumed by modern scholars that Shen-hui or one of his followers was the actual compiler of the *Platform Sutra*. Recent research by the distinguished Japanese scholar Yanagida Seizan has shown rather persuasively that the *Platform Sutra* was compiled by a certain Fa-hai, who was a member of the Ox-head school of Ch'an, a group that has been little studied but that flourished contemporaneously with the so-called Southern and Northern schools. The Ox-head school, as did all the Ch'an schools of the time, traced its origins to the early teachers of Ch'an but its major development as a school appears to have been during the last decades of the eighth century. The Ox-head school in all probability developed along independent lines, perhaps in reaction to the Northern and Southern schools. Four distinct lineages can be identified, each based on the teachings of specific masters, some of whom gained substantial recognition and for whom biographical materials remain. Less available, however, are texts that describe the content of the Ox-head teaching. It appears to have rejected the so-called gradual practices of Northern Ch'an and to have advocated a negation that did away with stated aims, techniques of meditation, and moralistic standards. The Ox-head school, together with groups that flourished in Szechuan, may well have served to transcend the sectarian distinctions of North and South and to have established a connection with the groups that were moving toward a new developing Ch'an.

There is no room here for a detailed discussion, but biographical information indicates that Fa-hai was a highly literate monk, concerned with the precepts, familiar with poetry, who was active around the year 780 when the *Platform Sutra* appears to have been written. By this time, most if not all schools of Ch'an had come to accept Hui-neng without reservation as the Sixth Patriarch. Internal evidence from the *Platform Sutra,* combined with known facts, give much credence to Professor Yanagida's view that the Ox-head monk, Fa-hai, was the actual compiler of the *Platform Sutra*. Making use of stories and legends current at the time, Fa-hai wrote a biography of Hui-neng, championed the Southern school of sudden enlightenment and condemned the gradual approach associated with Northern Ch'an. However, Fa-hai avoided the invective and violent accusations that accompanied Shen-hui's attack. The fact that the *Platform Sutra* makes little mention of Shen-hui and includes the lineage of twenty-eight Indian patriarchs that is accepted in both Northern Ch'an and the Ox-head school and is quite different from that espoused in Shen-hui's works, lends credence to the attribution. If one discounts the error-filled version that represents the Tun-huang text as nothing more than a copy by a less-than-literate monk, the identification of the work as a product of Fa-hai and the Ox-head school appears quite appropriate.

If we examine the texts of the sermons, we find that the major concepts are drawn from scriptural works. Although the autobiographical section places great emphasis on the *Diamond Sutra,* the concepts described derive more from the *Nirvana Sutra* and the *Awakening of Faith*. Hui-neng, in his sermon, is quoted as saying that the teachings derive from the sages of the past and are not his original concepts. Stress is placed on the identity of meditation and wisdom; to conceive that one precedes the other implies dualism. Wisdom is inherent; it is the original nature with which we all are endowed, and the realization of this is akin to enlightenment. Emphasized is the concept of no-thought. Thoughts are spoken of as progressing endlessly from past to present to future, and attachment to a single thought leads to attachment to a succession of thoughts; however, by cutting off this attachment one may achieve no-thought, which in itself is a state of enlightenment. The Perfection of Wisdom is given prominence in the *Platform Sutra,* indeed the term is contained in the original title of the work. The standard Ch'an doctrine of "seeing into one's own nature" is constantly invoked. One must not seek on the outside but always look within one's own mind and obtain awakening for one's self. Failing this, a good teacher may be sought as a guide, but in the end it is only you yourself who must perform the practice.

All these are concepts that are always associated with Ch'an, yet they are found in other schools of Mahāyāna Buddhism as well. The *Platform Sutra,* then, is not characterized by contributions that can be regarded as uniquely representative of Ch'an Buddhism. Yet historically the work is of great importance. That an unlettered "barbarian" from the south was able to attain to the highest position in Ch'an, emphasized the availability of the teaching to all. The work marks a shift in emphasis in Chinese Buddhism, a move from an abstract Nirvana to an individual enlightenment, available to anyone who seeks to realize through meditation the Buddha nature inherent within him. The content of Buddhism does not change; Ch'an is always Mahāyāna Buddhism, but the method of teaching assumes a different cast, with a greater emphasis placed on meditation. The decline of the T'ang court, domestic upheavals, persecutions of Buddhism, all contributed to the emergence of Ch'an as the dominant form of Buddhism in the early ninth century. Although we find no direct link between the T'ang of the *Platform Sutra* and that of the Hung-chou school that gained prominence at this time and from which all later Ch'an derives, the position of Hui-neng had become such that the founding fathers of this new form of Ch'an all traced their ancestry to him. Hui-neng always remains the Sixth Patriarch, the dominant figure in the early history of Ch'an Buddhism.

ENDNOTE

Two translations of the early Tun-huang version are available: Wing-tsit Chan, *The Platform Scripture* (New York: St. John's University Press,

1963); Philip Yampolsky, *The Platform Sutra of the Sixth Patriarch* (New York: Columbia University Press, 1967). Translations of the enlarged Yüan version have been made by Wong Mou-lam, *The Sutra of Wei-lang (Hui-neng)* (London: Luzac, 1953), and Lu Kuan-yu (Charles Luk) in *Ch'an and Zen teachings*, vol. 3 (London: Rider, 1963).

T'ang Poetry: A Return to Basics

Burton Watson

The history of Chinese poetry begins around 600 B.C. with the compilation of an anthology, the *Shih-ching* or *Book of Odes*, containing poems that probably date back several centuries earlier. It continues with barely a break down to the present day. Naturally, such an extended period of development saw the evolution of a number of different poetic forms and styles and countless ebbs and flows in the tide of artistic inspiration.

It has generally been agreed by Chinese critics—and non-Chinese students of the language have found no reason to dissent—that the highest peak in literary achievement in this long process of growth was reached during the T'ang dynasty, which ruled China from A.D. 618 to 907, particularly the middle years of this period. This was the age of Li Po, Tu Fu, Po Chü-i, and numerous other figures renowned in Chinese literary history, when the art of poetry seemed to reach levels of expressive force and universality of statement it had hardly known in the past and was seldom to rival again. I would like here to try to convey some idea of the nature of this poetry and its appeal for English readers of today. Rather than attempting generalities, I will center the discussion around specific examples of T'ang poetry, touching upon the qualities that can be effectively brought across in translation and those that must inevitably be lost.

Unlike the peoples of Europe and India, the Chinese did not develop a tradition of epic poetry. Though they had their internecine wars and campaigns against foreign invaders—Ezra Pound's "Song of the Bowmen of Shu" is a translation of an early work from the *Book of Odes* dealing with one such campaign—they seldom made feats of arms a theme of poetry. An overwhelmingly agricultural people, they have preferred in their poetry to focus mainly upon the scenes and events of everyday life, which accounts for the generally low-keyed and ungrandiose tone of so much of Chinese poetry. It is also one reason why many of their works, even those written centuries ago, sound strikingly modern in translation.

The first work to be quoted is by the government official and poet Po Chü-i (772–846). Po was one of the most prolific of the major T'ang poets, and his works are particularly well preserved, in part because he took the trouble to compile and edit them himself and deposit copies in the libraries of several important Buddhist temples. The poem was written in 835 and is addressed to Po's friend Liu Yü-hsi (772–842), a fellow poet and bureaucrat who was the same age as Po. The Chinese frequently exchanged poems with friends, often replying to one another's poems as one would reply to a letter, the practice constituting both an expression of friendship and an opportunity to exercise literary abilities and invite critical comment. When responding to a friend's poem, one customarily employed the same poetic form and sometimes the same rhymes or rhyme words as the original poem in order to add an element of challenge to the game.

*On Old Age, to Send to Meng-te (Liu Yü-hsi)**

The two of us both in old age now,
I ask myself what it means to be old.
Eyes bleary, evenings you're the first to bed;
hair a bother, mornings you leave it uncombed.
Sometimes you go out, a stick to prop you;
sometimes, gate shut, you stay indoors the whole day.
Neglecting to look into the newly polished mirror,
no longer reading books if the characters are very small,
your thoughts dwelling more and more on old friends,
your activities far removed from those of the young,
only idle chatter rouses your interest . . .
When we meet, we still have lots of that, don't we!

The subject of the poem is so universal an experience and the presentation so straightforward that comment seems almost superfluous. The poet, sixty-three at the time, begins by speaking directly to his friend Liu, but then quickly falls into a kind of private reverie on the subject of old age and the changes it brings. In the very last line he abruptly shakes himself out of his musings and addresses his friend once more. Unlike many traditional Chinese poems, this one employs no erudite allusions to earlier literature, though, as may readily be seen in the translation, it makes considerable use of verbal parallelism, a device common in both Chinese prose and poetry. The poem is in *shih* form, essentially the same form used in the *Shih-ching* or *Book of Odes*. It employs a line which is five characters or five syllables in length, and is in the relatively free "old-style" form, which means there is no limit on the number of lines. A single rhyme is employed throughout, the rhymes occurring at the end of the even-numbered lines.

Po Chü-i is particularly remembered for his relaxed, warmly personal works such as that just quoted. He himself, however, placed a much higher value on his poems of social criticism. Confucius had emphasized the didactic function of poetry, citing the poems of the *Book of Odes* as examples, and Confucian-minded officials in later centuries often employed poetic forms to voice criticisms of the government or expose the ills of society. Po Chü-i in his youthful years as an official enthusiastically carried on this tradition, writing a number of outspoken works that he hoped would bring about changes in government policy. The following is a famous example.

The poem is entitled "Light Furs, Fat Horses," an allusion to a passage in the Confucian *Analects* (6, 3) in which Confucius censures luxurious living among public officials. It was written in 810, when the poet held advisory posts in the capital and the region south of the Yangtze River was plagued by drought. The poet had previously asked that the government take steps to aid the drought victims, but his pleas went unheeded. The poem depicts a banquet at a military encampment in or near the capital. It is in the same form as the poem previously quoted.

Light Furs, Fat Horses

A show of arrogant spirit fills the road;
a glitter of saddles and horses lights up the dust.
I ask who these people are—
trusted servants of the ruler, I'm told.
The vermilion sashes are all high-ranking courtiers;
the purple ribbons are probably generals.
Proudly they repair to the regimental feast,
their galloping horses passing like clouds.
Tankards and wine cups brim with nine kinds of spirits;
from water and land, an array of eight delicacies.
For fruit they break open Tung-t'ing oranges,
for fish salad, carve up scaly bounty from T'ien-chih.
Stuffed with food, they rest content in heart;
livened by wine, their mood grows merrier than ever.
This year there's a drought south of the Yangtze.
In Ch'ü-chou, people are eating people.

T'ang poetry—at least, all that has come down to us—is almost entirely the product of a single group in society, the literati or scholar-bureaucrats, men who had received a firm grounding in the classical texts and had chosen to enter government service, often after passing the civil service examinations. For these men, the writing of poetry was no mere hobby or diversion, but an integral part of their lives as gentlemen and public servants, a means of airing their opinions, fulfilling their responsibilities to society, and furthering their spiritual cultivation.

The greatness of T'ang poetry probably derives first of all from this tone of moral seriousness that pervades so much of it. There were other periods in Chinese literary history when poetry was mainly a pleasant pastime for members of the court or aristocracy, a vehicle for displaying verbal ingenuity or embroidering upon the patterns of the past. The T'ang poets, though certainly not incapable of frivolous verse, generally had far more serious purposes in mind when they employed the medium, as we have seen in the example just quoted. They returned poetry to what they believed to be its original function, the addressing of important social and ethical issues.

At the same time, as evidenced in the first poem quoted above, they were not afraid to be frankly personal in their writing. Though this personal note was shunned in some periods of literary history, the best of the T'ang poets such as Tu Fu or Po Chü-i did not hesitate to record the experiences and emotional crises of their daily lives in their works, employing poetry much as the diary or autobiography forms are used in other cultures. To do so was for them a kind of literary and spiritual discipline.

The poet-official Wang Wei (699?–761), much of whose poetry describes the scenes of his daily life, purchased a country estate at a place called Wang River in the mountains south of Ch'ang-an, the T'ang capital. The estate had formerly belonged to another well-known poet-official, Sung Chih-wen (d. 712?). In the following poem, the first in a famous series describing scenic spots on the estate, the poet muses on the passing of time, as graphically exemplified in the dying willows planted by the former owner, his own feelings of pity for Sung Chih-wen, and the pity that owners of the estate in years to come will perhaps feel for him. This ability of the T'ang poets, often within the span of a scant four lines, to open out huge vistas in time or space is one of the qualities that endows their poetry with its chacteristic air of grandeur and mythic proportions.

Meng-ch'eng Hollow

A new home at the mouth of Meng-ch'eng;
old trees—last of a stand of dying willows:
years to come, who will be its owner,
vainly pitying the one who had it before?

The T'ang poets in their subject matter did not confine themselves to the autobiographical, however. Following a practice that is very old in Chinese poetry, they frequently adopted a persona from the folk song tradition in order to enlarge the breadth and social significance of their material, speaking through the voice of a peasant pressed into military service, a neglected wife, or a soldier on frontier duty. Here, for example, is such a work by Li Po (701–762), a poet particularly famed for his lyric gift and his works in folk song form. It is entitled "Tzu-yeh Song," Tzu-yeh being the name of a courtesan of earlier times who was noted for her brief and poignant songs. The poem is set in autumn, the time when women traditionally fulled cloth to make clothes to send to the soldiers at the border, and pictures a woman in the capital city of Ch'ang-an dreaming of her husband at Jade Pass in Kansu far to the west.

Tzu-yeh Song

Ch'ang-an—one slip of moon;
in ten thousand houses, the sound of fulling mallets.
Autumn winds keep on blowing,
all things make me think of Jade Pass!
When will they put down the barbarians
and my good man come home from his far campaign?

Before leaving the poem we may note that, according to some commentators, the first line should be interpreted to read, "Ch'ang-an—one swath of moonlight." The question, in effect, is whether one chooses to imagine the women working under the thin crescent of a new moon, or under a full moon that floods the ground with light. Famous as these poems are and as often as they have been commented upon, the nature of the classical Chinese language is such that differences of interpretation of this kind continue to exist.

The poems quoted so far have all dealt with the world of human affairs, but this does not mean that T'ang poets neglected the natural scene around them. In very early times, nature was looked on as rather fearful, the abode of fierce beasts or malevolent spirits. But from around the fifth century on, Chinese painters and poets began to show a much greater appreciation of the beauties of the natural world, particularly the mist-filled mountain and river landscapes of southern China. The period was one of foreign invasion and political turmoil, and these mountain landscapes came to be seen as places of peace and safety, where one might escape from the perils of official life and perhaps even acquire the secrets of longevity.

This interest in natural beauty continued to be an important theme in T'ang poetry, often bound up with religious overtones linking it to Buddhism or Taoism. The following poem, from a group of some three hundred poems attributed to a recluse known as Han-shan or The Master of Cold Mountain, is an example. Han-shan was said to have lived at a place called Cold Mountain (Han-shan) in the T'ien-t'ai mountains of Chekiang Province, the site of many Buddhist and Taoist temples. It is uncertain when he lived, though the late eighth and early ninth centuries is suggested as the most likely possibility. The poem is untitled.

I climb the road to Cold Mountain,
the road to Cold Mountain that never ends.
The valleys are long and strewn with stones,
the streams broad and banked with thick grass.

Moss is slippery, though no rain has fallen;
pines sigh but it isn't the wind.
Who can break from the snares of the world
and sit with me among the white clouds?

On the literal level the poem is a description of the scenery along the kind of mountain trail that I myself have climbed in the T'ien-t'ai range, with its rocky streambeds and pine-clad slopes. At the same time the imagery of the ascent suggests a process of spiritual cultivation and the attainment of higher realms of understanding, while the white clouds of the last line—clouds that the Chinese believed were literally breathed forth by the mountain itself—are a frequently recurring symbol in Chinese literature for purity and detachment.

The next poem to be quoted, by a ninth century writer named Kao P'ien, also deals with the natural scene. But this is nature carefully cultivated and seen in close conjunction with human habitation. As the title "Mountain Pavilion, Summer Day" tells us, the scene is a pleasant country retreat in the hush of a long hot summer's day. We are shown the masses of shade trees surrounding the house, the reflections of the building and terrace as they appear upside down in the pond that fronts them, the trellis of roses whose fragrance is so strong in the courtyard. Beyond the courtyard, a curtain strung with crystal beads stirs gently in the cool breeze, but just who is napping behind the curtains we are not told. The poem is an example of the kind of mood piece at which the T'ang poets excelled, deft sketches made up of a few artfully chosen details that serve to rouse the reader's curiosity and invite him to fill out the remainder of the scene from his own imagination.

Mountain Pavilion, Summer Day *

Thick shade of green trees, long summer day,
lodge and terrace casting their images upside down in the
  pond.

Crystal-beaded curtains stir, a faint breeze rising;
one trellis of roses, the courtyard full of its scent.

This poem, along with the Wang Wei poem quoted earlier, is written in a form known as *chüeh-chü* or "cut-off lines." The form is limited to four lines in length and usually employs a line of five or seven characters. Chinese is a tonal language and the *chüeh-chü* form, in addition to employing end rhyme, obeys elaborate rules governing the tonal pattern of the words. We do not know just how the four tones of T'ang period Chinese were pronounced, and even if we did, the effect of such tonal patterns could not be reproduced in a non-tonal language such as English. But it is well to keep in mind that, though translations of T'ang poetry may give an impression of relative freedom, the originals are often in highly controlled forms. The fact that the T'ang poets not only complied with the exacting prosodic restrictions placed upon them, but even succeeded in dancing in their chains, is one of the wonders of their poetry.

One writer who seems to have welcomed the challenges presented by such demanding forms and who produced in them works of great power and originality was Tu Fu (712–770), often referred to as China's greatest poet. He is particularly noted for the keen observations of nature recorded in his works, as well as for his tone of passionate sincerity and concern for the welfare of the nation. The following poem, entitled simply *Chüeh-chü*, was written in his late years, when conditions of unrest in the country forced him to live the life of a wanderer in the upper reaches of the Yangtze River, hoping always for an opportunity to return to his home in the northeast.

The poem begins with two lines in strict parallel form recording thoughtfully noted observations on the river scene: the fact that the river gulls appear whiter than ever when seen against the intense blue of the river, and that the buds of spring blossoms—probably peach tree buds—seem like so many flames about to burst into color. In the second couplet, however, the tense objectivity of the opening lines suddenly gives way to a rush of feeling as the poet realizes that yet another spring has come and is about to depart, while he is still far removed from his homeland.

*Chüeh-chü**

River cobalt-blue, birds whiter against it;
mountains green, blossoms about to flame:
as I watch, this spring too passes —
what day will I ever go home?

The last poem in my selection, like the first one, is addressed to a friend, and deals with the theme of friendship and separation. It was the custom of Chinese gentlemen to write poems of commemoration when they gathered for a banquet, outing, or other social occasion, and this was particularly true when the purpose of the gathering was to see one of their number off on a journey. Official assignments kept the scholar-bureaucrats moving constantly about the empire, and there are numerous works by T'ang poets bidding farewell to a friend or thanking friends for such a send-off. This poem is by Li Po and addressed to his friend Meng Hao-jan (689–740), who was sailing east down the Yangtze to Yang-chou (Kuang-ling) in Kiangsu. The farewell party was held at a place called Yellow Crane Tower overlooking the river at Wu-ch'ang in Hupei. All this information is carefully recorded in the heading of the poem, since the Chinese tend to feel that the circumstances that led to the writing of a poem are an important part of its meaning.

At Yellow Crane Tower Taking Leave of Meng Hao-jan as He Sets off for Kuang-ling

My old friend takes leave of the west at Yellow Crane Tower,
in misty third-month blossoms goes downstream to Yang-chou.
The far-off shape of his lone sail disappears in the blue-green void,
and all I see is the long river flowing to the edge of the sky.

Like Wang Wei's poem quoted above on the successive owners of his country estate, this one opens up vistas, here spatial ones that show us the sweeping mountain ranges and river systems of continental China. And unspoken but underlying it is the aching contrast between these vast, long-enduring features of the landscape and the frailty of human existence, as symbolized by the lone sail of Meng's boat fading from view on the horizon.

T'ang poetry, to sum up, stands out in the long history of Chinese poetic development because, eschewing the superficiality of an earlier age, the tendency toward bland impersonality and mannered manipulation of stock themes and images, it restored to Chinese poetry the lost note of personal concern. The T'ang poets were not afraid to employ poetry to record their deepest and most intimate feelings, crying out for the alleviation of social ills, noting with wry candor the waning of their physical powers, longing for absent friends or dreaming of the last journey home. And because they dealt with the basic impulses of the human being, their works easily survive the transition into another language and milieu. T'ang poetry, as one who reads it will readily perceive, is not just the product of a particularly golden age in China's literary history, but a part of the universal human heritage.

ENDNOTE

Poems marked with an asterisk were translated especially for this article and are published here for the first time. Other poems are taken from my *Columbia Book of Chinese Poetry* (New York: Columbia University Press, 1984).

A Dream of Red Mansions

C. T. Hsia

The Chinese novel *Hung-lou meng* is customarily known in English as *The Dream of the Red Chamber* (with or without the initial particle) because earlier partial translations bear this rather enigmatic title. Today, however, its continuing use is unjustified since we have a complete translation in three volumes by Yang Hsien-yi and Gladys Yang (Peking: Foreign Languages Press, 1978–80) under the apt title *A Dream of Red Mansions*. Another complete translation in five volumes by David Hawkes and John Minford is called *The Story of the Stone* (New York: Penguin Books, 1973–86), which accurately renders the novel's alternative title *Shih-t'ou chi*. However, since the work is best known in Chinese as *Hung-lou meng*, *A Dream of Red Mansions* should be its preferred title in English even though the Hawkes-Minford version is richer in style and more interesting to read.

A Dream of Red Mansions is the greatest novel in the Chinese literary tradition. As an eighteenth-century work, it draws fully upon that tradition, and can indeed be regarded as its crowning achievement. As that tradition is early distinguished by its poetry and philosophy, we expectedly find in *Dream* numerous poems in a variety of meters, including an elegy in the style of the *Ch'u tz'u* (*Songs of the South*, an ancient anthology), along with philosophic conversations that echo the sages of antiquity (Lao Tzu, Chuang Tzu, Mencius) and utilize the subtle language of Zen Buddhism. As a late traditional man of letters, its principal author is further aware of the encyclopedic scope of Chinese learning and the heritage of earlier fiction and drama. He has made obvious use of the Ming domestic novel *Chin P'ing Mei* and the romantic masterpieces of Yüan-Ming drama such as *The Romance of the Western Chamber* (*Hsi-hsiang chi*) and *The Peony Pavilion* (*Mu-tan t'ing*). But his novel is greater than these not only for its fuller representation of Chinese culture and thought but for its incomparably richer delineation of characters in psychological terms. That latter achievement must be solely credited to the genius of its principal author.

That author is Ts'ao Hsüeh-ch'in (1715?–1763), an ethnic Chinese from a family that had served the Manchu emperors of the Ch'ing dynasty for generations. Though mere bondservants to the throne in status, Ts'ao's great grandfather, grandfather, and father or uncle all held the highly lucrative post of commissioner of Imperial Textile Mills, first briefly in Soochow and then in Nanking. The grandfather Ts'ao Yin played host to the K'ang-hsi emperor during his four southern excursions from Peking. But the Yung-cheng emperor, who succeeded K'ang-hsi in 1723, was far less friendly to the Ts'ao house. In 1728 he dismissed Ts'ao Fu, most probably Hsüeh-ch'in's father, from his post as textile commissioner of Nanking and confiscated much of his property. Then thirteen or fourteen years old, Hsüeh-ch'in moved with his parents to Peking in much reduced circumstances. It is believed that the Ts'ao clan temporarily regained favor after the Ch'ien-lung emperor ascended the throne in 1736. But by 1744, when Hsüeh-ch'in started composing his novel, he had moved to the western suburbs of Peking, again living in poverty: the Ts'ao family must have suffered another disaster from which it never recovered. The novelist had lost a young son a few months before his death in February 1763 and was survived by a second wife, of whom we know nothing further.

By all indications Ts'ao Hsüeh-ch'in should have had ample time to complete *Dream* to his own satisfaction, but it would seem that at the time of his death this novel of autobiographical inspiration—about a great family in decline and its young heir—was not yet in publishable shape even though manuscripts of the first eighty chapters, known by title as *The Story of the Stone,* had been in circulation for some time. Scholars now believe that Ts'ao must have completed at least one draft of the whole novel, but went on revising it, partly to please the commentators among his kinsmen, prominently a cousin known by his studio name of Red Inkstone (Chih-yen Chai), and partly to remove any grounds for suspicion that his work was critical of the government in devoting space to the tribulations of a family justly deserving of imperial punishment. If Ts'ao had indeed completed the last portion of the novel but didn't allow it to circulate, it could have been due to fear of a literary inquisition.

A corrected second edition of the 120-chapter *Dream of Red Mansions* came out in 1792, only a few months after the first edition of 1791. The new edition contains, in addition to the original preface by Ch'eng Wei-yüan, a new preface by Kao Ê, and a joint foreword by the two. Earlier scholars have arbitrarily taken Ch'eng to be a bookseller who had acquired manuscripts of the later chapters and had asked the scholar Kao Ê to put them into shape and edit the work as a whole. Some would even regard Kao Ê as a forger. Now we know that Ch'eng Wei-yüan was a staff member of the gigantic imperial project to assemble a "Complete Library in Four Branches of Learning and Literature" *(Ssu-k'u ch'üan-shu).* Ho-shen, a Manchu minister enjoying the complete trust of the Ch'ien-lung emperor, was made a director general of the project, and according to a new theory advanced by Chou Ju-ch'ang, a leading authority on the novel, it was Ho-shen himself who had ordered Ch'eng and Kao to prepare a politically harmless version for the perusal of the emperor. This theory should be taken seriously inasmuch as Ch'eng and Kao could not have dreamed of putting out a movable type edition of a massive novel without the backing of a powerful minister like Ho-shen and without the printing facilities of the imperial court.

Whatever its faults, the Ch'eng-Kao edition has remained the standard text for Chinese readers for two hundred years. Scholars, of course, will continue to regret that Ts'ao Hsüeh-ch'in did not live long enough to complete or oversee the publication of his own novel, and belittle or give grudging praise to Kao Ê's contributions as an editor and continuator of the first eighty chapters. But if the last forty chapters are not what they should be, the first eighty are also by no means a coherent narrative of seamless unity. In addition to minor inconsistencies in the story line, Ts'ao's inveterate habit for revision would seem to be responsible for more serious instances of narrative ineptitude as well. One plausible theory (endorsed by David Hawkes) proposes that even before starting on his great project, Ts'ao Hsüeh-ch'in had acquired or himself written a manuscript called *A Mirror for the Romantic (Feng-yüeh pao-chien)*, about unhappy youths and maidens belatedly awakened to the illusory nature of love. He was apparently very fond of this manuscript and inserted some of its cautionary tales into his novel. He did so, of course, at the cost of upsetting its temporal scheme since the autobiographical hero and his female cousins lead quite unhurried lives while the trials of the deluded Chia Jui in chapter 12 and of the hapless Yu sisters in chapters 64–67 consume weeks in a matter of pages. Try as he might, Ts'ao could not have got himself out of this narrative impasse if he was determined to save these somewhat extraneous tales.

The story of the novel's composition and publication remains thus a very complicated affair demanding further research by specialists. The novel itself, however, should pose few difficulties for the Western reader unless he is intimidated right away by its sheer size. But the undaunted reader will be amply rewarded and will cherish the experience of having spent days and weeks with many memorable characters in a Chinese setting. *A Dream of Red Mansions* is about the aristocratic Chia clan which, like the Ts'ao family, has enjoyed imperial favor for generations. Its two main branches dwell in adjoining compounds in the capital, styled Ningkuofu and Jungkuofu. The nominal head of the Ningkuofu is a selfish student of Taoist alchemy who eventually dies its victim; his son Chia Chen and grandson Chia Yung are both sensualists. Grandmother Chia, also known as the Lady Dowager in the Yang translation, presides over the Jungkuofu. She has two sons, Chia She and Chia Cheng. Chia Lien, Chia She's pleasure-seeking son, is married to an extremely capable woman, Wang Hsi-feng. Despite her early triumphs in managing the household finances and driving her love rivals to suicide, this handsome and vivacious lady eventually languishes in ill health and dies. Her nefarious dealings are in large part responsible for the raiding of the Chia compounds by imperial guards and the confiscation of their property.

The Dowager's other son, Chia Cheng, is the only conscientious Confucian member of the family in active government service. A lonely man of narrow vision but undeniable rectitude, he has lost a promising son before the novel opens. Naturally, he expects his younger son by his legitimate wife, Lady Wang, to study hard and prepare for the civil service examinations. But Pao-yü, early spoiled by his grandmother, mother, and other female relatives, detests conventional learning and prefers the company of his girl cousins and the maidservants. Since late childhood, he has had as playmate a cousin of delicate beauty beloved by the Dowager, Lin Tai-yü. Some years later, another beautiful cousin, Hsüeh Pao-ch'ai, also moves into the Jungkuofu. In spite of Pao-yü's repeated assurances of his love, Tai-yü regards Pao-ch'ai as her rival and feels very insecure. As she progressively ruins her health by wallowing in self-pity, Pao-ch'ai replaces her as the family's preferred candidate for Pao-yü's wife. But the marriage when it does take place brings no joy to Pao-ch'ai since by that time Pao-yü has turned into an idiot. Broken-hearted and full of unforgiveness, Tai-yü dies on their wedding night.

Pao-yü eventually recovers and obtains the degree of *chü-jen*. But instead of returning home after taking the examination, he renounces the world and becomes a monk. The desolate Pao-ch'ai takes comfort in her pregnancy. A faithful maid, Hsi-jen (called Aroma in Hawkes and Minford) is eventually happily married to an actor friend of Pao-yü's. Another maid, Ch'ing-wen (Skybright in Hawkes and Minford), to whom Pao-yü was also much attached, had died of calumny and sickness long before his marriage.

Chinese novels before *Dream* are mostly about characters in history and legend. Though a type of short novel about talented and good-looking young lovers had become popular before his time, Ts'ao Hsüeh-ch'in quite properly dismisses these stereotyped romances in his novel for their palpable unreality. But his use of what we may call diurnal realism, the technique of advancing the novel with seemingly inconsequential accounts of day-to-day events and of lingering over days of family significance, clearly shows his indebtedness to the aforementioned *Chin P'ing Mei*, the only one of the four major Ming novels devoted to tracing the fortunes of a discordant large family. (The other three, all available in English translation, are: *Romance of the Three Kingdoms* [*San-kuo-chih yen-i*], *Outlaws of the Marsh* [*Shui-hu chuan*], and *The Journey to the West* [*Hsi-yu chi*].) But whereas *Chin P'ing Mei* is notorious for its graphic descriptions of Hsi-men Ch'ing's sexual life with his concubines and paramours, *Dream* is never pornographic despite its larger cast of male sensualists. The novel maintains instead a note of high culture by focusing attention on the hero and on several gifted young ladies whose poetic parties and conversations with him invariably touch upon intellectual and aesthetic matters. The life story of Chia Pao-yü, especially, is tested against all the major ideals of Chinese culture.

At the very beginning of the first chapter, Ts'ao places his hero in a creation myth that mocks his Faustian desire for experience, knowledge, and pleasure. When the goddess Nü-kua is repairing the Dome of Heaven, she rejects as unfit for use a huge rock of considerable intelligence, which consequently bemoans its fate and develops a longing for the pleasures of the mundane world. It can now turn itself into the size of a stone and, with the help of a Buddhist monk and a Taoist priest, it is eventually born with a piece of jade in his mouth as our hero (Pao-yü means "precious jade"). As a supramundane allegory, then, *Dream* is the transcription of a record as inscribed on the Stone itself after it had returned to its original site in the Green Fable Mountains. The Stone has found human life wanting, its pleasures and pains all illusory, and its detailed record—our novel—is by allegorical design a massive substantiation of that truth. Throughout the novel, the celestial agents of that allegory, the mangy Buddhist and lame Taoist, while watching over the spiritual welfare of Pao-yü, periodically mock or enlighten other deluded earthlings as well.

Chia Pao-yü is next characterized in chapter 2 by two knowledgeable outsiders as an unconventional individualist of the romantic tradition firmly opposed to the Confucian ideal of morality and service as represented by his father. To illustrate his propensity for love, our hero, while taking a nap in the bedchamber of Ch'in K'o-ch'ing (Chia Yung's wife) in chapter 5, is transported to the Land of Illusion presided over by the fairy Disenchantment. After warning him of the dangers of the kind of crazy love (*ch'ih ch'ing*) prized by the romantics, she introduces her own sister to him for the purpose of sexual initiation so that he may see through the vanity of passion and return to the path of Confucian service. The fairy Ko-ch'ing, who combines in her person the charms of both Tai-yü and Pao-ch'ai, of course enraptures Pao-yü, but he soon wakes up screaming after being chased by demons and wild beasts.

When lecturing Pao-yü, the fairy Disenchantment does allow a distinction between lust *(yin)* and love *(ch'ing)*, and as someone truly committed to *ch'ing* (also meaning "feeling"), our hero is in no danger of being confused with several of his kinsmen who are often driven by lust to trample upon human feelings. But Pao-yü is so free of the taint of lust that the dream allegory confuses matters by presenting him as someone desperate for salvation after only a brief interlude of sexual bliss. Contrary to popular belief among Chinese readers, Pao-yü is not a great lover, nor does he function principally as a lover in the novel. It is true that remembrance of the sweeter portion of the dream has led him to make love to the maid Aroma the same evening. For all we know they may continue to share sexual intimacy thereafter, but his enjoyment of her body, explicitly referred to only once and rarely emphasized again, alters not a whit his high regard for her as a person and a friend. Pao-yü is actually more drawn to his other maid Skybright because of her entrancing beauty and fiery temperament, but she dies complaining of being a virgin, untouched by her young master.

Pao-yü is every girl's true friend. Once the Takuanyüan, a spacious garden built in honor of his elder sister, an imperial concubine, becomes the residential quarters of Pao-yü and his girl cousins, he sees them and their maids all the time and gives daily proof of his unfeigned friendship and solicitude for their welfare. He admires each and every one of these girls as an embodiment of celestial beauty and understanding, but worries about the time when they will leave the garden to get married. He knows only too well that with marriage their celestial essence will be obscured and that, if they survive their unhappiness, they will become as mean-spirited as the older women in the Chia mansions.

As the sole young master in the Takuanyüan, Pao-yü therefore does his best to keep the young ladies and maids amused and to lull their awareness of the misery of approaching adulthood. But for all their lively parties and conversations, the young ladies have to leave one by one, by marriage, death, or abduction (in the case of the resident nun Miao-yü). It is these tragedies that reduce our helpless hero to a state of idiocy and prepare him for his eventual acceptance of his fate as an insensible Stone, regardless of suffering humanity. In that allegorical dream, the fairy Disenchantment has warned him only of his romantic propensity. But though he is grievously hurt when his elders rob him of his intended bride and marry him to Pao-ch'ai, ordinarily he is much more occupied by the tragic fate of Tai-yü, and of all other girls deprived of life or happiness. In accordance with the author's allegoric scheme, we should perhaps feel happy that he has finally gained wisdom and leaves this world of suffering for the life of a monk. But we cannot help feeling that his spiritual wisdom is gained at the expense of his most endearing trait—his active love and compassion for fellow human beings. Despite his irrepressible charm and gaiety, Chia Pao-yü must be regarded as the most tragic hero in all Chinese literature for ultimately choosing the path of self-liberation because his sympathy and compassion have failed him.

Pao-yü has a few like-minded male friends whom he sees occasionally, but inside the Chia mansions there are no men to whom he can unburden his soul. Even if he is not partial to girls, he has only these to turn to for genuine companionship. And it is a tribute to Ts'ao's extraordinary genius that he is able to provide him with so many sharply individualized companions to talk and joke with, to compete with as poets, and to care for and love. Among these, Lin Tai-yü naturally takes pride of place as the principal heroine with whose fate Pao-yü is most concerned. Alone of the major heroines, she is assigned a role in the supramundane allegory complementary to the hero's. She is supposed to be a plant that blossoms into a fairy after the Stone, then serving as a page at the court of Disenchantment, has daily sprinkled it with dew. The fairy has vowed to repay his kindness with tears if she may join him on earth, and judging by the occasions Tai-yü has to cry while living as an orphan among relatives, never sure of her status in the Jungkuofu nor of her marital future, she has certainly more than repaid her debt to her former benefactor.

Yet as is the case with Pao-yü's allegoric dream, Ts'ao Hsüeh-ch'in almost deliberately misleads with his fairy tale about Tai-yü as a grateful plant. The reality of the two cousins in love is far more complex and fascinating than any allegory can suggest. Long before Tai-yü is in danger of being rejected by her elders, she seethes with discontent. Her every meeting with Pao-yü ends in a misunderstanding or quarrel, and these quarrels are, for her, fraught with bitter and lacerated feelings. This is so because the two are diametrically opposed in temperament despite the similarity of their tastes. Pao-yü is a person of active sympathy capable of ultimate self-transcendence; Tai-yü is a self-centered neurotic who courts self-destruction. Her attraction for Pao-yü lies not merely in her fragile beauty and poetic sensibility but in her very contrariness—a jealous self-obsession so unlike his expansive gaiety that his love for her is always tinged with infinite sadness.

Tai-yü, on her part, can never be sure of Pao-yü's love and yet maintains a fierce pride in her studied indifference to her marital prospects. One could almost say that her tragedy lies in her stubborn impracticality, in the perverse contradiction between her very natural desire to get married to the man of her choice and her fear of compromising herself in the eyes of the world by doing anything to bring about that result. In time her temper gets worse, and so does her health. Ts'ao Hsüeh-ch'in never flinches from physiological details as he traces her growing emotional sickness in terms of her bodily deterioration. Her dream scene in chapter 82, where Pao-yü slashes open his chest in order to show her his heart and finds it missing, and her ghastly death scene in chapter 98 are among the most powerful in the novel. Kao Ê must be given high praise if he had indeed a substantial hand in the writing of these chapters.

Because Pao-ch'ai nominally gets her man, Chinese readers partial to Tai-yü are less sympathetic toward her, and find personal satisfaction in seeing her as a hypocritical schemer. This misreading is, of course, unwarranted. It is true that, as a sensible girl docilely accepting her place in a Confucian society, she may have less appeal for Pao-yü and for the modern reader than Tai-yü with her neurotic sensibility and volatile temper. Yet both are strictly comparable in talent and beauty, and both are fatherless children living more or less as dependents among relatives. Though Tai-yü is initially jealous, they become the best of friends after chapter 45:

two helpless pawns in the hands of their elders with no control over their marital fate. If the elders prefer Pao-ch'ai as Pao-yü's bride, at the same time they show little regard for her welfare. Though Pao-yü was once a desirable match, by the time the wedding is proposed he is a very sick person with no immediate prospect for recovery. Even more than Tai-yü, Pao-ch'ai is the victim of a cruel hoax, since there can be no doubt that the hastily arranged wedding is regarded by the elder Chia ladies as medicine for Pao-yü's health. For Pao-ch'ai's martyrdom their brutal and desperate self-interest is alone responsible.

As the wife of Pao-yü, Pao-ch'ai remains to the end a Confucian trying to dissuade him from the path of self-liberation. She is in that respect not unlike his parents in wishing to see him enter government service and get settled as a family man. But in the end she uses the Mencian argument to counter his Taoist resolve to leave the world. Even if the world is full of evil and suffering, or especially because it is so, how can he bear to sever human ties, to leave those who need his love most? How can one remain human by denying the most instinctive promptings of his heart? Pao-ch'ai cannot figure this out, and Pao-yü cannot answer her on the rational level of human discourse. It is only by placing human life in the cosmological scheme of craving and suffering that one can see the need to liberate oneself. It would be too cruel even for the enlightened Pao-yü to tell Pao-ch'ai that to cling to love and compassion is to persist in delusion: in the primordial antiquity of Taoism there was no need to love or commiserate.

As a tragedy, *A Dream of Red Mansions* has thus the overtones of a bitter and sardonic comedy. The Buddhist-Taoist view of the world prevails in the end, and yet the reader cannot but feel that the reality of love and suffering as depicted in the novel stirs far deeper layers of his being than the reality of Buddhist-Taoist wisdom. This Chinese masterpiece is therefore like all the greatest novels of the world in that no philosophic or religious message one extracts therefrom can at all do justice to its unfolding panorama of wondrous but perverse humanity. For any reader who would like a panoramic view of traditional Chinese life through the portrayal of many unforgettable characters in an authentic social and cultural setting there can be no richer and more fascinating work than Ts'ao Hsüeh-ch'in's *A Dream of Red Mansions.*

6 CLASSICS OF THE JAPANESE TRADITION

The Tale of Genji as a Japanese and World Classic

Haruo Shirane

The Tale of Genji, or the *Genji monogatari,* was written in the early eleventh century by a woman named Murasaki Shikibu. We know very little about the author except that she was the daughter of a scholar/poet, that she came from the middle ranks of the aristocracy, and that she served, at some point, as a lady-in-waiting to the empress, for whom she probably wrote at least part of this lengthy narrative. The title of *The Tale of Genji* comes from the surname of the hero, who is the son of the emperor regnant at the beginning of the narrative and whose life, marriage, and relationships with various women are described in the course of the first forty-one chapters. The remaining thirteen chapters are primarily concerned with the affairs of Kaoru, Genji's putative son.

Murasaki Shikibu's creation of highly individualized characters in a realistic social setting and her subtle presentation of inner thought and emotion have encouraged critics to call the *Genji* the world's first psychological novel. The appearance of a lengthy masterpiece of vernacular fiction toward the beginning of a literary tradition is indeed highly unusual. The Chinese tradition, for example, begins with poetry, history, and philosophy, all of which become classic genres. Vernacular fiction, which has a problematic place in the tradition, does not emerge until much later, and the novelistic masterpiece of Chinese fiction—*A Dream of Red Mansions* (*Hung-lou meng*), or *The Story of the Stone*—does not appear until the late eighteenth century (1792), about the time that the novel comes into its own in the Anglo-European tradition.

The Japanese, following the Chinese model, considered poetry, history, and philosophy to be the classic literary genres. But literary masterpieces failed to materialize, at least initially, from either history or philosophy, both of which had to be written in Chinese, the official language of religion and government. Of the three ideological centers—Buddhism, Confucianism, and Shintoism—two (Buddhism and Confucianism) are borrowed from the continent, and the third, Shintoism, the indigenous religion, while containing a body of intriguing myths, did not develop a self-conscious textual tradition. There is, in short, no Old Testament, no Plato, no Confucius. The impact of Buddhism and Confucianism, whose texts were considered literary classics by the Japanese priesthood and intelligentsia, cannot be underestimated. But these centers of thought did not directly give birth to great literature, at least not in the beginning.

Nor do we find epics, drama, or tragedy, the literary genres associated with the wellsprings of the Western literary tradition. Instead, there is poetry and, in particular, *waka*, the thirty-one syllable lyric, which was composed and exchanged by all educated Japanese from the ancient period onward. *Waka* was overwhelmingly private in nature and had little concern for politics, philosophy, or the larger humanistic issues that we normally associate with the Great Ideas, but it functioned superbly as a vehicle of aesthetic consciousness and led to an outstanding tradition of fiction, drama, essays, epics, and literary diaries, all of which are highly lyrical and poetic and of which the *Genji* is perhaps the most outstanding example.

The Tale of Genji also emerged out of a tradition of folk narratives, which can be traced back to the early histories and which had developed by the tenth century into a tradition of vernacular tales and Buddhist anecdotes. Of the two native genres, folk narratives and Japanese poetry, the latter took absolute precedence. Japanese poetry in fact was the only native, vernacular genre to be considered serious literature in Murasaki Shikibu's day. One consequence was that *The Tale of Genji* was not recognized as a classic in its own time.

Buddhism condoned storytelling as a parable, as a vehicle for transmitting higher truths, but it fundamentally distrusted prose fiction. Buddhist writers repeatedly condemned prose fiction for deceiving the reader, distorting facts, and encouraging immoral acts. Later medieval Buddhist anecdotes depict Murasaki Shikibu as suffering in hell for having written excessively of amorous affairs and of having "fabricated a tissue of lies." The early Anglo-European novel, which initially came under similar attack, defended itself by pretending to be a form of history, a kind of biography, or, as in the case of *Robinson Crusoe,* an authentic document. Probably for similar reasons, to borrow the prestige and apparent authenticity of the histories, Murasaki Shikibu gave her narrative a strong historical cast, interweaving historical names, places, and events, to the extent that parts of *The Tale of Genji,* which was written in the early eleventh century, can be regarded as a historical novel set a hundred years earlier. The title itself evokes the past, for the practice of conferring the surname of Genji, or Minamoto, upon a prince and thereby making him a commoner—which the emperor does in the opening chapter to provide the hero with political protection and opportunity—had ceased by the early tenth century. In an age in which the Fujiwara clan monopolized all phases of the imperial government, it was inconceivable for a Genji to gain power, let alone control the throne as the Shining hero eventually does.

In a famous discussion of fiction in the middle chapters of *The Tale of Genji*, the hero attacks *monogatari*, or vernacular tales, for being deceptive and worthless, but in the end he is persuaded, as Murasaki Shikibu no doubt hoped her readers would be, that there was more truth to be found in this admittedly fictitious tale than in the highly esteemed histories. It was, however, *The Tale of Genji's* poetic qualities that first earned it literary prominence.

When the *Genji* was finally recognized as a classic in the medieval period, from the early thirteenth century onward, it was recognized, not as a work of prose fiction per se, but as a sourcebook for poetry, a guide to the poetic diction, imagery, and sensibility required for composing poetry, which was de rigueur for all educated Japanese. Fujiwara no Shunzei, the leading poet of the late twelfth century, publicly remarked that "any poet who was not well versed in *The Tale of Genji* was to be deplored." Indeed, without an intimate knowledge of the *Genji* the subtle allusions upon which medieval poetry and linked verse, or *renga*, depended could not be comprehended. *The Tale of Genji* also lived in the popular imagination, in oral and written narratives, in Japanese drama, particularly the Nō plays of the late medieval period, and in the visual arts, where it graced everything from scroll painting to furniture engraving. But it was the medieval poet/scholars who were responsible for preserving, annotating, and explicating Murasaki Shikibu's masterpiece for future readers. In the premodern period alone, there are over a thousand commentaries.

One of the obvious attractions that the *Genji* holds for modern readers, particularly for those concerned with today's undergraduate curriculum, is the fact that it is a major classic by a woman. In Murasaki Shikibu's day, as in previous centuries, men devoted themselves to writing prose in Chinese, the official language of religion and government. (The only prose writing that was taken seriously was historical and philosophical writing, all of which was done in Chinese and little of which is read today.) One consequence was that women, who were not obligated to write in a foreign language and who were in fact discouraged from doing so, were the first to create a substantial body of prose texts in the vernacular. If Virginia Woolf lamented the silence of Shakespeare's sister, Japan's Shakespeare was a woman who had many literary sisters. In the tenth century, vernacular prose, particularly literary diaries, belonged to women to the extent that the leading male poet of the day, Ki no Tsurayuki, pretended to be a woman in order to write a literary diary in Japanese—a reversal of the George Eliot phenomenon.

Male scholars, however, were the first to write vernacular tales, or *monogatari,* though they did so anonymously for such writing was considered a lowly activity directed only at women and children. These early vernacular tales, which begin with the *Taketori monogatari* (*The Tale of the Bamboo Cutter,* early tenth century), tend to be highly romantic, fantastical, and dominated by folkloric elements. Women, by contrast, wrote highly personal, confessional literature based on their private lives and centered on their own poetry. The author of the *Kagerō nikki,* the first major literary diary by a woman, wrote out of a profound dissatisfaction with contemporary *monogatari,* which, in her view, were "little more than gross fabrications." Standing at the crossroads of literary history, Murasaki Shikibu was able to combine both traditions. *The Tale of Genji* carries on the *monogatari* tradition in its larger plot and its amorous hero. But in its style, details, psychological insight, and portrayal of the dilemmas faced by women in aristocratic society, *The Tale of Genji* remains firmly rooted in the women's tradition.

It was a plot convention of the vernacular tale that the heroine, whose family has declined or disappeared, is discovered and loved by an illustrious noble. This association of love and inferior social status appears from the opening line of the *Genji.*

> Which imperial reign was it? Of the many consorts who were in the service of the emperor, there was one who was not of particularly high status but who received the special favor of the Emperor. (Translation mine)

In the opening chapter, the emperor regnant, like all Heian emperors, was expected to devote himself to his principal consort (the Kokiden lady), the lady of the highest rank, and yet he dotes on a woman of considerably lower status, a social and political violation that eventually results in the woman's death. Like his father, Genji pursues love where it is forbidden and most unlikely to be found or attained. In the fifth chapter, Genji discovers his future wife, the young Murasaki, who has lost her mother and is in danger of losing her only guardian when Genji takes her into his own home.

In Murasaki Shikibu's day, it would have been unheard of for a man of Genji's high rank to take a girl of Murasaki's low position into his own residence and marry her. In Heian aristocratic society, the man usually lived in his wife's residence, either in the house of her parents or in a dwelling nearby. As a rule, the wife did not leave her family after marriage. She received her husband at her own home, reared her children there, and continued to be supported by her family. Though political power lay in the hands of men, the succession to marital residences remained matrilineal. The prospective groom thus had high stakes in marriage, for the bride's family provided not only a residence but other forms of support as well. When Genji takes a girl with absolutely no political backing or social support into his house and marries her, he openly flouts the conventions of marriage as they were known to Murasaki Shikibu's audience. In the *monogatari* tradition, however, this action becomes a sign of excessive, romantic love.

A number of other sequences in the *Genji*—those of Yūgao, Suetsumuhana, Tamakazura, the Akashi lady, Oigimi (Agemaki), and Ukifune—start on a similar note. All of these women come from upper or middle-rank aristocratic families that have, for various reasons, fallen into social obscurity and must struggle to survive. The appearance of the highborn hero signifies, at least for those surrounding the woman, an opportunity for social redemption, an expectation that is usually fulfilled in the earlier *monogatari*. Murasaki Shikibu, however, focuses on the difficulties that the woman subsequently encounters, either in dealing with the man, or in making, or failing to make, the social transition between her own class and that of the highborn hero. The woman may, for example, be torn between pride and material need, or between emotional dependence on the man and a desire to be more independent, or she may feel abandoned and betrayed—all conflicts explored in Heian women's literature. In classical poetry, which had a profound influence on the *Genji,* love has a similar fate: it is never about happiness or the blissful union of souls. Instead, it dwells on unfulfilled hopes, fear of abandonment, deep regrets, and lingering resentment. One of the most prominent poetic stances in the *Kokinshū,* the first imperial anthology of Japanese poetry (early ninth century) is that of the lonely woman. As the medieval aesthetic term *sabi* (which comes from the word *sabishii,* or "lonely") suggests, loneliness is not only a state of being, it is part of a larger aesthetic consciousness that finds melancholy beauty in loneliness.

The Tale of Genji has often been called the world's first psychological novel, a notion reinforced by Arthur Waley who transformed *The Tale of Genji* both stylistically and socially into a Victorian novel. The label of novel is obviously meant to be a compliment, but it can be misleading. First of all, *The Tale of Genji* need not be read from front to back, as a single monolithic work. *The Tale of Genji* was not conceived and written as a single product and then published and distributed to a mass audience as novels are today. Instead, the chapters were issued in limited installments to a small aristocratic audience, and possibly to a single reader (the empress). Furthermore, the chapters probably did not appear in the order that we have them today. In all likelihood, the *Genji* began as a short story, and in response to reader demand, Murasaki Shikibu produced another story or sequel.

The *Genji* is probably best appreciated as Murasaki Shikibu's oeuvre, or corpus, as a closely interrelated series of texts that can be read either individually or as a whole and that is the product of an author whose attitudes, interests, and techniques evolved significantly with time and experience. For example, the reader of the Ukifune story (the last five chapters, devoted to Ukifune) can appreciate this sequence both independently and as an integral part of the previous narrative. It is thus possible for undergraduates to read only a part of *The Tale of Genji* and still appreciate many of its finer qualities. In fact, it is sometimes better to start with the later, more mature, sequences and then, having acquired a taste for the narrative, go back to the earlier chapters.

Japanese poets were well aware that meaning is dependent on context and that the significance of a 31-syllable *waka* could be profoundly altered by the prose context or by contiguous poems. An entire poetic genre—*renga,* or linked verse—eventually grew out of the pleasure derived from deliberately changing the meaning of a preexisting verse by adding another verse to it. In a similar fashion, Murasaki Shikibu altered the significance of her existing text, or body of texts, not by rewriting it, but by adding and interlacing new sequences. To take a larger example, love, glory, and *miyabi* ("courtliness"), the secular ideals assumed in the earlier volumes, are placed in relative and ironic perspective in the latter chapters by the emergence of their opposite: a deep-rooted desire to renounce the world and achieve detachment.

The fact that *The Tale of Genji* is an evolving narrative, however, does not mean that Murasaki Shikibu ignores or forgets the earlier stages of the narrative. The author links many of the women by blood or physical appearance, in the form of surrogate figures. For example, in the opening chapter, after losing the Kiritsubo consort (Genji's mother), the emperor finds consolation in Fujitsubo, a lady of similar countenance. Genji, longing for his deceased mother, is likewise drawn to his father's new consort. Frustrated by Fujitsubo's stiff resistance and the barriers that separate them, he eventually finds a substitute and a wife in the young Murasaki, who is Fujitsubo's niece and almost identical in appearance. In each case, the loss of a woman leads the man to find a surrogate, who is similar in appearance, or closely related, or both. The notion of the surrogate lover enabled Murasaki Shikibu not only to explore one of the great themes of the *Genji*—the pseudo-incestuous nature of male/female relationships—but to move smoothly from one new sequence to the next.

An equally significant form of linkage exists between characters who are *not* associated by blood or appearance but who bear common social, spiritual, and emotional burdens. Perhaps the most revealing of these analogous relationships involves Asagao, Princess Ochiba, and Oigimi, three royal daughters who appear in three different parts of the *Genji*. Owing to an unfortunate turn in family circumstances, all three women have been placed in difficult positions. But despite the obvious rewards of marriage, each one rejects the advances and generous aid of a highborn, attractive noble: Genji, Yūgiri, and Kaoru, respectively. None of these women is directly related to the other. Nevertheless, each successive sequence explores, with increasing intensity, the problem of honor, pride, and shame in regard to the spiritual independence of a highborn but disadvantaged lady.

The *Genji* can also be thought of as a kind of bildungsroman, in which the author reveals the development of the protagonist's spirit and character through time and experience. In the *Genji* this growth occurs not only in the life of a single hero or heroine but over different generations and sequences, with two or more successive characters. Genji, for example, gradually attains an awareness of death, mutability, and the illusory nature of the world through repeated suffering. By contrast, Kaoru, his putative son, begins his life, or rather his narrative, with a profound grasp and acceptance of these darker aspects of life.

The same is true of the mature Murasaki, the heroine of the first half, and Oigimi (Waley: Agemaki), the primary figure of the last part. By the beginning of the middle chapters, Murasaki has long assumed that she can monopolize Genji's affections and act as his principal wife. Genji's unexpected marriage to the high-ranking Third Princess (Waley: Nyosan), however, crushes these assumptions, causing Murasaki to fall mortally ill. Though Oigimi never suffers the way Murasaki does, she quickly comes to a similar awareness of the inconstancy of men, love, and marriage, and rejects Kaoru even though he appears to be the perfect companion. Building on the earlier chapters, Murasaki Shikibu makes a significant leap, moving from a narrative about the tribulations of love and marriage to one that explores a world without men.

The form of the *Genji* is closely bound to its aesthetics. Beauty in the West has often been associated with the eternal, the sublime, with the uplifting, and in form it has been often tied to unity and balance. In Heian literature, however, beauty is found in the fleeting, in the uncertain, in the fragmentary, and in the inherently sorrowful aspects of the world. The cherry blossoms—the quintessential image of Japanese aesthetics even today—were loved by Heian poets not only because the delicate, multi-petaled flowers reminded them of the glories of this world but because the same blossoms, in a matter of days, turned color, faded, and scattered in the wind like snowflakes, a sorrowful reminder not only of the brevity of life and fortune but of the uncertainty and fickleness of the human heart. In the *Genji* the essence of nature and human life tends to be grasped in terms of their end, in their dying moments rather than in their birth or creation. The dominant season of the *Genji* is autumn, when nature, in all its melancholy hues, seems to wither and fade away.

In one of the opening chapters of the *Genji* the young hero discovers in a run-down residence on the outskirts of town a fragile young woman, Yūgao, or the Evening Faces. Unable to resist her beauty and charm, he whisks her off to a deserted mansion where they spend the night together. Suddenly, in the darkness, she is seized by an evil spirit (presumably that of the Rokujō lady) and expires in the hero's arms. The hero comes, as he does elsewhere, to an understanding of his love, not in its fulfillment, but in its all-too-sudden and incomprehensible loss. Indicative of the symbolism that permeates the *Genji* is the woman's name, Yūgao, a gourd-like plant (suggesting her lowly origins) whose beautiful white flowers, at the height of summer, bloom in the dusk and fade before the sunrise.

Perhaps the most important critical concept in Japanese poetry from the classical period onward is the notion of *yojō* 余情, or *yosei,* which has two broad meanings. On the one hand, *yojō* refers to poetry or art as an expression or product of excessive, irrepressible emotions. When we compare Genji to the heroes of the Western classics, to Achilles and Odysseus, a strikingly different set of human values emerges. Genji does not triumph through strength and courage, by cunning and intelligence, by resisting temptation, or through acts of benevolence and insight. In fact, he fails in almost every one of these categories. Instead, heroism lies in his capacity not only to be deeply moved and rendered vulnerable but to express that inner weakness and deep emotion through aesthetic means, through poetry, painting, music, and other aesthetic forms.

Yojō also means overtones, what is beyond the referential meaning of words, what is implied rather than stated. Visually, *yojō* implies that the shadows—for example, the dusk and early dawn—have more allure and depth than light or darkness. Musically, *yojō* suggests that the faint echoes, the reverberations that linger in the ear, are often more moving than the melodic notes themselves. *Yojō* also implies that the fragrance, wafting on a gentle breeze, is often more memorable than the flower itself. Such is Kaoru, the Fragrant One, whose bodily scent reaches into the houses of unsuspecting women. The name borne by Oborozukiyo, the daughter of the Minister of the Right, with whom Genji is caught sleeping in the early chapters, literally means "The Evening of the Misty Moon." As in Japanese poetry, the softly enshrouded moon is more erotic and seductive than a brightly shining crescent.

Yojō also refers to the intertextual fabric of poetry. *The Tale of Genji* is not only an exquisite weave of poetry and prose, but is interwoven with elaborate allusions to Chinese poetry and literature, to Buddhist scriptures, and to *waka.* Many of the places in the *Genji*—Suma, where Genji is exiled, or Uji, where Kaoru discovers two beautiful sisters—are *utamakura,* famous place-names in

Japanese poetry, with rich clusters of associations that are woven into the drama. *The Tale of Genji* unfolds over seventy-five years, three generations, four imperial reigns, and presents over five hundred characters, and yet it gravitates toward intensely emotional and meditative scenes in which the language, rhetoric, and themes of poetry are foregrounded and in which the primary reference is not to an "external" world so much as to other literary and poetic texts. (It is thus no accident that the *Genji* was first regarded as a classic of poetry.)

The notion of *yojō,* or overtones, also extends to the structure of the *Genji,* in which the aftermath, the lingering echoes, and the memories are often more central to the narrative than the event of action itself. The opening chapter, for example, describes the tragic love affair between the emperor and Genji's mother. The greater part of the chapter, however, is an extended meditation on the death of the lover, climaxed by poetry and allusions to Yang Kuei-fei and "The Song of Sorrow" by Po Chü-i, Japan's favorite Chinese poet. In the manner of lyrical narratives, the tone is elegant, poetic, and uplifting even though the subject matter is tragic. These scenes belong to a familiar topos, the lament (*aishō*), which can be traced back to the elegies by Kakinomoto no Hitomaro (d. 709) and other *Manyōshū* (c. 771) poets. The meditations on personal loss—due to either death, separation, or abandonment—also derive from the women's tradition. If the earlier *monogatari* written by men revolved around action and plot, the literary diaries by women, often written in memoir or autobiographical form, ruminate on the consequences and significance of the past.

Western literary criticism, from the time of Aristotle onward, has stressed formal unity and balance, particularly beginnings, middles, and ends. But in *The Tale of Genji,* as in much of Japanese literature, the fragment or the part is often more aesthetically important than the whole. Literature is more akin to a trailing cloud, to use a recurrent image from the *Genji,* than a figure carved in stone. It is revealing that we do not know if the *Genji* is in fact finished. The last chapter, "The Floating Bridge of Dreams," suggests both an end and a new beginning, and is no more closed than a number of other earlier chapters. The ending, or a lack of it, has disturbed some Western scholars, but Japanese critics have never made it an issue, for the notion of an open, unbound text is a given, just as is the poetics of overtones, fragmentation, and uncertainty.

ENDNOTE

There are two English translations, complete or nearly so. That by Arthur Waley appeared in installments more than a half century ago and is available in Modern Library. That by Edward Seidensticker was published by Alfred Knopf in 1976. A selection from the latter translation, about a fifth of the whole, was published by Vintage in 1985.

Earlier essays on the *Tale of Genji* by Donald Keene and Edward Seidensticker may be found in *Approaches to the Oriental Classics* (1959), pp. 186–195; and *The Great Ideas Today* (Chicago: Encyclopedia Britannica, 1987), pp. 286–291.

"An Account of My Hut" *(Hōjōki)*

Paul Anderer

Kamo no Chōmei was born in 1153, and at the age of fifty, he tells us, he renounced the world and became a Buddhist monk. He was of a hereditary line of Shinto priests, and in better times may well have succeeded his father as a priest at the Kamo Shrine in Kyoto. But the late twelfth century was among the most strife-torn and transforming of all periods in Japan, and this was not to be.

In 1212, ten years after he took the tonsure and assumed a Buddhist name, after he adopted, too, the life of a recluse in the mountains, Chōmei wrote a brief essay. His "Account of My Hut" seems a simple, almost a fragile, literary structure, yet has proved to be among the most resilient and enduring of Japanese texts. Indeed, when we recall how frequently Japanese writing—whether a thirty-one syllable lyric or a Nō play or a narrative of over a thousand pages—coheres around the site of a hut, of a small sequestered dwelling, in the mountains or a strand of desolate beach, at a discrete remove from the pressures of politics and society, we begin to understand the range and importance of Chōmei's account. We might also adjust our sense of a literary "monument," of a "classic" work of canonical stature, to accommodate other understandings of how literary strength or spiritual value can be recognized or measured.

The "Account of my Hut" has been variously described, but to begin simply we can say that it is written in two parts. The first is an illustration of suffering in the world. Here the writing is reminiscent of the apocalyptic Buddhist commentary and parables popular at the time, and finds a visual analogue in those medieval picture scrolls depicting a desiccated world haunted by hungry ghosts. The second part, though nostalgic and often brooding in tone, is yet a celebratory record of how the author recovered, under specific conditions, at a particular place, what he calls "peace," or else minimally, "absence of grief." It is an account, finally, of a cultural survivor, who had witnessed dramatic and ultimately far-reaching changes. No modern Tokyo writer, sipping coffee under a naked light bulb, recollecting the glow of fireflies, had greater material cause for nostalgia than did Chōmei.

Plainly, this short, diary-like rendering we know as "An Account of My Hut" offers no thorough historical record of occurrences in the second half of the twelfth century (in brief, the advent of the medieval age at this time brought with it the rise to power of the provincial military or samurai class, accompanied by warfare and widespread disorder). But neither does Chōmei ignore completely the sights and the consequences of that history, as does much later medieval writing, where concrete reference to worldly distress seems but a lapse of concentration, so strong is the meditative urge. The "Account," to be sure, is the work of a cleric, whose adopted faith teaches most fundamentally that the world is a place of suffering, that the things of the world are illusory, inconstant, impermanent. It is a work moreover which, from beginning to end, means to be instructive (when Chōmei claims that he is writing to please himself, as though he had no audience, he is affecting a familiar stance taken, among others, by Sei Shōnagon when she wrote her *Pillow Book* ca. 996). Yet the didactic tone is modulated, where it does not break off altogether. The will to transmit abstract religious truth fades away, and in its place we find another impulse: to speak in a personal, lyrical way of suffering and a path toward tranquility. In this sense, the "Account" is no mere tract which heaps scorn on this "cracked husk of a world," but rather a guide directing us to a remote mountain hut, where in solitude Chōmei reveals affection for all that the world has torn and scattered—for a whole culture uprooted, unhoused, in need of shelter, however fragile or temporary.

For many, it seemed, religion itself was to provide that shelter. In fact, a number of popular Buddhist revival movements had emerged and were enthusiastically embraced in Chōmei's day. Their popularity sprang, no doubt, from the sheer scale of change, wherein people of every place in society were daily brought face to face with uncertainty. This historical predicament was given heightened significance in the notion of *mappō*, or the "last days of the Law." According to Buddhist chronology, in this phase the world would lapse into degeneracy, laws and rites would be imperfectly observed, and merely ordinary suffering would yield to chaos. This age was to have begun fifteen hundred years after the Buddha's birth, and so by a numerical estimate, in 1052, and was to continue for an indefinite period. This put Chōmei and his culture squarely within a sick, decadent cycle, and gives a distinctly religious aura to that litany of disasters by which the "Account" begins.

And so the Fire which sweeps the capital, which was a fire in fact and can be documented, assumes figural significance as an inevitable inferno, brought on by the vanity of city-dwellers. The Whirlwind, given realistic detail as "roofs of bark or thatch were driven like winter leaves in the wind," also reminds the author of "the blasts of Hell," and is of such uncommon force that "it must be a presage of terrible things to come." The Moving of the Capital, which was a historical occurrence, seems a pure sign of instability, the unexpected, provoking both anxiety and a painful comparison between these days and the past, when rulers were wise and forbearing, and people presumably did not "all feel uncertain as drifting clouds." With the Famine there is the graphic scene of bodies decomposing along the banks of the Kamo River, and of an infant, unaware its mother was dead, still sucking at her breast; yet it also totalizes the author's vision, as he sees that the world is one of "foulness and evil." Finally, the Earthquake seems to signal the end, as "mountains crumbled and rivers were buried, the sea tilted over and immersed the land"; as for damage throughout the capital, "not a single mansion, pagoda, or shrine was left whole." Considered the most benign of the four elements, the earth itself had thus broken apart to afflict the people. With this, Chōmei concludes his litany of disaster and extraordinary suffering, drawing out the ultimate lesson: "of the vanity and meaninglessness of the world."

As mentioned earlier, Chōmei's language in this section has parallels in other religious or secular writings of this general period. In the monk Genshin's *Essentials of Salvation,* for example, a widely known catechetical text, the Hell which awaits karmic evildoers is described as horrifyingly as is Chōmei's Kyoto-Hellfire, even as the heavenly rewards awaiting those who attain salvation, in Genshin's portrayal, assume a certain this-worldly form in the pleasures of his hut, in the way Chōmei will describe them as he continues his "Account." Also, in the warrior tales, and notably in *The Tale of the Heike,* which grew from oral stories which had begun to circulate in Chōmei's day, we find episodes of fire, earthquake, and moving capitals, examples of unnatural disaster and disease, with the reiteration that clearly "the world was fixed on the path of chaos," or again, that "for men of sensitive soul, the world now seemed a hopeless place." Also to be noticed about the *Heike,* whose theme is that of impermanence and the fall of the mighty, and whose subject is the historical struggle between the Heike and the Genji clans, is that the reach toward a certain epical breadth is often interdicted by lyrical intensity ("the blood stained the sand like dark maple leaves"). Here, as in Chōmei's "Account," a way out, a path toward salvation, follows the path of the exile, haunted by the loss of past glory. Here, too, tranquility is recovered in the quiet of a mountain retreat, where the former empress, now a Buddhist nun, waits for death "on a velvety green carpet of moss."

When Chōmei concludes his opening section with a reflective passage on "Hardships of Life in the World," and when he tells us that in his fiftieth year he renounced the world and took Buddhist orders, we are at once given certain biographical facts, as well as the sketch of a literary archetype. For even in better times, indeed, in some of the memorable writing of the lost Heian golden age, we regularly come across the figure of an emperor abdicating or a love-stricken courtier withdrawing in the direction of outlying hills and the contemplative life, even though many such world-weary figures never finally make their vows, or return at intervals to the colorful complications of the city.

In that sense, and just when he seems most "original," setting off on his own solitary path, leaving the vanities of culture and society behind, Chōmei moves modestly but with grim, focused determination, along a literary path once taken. Then he fashions a hut "where, perhaps, a traveler might spend a single night." It is this kind of path, this type of dwelling, which will carry and shelter Saigyō and later Bashō along their own protracted period of exile and wandering. Here too we identify the traveling priest who, in some out of the way but culturally resonant place in Nature, will discover the heroes and heroines of many Nō plays. The hut which Chōmei builds is made of wood and thatch. But it assumes shape because of certain cultural materials which Chōmei knew and used, and sought to rescue.

Like other influential medieval literati, Chōmei was a writer (essayist, compiler of miracle stories, travel diarist, but primarily a *poet*) and a monk. Literature, and especially poetry, came thus to be practiced and preserved as a religion. And the poet's life, like the monk's life, was one of seclusion or exile. It was spare, unadorned, in any practical sense, marginal and precarious. Yet it did have formidable precedents. Genji himself was exiled to a forlorn dwelling on Suma beach, a dark but crucial chapter in Murasaki's great narrative, one of its several illustrations of karma leading even the brightest of lives into darkness. And beside the figure of Genji in this scene is that of Po Chü-i, the most influential of all Chinese poets for classical writers in Japan, who himself built a hut on Mt. Lu (just as beyond Po Chü-i emerges the figure of the Indian recluse-sage, Vimalakīrti).

This is exile, then, but an enabling deprivation. Lacking color, variety, action, its very *blandness* (a trait widely celebrated in Taoist and later Ch'an or Zen texts) generates other insights, other tastes. These Chōmei attempted to identify in his *Mumyōshō* (Notes Without a Name), one of the most famous of all medieval treatises on poetry and aesthetics. Chōmei himself had written poetry in a so-called "new style," notable for its "mystery and depth," or *yūgen*, an aesthetic category of crucial importance to medieval culture. But here, in the question and answer form typical of such discussion, Chōmei feigns ignorance, and asks what "new style" poetry, and its alleged "mystery and depth," might possibly mean. The answer, his own of course, but deferentially attributed to his master, the priest-poet Shunei, gives no definition, but a series of metonymical illustrations:

> on an autumn evening, for example, there is no color in the sky nor any sound, yet although we cannot give any reason for it, we are somehow moved to tears. . . .
>
> again, when one gazes upon the autumn hills half-concealed by a curtain of mist, what one sees is veiled yet profoundly beautiful; such a shadowy scene, which permits free exercise of the imagination in picturing how lovely the whole panoply of scarlet leaves must be, is far better than to see them spread with dazzling clarity before our eyes. . . .
>
> it is only when many meanings are compressed into a single word, when the depths of feeling are exhausted yet not expressed, when an unseen world hovers in the atmosphere of the

> poem, when the near and common are used to express the elegant, when a poetic conception of rare beauty is developed to the fullest extent in a style of surface simplicity—only then, when the conception is exalted to the highest degree and the words are too few, will the poem, by expressing one's feelings in this way, have the power of moving Heaven and Earth within the brief confines of a mere thirty-one syllables, and be capable of softening the hearts of gods and demons. (269)

In the atmosphere of all that Chōmei writes, in the contours of his fragile hut and the misty views of autumn twilight it provides, what if not the old lost world of the Heian court "yet hovers like an unseen world," waiting to be apprehended? Nature immediately and clearly surrounds Chōmei in the mountains, but it is the distant world of a fading culture which he consciously gathers about him:

> On mornings when I feel short-lived as the white wake behind a boat, I go to the banks of the river and, gazing at the boats plying to and fro, compose verses in the style of the Priest Mansei. Or if of an evening the wind in the maples rustles the leaves, I recall the river at Jinyō, and play the lute in the manner of Minamoto no Tsunenobu. If still my mood does not desert me, I often tune my lute to the echoes in the pines, or pluck the notes of the Melody of the Flowering Stream, modulating the pitch to the sound of the water.

What Chōmei sees in Nature are not "unmediated visions," generated by the force of the poet's free imagination. Setting out on an "ambitious journey," Chōmei passes through the fields of Awazu, there to "pay my respects to the remains of Semimaru's hut"; crossing the Tanagami River, he visits the tomb of still another Heian poet, Sarumaru. These are lyrical movements in prose, through sights and sounds recorded by other wanderers. Even "the hooting of owls," a startling sound suggestive of the stark isolation of the mountain, contributes to Chōmei's "endless pleasure," since Saigyō had also heard and sung of the owl's "eerie cries." Far beyond Chōmei's hut, in the city, the world rages and people fall victim to a dizzying flux. But inside the hut, where on a shelf rest his books of poetry and music and extracts from the sacred writings, and beside them a folding koto and a lute, or in the Nature which immediately surrounds it, Chōmei lives both in solitude, and in the company of a tradition he willfully places in all he hears and sees.

Throughout the medieval period, it is the poet who most movingly illuminates this forlorn, tumble-down, autumnal scene. But it is in the prose-poetry of Chōmei's "Account" that within this scene, if dimly and in monochrome, emerges a human figure—a medieval portrait of the artist, though here an old man. The "Account" warns us of disaster and hardship in the world. And it reveals the path of renunciation, which leads into Nature and the crude but comforting arrangement of a hut ten feet square. Still, it is Chōmei himself, the aging poet-priest, who is the hidden, and so in the terms of medieval aesthetics, the truly valuable subject of this "Account."

Chōmei is "hidden" insofar as he does not stand forward in this work and present a whole life for our scrutiny and judgment, which seems to be the dramatic burden St. Augustine or Rousseau bear. His are modest claims: "I seek only tranquility. I rejoice in the absence of grief." When he tells us what he knows, of the world, of human dwellings, and finally of attachment, Chōmei reveals himself as an all too human monk. He is weak both by the standards of the world he has renounced; and weak before his religion's imperative, since he remains attached to what is, after all, illusory.

But Chōmei is strong in a way that is comprehensible, given the history he experienced. He knew that much of the past was gone, and much else would not last. He mourned what was lost, and gathered about him what was left. In a hut on Toyama in 1212, he recorded the exact site, the day-to-day moments, where he eked out his own, and his tradition's survival.

The Tale of the Heike

H. Paul Varley

The Tale of the Heike is a lengthy war tale (416 pages in the translation into English by Helen McCullough) that recounts the rise and fall of the warrior house of Taira (or Heike) in Japan in the late twelfth century, culminating in the Gempei War of 1180–85 fought by the Taira against the Minamoto (or Genji).[1]

The version of the *Heike* that has been most widely read for many centuries is a 1371 text attributed to an itinerant, blind storyteller named Kakuichi. It is the product of a long process of both written and oral development. According to the best scholarship, the original *Heike* was written by a courtier named Yukinaga sometime about 1220, a quarter of a century or so after the events with which it deals. During the later thirteenth century and the early fourteenth century, it was greatly expanded in size and fictionally embellished, especially by blind storytellers like Kakuichi, who accompanied themselves with lute-like musical instruments called *biwa.* The accretions to the original *Heike* that we attribute to these storytellers were designed in particular to appeal to the dramatic expectations of the storytellers' audiences.

Although usually categorized as a war tale, the *Heike* deals with much more than just warriors and their battles. It is a rich evocation of life in Japan during the tumultuous period of transition from ancient to medieval times, focusing primarily on the affairs of the courtier and warrior aristocrats who were the principal actors of the age.

The war tales as a literary genre are loosely structured and episodic. But the *Heike,* virtually alone among them, also possesses narrative unity because of its powerful and consistently maintained theme of the decline and destruction of the Taira. This sad, ultimately pathetic story must be seen against prevailing attitudes in Japan—at least at the aristocratic level of society—during the years that ushered in medieval times, which brought the warrior or samurai class to national leadership after a long period of growth in the provinces.

The ancient Japanese believed that, beginning in the late eleventh century, the world entered the age of *mappō* or the "end of the Buddhist Law," a time of decline and disorder. To the courtier class, it seemed that not only the Buddhist Law but also the "Imperial Law"—rule by the emperor with the assistance of his courtiers in Kyoto—was in sharp, perhaps irreversible decline. Under such circumstances, it appeared that only warriors, with their coercive powers, might be able to restore order to the country.

Acceptance of the idea of *mappō* was accompanied by the stirring of fervent religious belief in salvation, especially in the form of Pure Land Buddhism based on the promise of the Buddha Amida to save all beings who placed their faith in him by transporting them upon death to a Pure Land paradise in the western realm of the universe. In historical fact, the Pure Land sect was just being established as an independent sect of Buddhism by the priest Hōnen in the final years of the Taira-Minamoto conflict of the late twelfth century, and the sect did not become widely popular until the thirteenth century. In this sense the *Heike,* in which we find one character after another imploring Amida to be saved, is clearly more a product of the thirteenth than the twelfth century.

In addition to its bleakness of outlook based on conviction that the world had entered the age of *mappō,* the *Heike* is suffused with an acute awareness of impermanence *(mujō),* that all things are fleeting, ephemeral, ever-changing. Although impermanence is fundamental to the Buddhist view of life, it is presented with particular intensity in the literature of the medieval age. Thus the *Heike* begins with the famous statement that:

> The sound of the Gion Shōja bells echoes the impermanence of all things; the color of the *sala* flowers reveals the truth that the prosperous must decline. The proud do not endure, they are like a dream on a spring night; the mighty fall at last, they are as dust before the wind. (McCullough, p. 23)

It is the Taira who have prospered, who have become mighty and proud, and who will inevitably fall. The Taira chieftain Kiyomori, having led his clan, although warriors, to preeminence as ministers at the emperor's court in Kyoto, is described as guilty of sins and crimes that are "utterly beyond the power of mind to comprehend or tongue to relate" (p. 23). He has treated members of both the imperial family and the courtier class abominably, and has, against all precedent, made himself the grandfather of an emperor by marrying his daughter into royalty.

The *Heike* is the story of the tragedy of the Taira. But "tragedy" cannot be understood in any classical Western sense. The course of decline and ultimate destruction of the Taira, once begun, is governed by an unrelenting fate *(unmei),* and the Taira themselves become the merest pawns in the functioning of this great, dark force.

In this regard, the *Heike* divides roughly into two parts. In part one, up to the death of Kiyomori in 1181 (he literally boils to death in a fever), we feel little more than contempt for the haughty and arrogant Taira, who believe that "All who do not belong to [our] clan must rank as less than men" (p. 28). But the Minamoto have already begun their rebellion in the provinces against the Taira—the Gempei War started in the eighth month of 1180—and there is no question, from this point, that the Taira will in the end be completely destroyed, so completely that at the finish of the book it is stated: "Thus did the sons of the Heike vanish forever from the face of the earth" (p. 425).

In the second half of the *Heike* the Taira, heretofore despised, increasingly elicit our sympathy, as they suffer defeat after defeat at the hands of the Minamoto. In 1183 they are driven from Kyoto, and thereafter are hunted (by the enemy) and haunted (by memories of their former, glorious existence in the capital). Fleeing from lost battles, they find themselves "drifting on the waves of the western seas" (p. 404), "drawn onward by the tides" (p. 255), and "in aimless flight" (p. 370).

Like most of the war tales, the *Heike* is primarily concerned not with the victors of medieval warfare but with those, such as the Taira, who lose out. As the fate of the Taira moves steadily toward oblivion, the fortunes of the Minamoto rise. Yet the author of the *Heike* (to speak of him in the singular, for convenience) never shifts his focus from the Taira and their somber story. Even the Minamoto chieftains who appear most importantly in the *Heike*, Yoshinaka and Yoshitsune, are prominent losers, victims of the suspicion and jealousy of the supreme Minamoto commander, Yoritomo. At the same time Yoritomo, founder of the Kamakura Bakufu and, by any standard, one of the great victors in Japanese history, appears in the *Heike* as a remote, indistinct figure.

The tragedy of the Taira, as they are driven inexorably toward their destruction, is made more poignant by the portrayal of them as elegant, refined, and courtier-like. Thus we find Kiyomori's brother Tadanori, shortly before he is killed in battle, imploring the famous poet Fujiwara no Shunzei to include even one of his poems in a forthcoming imperially authorized anthology. Tadanori claims that he will "rejoice in [his] grave and become [Shunzei's] guardian spirit" (p. 247). And when the slayer of the youthful Taira general

Atsumori at the battle of Ichinotani discovers a flute in a brocade bag at Atsumori's waist, he cries out:

> There are tens of thousands of riders in our eastern [Minamoto] armies, but I am sure none of them has brought a flute to the battlefield. Those court nobles (i.e., the Taira) are refined men! (p. 317)

Even the dashing Minamoto chieftain Yoshitsune, who is destined to go down in history and legend as probably the most famous and best-loved of all Japanese samurai, is described in the *Heike* as, in appearance and bearing, "not the equal of the dregs of the Heike" (p. 357).

Perhaps the best example in the *Heike* of a Taira who is portrayed much like a court noble is Koremori, grandson of Kiyomori and father of Rokudai, the "last of the Taira." We first encounter Koremori, apart from passing references, in the early stages of the Gempei War, where he shows himself to be an inept military commander. When the time comes for the Taira as a group to depart from Kyoto, Koremori alone among the clan's leaders cannot bring himself to take his wife, the daughter of a courtier, and children with him to face the hardships that undoubtedly lie ahead. He leaves his wife "prostrated . . . in a passion of weeping" and his two children and the ladies-in-waiting "shrieking and screaming without caring who heard them" (p. 245).

As the Taira are forced to move from one place to another, defeated in their battles with the Minamoto, Koremori becomes increasingly despondent and suffers a constant agony of yearning for the capital. He finally absconds from the Taira camp at Yashima on Shikoku Island and, making his way to Mount Kōya, shaves his head and becomes a Buddhist monk. This is in preparation for committing suicide, which he does by drowning himself after making a pilgrimage to Kumano.

While on the pilgrimage, Koremori encounters a monk at a retreat who remembers him from the former, glory days of the Taira. The monk recalls in particular a celebration in the capital years earlier for Retired Emperor Goshirakawa, which was attended by the leading Taira and at which the youthful Koremori danced:

> [Koremori] emerged [from among the Taira], dancing "Waves of the Blue Sea," with a sprig of blossoming cherry tucked behind his headgear. His figure was like a flower coquetting with the dew; his sleeves fluttered in the breeze as he danced; his beauty seemed to brighten the earth and illumine the heavens. (p. 348)

Here, on the eve of his suicide at age twenty-seven, Koremori is remembered in a setting that the *Heike*'s author has clearly taken from the *Tale of Genji*, likening Koremori to the Shining Genji himself, the fictional prototype of the cultured Heian courtier.

In a sense, the courtier-like Taira serve as surrogates in the *Heike* for the courtier class itself, which is losing out to the warriors as the new rulers of the country. But, in combining the qualities of the cultural *(bun)* and the military *(bu)*, the Taira also set a standard as courtier-warriors that was very much admired by later samurai leaders, especially during the Muromachi period (1336–1573).

Many memorable women appear in the pages of the *Heike*, including: Giō and Hotoke, court dancers who are brutally exploited by Kiyomori for his sensual pleasure but who ultimately achieve spiritual fulfillment as nuns; the Minamoto partisan Tomoe, who was both a "remarkably strong archer, and as a swordswoman . . . was a warrior worth a thousand, ready to confront a demon or god, mounted or on foot" (p. 291); and Kiyomori's widow, the Nun of Second Rank, who leaps into the sea with her grandchild, the seven-year-old Emperor Antoku, in the climactic naval battle of Dannoura in 1185, which marked the destruction of the Taira and the end of the Gempei War.

But many other women in the *Heike*, especially those who have married into or serve the Taira, are consigned to the roles of waiting for and mourning their men. Grandmothers, mothers, wives, daughters, nurses, they are the secondary victims of the battlefield casualties of the Gempei War. These sad personages are essentially stereotypes, the creations of storytellers, who typically either become Buddhist nuns to pray for the souls of dead warriors or commit suicide, usually by drowning, in an agony of grief over the warriors.

Stereotypes abound as well among the male characters in the *Heike*. Indeed, apart from the leading performers in the tale, such as Kiyomori, Yoshinaka, Yoshitsune, and Koremori, most of the warriors are stock figures, representing the values that were most esteemed by the samurai class—selfless loyalty to one's lord, military prowess in the "way of the bow and horse," an exaggerated regard for personal honor, a bold and ferocious fighting spirit, and pride in family traditions. There are, in addition, stock villains among the warriors in the *Heike*—although they are far fewer in number—who disgrace their samurai status through acts of cowardice, betrayal, and the like.

We also find in the *Heike* recurrent narrative devices and themes that were used by its storyteller authors, often extemporaneously, to develop and enhance their recitations. Two of these devices were "dressing the heroes," or descriptions in minute detail of the armor and weapons of the leading warriors as they entered battle, and the "naming of names," pre-battle declamations by the heroes in which they recited in booming voices their family lineages and family and personal achievements and, in the process, sought both to bolster the morale of their troops and to intimidate their opponents psychologically.

Still another common narrative device was the description of a battle in terms of "summary" and "scenes"; that is, the presentation first of a general overview of a battle and its contending armies and then the recapitulation of a series of close-up encounters among smaller groups or between individual warriors. Although this division of a battle into summary and scenes was a device convenient to the storyteller's art, it also cohered, in fact, to the actual conditions of warfare in the late twelfth century. The main participants in a battle in this age were mounted warriors who, after an exchange of arrows and a charge, quickly broke ranks to seek worthy opponents—opponents of equal or higher rank—with whom to engage in essentially one-to-one combat.

Among the narrative themes that appear frequently in the *Heike* are those of the loyal retainer or servant following his lord in death, the warrior bidding farewell to a lover or wife before leaving for battle, and—a theme already discussed—the female survivor either committing suicide in grief or taking Buddhist vows to pray for a lover, master, or kin killed in battle. A particularly interesting theme, which appears twice in the *Heike,* is that of "the older warrior who spares (or wishes to spare) a younger enemy because the younger enemy reminds him of his son." This theme is the basis, for example, of the "Death of Atsumori," one of the most cherished stories in the *Heike.*

In this story a Minamoto adherent, Kumagai no Naozane, attacks and wrestles the Taira general Atsumori from his horse at the battle of Ichinotani, wrenching off Atsumori's helmet to cut off his head. To his amazement, Naozane finds himself gazing at a youth "sixteen or seventeen years old, with a lightly powdered face and blackened teeth—a boy just the age of [his] own son . . . and so handsome that Naozane could not find a place to strike" (p. 317). Naozane would willingly free Atsumori, but is forced to kill him to prevent his being captured, and more poorly treated, by others on the Minamoto side. Much of the appeal of this story lies in Atsumori's courtier-like appearance and in Naozane's discovery that Atsumori possesses a flute (a fact mentioned earlier, in the discussion of Taira courtliness).

Throughout the *Heike* there are references to the "luck" of the Taira "running out," and the last chapters of the book are devoted to the final, awful retribution that fate has ordained for them. The Minamoto were not content with crushing the Taira militarily at the battle of Dannoura, which claimed the lives of many Taira leaders; they also killed most of the other leaders they took as prisoners and even tracked down and murdered surviving male children of the clan. Thus, for example, the Taira commander at Dannoura, Kiyomori's second son, Munemori, and his grown, warrior son were executed; and another of Munemori's sons, the eight-year-old Fukushū, was torn from the breast of a nurse and beheaded.

This brutal conduct did not reflect any particular perversity of the Minamoto, but was dictated by the harsh laws of the "way of the warrior." Thoughout their history, the samurai followed the law of the vendetta: that a warrior "must be determined not to live with the slayer [of a parent or lord] under the same heaven" (*Book of Rites*). A corollary to this law was that victors in battles were virtually compelled to exterminate remaining male kin to prevent them from carrying out acts of revenge against them, the victors, in the future. Taira no Kiyomori had ignored this need for extermination and, yielding to the persuasive pleas of women, had allowed the youthful Yoritomo and Yoshitsune of the Minamoto to live after Kiyomori caused the death of their father in 1160. According to the *Heike*, Kiyomori, angrily regretting his error twenty years later, after Yoritomo had launched the Gempei War, blasphemously forswore on his deathbed any posthumous tributes to him, instead demanding of his wife, who sat attending him, to: "Build no halls or pagodas after I die; dedicate no pious works. Dispatch [a] punitive force immediately, decapitate Yoritomo, and hang the head in front of my grave. That will be all the dedication I require" (p. 211).

The last chapter of the *Heike*, "The Initiates' Chapter," is thought to have been created at a date much later than the other twelve chapters, and is not included in some versions of the *Heike*. It contains, however, some of the work's loveliest and most moving passages, as it recounts the final, pathetic years of Kenreimon'in, the Imperial Lady who was both the daughter of Kiyomori and the mother of the tragic young Emperor Antoku. The chapter's story is simple. Kenreimon'in, agonized with grief over the virtual extermination of the Taira—especially the death of the "Former Emperor"—and filled with guilt that she did not drown with so many of her kinsmen and kinswomen at Dannoura, becomes a nun and retires to a Buddhist temple at Ōhara, a remote place in the mountains a short distance to the northeast of the capital. She is visited there by Retired Emperor Goshirakawa, tells him of the religious practices she is engaged in, and recites with much feeling the account of the decline and destruction of her family. Some time after the retired emperor's visit, Kenreimon'in falls ill and dies, praying fervently for rebirth in the Pure Land.

The language and tone of "The Initiates' Chapter" are very much like those of the fictional and historical tales of the Heian period, including the *Tale of Genji*. There are many other passages scattered through the *Heike* of similar language and tone, including those that tell of the wandering of the Taira after their expulsion from Kyoto. Such passages, and "The Initiates' Chapter" as a whole, establish a literary link between the *Heike* and the mainstream of Heian prose writing. They also contribute a sense of sadness and nostalgia based on the classical Heian aesthetic of *mono no aware*, which may be translated as a "sensitivity to things," especially the perishable beauties of human life and nature.

The complex textual and tonal qualities of "The Initiates' Chapter" can be illustrated by the description it contains of the hut (or "hermitage" in the McCullough translation) that Kenreimon'in has constructed for herself at Ōhara:

> The crudely thatched cryptomeria roof seemed scarcely capable of excluding the rain, frost, and dew that vied with the infiltrating moonbeams for admittance. Behind, there were mountains; in front, barren fields where the wind whistled through low bamboo grass. The bamboo pillars, with their many joints, recalled the manifold sorrows of those who dwell apart from society; the brushwood fence, with its loose weave, brought to mind the long intervals between tidings from the capital. (p. 431)

The chief purpose of the hut is to provide an austere setting in which Kenreimon'in can pray not only for her personal salvation but also for the redemption of the Taira clan, which although guilty of grave sins has also been the collective victim of catastrophic forces, described variously as fate, a bad karma, and the will of the gods, that are utterly beyond the comprehension and control of humans. We are told that Kenreimon'in was "zealous . . . in reciting the sutras and invoking Amida's name so that they (the Taira dead) [might] achieve enlightenment."

The above-described hut, then, is a place for the gravest, most serious kind of business, involving release from the toils of what Buddhism regards as an unceasingly sorrowful, suffering existence, salvation, and, ultimately, enlightenment. Yet the hut's setting is pictured in words that also finely evoke the sensibilities of the Heian poet to the perishable, sad beauties of nature as implied in *mono no aware*. And the hut itself—like the hut in Kamo no Chōmei's *Hōjōki* (An Account of My Hut)—is representative of a central image in the aesthetics of deprivation, the aesthetics of the lonely *(sabi)*, withered *(kare)*, and cold *(hie)* that evolved in the medieval age.

The *Heike*, we know from modern scholarship, is largely fictional; but for most of its existence it has been regarded as largely historical, a generally reliable account of the exciting, violent years that led Japan into its medieval age. In any case, no other work of fiction or history is comparable to the *Heike* as a source from which the Japanese over many centuries have derived their sense of the character and ethos of the samurai class. The stories of the *Heike* have been told and retold by countless generations and in countless forms, including the Nō, puppet, and Kabuki theaters, historical novels, the radio, cinema, and television. The appeal of these stories and the characters in them seems to be timeless.

ENDNOTE

The best translation of the *Heike* into English is the one cited in this article: Helen Craig McCullough, tr. *The Tale of the Heike* (Stanford: Stanford University Press, 1988).

1. The Taira and the Minamoto had, by the late twelfth century, become multi-branched clans living in many parts of Japan. The Taira who

play the leading roles in the *Heike* were simply one branch, from Ise province, of this great clan. The leaders of various branches of the Minamoto rose against the Ise Taira in the Gempei (Gem or Gen for Genji and Hei or Pei for Heike) War; and some Taira branches, from the eastern provinces and elsewhere, joined the Minamoto against the Ise Taira.

Kenkō: *Essays in Idleness (Tsurezuregusa)*

Donald Keene

Tsurezuregusa is a collection of essays and observations that range in length from a sentence or two to several pages. The title is derived from a phrase in the preface where the author reveals that he has spent whole days "with nothing better to do" *(tsurezure naru mama ni)*, jotting down whatever thoughts happened to enter his head. The work belongs to a tradition known in Japan (following Chinese examples) as *zuihitsu*, or "following the brush," meaning that the author allowed his writing brush free rein to scribble down anything it chose.

The author of *Tsurezuregusa* is most commonly known by his Buddhist name, Kenkō. His name before he took Buddhist orders is usually given as Urabe no Kaneyoshi, but also sometimes as Yoshida no Kaneyoshi, presumably because he at one time resided in the Yoshida district of Kyoto. The Urabe family were hereditary Shintō diviners, but this background did not keep Kenkō from pursuing

Buddhist studies. The dates of his birth and death have yet to be determined, but it is generally agreed that he was born in 1283 and died in 1352 or somewhat later. As a young man he served at first in a nobleman's household. Later, after his talents were recognized, he was granted official rank, enabling him to serve at the court, where his skill at composing poetry was prized. The knowledge of court precedents and distaste for novelty characteristic of *Tsurezuregusa* may reflect the years he spent in the conservative milieu of the court. At some time before 1313 Kenkō took orders as a Buddhist monk. It is not known why he took this step, but there are strong suggestions in the poetry he composed about this time of increasing disenchantment with the world.

Even after he took orders, however, Kenkō did not reside in a temple but lived by himself at various places around the capital, occasionally traveling elsewhere. During his lifetime he enjoyed a considerable reputation as a poet, and was even known as one of the "four heavenly kings" of the poetry of his time. Some of his poems were included in imperially sponsored anthologies, but they are no longer so highly esteemed. The poems, in the conservative traditions of the Nijō school of poetry, are apt to strike modern readers as being tepid if not downright boring.

Tsurezuregusa was by far Kenkō's most important literary achievement. We do not know just when he wrote the preface and 243 essays that make up the work. Some scholars have suggested that many years elapsed between the composition of the first and last of the essays, but it is more common to date the work between the years 1330 and 1332. This was not a propitious time for a work of reflection. In 1331 the Emperor Go-Daigo staged a revolt against the Hōjō family, who had ruled the country as surrogates of the shoguns in Kamakura, but he was defeated and exiled the following year to the lonely Oki islands in the Sea of Japan. The Hōjō family subsequently set up another imperial prince as the emperor. In 1333 Go-Daigo returned from exile and this time he and his supporters succeeded in overthrowing the Hōjōs. These events often divided families because of conflicting allegiances, but they hardly ruffle the surface of *Tsurezuregusa;* it neither grieves over the turbulent times nor rejoices over the victories of one side or the other, but presents instead the reflections of a strikingly civilized man.

At first glance there seems to be no apparent order to the 243 sections. According to one old tradition, Kenkō wrote down his thoughts as they came to him on scraps of paper which he pasted to the walls of his cottage. Years later, the distinguished poet Imagawa Ryōshun, learning of this unusual wallpaper, had the various scraps of paper removed and arranged them in their present order. This account was long accepted, but modern critics tend to reject it, because they can detect subtle connections linking one section to the next that suggest associations in the writer's mind that would probably not have occurred to another person. At least four clusters of essays were unmistakably composed in sequence, and other links have been found. The oldest surviving text, dated 1431, bears the title *Tsurezuregusa,* but we cannot be sure that this title was given by Kenkō himself. The present arrangement of a preface and 243 numbered sections goes back only to the seventeenth century.

Tsurezuregusa seems to have been unknown to anyone but the author during Kenkō's lifetime. It was first given attention by the poet and critic Shōtetsu (1381–1475), to whom we owe the 1431 text, but the popularity of the work dates only from the seventeenth century. In 1603 the haiku poet Matsunaga Teitoku (1571–1633), who had previously been instructed in *Tsurezuregusa* by a scholar of the old school, offered lectures to the general public on the work, breaking the tradition of secret transmission of the traditions surrounding the classics. *Tsurezuregusa* subsequently became one of the books that every educated Japanese was expected to have read, and Kenkō's thoughts affected many people. The influence of *Tsurezuregusa,* especially on the formation of Japanese aesthetic preferences, can hardly be exaggerated.

Buddhist thought naturally supplied the background for much of what Kenkō wrote. Specifically Buddhist doctrine is sometimes expressed, but more typical of the work are the general Buddhist beliefs that colored Kenkō's thinking—that the world is no more than a temporary abode and that all things in this world are impermanent. Kenkō also described the full cycle of birth, growth, sickness, and death, followed by rebirth: "With the falling of the leaves, too, it is not that first the leaves fall and then young shoots form; the leaves fall because the budding from underneath is too powerful to resist." But the predominant tone is provided by Kenkō's conviction that worldly achievements and possessions are without lasting significance in a world that it is itself no more than transitory. Many passages in *Tsurezuregusa* convey this belief, including, "The intelligent man, when he dies, leaves no possessions." "If you have power, do not trust in it; powerful men are the first to fall. You may have possessions, but they are not to be depended on; they are easily lost in a moment." "When I see the things people do in their struggle to get ahead, it reminds me of someone building a snowman on a spring day, making ornaments of precious metals and stones to decorate it, and then erecting a hall to house it."

Kenkō again and again reproached the man who delays taking the Great Step of entering the Buddhist priesthood until he has achieved desired success: "My observation of people leads me to conclude, generally speaking, that even people with some degree of intelligence are likely to go through life supposing they have ample time before them. But would a man fleeing because a fire has broken out in his neighborhood say to the fire, 'Wait a moment, please!'? To save his life, a man will run away, indifferent to shame, abandoning his possessions. Is a man's life any more likely to wait for him? Death attacks faster than fire or water, and is harder to escape. When its hour comes, can you refuse to give up your aged parents, your little children, your duty to your master, your affection for others, because they are hard to abandon?" Again, "You must not wait until you are old before you begin practicing the way. Most of the gravestones from the past belong to men who died young."

Such passages are testimony to the depth of Kenkō's religious convictions. Sometimes he also found unusual implications in Buddhist doctrine, as when he traced the close relationship between impermanence and beauty, a particularly Japanese aesthetic principle. He wrote, "If man were never to fade away like the dews of Adashino, never to vanish like the smoke over Toribeno, but lingered forever in this world, how things would lose their power to move us! The most precious thing in life is its uncertainty." Other Buddhists rarely suggested that impermanence itself was valuable; like the ancient Greeks who declined to call a man happy until he was dead, the uncertainty of life was frequently called a source of grief. But unless (like Kenkō) the Japanese had appreciated impermanence, they surely would not have displayed such love for cherry blossoms, which hardly bloom before they fall; and their preference for building houses of perishable materials like wood and paper, rather than of brick or stone, was surely not due only to a fear of earthquakes. The falling of the cherry blossoms is regretted in innumerable poems, but the very brevity of their blossoming imparts a special beauty and makes them more precious than hardier flowers.

Ironically, wooden statues and temples erected in Japan a thousand years ago survive, despite the perishable nature of the materials, but the Japanese made no conscious effort to achieve the permanence of marble. Whatever has survived has also aged, and this faded quality, the reminder of impermanence, has been prized. Kenkō quoted with approbation the priest Ton'a who said, "It is only after the silk wrapper has frayed at top and bottom and the mother-of-pearl has fallen from the roller, that a scroll looks beautiful." Kenkō constantly warned of the shortness of life and the close presence of death, and urged people to hasten in the path of Buddha, but he also found in the shortness of human life the source of its poignance. His delight in the worn, the obviously used, contrasts with the Western craving for objects in mint condition and the desire to annihilate time by restoring works of art to so pristine a state as to make people exclaim, "It might have been painted yesterday!" The Japanese craftsman who repairs a broken or chipped bowl fills in the cracks with gold, as if to emphasize the ravages of time.

Kenkō's preference for objects that reveal the effects of impermanence was accompanied by a similar preference for the irregular and the incomplete. He wrote, "In everything, no matter what it may be, uniformity is undesirable. Leaving something incomplete makes it interesting, and gives one the feeling there is room for growth." Again, "It is typical of the unintelligent man to insist on assembling complete sets of everything. Imperfect sets are better."

No doubt most people in Kenkō's time preferred to own complete sets rather than odd volumes, but as anyone knows who has ever confronted the grim volumes of a set of the Harvard Classics or the Complete Works of Sir Walter Scott, they do not tempt one to browse. Asymmetry and irregularity not only allow the possibility of growth but the participation of the outsider; perfection tends to choke the imagination.

Kenkō's love of the imperfect led him to stress also the importance of beginnings and ends: "Are we to look at cherry blossoms only in full bloom, the moon only when it is cloudless? To long for the moon while looking on the rain, to lower the blinds and be unaware of the passing of the spring—these are even more deeply moving. Branches about to blossom or gardens strewn with faded flowers are worthier of our admiration." Even in Japan a fondness for the imperfect has usually not caused people to rush to see cherry blossoms before they open, or to wait until they are scattered before paying a visit; and in the West the climactic moments—when Laocoön and his sons are caught in the serpent's embrace or the soprano hits the much-awaited high C—have been given greatest attention. But for Kenkō the climax, whether the full moon or the full flowering of the cherry trees, was less suggestive than the beginnings and ends: the full moon and the cherry blossoms at their peak do not suggest the crescent moon or buds, but the crescent and the buds (or the waning moon and strewn flowers) can evoke with poignance the full cycle. In Japanese poetry hoped-for love affairs and regretted affairs that have ended are often treated, but hardly a poem expresses the pleasure of requited love.

Irregularity and incompleteness accord with another element of Japanese aesthetics emphasized by Kenkō: simplicity, the art of suggesting more than is stated. He wrote, "A house which multitudes of workmen have polished with every care, where strange and rare Chinese and Japanese furnishings are displayed, and even the grasses and trees of the garden have been trained unnaturally, is ugly to look at and most depressing." It is easier for us to assent to this opinion than it would have been for Western readers of a century ago. In the West the house "which multitudes of workmen have polished with every care" was for long considered beautiful, as we know from photographs showing the profusion of treasures with which the drawing rooms of the rich were adorned. Gardens where even the trees and plants have been trained unnaturally still attract visitors to the great houses of Europe.

Kenkō elsewhere stated, "People agree that a house which has plenty of spare room is attractive to look at and may be put to many different uses." By a curious coincidence, this preference is now a commonplace of decorators in the West, for whom "less is more" has replaced richness of effect as an ideal. No doubt Kenkō's tastes were formed by earlier traditions, but he was probably the first to define these tastes, and when *Tsurezuregusa* came to be generally circulated it surely influenced the tastes of later Japanese.

Kenkō exercised even greater influence with his descriptions of the proper behavior of the well-bred man. Indeed, *Tsurezuregusa* is a kind of manual of gentlemanly conduct. "A man should avoid displaying deep familiarity with any subject. Can one imagine a well-bred man talking with the airs of a know-it-all, even about a matter with which he is in fact familiar? . . . It is impressive when a man is always slow to speak even on subjects he knows thoroughly, and does not speak at all unless questioned." Kenkō often contrasted his gentleman with the insensitive, boorish people who make up most of society: "The man of breeding never appears to abandon himself completely to his pleasures; even his manner of enjoyment is detached . . . When the well-bred man tells a story he addresses himself to one person, even if many people are present, though the others too listen, naturally . . . You can judge a person's breeding by whether he is quite impassive even when he tells an amusing story or laughs a great deal even when relating a matter of no interest." "The well-bred man does not tell stories about prodigies." "When a person who has always been extremely close appears on a particular occasion reserved and formal towards you . . . some people will undoubtedly say, 'Why act that way now, after all these years?' But I feel that such behavior shows sincerity and breeding."

Early in the work Kenkō stated the cultural qualifications of a gentleman: "A familiarity with orthodox scholarship, the ability to compose poetry and prose in Chinese, a knowledge of Japanese poetry and music are all desirable, and if a man can serve as a model to others in matters of precedent and court ceremony, he is truly impressive. The mark of an excellent man is that he writes easily in an acceptable hand, sings agreeably and in tune, and, appearing reluctant to accept when wine is pressed on him, is not a teetotaler." These abilities continued until recent times to be the marks of a gentleman in Japan.

Kenkō's insistence on the importance of knowing precedents and court ceremony accounts for his inclusion of the least interesting parts of the text of *Tsurezuregusa*. He clung to each usage sanctified by tradition, even though some were surely meaningless even in his day. He wrote, "It is best not to change something if changing it will not do any good," but gave no instances of desirable changes. Instead, he lamented each violation of precedent and praised each act of fidelity to the old ways. He described, for example, how an official, deciding that the file chest in his office was unsightly, ordered it to be rebuilt in a more elegant style. Other officials, familiar with court precedents, voiced the opinion that the chest was not to be altered without due consideration: "This article of government property, dating back many reigns, had by its very dilapidation become a model." Kenkō enthusiastically approved the final decision not to remodel the chest.

His nostalgia for the past is eloquently described in various sections, notably: "When I sit down in quiet meditation, the one emotion hardest to fight against is a longing in all things for the past." Such feelings made him treasure even the least important tradition. He was impressed by the Abbess Genki who remembered from childhood that the "bell-shaped windows in the Kan'in Palace were rounder and without frames." For Kenkō even a window whose shape was slightly at variance with tradition was indicative of the degeneracy of the age. He was dismayed that no one knew any longer the proper shape of a torture rack nor the manner of attaching a criminal.

Various essays devoted to precedents and correct usage were omitted from eighteenth and nineteenth century editions of the work, evidence that they had lost their interest, but they are no less typical of Kenkō than the more celebrated essays. He so startles us again and again with his insights into the characters of people, the nature of beauty, the passage of time and other eternally moving subjects that we are likely to forget that he was acutely aware of belonging to a particular age. He feared that people of his time might be so involved in the turbulent changes that affected everyone as to destroy by ignorance or indifference the civilization that had been created in Japan. It probably seemed just as important to him to preserve the correct nomenclature for palace ceremonies as to preserve the old texts or the works of art that survived from the past. His work is not systematic, and its pages even contain contradictions, but it is central to an understanding of Japanese taste. Kenkō was not the first to be aware of the principles he enunciates, but he gave them permanence by his eloquent and affecting presentation.

ENDNOTE

A full translation of the *Tsurezuregusa* has been made by Donald Keene and published under the title *Essays in Idleness* (New York: Columbia University Press, 1967).

The Poetry of Matsuo Bashō

Haruo Shirane

Modern *haiku* derives from the seventeen-syllable *hokku,* or opening verse, of *haikai,* or comic linked verse. In the early Edo period, when Matsuo Bashō (1644–94) began his career as a *haikai* poet, the seventeen-syllable *hokku* was regarded primarily as the beginning of a linked verse *(renga)* sequence, which usually consisted of thirty-six or a hundred links (5/7/5, 7/7, 5/7/5, 7/7 etc.), composed alternately by one or more poets. Bashō considered himself to be, first and foremost, a comic linked-verse poet and made a profession as a *haikai* teacher, but he often composed independent *hokku*—commonly referred to by modern readers as *haiku*—for which he is primarily known today and which lie at the heart of his prose narratives.

In a linked verse session, the author of the *hokku* was required to include a *kigo,* a seasonal word, which functioned as a greeting to the gathered poets and which established a special line of communication between the poet and the audience—a pipeline that proved crucial to the independent *hokku*. In the course of poetic history, the seasonal words used in classical poetry (the thirty-one syllable *waka* and then later orthodox linked verse, or *renga*) had come to embody particular emotions, moods, and images. Thus, the word "spring rain" *(harusame)*, which always meant a soft, steady drizzle, brought sweet thoughts; the long, oppressive "summer rain" *(samidare)* meant depression; and the cold and sporadic "early winter showers" *(shigure)* became associated with the uncertainty and impermanence of life. The importance of seasonal words in the *hokku* is evident in the following poems from the beginning and end of Bashō's *The Narrow Road to the Deep North (Oku no hosomichi)*.

yuku haru ya
tori naki uo no
me wa namida

The passing of spring:
Birds cry, and in the eyes
Of the fish are tears.
(1689)

hamaguri no
futami ni wakare
yuku aki zo

A clam being parted
From its shell at Futami—
The passing of autumn.
(1689)

The two respective seasonal words, "the passing of spring" *(yuku haru)* and "the passing of autumn" *(yuku aki)*, indicate more than the temporal dimensions of the poems; in the classical tradition they are strongly associated with the sorrow of separation, particularly that caused by a journey. In the first poem, nature at large—

here represented by a bird and a fish—reveals its sorrow at the departure of spring. Through the connotations of the seasonal word, the same poem also expresses Bashō's sorrow at leaving behind his friends. In the last poem, the departure of autumn (and implicitly that of Bashō) becomes as difficult and as painful as prying apart the shells of a clam.[1] On the surface, the two poems appear to depict only nature, but the seasonal words, coupled with the larger context, underscore a recurrent theme of *The Narrow Road to the Deep North*: the sorrow of the eternal traveler.

Haikai deliberately employs contemporary language and subject matter, which classical poetry (the thirty-one syllable *waka*) was forbidden to use. *Haikai* is also informed by a sense of the comic, which usually derives from humorous subject matter, from verbal play, or from parody of traditional poetry and literature. Ichū, a *haikai* theorist of the Danrin school, once stated that "A poem that draws on the literary tradition and at the same time parodies it is *haikai*." The same is true of much of Bashō's poetry, though in a more subtle manner than in earlier *haikai*. A good example is Bashō's famous frog poem, which marks the beginning of his mature poetry, of the so-called "Bashō-style."

furu ike ya
kawazu tobikomu
mizu no oto

An ancient pond—
A frog leaps in,
The sound of water.
(1686)

Kawazu ("frog"), a seasonal word for spring, was a popular poetic topic, appearing as early as the *Manyōshū* (mid-8th c.). The following *waka* appears in a section on frogs (vol. 10, no. 2161–65).

kami tsu se ni
kawazu tsuma yobu
yū sareba

koromode samumi
tsuma makamu toka

On the upper rapids
A frog calls for his lover.
Is it because,
His sleeves chilled by the evening,
He wants to share his pillow?
(vol. 10, no. 2165)

By the Heian period (late 8th to late 12th c.), the *kawazu* became almost exclusively associated with the blossoms of the *yamabuki* (kerria), the bright yellow mountain rose, and with limpid mountain streams, as in the following poem from *Kokinshū* (early 9th c.).

kawazu naku
Ide no yamabuki
chirinikeri
hana no sakari ni
awamashi mono o

At Ide, where the frogs cry,
The yellow rose
Has already scattered.
If only I had come when
The flowers were in full bloom!
(Spring II, no. 125, Anonymous)[2]

In medieval poetry, the poet was often required to compose on the poetic essence *(hon'i)* of a given topic, which, in the case of the *kawazu*, became its beautiful voice. In a fashion typical of *haikai*, or comic linked verse, Bashō's poem on the frog works against these traditional associations. In place of the plaintive voice of the frog singing in the rapids or calling out for his lover, Bashō gives us the plop of the frog jumping into the water. And instead of the elegant image of a frog in a fresh mountain stream beneath the bright yellow rose, the *hokku* presents a stagnant pond. According to *Kuzu no Matsubara* (1692), one of Bashō's disciples suggested that the first line be "A yellow rose—" *(yamabuki ya)*, an image which would have remained within the associative bounds of traditional poetry. Bashō's version, by contrast, provides a surprising and witty twist on the classical perception of frogs.

This is not to say that Bashō rejects the seasonal association of the frog with spring. The *kawazu* appears in spring, summer, and autumn, but in the seasonal handbooks used by both Bashō and his readers, the frog is listed in the category of mid-spring along with other insects and reptiles that emerge from underground hibernation in mid-spring. As a seasonal word, the frog thus deepens the contrast or tension between the first half of the poem, the image of an old pond—the atmosphere of long silence and rest—and the second part, a moment in spring, when life and vitality have suddenly (with a surprising plop) returned to the world.

In Bashō's time, the seasonal words in *haikai* formed a vast pyramid, capped at the top by the key seasonal topics *(kidai)* of the classical tradition—the cherry blossoms (spring), the cuckoo (summer), the moon (autumn), and the snow (winter)—which remained the most popular topics even for early Edo *haikai* poets. Spreading out from this narrow peak were the other seasonal topics derived from classical poetry. Occupying the bottom and the widest area were the *kigo*, which literally numbered in the thousands by Bashō's day, used by *haikai* poets. In contrast to the seasonal topics at the peak, which were highly conventional and conceptual, those that formed the base were drawn from and directly reflected contemporary life. Unlike the elegant diction at the top of the pyramid, the new, ever-expanding words at the base were earthy, sometimes vulgar, and drawn from a variety of "tongues," particularly those of popular Edo culture and society.

Bashō's place in *haikai* history can be defined as an attempt to tread the "narrow road" between the complex, rigidly defined, aesthetic order centered on traditional seasonal topics and a strongly anti-traditional movement that sought to break out and explore new topics, new subject matter, and new poetic language. As the frog poem suggests, Bashō draws on the classical tradition, not in order to return to it, but to provide it with new life. Indeed, for those aware of the cluster of associations that have accumulated around the seasonal words, the beauty of Bashō's poetry often lies, as it does in the frog poem, in the subtle and ironic tension between the traditional associations and the new presentation.

It has often been noted that the effect of the frog poem derives from the intersection of the momentary and the eternal, of movement and stillness. The two parts of the poem, divided by the cutting word, interpenetrate, the sound of the frog accentuating the stillness of the ancient pond and the quiet atmosphere highlighting the momentary. A similar effect can be found in the following poem in *The Narrow Road to the Deep North.*

shizukasa ya
iwa ni shimiiru
semi no koe

How still it is!
Into the rock it pierces —
The cicada shrill.
(1689)

In this summer poem, the cries of the cicada, which seem to sink into the surrounding rocks, deepen the profound feeling of silence. According to one modern commentator, the spirit of the speaker becomes one with the voice of the cicada and penetrates the rocks, arriving at a deep, inner silence.[3] In a number of *hokku* written by Bashō at this time, a small, vulnerable, or fragile creature—a cicada, a frog, a cricket, etc.—is cast against a temporally or spatially unbounded setting, creating a feeling of "loneliness" *(sabishisa)*, a poignant and tender mood that is savored and appreciated for the inner peace and quiet communion it brings with nature.[4]

Shikō, one of Bashō's foremost disciples, once noted that "loneliness and humor are the essential style of *haikai.*" "Humor is the name of *haikai*, and loneliness the essence of its poetry" *(Zokugoron).* Bashō referred to this unique combination as *sabi*, which is to be distinguished from *sabishisa* ("loneliness"), a medieval poetic and aesthetic ideal that represents only part of *sabi*. Kyorai, another of Bashō's prominent disciples, reminds us of the distinction between the two: "*Sabi* is the complexion of a verse. It does not mean a tranquil and lonely verse. *Sabi* exists in both lively and quiet verses" *(Kyoraishō).* As the word *haikai*, which literally means "comic," suggests, *haikai* was originally comic verse. In early Edo *haikai*, the comic element derived almost entirely from parody of classical poetry (*waka* and orthodox linked verse), from the playful destruction of the aesthetic world created by classical tradition. Many of Bashō's earlier poems are in fact amusing, clever displays of wit that make light of the conventions of classical poetry. However, Matsuo Bashō's mature poetry, which begins from the period of the frog poem, transformed *haikai* into a serious form that embraced larger human and worldly concerns even as it retained its comic roots. The *haikai*, or comic, element in Bashō's mature poems usually derives from a sense of "newness" *(atarashimi)* or the unexpected, which brings a smile rather than the laughter typical of earlier *haikai*. In the frog poem, it is the unexpected, sudden plop of the frog that provides the comic overtone.[5] The solemn opening line, "An ancient pond—" *(furuike ya)*, however, tempers and internalizes this comic aspect, making it part of a highly meditative poem. This ironical movement or tension, which is both serious and light, profound and minor, is *sabi*, a hallmark of Bashō's mature style.

Bashō and his disciples speak broadly of two fundamental kinds of *hokku*: the "single-topic" *(ichimotsu shitate) hokku* and the "combination" *(toriawase) hokku*. The "single-topic" *hokku* treats only one subject, as in the following examples by Bashō.

kegoromo ni
tsutsumite nukushi
kamo no ashi

In fur robes,
They are warmly wrapped—
The feet of the wild duck.
(1693)

bii to naku
shirigoe kanashi
yoru no shika

Crying "Bee—,"
The sadness of the trailing voice.
A deer at night.
(1694)

Both poems describe a single topic, the feet of a wild duck and the voice of the deer, albeit in a surprising and fresh manner.

The "combination" *(toriawase)*, by contrast, combines two or more different images into one *hokku*. Bashō's disciples further divided the "combination" into two types: those "outside the circumference," which bring together two (and sometimes more) images that traditionally have not been found together, and those "inside the circumference," which combine images that have been associated with each other in the classical tradition. Bashō once said that "Combinations that emerge from within the circumference are rarely superior, and all of them are old-fashioned" *(Udanohōshi)*. As we have seen, in classical poetry the frog was usually combined with fresh water and the yellow rose *(yamabuki)* to form an elegant and bright image. Bashō's poem effectively goes outside that "circumference," but had Bashō used "A yellow rose—" *(Yamabuki ya)* instead of "An ancient pond—," as one of his disciples suggested, he would have stayed within the "circumference."

Sometimes a "combination" of distant, extra-"circumference" images is held together by an intermediary image, as in the following poem by Bashō.

aoyagi no
doro ni shidaruru
shiohi kana

Branches of the willow
Drooping down into the mud—
The tide is out.
(*Sumidawara*, 1694)

The gap between the two elements of the "combination," the "willow" *(aoyagi)* and "low tide" *(shiohi)*, two classical images never associated in the poetic tradition, is bridged by the earthy, nonclassical image of "mud" *(doro)*. The *haikai*, or comic, element derives from the vernal, feminine image of the elegant willow, admired for its gracefully drooping branches, being unexpectedly soiled by the mud on the bay bottom.

Bashō's distant "combinations" are closely associated with the "fragrant links" *(nioi-zuke)* that he regarded as an aesthetic and literary ideal in *haikai* linked verse. The following example is from a thirty-six link verse sequence in *Sarumino (The Monkey's Raincoat*, 1691).

sō yaya samuku
tera ni kaeru ka

A priest returning to a
Temple as he grows cold?
(Bonchō)

saruhiki no
saru to yo o furu
aki no tsuki

A monkey trainer,
Passing through life with a monkey —
The moon of autumn.
(Bashō)

In the first verse, a priest has come back from a chilly day of begging for alms, and in the second verse a monkey trainer, fated to pass his days with a monkey, is juxtaposed to an autumn moon, an image of loneliness. The two scenes are completely unrelated to each other on both the referential and rhetorical levels, and yet they are linked by a common mood, by the solitary and humble sadness of two individuals who stand outside the warm embrace of society. The second verse (by Bashō) probes the chilly atmosphere and loneliness of the previous verse (by Bonchō) even as it stands at a distance. To use *haikai* terminology, the new verse "lets go" *(tsukihanasu)* of the previous verse even as it catches its "fragrance" *(nioi)*.

The same kind of "fragrant" link can be found within the confines of a single *hokku*, as in the following verse by Bashō.

kiku no ka ya
Nara ni wa furuki
hotoketachi

Chrysanthemum scent —
In old Nara the ancient
Statues of Buddha.
(1694)

The chrysanthemum, which blooms amidst the bright colors and leaves of autumn, possesses an old-fashioned but refined fragrance. The dignified and elegant statues of the Buddha that fill the temples in the old capital of Nara have no overt connection to the scent of chrysanthemums—the statues are not surrounded by flowers—and yet the overtones of the two parts overlap: both possess an antique, elegant atmosphere that is at once familiar.

The "distant combination" can take the form of a question and an answer, one of the formats from which Japanese linked verse first arose. The following poem was written shortly after Bashō fell ill on a journey.

kono aki wa
nande toshi yoru
kumo ni tori

Why have I aged
This autumn?
A bird in the clouds.
(1694)

According to one of Bashō's disciples, the speaker, hampered by the vicissitudes of old age, looks enviously at the bird in the floating clouds, symbolic of eternal travel. The bird in the clouds also reflects the speaker's loneliness. Whatever connection one finally decides to draw, the reader must leap from one mode or state to another (in this instance, from a subjective, lyrical statement to an objective description).

The "combinations" found in Bashō's *hokku* do not usually employ simile or metaphor proper, in which a direct transference is made between one image and another. Instead, Bashō relies on selective juxtaposition, in which the connections are only suggested. The *hokku* usually juxtaposes either two antithetical items or two similar elements. In either case, the combination is usually unexpected and "new"—that is to say, it works against traditional associations, shedding new light on both sides of the "combination" and often joining a classical topic with a nonclassical image or phrase.

The notion of "fragrance" *(nioi)* also applies to the relationship between Bashō's prose and the embedded poetry. Like the two parts of the *hokku*, the poem and the surrounding prose often highlight each other even as they can be read and appreciated independently of each other. The linking by "fragrance," or overlapping overtones, also occurs between poetry and painting. Instead of the poem simply reflecting the content of the painting or sketch on which it appears, we often find the two juxtaposed, creating a montage effect, in which the poetry and the painting are joined only by "fragrance."

The *toriawase* ("combination") is usually made possible by the "cutting word" *(kireji,)* one of the formal requirements of the *hokku,* which severs the semantic, grammatical, or rhythmic flow of the poem. The "cutting word" frequently takes the form of the exclamatory particle *ya* at the end of the first or second line, or the exclamatory particle *kana* at the end of the poem.[6] According to Bashō, any of the seventeen syllables of the *hokku* can function as a "cutting word" as long as it "severs" the poem. In the frog poem, the "ya" (translated by a dash) at the end of the first line splits the poem into two parts, causing the two halves to reverberate against each other. In typical Bashō fashion, the "cutting word" sets up an opposition or parallel between a visual image and an auditory sensation.

The "cutting word," like the seasonal word, vastly increases the complexity and power of the seventeen-syllable *hokku,* commonly recognized as the shortest poetic form in world literature. The cutting word, however, can only be effective if the recipient makes it so. In linked verse, the *hokku,* or opening verse, was followed by a second verse, that drew on or emerged out of the overtones of the first verse. In the independent *hokku,* or *haiku,* the reader must perform the same task in his or her imagination. To "cut" a verse is to entrust the final meaning to the reader, to allow the audience to participate actively, an aesthetic process similar to the cadenza in pre-Romantic music, in which the composer leaves part of the musical notation blank for the performer. It is no accident that Matsuo Bashō once said, "those verses that reveal seventy or eighty percent of the subject are good. Those that reveal fifty to sixty percent, we never tire of."

Many of the literary characteristics of Bashō's *hokku* are also to be found in his literary travel journals, where much of his best poetry appears. In addition to hundreds of *haibun* (poetic prose) vignettes and essays, Bashō wrote a series of more extended works (all available in English translation), *Nozarashi kikō (Record of a Weather-Exposed Skeleton), Kashima mōde (A Visit to Kashima Shrine), Oi no kobumi (Record of a Travel-Worn Satchel), Sarashina kikō (A Visit to Sarashina Village), Oku no hosomichi (The Narrow Road to the Deep North),* and *Saga nikki (The Saga Diary),* all of which are based on journeys to various parts of Japan. Most of these journeys, particularly that which led to *The Narrow Road to the Deep North,* Bashō's masterpiece, involve a search for or visit to *utamakura,* famous places in Japanese poetry.

Like seasonal words, *utamakura* ("poetic places") were aesthetic clusters, which, as a result of their appearance in famous poems, possessed rich overtones. When used in a poem (or, as Bashō often did, in prose), the established associations radiated out from the *hokku,* providing depth to the seventeen-syllable verse. From as early as the classical period, *utamakura* became popular topics for classical poetry; and like seasonal topics, they assumed fixed associations that the *waka* poet was required to employ. Relying on poetry handbooks, classical poets could easily write about places that they had never seen, just as they composed about aspects of nature that they had never encountered. Bashō broke from this tradition, and in a manner that deliberately recalled certain poet/priests of the classical and medieval past—Nōin, Saigyō, and Sōgi—he journeyed to numerous *utamakura,* where the present met, sometimes in ironic and violent disjunction, with the literary past. If, for most classical poets, the *utamakura* represented a beauty that transcended time and place, Bashō's travels brought him face to face with the impermanence of all things. This tension between the unchanging and the changing, between literary tradition and intense personal experience, between classical diction and the contemporary language lies at the heart of both Bashō's prose and poetry.

The following is from *Record of a Weather-Exposed Skeleton.*

akikaze ya
yabu mo hatake mo
Fuwa no seki

The autumn wind!
Nothing but thicket and fields
At Fuwa Barrier.

Fuwa Barrier (in present-day Gifu Prefecture), originally one of the three main checkpoints in Japan, was abandoned in the late eighth century, but it continued to exist in literature as an *utamakura,* immortalized by the following poem in *Shinkokinshū* by Fujiwara no Yoshitsune.

hito sumanu
Fuwa no sekiya no
itabisashi
arenishi nochi wa
tada aki no kaze

The shingled eaves
Of the guard post at Fuwa,
Where no one lives,
Have collapsed, leaving only
The winds of autumn.
(Msc. 2, no. 1599)

Coming upon the guard post at Fuwa (which literally means "Unbreakable"), the speaker in Bashō's poem finds that even the building has disappeared, leaving only thickets and open fields swept by autumn winds. The *hokku* follows the "poetic essence" *(hon'i)* of Fuwa Barrier (the pathos of decay) as well as that of the "autumn wind" (loneliness). But these classical associations, which are embodied in Yoshitune's *waka,* are re-presented in a new and striking manner, using nonclassical diction: "nothing but thickets and fields," a phrase which subtly contrasts the present with the poetic past.

Bashō repeatedly told his disciples that they "should awaken to the high and return to the low" *(takaku kokoro o satorite, zoku ni kaerubeshi)*. Matsunaga Teitoku, the founder of Edo *haikai*, defined *haikai* as linked verse with *haigon*, vocabulary that classical poetry had excluded as being vulgar and "low" *(zoku)*. The use of *haigon* (literally "*haikai* words") transformed *haikai* into a highly popular form that could be enjoyed by all classes. At the same time, however, *haikai*'s poetic "liberation," particularly the free use of *haigon*, seriously threatened the literary life of *haikai*, making it more a form of amusement than a serious literary genre. Bashō was the first major poet to bring a heightened spiritual and literary awareness to *haikai*, to infuse the "high" *(ga)* into the "low" *(zoku)* of *haikai*, or rather, to seek the "high" in the "low," a pursuit that ultimately transformed the *hokku* into a powerful poetic form. As the frog poem suggests, Bashō sought to find the new in the old, the "high" in the "low," the profound in the trivial, the serious in the comic.

"Awakening to the high" also meant exploring and sharing in the spirit of the "ancients," the superior poets of the past. The long and difficult journeys to *utamakura* were a means of communing with the spirits of the great poets of the past, of sharing in their poetic experience. For Bashō, the great figures were Li Po, Hanshan, Tu Fu, Po Chü-i, in the Chinese tradition, and Saigyō, Sōgi, Rikyū, and Sesshū in the Japanese tradition—most of whom, significantly, had been recluse poets or artists. The work of these "ancients" was bound together, in Bashō's mind, by a common literary spirit, in which the best of *haikai* should share. It was not enough, however, simply to imitate and borrow from the "ancients," whose "high" *(ga)* art—particularly Chinese poetry, *waka*, and *renga*—had become, by Bashō's day, aristocratic, refined, and exclusive. One must also—and here Bashō parts company with his medieval predecessors—return to the "low" *(zoku)*, to the popular, to everyday life, to immediate personal experience, and to the language and "tongues" around us, all of which would continue to change from day to day. It was only by "returning to the low" that one could create poetry with "newness" and lightness, which were critical to the life of *haikai*. For Bashō, it was ultimately the harshness of travel on foot, which combined the pursuit of *utamakura* with the vicissitudes of everyday life, that became the quintessential means of "awakening to the high and returning to the low" and that led to much of his finest poetry.

ENDNOTES

1. Futami, Bashō's destination and a place known for clams, is also a homonym for "shell" *(futa)* and "body" *(mi)*.

2. The phrase "the frogs cry" *(kawazu naku)* functions as an epithet *(makurakotoba)* for Ide (in present-day Kyoto Prefecture), a place famous for its frogs.

3. Ogata Tsutomu, in Ogata Tsutomu, ed., *Haiku no kaishaku to kanshō jiten* (Obunsha, 1979), p. 82.

4. Another famous example is:

> shizukasa ya
> e kakaru kabe no
> kirigirisu
>
> How quiet it is!
> On a wall, where a picture hangs,
> A cricket.
> (Genroku 4, 1691)

5. Another example of the unexpected is:

> hototogisu
> kieyuku kata ya
> shima hitotsu
>
> A cuckoo
> Fading into the distance—
> An island.

The poet, standing on the shores of Suma Bay, hears the sound of a *hototogisu* ("cuckoo"); and as he watches it fade into the distance, it suddenly becomes a small island, presumably Awajishima, a small island across from Suma. In contrast to the first two lines, which have the lyricism of *waka,* the last line possesses the element of *haikai* in the unexpected transfer between an aural and a visual image.

6. The eighteen standard *kireji* established by the Muromachi *renga* masters and generally followed by Edo *haikai* poets include four imperative verb endings, four auxiliary verbs, and one speculative adverb.

7

SYMPOSIUM ON THE ORIENTAL HUMANITIES

Oriental Humanities in America: The Next Forty Years

Robert P. Goldman

Fortieth anniversaries are, inevitably, occasions for nostalgia, for looking back fondly on days of new beginnings, of youthful optimism and energy, days that loom, in memory at least, larger—more expansive—than the cramped and stress-filled routines of today. This is only appropriate and many of those assembled here, Professors de Bary, Embree, Meskill, and the rest, have surely more than earned the right to reminisce proudly on their role in the creation of the Oriental Humanities and Oriental Civilizations programs here at Columbia and of the accomplishments of these programs in terms of students educated, scholars trained, and scholarship produced. Truly these programs, perhaps more than any others, have stimulated and kept alive the tradition of humanistic scholarship on Asia in this country.

I, too, who have not stood here among this group of scholars on this campus for nearly twenty-five of these forty years, find myself somewhat smitten with a sense of nostalgia for the "good old days," a sense so vividly captured in Bhavabhūti's often quoted verse:

> *jīvatsu tātapādeṣu nave dārāparigrahe |*
> *mātṛbhiś cintyamānānāṃ te hi no divasā gatāḥ |*
> *(Uttararāmacarita,* 1.19)
>
> *Father was alive then, and we but newly married.*
> *And how our mothers fussed over us! Those days we*
> *had are gone forever.*

Indeed those days we had are gone. And it is only fitting, as I reflect on my own early experience of the Oriental Humanities colloquium, when I sat as an undergraduate at the feet of my teachers, to recall and acknowledge my enormous debt to the people whose learning and guidance set both the model and the direction of my subsequent career. After all, in the words of Śaṅkarācārya:

> *na hi suśikṣito 'pi naṭabaṭuḥ svaskandham adhiroḍhuṃ*
> *paṭuḥ ||*
> (*Bhāṣya* on *Brahmasūtra* 3.3.54)
>
> *No matter how well you train a young actor, he still*
> *won't be clever enough to stand on his own shoulders.*

Yet, even as we recall the past, it is also appropriate for us to give thought to the present and future as well. The status and the future of the Asian Humanities or "Oriental Studies" (to use the older and perhaps now somewhat controversial term) in the curriculum at American institutions of higher learning have been the subject of a lively and highly publicized debate stimulated to a great extent by the remarkable sales of Allan Bloom's book *The Closing of the American Mind,* a work that consists largely of a series of attacks on various contemporary phenomena among which the inclusion of the study of non-Western cultures is given a prominent place, and by a similar call for a return to an entirely Western humanities based core curriculum on the part of the Secretary of Education. This latter official, it may be noted, has only recently castigated the faculty of Stanford University for replacing their core course in Western civilization with a course drawing on Asian as well as other sources in an act he viewed as one of reprehensible capitulation to student pressure. This debate has raged furiously in academic and literary journals for some months and I note that—again just recently—the community of Asian Humanists represented in part by no less distinguished a voice than that of Professor de Bary took collective defensive action in the form of an entire panel at the annual meeting of the Association for Asian Studies consisting of a response to Bloom.

Now while I certainly share my Asianist colleagues' dismay at the celebration in many quarters of Allan Bloom's know-nothing-ism and clarion call for ignorance of anything other than the limited corpus of "classics" that he personally regards as appropriate to the molding of the minds and souls of American students, a cry echoed embarrassingly by his crony Saul Bellow in a recent piece on Bloom in the *New York Times Magazine*, I do not frankly find the book and the attitude it represents as menacing as do many. Indeed I wonder, for example, if the refutation of Mr. Bloom's assertions (they can hardly be called arguments in any meaningful sense) really requires dignifying them with the dedication of a panel of serious scholars to the effort. In any case the Asianists on such a panel and those, including myself, likely to attend it are hardly in need of being persuaded as to the importance of modern humanistic research and education's expanding beyond the narrow limits within which the Blooms of the world feel secure.

The efforts of Allan Bloom and others to attempt a retrenchment in what should constitute the limits of humanistic inquiry, and the evidently responsive chord his book has struck in many quarters of the American intellectual community, can be viewed, I would argue, as artifacts of an attitude fostered by the history of the past two decades and its implications for many Americans' view of this country's role in the world in terms of political, economic, cultural, and intellectual influence. These conditions are, or at any rate are perceived to be, radically different from those that prevailed at the time, forty years ago, when Columbia pioneered the broad-based, interdisciplinary academic study of Oriental Humanities that we are celebrating here today. Thus, as we reflect on those early, heady days in which the fruits of a multicultural study of the human experience as reflected in the cherished and influential cultural legacy of all the world's peoples, were at last beginning to be widely available to American undergraduates, we should keep in mind the enormous changes that have taken place since then.

The Second World War marked in many ways a watershed in the development of American awareness of Asia. Service in the Pacific Theater as well as intelligence work brought dozens of American scholars and intellectuals into contact with the cultures, languages, peoples, and literatures of Asia. In not a few cases this exposure led to significant changes in the direction of these peoples' careers and some of them brought their new interests to the rapidly expanding academic world of postwar America.

At the same time the war marked the beginning of an era of unprecedented American global expansiveness in terms of economic and political influence and general self-confidence. This sudden sense of centrality led, I believe, to a number of shifts in attitudes concerning non-Western cultures on the part of governmental and academic circles in this country. Running rather counter to the equally strengthened sense of unique superiority, the "ugly American" syndrome that has had such negative consequences in the area of foreign policy, was a new sense of openness to, of curiosity about, the "provinces," if you will, of the emergent global American imperium. This was particularly to be seen in the corps of Americans in the foreign service and the burgeoning development agencies which arose in the wake of our interactions with postcolonial Asia. This community was, as it is now, separated from the academic community by a thin and highly permeable line and given the new needs of the society for specialists it was not surprising that a corresponding development of Asian and other area studies at influential American universities should take place. The situation may be viewed as in some ways comparable—even parallel—to the dramatic development of Oriental Studies, particularly, with respect to traditional India, which accompanied the opening of Bengal to the mercantile and colonial influence of the British East India Company at the end of the eighteenth century with its concomitant rise to prominence of scholar-administrators such as Jones, Wilson, Colebrook, et al., and the institutionalization of Oriental studies at the great British universities.

Consider the situation now. In many ways the Vietnam War marked the beginning of the recent decline in American self-confidence and self-assured global dominance that marked the twenty years following the defeat of the Axis. The twenty years or so since the fall of Saigon have witnessed a major and ongoing crisis of this confidence, the inability of the American government to impose its will and values upon—in some cases even to avoid humiliations at the hands of—even seriously under-developed nations in Asia and, more recently, the dramatic shift in industrial, financial, and trade dominance to small Asian countries which forty years ago were clearly American client states. Parallel with these developments, and indeed connected with them, has been the social and intellectual ferment of the past two decades in which previously static patterns of social hierarchy and authority have been increasingly and often violently challenged. This has been reflected in the new militancy of many groups—students, ethnic minorities, women, gays, and so on—precisely the phenomenon that the political movement we have come to know as the Reagan Revolution and its academic counterpart, Bloomism, have found so alarming and which they seek so desperately to suppress. In other words the new stress on the values of Western culture as it is imaginatively reconstructed by the neo-conservatives can be read as a desperate and finally hopeless effort to deny reality.

The question for us is what should be our response? How, in other words, should we, as exponents of what we have been calling the Oriental Humanities, approach the coming forty years in terms of the shifting role of the United States in the world, the dramatically shifting demography of our student audiences, the exclusionist efforts of some of our colleagues, and the increasing substantive and theoretical sophistication of humanistic research in general?

Well, for one thing, I think we should prepare for the acceleration of the growth of interest in our fields. The dramatic emergence of Asia as one of the great political and economic centers of the contemporary world has sparked considerable interest in governmental and business circles; and the number of students who need training in the languages and civilizations of the region has been increasing and we must be prepared to provide it. In addition, we are now seeing at many American universities a great influx of highly motivated and enormously talented students of Asian backgrounds who, although they may not be interested in the field of Asian Humanities as a career goal, are extremely eager for systematic education in the cultures and civilizations from which they and their families derive. My expectation is that despite or perhaps even in part because of the cries of the Blooms, our field will in fact be experiencing growth in the next several decades.

But the more interesting question, to my mind, is to be derived from the nature of our area itself and its traditional relationship to the well entrenched curricula in the study of the literary and ideological history of Western Europe, an area known best under the brave term "the Humanities." The use of this term and the consequent relegation of the things we do to the marked category "Oriental Humanities" must, in the light of the issues touched upon above, lead us to a serious reconsideration of what exactly it is we are trying to do and on whose terms. To what extent should we be content to allow the proponents of one small portion of the humanistic heritage of our species to continue to define the very terms in which we approach other portions and the whole itself?

Let me give an example that strikes rather close to home. In the most recent issue of *Columbia College Today*, Jacques Barzun has a typically learned and entertaining piece on the "Birth of the Humanities Course (Humanities A) at Columbia," an event whose fiftieth anniversary the College is celebrating even as we celebrate our fortieth. Professor Barzun closes his article with what he evidently regards as a focally illustrative anecdote. He tells us that when Gilbert Highet was first asked to teach the Humanities A course he was in the habit not only of writing Greek words on the board but—horror of horrors—of tracing their etymologies "all the way back to Sanskrit." This tragic situation was, however, soon remedied. Someone close to Professor Highet (certainly, as I recall my days in the College, not a student) spoke a kind word in his ear. Highet saw the point and from then on "taught the humanities in a humanistic manner, with not a thought of Sanskrit." "Humanism in the humanities," Barzun concludes, "is the slogan that makes these courses work." Now perhaps Professor Barzun did not mean to suggest it, but to many his remarks must appear to reflect a notion that somehow the study, even the mention, of the linguistic and intellectual connections between Sanskrit and the classical languages of the Mediterranean, is antithetical to a humanistic approach to the humanities. Many of us here are aware that this is in fact far from true, and I need not spend time demonstrating it. The point is that many of our colleagues who specialize in the study and teaching of the literatures and cultures which, since the fifteenth century or so, like to trace their heritage to the ancient civilizations of the Mediterranean are to an extraordinary degree simply unaware of the cultural and intellectual configurations of the civilizations of Asia and to an even greater degree innocent of their interconnectedness with many of those of Europe. One way in which we can work to break down these barriers of incomprehension is to move away from the tradition of separating humanistic areas of inquiry into separate categories in which our interests become part of a marked category, "Oriental" or "non-Western," as though such categories necessarily imply greater sets of affinities within their boundaries than exist between some of the cultures so defined and those not so defined. One way in which this approach might take concrete form would be to devise and institute a series of undergraduate seminars on larger topics such as an intellectual history of the ancient world in which the major traditions of the major cultural areas to which we have textual access could be studied and compared. Similar topical, chronological, and other non-geographical approaches to the humanistic legacy of the human race will come easily to mind.

Finally, what exactly should we be studying and teaching under the rubric of Oriental Humanities or just plain (this time in a universal sense) Humanities? Let me try to answer this by first suggesting what perhaps we should not do or continue to do. That is to permit, even as we assert the claim of distinctiveness for Oriental Humanities and its sub-disciplines, the inherited schemata of the Western classics derived humanities, to determine our subject matter and the ways in which we view it. I am referring to the concept of the Great Books. Even if we accept the, to me, highly arguable point that there is a relatively small discrete set of literary documents that somehow among them define the intellectual history of Western Europe must it follow that a similar set can and should be adduced from every other culture with pretensions to the title civilization? I would think not. For if we unquestioningly apply the highly bibliocentric West's concept of Great Books to some cultures we may be in fact imposing an alien and even irrelevant set of criteria that may serve to falsify our conception of both the cultures and the documents we are so elevating. Does every culture really have a "Bible"? Not necessarily, but if we are trained to look for bibles we will certainly be able to find them. The result, however, of such an effort may well be artificially to center a text or a set of texts in a culture which may have only a very diffuse notion of this document or which, worse, as a result of and reaction to a long history of asymmetrical contact with the West, may seize upon the document so presented and follow through on its exaltation. One result of this process is to be seen in our tendency to represent the highly diffuse and complex tradition of Hinduism which lives chiefly through its rootedness in the tantric-āgamic traditions of ritual praxis and temple cults as a written text-driven set of lofty metaphysical ideologies with its *Upaniṣads, Vedas, Gītā,* and so on, its courtly dramas that could never have had more than a miniscule audience, and whole hosts of documents that are often of only the most peripheral use, in an effort to apprehend a central intellectual tradition or civilization. It is very likely that reflection on issues such as this will lead us to very different conclusions about the different regions of Asia, but in any case let us not run the risk of casting in bronze our current state of knowledge about Asian cultures as have so many of our Westernist colleagues in their own fields by skewing our students' and our own understanding of Asia's complex, vital, and still very much alive civilizations through the self-validating notion of "Great Books."

Those of us who are engaged in the humanistic study of East Asia, South and Southeast Asia, and West Asia where some of the great civilizations of the world not only arose but continue to live, should take full advantage of the opportunity not available to our colleagues in the Western classics, to study culture not only as it is written but as it is lived. If this means breaking down not only the geographical and conceptual boundaries that seem still to divide humanists but also the often unproductive barriers that divide what we call the humanities from the social sciences, then by all means let us do so. For in this way we and our students may continue—in the proud tradition Columbia is celebrating this year—to add to the sum total of humanistic scholarship while extending its very boundaries.

An Appreciation of Oriental Humanities

David Johnson

I do not know if any of the students who took my section of Oriental Humanities were actually influenced by the experience. Quite a few enjoyed the course, I think, but that does not mean it changed the way they thought. But I know that Oriental Humanities influenced *my* thinking, both about teaching (and liberal education), and about China. So I thought I would say a little under both these heads as my contribution to this celebration of a great educational idea.

I knew nothing about teaching and not very much more about China when I came to Columbia in 1970 to teach Chinese history. In fact, I can remember going to the bookstore to buy a copy of Gilbert Highet's *The Art of Teaching*, since it seemed likely to contain some useful tips. I found the book and glanced at the opening sentence, which as I recall went something like this: "To be a good teacher you must know your subject."[1] I knew at once that Highet was right, and that therefore I was not qualified to teach about China, or anything else. I put the book back on the shelf and crept quietly out of the store.

So it was learning by doing, and Oriental Humanities was where I learned most. Oriental Humanities is an undergraduate colloquium, a seminar for students just beginning to assemble and articulate their views of themselves and the world. As time passed, my experiences in the class left me with a clear sense of what I wanted to happen in an undergraduate seminar: there should be a kind of controlled spontaneity, in which *my* favorite ideas emerged in good order but were augmented by those marvelous insights of which even ordinary students are capable when they let themselves really respond to the strange material the syllabus has required them to read that week.

Every now and then, when a class went well, it was like what I imagine a successful jazz improvisation is—a foundation of familiar elements made new by moments of true inspiration, all combined in a coherent whole. Of course, one wants all one's seminars to be like this, and they aren't. But the memory of the best moments does not fade—indeed, like my memory of the Higher quotation, may grow more vivid with time. I continued to look for little epiphanies in my classes. This is a rather impractical attitude, especially if one's students have not gone through something like the Contemporary Civilization/Humanities core curriculum; romantic, really, when you get right down to it. But that is what Oriental Humanities did to me. I still believe that with the right material, and with close attention to the texts, epiphanies are possible.

Of course, Oriental Humanities has the right material—the right stuff indeed—though I must confess to a slight wavering from the Original Doctrine here, since I had a very strong preference for the Chinese and Japanese texts: comparing them with each other, and with their European analogues. And within the spring semester readings, it was the first five weeks or so that I really loved: *Analects, Mencius, Lao Tzu, Chuang Tzu, Han Fei Tzu, Hsün Tzu.*

I had never read those works with any care, and most of them utterly baffled me when I had to prepare my classes for the first time. Why were they like *this?* Was this philosophy? Here were China's great thinkers—but they seldom defined their terms or examined their premises; they did not argue, they asserted; they did not construct complex logical structures, but simply moved from topic to topic apparently at random. They were so . . . un-Greek! Just what were they trying to do?

Eventually I went back to the Chinese originals—especially *Mencius* and *Hsün Tzu*—and pored over the indispensable translations of Burton Watson, who was then a colleague in the Department of East Asian Languages and Cultures. Then I began to read Plato again, with new eyes because of my struggles with the likes of Mencius. And gradually some basic ideas began to take shape: that Chinese "thinkers" were more interested in behavior than in ideas, by which I mean that they seemed concerned not with creating formulas of words (which is what it now appeared to me that the Greeks were aiming at when they were doing ethics, metaphysics, or aesthetics), but rather with describing ideal patterns of action. From this it followed that my definition of philosophy was thoroughly parochial, and it did not take long to realize that my ideas about the nature of "religion," "art," "history," and so on were equally limited.

By paying close attention to what the texts were actually saying, I came to see more and more clearly how profoundly different Chinese thought was from Western thought. Yet it could not be dismissed as an imperfect approximation of "real philosophy"; it was what it was, with its own kind of perfection; and it had to be comprehended (I couldn't forget Highet's precept). This meant calling into question many of my fundamental assumptions; or rather, *seeing* those assumptions for the first time and so being able to assess them. For example, curiosity about the natural world and the desire to understand how it operates, the urge to discover more and more, to keep pushing back the frontiers of the unknown forever, never stopping—this whole cast of mind, which seemed to me to be perfectly natural and admirable, was directly challenged by Hsün Tzu's cautious, humane skepticism.

Eventually it began to appear to me that European civilization may have been a kind of aberration; that a culture had to be a bit crazed to follow the path we have taken, in which the drive to understand the operations of the natural world has led us to the brink of destruction, and our mastery of the techniques of production has made us slaves of our possessions. And this necessarily led to a growing appreciation of traditional Chinese civilization.

Well, I was getting a liberal education. The heart of it was the perception of *difference,* and the challenge to my preconceptions this necessarily entailed. Teaching about similarities between people of various cultures, well-intentioned though it is, does not take the student nearly as far, at least on the level of high culture. With non-elite culture it is another matter, since the poor and uneducated are not burdened with so much culture-specific self-consciousness, and therefore probably share important attitudes and values throughout the world. But Oriental Humanities is not concerned with popular culture, and for good reason.

What Oriental Humanities does do is allow students (and teachers) to see for themselves what the central documents of Chinese (or Japanese, or Indian, or Islamic) civilization actually say, and then challenge them to understand those texts in their own terms and come to grips with the depth of difference between their preconceptions and assumptions and ours. The resulting kind of self-comprehension is the foundation of a true liberal education.

ENDNOTE

1. The exact words, which I have recently looked up, are these: "What are the qualities of a good teacher? First, and most necessary of all, he must know the subject." But they are on page 12, not page 1—an interesting example of the way memory can "touch up" the past to make it more dramatic.

Recollections of Oriental Humanities

Jonathan Cott

It is, of course, a bit daunting to speak, from the point of view of an ex-student, to this gathering of distinguished professors; and it *is* as a kind of "continuing student" that I am happy to be here today to say what Oriental Humanities—which I took some twenty years ago—meant, and still means, to me as a journalist, a writer of a number of books, and a poet.

I think I came to Oriental Humanities in the following way: In 1962, the financial pressures and burdens of the world did not seem to motivate almost every other student to take business courses and to study the cost of capital and other such subjects as they do today. I believed, along with Ralph Waldo Emerson, that "Life consists in what a man is thinking of all day"; and I was either curious enough (or unstable enough, depending on how you looked at it) to want to explore as many non-business subjects as I could while being a literature major at Columbia College (a matter of *pluralism,* not *relativism*—*pace* Allan Bloom). What I discovered was that if you could just maneuver yourself around or rush through certain physical education requirements (I took bowling, believe it or not, one semester!) and Set Theory and Botany courses, you could somehow get permission to take, or sit in on, all kinds of extraordinarily fascinating and unusual courses that Columbia offered in its various departments or divisions.

I remember, for instance, following C. Wright Mills, caparisoned in a black leather jacket, as he got off his imposing Harley-Davidson-type bike one afternoon and led some of his students into a college sociology classroom for a radical analysis of American society. I remember sitting in on Meyer Shapiro's breathtakingly inspired lectures on Impressionism; I remember taking a General Studies course on Jungian approaches to literature—and this at a time when the Columbia psychology department was a bastion of rat research and behaviorism, and when the Columbia English department was promulgating an orthodox Freudian aesthetic—a course filled with extremely "far-out," gentle-looking students who enjoyed discussing . . . their dreams—students the likes of whom I would meet two years later in the streets of Berkeley, California. I remember being deeply moved at that time by Balkan music—especially the folk music of Bulgaria and Macedonia — so I decided to take a graduate course in Balkan Literature, taught by a charming, eccentric Albanian professor—a dead ringer for Nabokov's Pnin—who read from his notes on his desk—never once looking up at the four students taking his class—in a number of the twelve or so languages he was master of—and, as the lectures continued through the semester, I remember reading the "famous" Bulgarian novel *Under the Yoke* by Vazov and some wonderful Macedonian and Serbian ballads (decimated in translation). Professor Pnin never really noticed that on the last day of class only two students (myself included) were still in attendance; I am not even sure he noticed that the term was even coming to an end. And finally, I remember taking the one course in ethnomusicology offered by the College Music Department, for I had toyed with the idea of becoming an ethnomusicologist (I could not imagine anything more appealing than spending one's life with one's tape recorder traveling into bush, forests, and deserts to record the music of the world's peoples). In this class the students would listen to old 78 rpm recordings (of southwest and northwest American Indians) made by Alan Lomax, who, when he had us listen to them in our class, went into a semi-trance and sang and chanted and danced around the classroom in time to the music and in remembrance of the rituals he had recorded and obviously loved, far away from the plateau of 114th Street and Broadway.

In my senior year, I decided to rein in my global curiosity, and was fortunate to be accepted into the College Colloquium Seminar —the weekly Great Books symposium, which concentrated on the Western tradition from the Greek tragedians to Dostoyevsky. But on glancing through the college catalog, I noticed a listing for a year-long Oriental Humanities program, got hold of the reading list, and discovered at least forty or more obviously "great" books that I had never even heard of—from *The Assemblies of Al-Ḥarīrī* and Kālidāsa's *Śakuntalā* to *A Dream of Red Mansions* and *The Tale of Genji*—works that were certainly not being read or talked about in the Colloquium program.

I remember that, in a Romantic English poetry class I had taken the year before, I had discovered that William Wordsworth (many of whose sonnets, ironically, are so reminiscent of the world of the Chinese Sung poets) had stated that when he was fourteen years old, he had been totally carried away by the sight of an ordinary row of boughs silhouetted against a bright evening sky—so much so that he knew that at that very instant he would have to become a poet. But what he wrote about that moment really bothered me: "The moment was important in my poetical history," Wordsworth stated, "for I date from it my consciousness of the infinite variety of natural appearances which had been unnoticed *by the poets of any age or country*" (emphasis added). And it was this kind of provincialism (no matter that Chinese poets were writing poems better than most of Wordsworth's before the Norman invasion!)

that had led one of my English professors to dismiss Walt Whitman as "hairy Walt," leaving him and his poetry—a poetry that has influenced poets in almost every country throughout the world—at that. William Carlos Williams was similarly dismissed in favor of minor, technically competent versifiers. And so on.

This was, of course, the era of New Criticism—not only at Columbia but even more so at English literature departments around the country. And later, I remember coming across the following poem by Yang Wan-li, the Sung poet, in a translation by Jonathan Chaves:

The Fishing Boat

It is a tiny fishing boat, light as a leaf;
no voices are heard from the reed cabin.
There is no one on board—
no bamboo hat,
  no raincoat,
    no fishing rod.
The wind blows the boat, and the boat moves.

To New Critical explicators, there would be nothing happening in the above poem to merit discussion—*no* bamboo hat, *no* raincoat, *no* fishing rod, *no* person. No *poem*, in fact! But that, in a sense, was exactly what the poem was about: to enable one to see and feel how one can see and feel *nothing* happening—and be moved by that, just as the boat moves—and to realize and feel how nothing can move *you*. It was, after all, so much *easier* to talk about a wry Philip Larkin poem, for example, or a pseudo-metaphysical set of ironies in some easily forgettable (if analyzable) academic poem. Of course, this same kind of aesthetic debate inevitably went and goes on in every culture. But what was most reprehensible to me was to hear teachers apodictically asserting that *Don Quixote* was *of course* the first great world novel, or that the religious texts of the East lacked the subtlety and vision of the Gospel According to St. John.

This was in 1963, which, as I sometimes still think—in spite of

Allan Bloom and revisionists of his ilk—was the very end of the Dark Ages, at least as far as intellectual provinciality regarding things and subjects east of the Suez were concerned. First, because *I* was fortunate enough to take Oriental Humanities! And second, because James Joyce's punning remark "that European end meets Ind" was clearly revealing itself to be a profound and ineluctable truth. The East had, of course, influenced the West for centuries, but never more so than during the past thirty years, especially in the fields of music, painting, dance, literature, spiritual practices, medical approaches, etc. In 1977, for example, the poet, critic, and translator Kenneth Rexroth had stated that he could easily name at least one hundred American poets whose work was primarily influenced by Chinese and Japanese verse—and that was probably an understatement. In music, moreover, it was clear that works by composers as diverse as Olivier Messaien, Pierre Boulez, Roger Reynolds, Steve Reich, and by groups and musicians such as John Coltrane and the Art Ensemble of Chicago were deeply influenced by gagaku and gamelan music and by Indian ragas, as well as by the radical concept of "living tones" and the complex notion of tone's unlimited possibilities of color, articulation, and inflection. The same influences, *mutatis mutandi,* applied to painting and many other art forms and fields.

There are no longer any centers of the known world. And if Copernicus had not taught me that, Oriental Humanities did. Today, the seeds that Oriental Humanities was planting have blossomed into all kinds of multitudinous, elaborate, sometimes strange, sometimes fascinating growths. Many of my friends, who profess allegiance to Zen or Tibetan Buddhist or Sufi teachings, often do not have the overarching multicultural perspective that Oriental Humanities, which allowed one to believe and think for oneself, provided. But the seeds it planted in *me* have continued to make me as curious as ever and anxious to read new and in many cases now-complete translations of works I had only read part of in class: *The Journey to the West* (which took me about six months to traverse); the two-volume edition of Ssu-ma Ch'ien; many of the beautiful new translations of poets like Ryōkan, Lu Yu, Saigyō, and Li Ch'ing-chao; *The Muqaddimah, an Introduction to History* by Ibn Khaldūn; and the complete version of Kenkō's *Essays in Idleness,* as well as books that were not offered in the course: *The Confessions of Lady Nijō, As I Crossed A Bridge of Dreams (Sarashina nikki),* and many Ming poets, all new to me.

One thing led to another. I remember coming across Jonathan Chaves' brilliant translation of the Ming poet Yüan Hung-tao, noticing a reference to the philosopher Li Chih and a footnote advising me to check out Professor de Bary's essay "Individualism and Humanitarianism" in a book called *Self and Society in Ming Thought,* in which I found out about Li's notion of the "Childlike Mind," and read the following extraordinary text by Li:

> Once people's minds have been given over to received opinions and moral principles, what they have to say is all about these things, and not what would naturally come from their childlike minds. No matter how clever the words, what have they to do with oneself? What else can there be but phony men speaking phony words, doing phony things, writing phony writings? Once the men become phonies, everything becomes phony. Thereafter if one speaks phony talk to the phonies, the phonies are pleased; if one does phony things as the phonies do, the phonies are pleased; and if one discourses with the phonies through phony writings, the phonies are pleased. Everything is phony, and everyone is pleased.

As far as I am concerned, these powerful words go right to the heart of the Social Lie—in whatever society. But this is no reason to go on permanent student strike. As Professor de Bary points out, Li Chih did not attack as useless all art, culture, and technology; and he felt that when people read books, they had much to learn from them as long as they read them afresh.

I certainly cannot think of another college or university course that nurtures and purveys this approach to reading and thinking with more openness and human-heartedness than Oriental Humanities. To read *The Tale of Genji* or *A Dream of Red Mansions* for the first time is an amazing, mind-opening experience. Without having done so, moreover, I know I would have missed an enormous amount in the great films of Kenji Mizoguchi *(New Tales of the Taira, The Empress Yang Kuei-fei)*. Similarly, without the *Jātaka Tales*, the *Pañcatantra*, and *The Thousand and One Nights*, I would have missed much in Western fables, fairy tales, and a work like Kipling's *Just So Stories*, for example. (Not to speak of Indian, Japanese, and Chinese art.) Re-reading, as I did several years ago, some essays by Montaigne, Isaac Walton's *The Compleat Angler*, and Mark Twain's *Huckleberry Finn*, I know that my love for Arthur Waley's *The Way and Its Power*—his translation of Lao Tzu—deepened my experience of those three works, each one of them manifesting, in its own way, the nature of that Power, unknown to or maligned by phonies at any time and any place, East or West.

Ultimately, it is the *process* itself of being guided through four major traditions that, I am sure, has a subtle but sure effect on everyone who takes Oriental Humanities. When I re-read *Essays in Idleness*—something I do very often since it is one of my favorite books—I am always astonished by the audacious and amazingly modern manner in which Kenkō seems to explore, experiment, and play with ways of beginning, expanding, cutting off narrative, allowing the reader to meditate on or simply imagine the implications of and possible conclusions to a thought, a moral, an observation, a miniature essay, a legend, a story, even the false beginning of a novel—and I think to myself: "It certainly would be great to test this idea out in an Oriental Humanities class in order to determine its validity or stupidity!" But from Kenkō I have learned that Oriental Humanities is a life-long, ongoing approach to teaching and learning, and one that does not end at the end of spring. "Leaving something incomplete," Kenkō writes, "makes it interesting, and gives one the feeling that there is room for growth. Someone," Kenkō continues, "once told me, 'Even when building the imperial palace, they always leave one place unfinished.' "

And I am grateful and happy that after forty years Oriental Humanities is still not finished—still not finished fulfilling what the Confucian philosopher Mencius said was the end and aim of all learning: "To seek and find the feeling we have lost."

Are the "Great Books of the East" Necessary?

John Van Doren

It appears that almost everyone, including myself, believes that the works read in the Oriental Humanities course are important ones that should be known so far as possible, even in translation, by every educated person. There may be some who dispute this, and possibly the dispute is worth airing, but we need not consider it now. The importance of these readings is taken for granted here—indeed, it is warmly affirmed. Though I cannot help wondering if our parochial ignorance is any greater than that which the several Eastern traditions have of each other, it seems clear that such works should be part of our Western experience.

As much could be said, however, about a great many things and a great many books which ought to be discovered and studied by us over the course of a lifetime of learning—the kind of lifetime that all human beings ought to have, whatever they make otherwise of their days on earth.

The practical question is harder. It is whether the texts under consideration—the books read in the Oriental Humanities course, and other works of the Eastern traditions which could be read as well—are *necessary* in the sense that the works read, at least at Columbia, in the Western Humanities course, may be said to be necessary—that is, are thought impossible to omit from the undergraduate curriculum.

Before we conclude that they are, it might be well to recall the logic, as I think it is, according to which Western Humanities readings have generally been required—or at least I should say, according to which they have maintained themselves, not without occasional dissent and sometimes rather precariously, in undergraduate programs. This is, I think, that such works already inhabit the minds of students when they come to college (assuming they are students of Western background and upbringing—even perhaps if not), and that they have to be duly recognized if these minds are to develop properly—that is, with adequate command of their own mental furniture.

I do not mean, of course, that the students have literally read such works before they come to college. I mean that the works exist within them in the sense that the kind of language they speak, the terms they use, and the ideas they have about themselves and the world around them are derived from such writings. Of course the language is not spoken very well, nor are the terms used with much precision, nor are the ideas sufficiently understood. That is why it is necessary for students to undertake this reading in their college years, and preferably, I should think, at the beginning of their course of study. They have to discover what it is that they think they know, and perhaps how little they really know it, before they can move on to other things—before, indeed, they can grasp the works themselves that make up the Western Humanities course—grasp them, that is, with comprehension.

I am glad to think, as I do think, that this is understood at Columbia, where the Western Humanities course is a long-standing tradition—as it is understood also at St. John's College, for example, where I went years ago, and where a much expanded "Western Humanities" course, including a lot of science and mathematics, constitutes the entire curriculum.

But I have to admit—if I am not merely to beg the question that seems somehow implicit on this pleasant and learned occasion—I am not convinced that what is true of the Western Humanities, at least in my view, is true also of the Oriental Humanities. Worthwhile as these are, and such as no educated person can finally be ignorant of, they do not seem to me to be *necessary* to the undergraduate curriculum in the same way. The reason is simply that they are not, by definition, present in the same way in the minds of the students that Western universities must endeavor to educate—that is, to start upon the adult phase of what must be, again, a lifetime of learning. But if they are not necessary at this stage of the game, then it is open to question, I should think, whether they should be included, as requirements, at the expense of other things that *are* necessary.

I may be quite wrong, of course, in this doubt I confess that I have. It is only too likely, perhaps, that I *am* wrong, since my own education in the materials of the Oriental Humanities course has only begun—since I am invited to participate here as one who is, so to say, on the outside looking in, not as one having experience, still less scholarly attainments, in the field of Oriental Humanities. Still, I do feel a doubt, and I suppose, being called on to say something, that I cannot do otherwise than express it.

But I do not wish to go on. I assume the anxiety I acknowledge is not shared here by anyone else. If it is not, and if the Oriental Humanities are in fact to be considered among the options to satisfy a requirement in the "extended core" curriculum of Columbia College, as I am informed is the decision which has been reached, then I am glad to learn that the requirement will not be at the expense of the Western Humanities readings. For the selection there, as in other universities, is at best and perforce a small one, and can hardly afford to be reduced any further. Presumably the

Oriental Humanities requirement will be at the expense of electives which the students could otherwise take, and that may be a test of the faculty's devotion—a yet further test of its devotion—to the whole idea of Humanities. But I like to think this idea is so well established at Columbia that nothing can undermine it.

Comparative Literature and Its Discontents

Pauline Yu

It has always seemed undeniable to me that the values of stepping across cultural lines in the study of literature, the arts, philosophy, or whatever outweigh the possible risks and problems, although since I am a comparatist by training and profession it would perhaps be unwise of me to hold any position to the contrary. Any close reading of an early Chinese philosophical text, for example, will reveal questions that—by the very fact of their formulation as well as by virtue of the sorts of answers that may be provided for them—may stimulate students to take another look at those they have been trained to ask about and within the Western tradition. Equally illuminating, of course, will be the questions—and answers—that do not appear in the Chinese text, which may similarly move readers to rethink ideas they have always taken for granted because of the culture-bound nature of the discourse to which they have been exposed. This broadening of perspective may thus not only lead students to rethink the *content* of questions and answers—e.g., whether human nature is fundamentally good or evil, or whether the universe is created or uncreated—it may also focus an interesting and important light on the variety of forms within which the inquiry itself can proceed. Reading a work like the *Analects* or the *Mencius*, for example, they will encounter an unfamiliar reluctance to define concepts in the abstract, a rejection of an overarching theoretical framework—or even narrative—and the preference instead for embedding discussions in particular circumstances. Such observations about form not only bear directly on issues of content but may also, along with the latter, help students to reformulate their notions of norms of philosophical discourse. Similar exercises in rethinking are of course equally possible and pertinent to the literary tradition as well.

Needless to say, however, we have heard from more than one quarter that a curriculum that has always focused on Western canonical "masterpieces" may be diluted, if not utterly violated, when revised to include works from other cultures, not to speak of previously unsanctified texts from within the West itself. Yet quite apart from voices like those of Allan Bloom, others with less objectionable agenda have raised serious doubts about the merits of such juxtapositions and comparisons or, often, displayed an utter lack of interest. I have found, for example, the disincentives to studying classical Chinese literature from a comparative perspective frequently extremely powerful. Many scholars of Western literatures may lend an interested ear briefly, but then lapse quickly from what turns out to have been a rather patronizing tolerance to an all-too-visible impatience to get back to what really matters, muttering excuses, perhaps, about the unbridgeable linguistic or cultural gaps. (One extremely well-known literary theorist, who shall remain unnamed, reviewed for publication a colleague's manuscript, one which ranged widely over centuries, countries, and cultures. He submitted a favorable review to the publisher but did confess to the author, over dinner, that while he had liked it very much, in his reading he had "skipped over" all the Chinese stuff.)

In all fairness, however, I should point out that the resistance has entrenched itself equally stubbornly from the other side—that of sinology, as it has evolved in some Western academic institutions. Hard-core sinologists are often more than willing to confirm the opinions of scholars of Western literature as to the unique difficulty of their own special enterprise and cast a suspicious, if not outright contemptuous, eye on those who would claim to know about China *and* about something else as well. Audible sniffs casting aspersions on the presumptuous scholars' knowledge of Chinese, for example, convey a widespread skepticism, and even hostility, toward those not content to remain within the safe confines of a single dynasty, genre, or—best of all—botanical species. I should clarify that I am speaking here only—and the irony should be apparent—of Western-trained sinologists, for in my experience those trained in Asia could by no means, whether in the past or in the present, be characterized by what, quite baldly, strikes me as a modern academic kind of chinoiserie.

Now, as frustrating as such (anti)pathetic parochialisms may be, there are unfortunately a number of good reasons for their dogged persistence. Bad comparative work has been done—about this there cannot be any doubt. Individual comparisons of authors, works, or movements may be conducted without attention, for example, to cultural assumptions and institutions and concrete extra-literary conditions and are therefore so inconclusive as to seem pointless. More than once, alas, I have found myself forced to dampen the enthusiasm and hopes of students who come into my office wanting simply "to compare." Many Western approaches find no counterparts in the Chinese critical tradition and are based on very different sets of philosophical and literary presuppositions; improperly justified, they can be castigated as irrelevant at best, culturally imperialist at worst. Similarly, literary "universals" on close examination almost invariably turn out to be Western ones, and when used as the framework for the study of Chinese literature they cannot but elicit, for instance, great expenditures of energy on arguments to show why China lacks tragedy, or epic, or, conversely, to argue that these did develop after all, albeit in (extremely effective) disguise. Significant differences over time and space evaporate in the hypostasis of forms and genres (although there is equally significant disagreement over how those characterizations should be frozen). And finally, entire richly varied traditions become, without qualification, monoliths in the face-off of "East-West" comparative literature.

As an admitted perpetrator of many of the embarrassments just catalogued, I am nonetheless reluctant to throw my hands up in despair and dismiss the integration of Asian texts into the general humanities curriculum as a hopelessly flawed enterprise. It seems to me that both sides lose when major traditions, on the one hand, are consigned to the margins of serious critical and theoretical study, or, on the other, choose to retreat behind the inviolable walls of esoterica. The traditions discussed in this volume may indeed be "other," but, arguably, not significantly more so than the Middle Ages or Greek antiquity are to our students, as has often been pointed out. And it seems to me that one can insist upon a minimum of conditions to ensure the validity of integrative, cross-cultural study, all of which, one would hope, would also be met in the study of Western texts as well. First, for example, we can acknowledge the undeniable linguistic difficulties posed by texts written outside the European cultural sphere, but we can also, however, render them provocative rather than paralyzing by offering students a number of translations among which they can triangulate (and in the case of short texts I have found that supplying a sample poem or two in the original with all the necessary apparatus is often extremely useful). Second, we should accept the necessity of providing as much historical, contextual, intertextual, and textual background as possible to the materials under study; close readings are necessary, but not sufficient. And third, we should recognize the value of using these juxtapositions as an occasion to step back and examine the assumptions behind the very questions one would ask of any sort of text—literary, philosophical, or historical—and the frameworks within which one would place them.

Gerald Graff has written that "literary theory" is no mere "passing fad," but rather "simply the kind of discourse that is generated when presuppositions that were once tacitly shared about literature, criticism, and culture become open to question. Theory is what breaks out when agreement about such terms as *text, reading, history, interpretation, tradition,* and *literature* can no longer be taken for granted so that their meanings have to be formulated and debated."[1] And at a session on comparative literature at a recent convention of the Modern Language Association, Sarah Lawall argued that such debate is especially crucial in questions of canon formation and evaluation. "A canon," she pointed out, "is presented as a system, but it is a blind system that does not carry with it its own critique." If we attempt to expand it by simply squeezing in texts similar to those already enshrined, the very ease with which they can be subjected to traditional reading strategies may only end up co-opting them. "New works must teach us how to read, or at least how not to misread, if they will truly renew cultural tradition. Only a discipline that makes a point of being aware of how it reads, and with what assumptions and intertextualities, is in a position to attempt either a broadening of literary understanding or an authentic expansion of canonical texts."[2] What Graff defines as theory has found congenial ground within the discipline of comparative literature, and the challenge Lawall recommends, I suggest, is one that informed comparisons across cultural lines can meet in particularly provocative and fruitful ways. We may find more that is different than is the same, but we are not, I think, looking for universals anyway, and if we can encourage students to expand their perspectives in a critical yet non-judgmental way, then we have surely done something worthwhile.

ENDNOTES

An earlier version of these remarks was delivered as a commentary on a presentation by Professor Irene Bloom on "Mencius and the Chinese Classics" at a symposium on the Oriental Humanities held at Columbia

University in the spring of 1988. Brief portions have also appeared, in different form, in my essay entitled "Alienation Effects: Comparative Literature and the Chinese Tradition," included in a volume on *The Comparative Perspective on Literature: Approaches to Theory and Practice,* edited by Clayton Koelb and Susan Noakes (Ithaca: Cornell University Press, 1988), pp. 162–175.

1. "Taking Cover in Coverage," *Profession 86*, p. 41.

2. "The Canon's Mouth: Comparative Literature and the World Masterpieces Anthology," *Profession 86*, p. 25.

From Oriental Humanities to the Humanities

Paul Anderer

The essays collected here document a compelling educational initiative, the Oriental Humanities program of Columbia College. Most discuss specific books which are used in this program, illuminating how these books, no less than Western classics, challenge us in complex ways to engage the range and depth of our humanity. This program possesses, of course, its local history as an outgrowth of pre-existing courses focused on "important" books of the Western cultural tradition. In this way, the Oriental Humanities have evolved as an elective complement to the required Western Humanities courses in the College. And so it is no wonder why this program, given its present place in the curriculum, would seem to intersect broader questions—about a core curriculum, general education, canon formation, tradition and modernity, West and non-West—which at the moment are generating intense campus controversy and even public (or media-inspired) debate.

In the main these essays do not represent position papers, but together read as a manual of sorts, intended for teachers, which reflects our own teaching situation. No doubt there is a philosophy of education here, even an ideology, since the idea of the Humanities—extended now to include works outside the cultural arena within which it originally functioned—emerges intact. Still, even this idea—that the Humanities is too valuable and broad a term to exclude all but Western classics—owes its existence not to rhetoric but to forty years of teaching practice. Moreover, a practical task remains; namely, to make this idea and teaching practice a more central part of the basic, required curriculum at Columbia College, and elsewhere.

I call attention to this task we face, to our teaching situation, because it seems to me that in the broader debate over the relative place of the West and "other" cultures in the core curriculum, the questions typically devolve on what books to teach, not on who is to do the teaching (much less, as Wm. Theodore de Bary points out, on student expectations or needs). Either to fashion a revolutionary or a revisionist book list, or stolidly to put forward a perennial canon, seems to be the order of the day. Who will teach any of these books, however hegemonic or heterodox, with what degree of enthusiasm and thanks to what sort of training or institutional reward, are questions seldom asked. Instead, we quantify our judgments, and based on what percentage of a particular culture or period or gender a given syllabus contains, we reduce its teachers to caricature. Proudly brandishing our preferred syllabi on high, but ourselves diminished and deformed, we are cast in the role of male reactionary, carping feminist, ethnic agitator. This crude stereotyping will no doubt continue, so long as the focus of "dealing with" the Humanities or liberal education is on the quick, managerial fix—the imposition of an old or a new book list—and not on the more difficult, human issues of who will teach the Humanities, using what language, to whom.

My title, as well as some remarks above, gives indication of my own position on the matter of education in the Humanities, which

I would like to clarify here. If a college is to maintain a core requirement in the Humanities, then these courses should expose students to intellectually challenging work of several cultures, and from modern and not only classical traditions. This should not be construed as a position which would simply displace the Western classics. Rather I see it as responding to some of that culture's deepest, exploratory urgencies—to journey, to go into exile, which, from the *Odyssey* to *Genesis*, becomes a precondition of wisdom and a test of cultural strength.

Yet in proposing a more central place for the Oriental Humanities (or similar courses) in the overall Humanities curriculum, I am not proposing some "return of the repressed," or of the marginalized, or banished, much less cautioning that, in the going jargon, any such recuperation or return would domesticate and tame the truly alien and subversive power of these various "others." Instead, I want to question how we read certain books and not others with our students in a spirit of common inquiry. How conscious are we of the claim we make in maintaining a required "core" course—the claim that as a faculty, we have taken on a responsibility to determine a set of intellectual and moral parameters and values. Core courses are where certain freedoms are abridged, and we should understand that. It is not my argument that such freedoms should be extended without limit, or be completely taken away. But we need to talk more openly, more publicly, and in plain language, about the ways Columbia College and many others will continue to maintain, or responsibly redefine, what educational values it holds to and wishes to share, not with some but with all of its students.

"That things are unequal is part of their nature." Mencius said that. "Writing is a pact of generosity between author and reader. Each one trusts the other." Mencius could have said that. It is in his idiom. But he did not. Jean-Paul Sartre said it, in the late 1940s, a time, as it happens, when the Oriental Humanities Program was just beginning. In different ways, I think these are challenging, humanistic propositions. But do either of them, for all the cultural and temporal remoteness of the one and the apparent proximity of the other, seem at all close to us now? Or are both equally strange to the ways we have come to think of ourselves, as teachers, in our relation to a culture and a society? When we read and when we talk about books we regard as important—not in the privacy of our offices, not in the privacy of our scholarship, not in the privacy of our specialized languages by which we dismantle texts—but when we are speaking in public (or what is for the teacher its closest analogue, the Humanities classroom) about books and the values they hold, do either of these propositions compel our attention? Or, in the self and culture-annihilating claim that any text is deceptive and untrustworthy, have we condemned ourselves to silence, or to a self-referential monologue?

The classical texts of either the East or the West are neither silent, nor do they speak to us simply because some of us, or some alumni, say they do. If it is plausible to accept a persistent claim—that knowledge proceeds from the known to the unknown—we should not assume that for American students at this time, knowledge begins with the West and proceeds in other, stranger directions. One need not be an extremist, like Emerson—who claimed Homer and Milton were of a "feudal school," that Shakespeare and Plato, "would not do," and wished to "extract this tape-worm of Europe from the brain of our countrymen"—to admit that the known American cultural environment is composed of more than a set of classic texts.

At any rate, it seems to me less a spatial issue (America vs. Europe, West vs. non-West) than a temporal one. We know the family, the neighborhood, the religious and social history we were born into; for the typical American college student, now, if not fifty years ago, this personal history may embrace a range of linguistic and cultural experience, exceeding even Whitman's imaginings. As we mature intellectually, we move toward the unknown—both past and future. And so if we maintain that classical books still "talk" to us, certain modern books, books from our known environment, should talk to us as well.

It is likely that any configuration of readings in either a Western or an Oriental Humanities course, would always include ancient or "pre-modern" books. Yet how guarded and ungenerous our definition of the Humanities would seem, if somewhere within our modern world, we could not find important books to which it might apply. In fact, if we could not walk into a Humanities classroom feeling strongly about the literature being written in or near our own time, then we may not be prepared to speak of older books, from either Western or Oriental traditions, in a way that truly challenges contemporary prejudice and conceit.

For example, the South African author Nadine Gordimer has written books which, over the years, by force of their aesthetic grace and a seriousness both intellectual and moral, have shaped my sense of existing excellence and possibility in English literature. In that way, she has written what are for me "important books" (the criterion, however vague, on which both Erskine and Barzun based their Colloquia). Her writings strike me as all the more important, for present teachers of the Humanities, since a central issue in her work—the survival, collision, or extension of traditions across time and different cultures—is precisely our own. Here is a sample passage. It is from *A World of Strangers:*

> The atmosphere of ideological flux which I have breathed all my life sometimes seemed terrifyingly thin, a rare air, in which one must gasp for the want of the oxygen of certainty, of an established way of life. Paradoxically, there had been bred into me a horror of the freedom that is freedom only to be free; I wanted to be free to cling to what I should break from, if I wished. I did not think that a man should have to lose himself, in Gide's sense, in order to find himself. Something in me clung strongly to the need for mediating powers—tradition, religion, perhaps; a world where you might, if you wished, grow up to do what was expected of you. My mother and father gave up a great many small, unworthy things that together, constituted a workable framework of living, but what did they have to offer in their

place? Freedom; an empty international plain where a wind turns over torn newspapers printed in languages you don't understand.

Learning, even humanistic learning, too far removed from the contingencies of life, breeds ideology. Both an abstract appeal to the pre-nineteenth century classics, and a revolutionary call for their displacement, sound equally vacant, mere ideological echoes over "an empty international plain." This is not, of course, the place where we teach. Instead, we face students in a classroom, within a college whose curricular structure possesses local traditions which we should be conscious of and understand, since the great traditions got their start in something littler, more local and contingent.

Wm. Theodore de Bary has supplied a thorough and balanced description of the history of general education at Columbia (see opening chapter). I would like here to reiterate, or emphasize, a few facts and characteristics. Arriving at Columbia in 1916, John Erskine established an Honors course, from which would emerge an idea of general education. A recent report on the curriculum noted that however many other notions have entered into an understanding of what the Humanities and general education mean at Columbia, the idea set forward by Erskine at that time—"to help students understand the civilization of their own day and participate effectively in it"—has been present. It should also be noticed that it took time and effort for a variation of the Erskine Honors course to become part of the required curriculum. Begun in the combative cultural atmosphere of the First World War, the Honors course collapsed along with the stock market and the structure of the disciplines in 1929, was revived as a "Colloquium on Important Books" in 1932, and was subject to five years of faculty debate until, in 1937, it became part of the required, core curriculum.

In this process, what also seems notable is that the teachers of these courses regarded themselves as amateurs (including such amateurs as Jacques Barzun, Mark van Doren, Moses Hadas, and Lionel Trilling). Perhaps better, they were intellectuals who were part of a university environment, yet conscious of and attentive to public life. Some taught, concurrently, at teacher institutes and union halls. They shared a common, accessible idiom, and believed there was a place in undergraduate education to use it.

This was a teaching situation which prevailed at Columbia College through the 1940s, when the Oriental Humanities program began. It was initiated by scholar-teachers who, though trained in a limited area of study, felt a commitment to move the existing Humanities curriculum beyond its European focus.

Yet since the late '40s until recently, Oriental Humanities has remained a highly respected, but elective course within Columbia's curriculum. Now it is an option within a second tier requirement, but does not infringe directly on the freedom of an undergraduate and, to that extent, cannot lay claim to the attention of all students. Like other non-Western courses in the College, it fulfills, in curricular terms, a supplementary function. Plainly, it is not a part of the primary "core"—those courses or books judged important enough to be confronted by everyone.

Here we face a Mencian problem: the existence of two related but unequal courses, and the task of trying to draw them, and others, closer together. It is not a problem which will be solved in isolation, or at a conference, or at some point abstracted from the situation in which we teach. Yet I wonder, not cynically, if in our present academic environment, we possess the language or the nerve to engage this task. Can we still speak clearly with each other about some books we would commonly regard as being important to any tradition? As teachers, can we still see some open, public space, beyond the smokescreen of our specializations? It is in general education, in core courses, that we must hand over some of our freedom, bias, and privacy, to serve a common good. I wonder if we still have the will or the commitment to stake out and hold that common ground.

These are open questions. But we need to know if faculty remain committed to teaching books in an amateur tradition, to speaking about books in a public style, before we speculate on what books might be taught in a core curriculum. A given college faculty may decide to retain an existing requirement in the Western Humanities, or it may commission more inclusive Humanities courses. But neither what we presently have, nor any new model we might offer, addresses what seems to me the basic, gut issue in all of this: the attitude teachers have toward books, and toward the students they teach.

Is there a pact, to paraphrase Sartre, which still exists between teacher and student? Is there a conviction that books are more than machines producing either absolute truths or contextualized lies—that there is a voice within books, and within ourselves, worth exploring? It is not at all clear that most present teachers, or those who will shortly join college faculties, have been educated to hold such convictions, much less to pass them on. We may harbor such feelings about books privately, but probably view teaching any book which falls outside our chosen area of expertise as being "unprofessional." This should not be ascribed to a generation's fears, some meek withdrawal into careerism. College administrations and national agencies played a part in this. The reward and punishment systems within higher education encouraged this drift toward a personal, private language, meant for other professionals or for a discipline, though not for public, general education. Reflection on the present or a future Humanities curriculum should not overlook changes in the training, hiring, and promotion of teachers over the last two decades—which in turn have caused changes in the way we talk about and regard books.

Given the skittishness of this environment, some might reasonably argue to leave well enough alone. That is, to maintain existing Western Humanities requirements, and perhaps encourage students to complement them with a course like Oriental Humanities, either as an elective or as an upper-level distribution requirement. But to preserve the status quo, prior to thorough public discussion, involving faculty of every rank and most disciplines, seems to me a prescription for the end of general education, at Columbia and elsewhere. The original Humanities courses grew out of and were sustained by a public, not a hermetic tradition. Yet as academics today, not only those at Columbia and not only the younger faculty among us, we have been educated within and employed to serve essentially private institutions. Moreover, the connections and responsibilities between these institutions and the wider, public culture are no longer forcefully articulated and made clear—least of all by our leaders.

Surely there are other, perhaps even more effective ways, to preserve and extend the legacy of past literary traditions than to line up in defense of "classic works," calling only such works the Humanities. It was in the modern world, we must remember, that the idea of the Humanities came into being, carried forward by such as Matthew Arnold's "remnant," who converted a fear of intense social and cultural change into a confidence it could know and define "the best that has been thought and said." There remains an educational need to engage both the excellence and the limits of Western culture. But this becomes all the more possible if we also engage, as a primary and not a secondary activity, the excellence of other cultures and their limits. It is, as well, an educational and a cultural need to face and not evade the difficulties posed by our increasingly interconnected, if fractious, modern world, and to recognize that it has produced excellence of its kind, which deserves to be part of the Humanities.

The essays gathered in this volume introduce classic works of the Oriental traditions and indicate how they may be taught as "Humanities." Here I would like to propose another teachable book, which, like Gordimer's, is part of our modern tradition. The book is *Grass on the Wayside*, written by Natsume Sōseki in 1915.

Like most educated Japanese prior to this century, Sōseki received early training in the Chinese classics. This represented both aesthetic and moral learning, and from it Sōseki would have gleaned a Neo-Confucian sense of an ordered universe, subject to violation by selfish excess. But to enter Tokyo University in the mid 1880s, Sōseki felt compelled to study English, seeing it as a way to enter a wider cultural world. With the dedication he had earlier applied to the classics of his own tradition, Sōseki devoted himself to English literature. He wrote trenchant criticism, ranging from Arthurian legend to Swift, *Tristram Shandy* to George Meredith. At the turn of the century, he spent two years in London. He had left Japan with great expectations, hoping to meet renowned English scholars, and to exchange his ideas with them. Instead (and without cataloguing the manner and degree of his humiliation) he was ignored. He had studied the West and, even later, would not disparage the excellence of English literature. Yet the West, in the persons of the educated men he met, who revealed no corresponding interest or enthusiasm to know about the Japanese or Asian literary heritage, had turned its back on him. Returning to Japan, he succeeded Lafcadio Hearn as Lecturer in English at Tokyo University. Later, to serve a more public role, he became a cultural editor at a mass circulation daily newspaper. Between 1906 and 1916, he wrote over a dozen novels which established him as the dominant presence in Japanese fiction down to our own day. In books like *Grass on the Wayside*, Sōseki confronted the various ways Japanese have become —or been made—strangers in their own land. The following passage illustrates this predicament:

> Kenzō felt quite lonely as he left his sister. He walked vaguely in the direction of his house, knowing that his familiarity with Tokyo geography would get him to his destination eventually. After a while he found himself in a very busy quarter which had that cheap, dirty look peculiar to newly developed areas. There was nothing in the surrounding scene that he could recognize, despite the fact that he had certainly been to this part of Tokyo before. Over the ground from which all vestiges of the past had been taken away, he walked like a man lost.
>
> There had been rice paddies here once, with straight footpaths running between them. Visible on the far side of the paddies were the thatched roofs of farmers' cottages. He could remember seeing a man seated on a bench somewhere around here, his sedge hat beside him, eating jelly. Nearby had stood a large paper

> mill. One followed the path around the mill and came to a little stream with a bridge over it. The banks were built up high with stones, so that the stream seemed much further below than one had expected. The old-fashioned signs on the bathhouse at the foot of the bridge, the pumpkins lying in front of the grocer's next door—these had often reminded the young Kenzō of Hiroshige's prints.
>
> Now everything was gone like a dream; all that was left was the ground he stood on. "But when did it all go?" He was shocked to see how a place too could change—as though until then he had imagined only people changed.

The sense of loss here is rooted in the history of late nineteenth-century Japan. Yet it echoes the tone and style of a traditional Japanese book, one which we do presently teach in the Oriental Humanities, the priest Chōmei's "Account of My Hut." This is a Buddhist parable on the evanescence, the illusory nature of things, the instability of worldly structures. Ironically, while he was still a student in college, Sōseki translated this "Account" into English. His translation, remarkable for its elegance, may not be as "correct" and fluid as the one we use, but I want to cite this passage in Sōseki's newfound language, in respect for what it cost him:

> Incessant is the change of water where the stream glides on calmly. The spray appears over a cataract, yet vanishes without a moment's delay. Such is the fate of men in the world and of the houses in which they live. Walls standing side by side, tiles vying with one another in loftiness. These are through generations past the abodes high and low in a mighty town, but none of them has resisted the destructive work of time. Some stand in ruins; others are replaced by new structures. Their possessors, too, share the same fate with them.

If Chōmei's classic "spoke" to Sōseki, it did so through a foreign language. And so its deepest message—about transformation and change—was preserved paradoxically by way of a "modern" idiom. In his fiction, Sōseki seems haunted by old sights and sounds and traditions, even as he vigilantly observed the new, if precarious, structures of his own time. He is an exemplary humanist, who engaged the past, did not flinch from the present, and subjected his intelligence and moral imagination to the test of different languages and cultures.

I think it would be possible in any Humanities course to read a Sōseki book. I am not narrowly suggesting that this particular book, or Gordimer's, or a specific percentage of modern books, should comprise a revised syllabus. But it strikes me that such works, using an idiom and reflecting conditions we recognize as part of our shared modernity, speak to us with urgency about the hard task of carrying on and extending cultural traditions. They clarify the nature of the charge, the work which lies before us, as teachers of the Humanities.

Contributors to Chapters 1 to 6

Paul Anderer is Professor of Modern Japanese Literature and Chair of the Department of East Asian Languages and Cultures at Columbia University. He is author of *Other Worlds: Arishima Takeo and the Bounds of Modern Japanese Fiction* (1984).

Robert Antoine, S. J., was formerly Professor of Sanskrit, Xavier College, Calcutta, India.

Peter Awn is Professor of Religion at Columbia University, and the author of *Satan's Tragedy and Redemption* (1983).

Irene Bloom is Wm. Theodore de Bary and Fanny Brett de Bary and Class of 1941 Collegiate Associate Professor of Asian Humanities at Columbia University, Associate Professor and Chair of the Department of Asian and Middle Eastern Cultures at Barnard College, and Program Director of the Columbia University Committee on Asia and the Middle East. She is editor/translator of *Knowledge Painfully Acquired: The K'un-chih chi of Lo Ch'in-shun* (1987).

Joel Brereton is Associate Professor of Religion at the University of Missouri. He is author of *The Ṛgvedic Ādityas* (1981).

Contributors

Wing-tsit Chan was Professor Emeritus of Chinese Culture and Philosophy at Dartmouth College, Anna R. D. Gillespie Professor of Philosophy Emeritus at Chatham College, and Adjunct Professor of Chinese Thought at Columbia University. He is author and translator of many books, including *A Source Book in Chinese Philosophy* (1963), *Instructions for Practical Living and Other Philosophical Writings by Wang Yang-ming* (1963), *Reflections on Things at Hand: The Neo-Confucian Anthology* (1967), and *Neo-Confucian Terms Explained: The Pei-hsi tzu-i, by Ch'en Ch'un* (1986).

Wm. Theodore de Bary is Special Service Professor and Provost Emeritus of Columbia University. A former president of the Association for Asian Studies (1969–1970), he also served as Vice President and Provost of Columbia from 1971 to 1978. In addition to many books on Asian civilizations prepared for use in general education, his published works include more specialized researches in Neo-Confucianism, the latest of which is *The Message of the Mind in Neo-Confucianism* (1988).

Ainslie T. Embree is Professor Emeritus, former chair of the History Department, and former Acting Dean of the School of International and Public Affairs at Columbia University. He is past president of the Association for Asian Studies and editor-in-chief of the *Encyclopedia of Asian History*.

C. T. Hsia is Professor Emeritus of Chinese Literature at Columbia and the author of many books including *The Classic Chinese Novel* (1968).

Donald Keene is Shinchō Professor Emeritus of Japanese Literature and University Professor Emeritus at Columbia and the author of three volumes on the history of Japanese literature, including *World Within Walls* (1976) and *Dawn to the West* (1984).

Mushin Mahdi is Jewett Professor of Arabic at Harvard University and the editor of a definitive edition of the *Thousand and One Nights (Alf Layla wa Layla) from the Earliest Known Sources* (1984).

Barbara Stoler Miller was Samuel R. Milbank Professor and Chairman of the Department of Asian and Middle Eastern Cultures at Barnard College. She was the author and translator of numerous books on Indian literature, including *Bhartrihari: Poems* (1967), *Phantasies of a Love Thief: The Caurapañcāśikā Attributed to Bilhaṇa* (1971), *Love Song of the Dark Lord: Jayadeva's Gītagovinda* (1977), *Theater of Memory: The Plays of Kālidāsa* (1984), and *The Bhagavad Gita: Krishna's Counsel in Time of War* (1986).

James W. Morris is Professor of Religion and teaches Islamic studies at Oberlin College. He is the author of *The Wisdom of the Throne: An*

Introduction to the Philosophy of Mulla Sadra (1981) and coauthor, with Michel Chodkiewicz and William C. Chittick, of *Ibn ʿArabi: The Meccan Illuminations* (1989).

Haruo Shirane is Professor of Japanese Literature and Chair of the Administrative Committee of the Donald Keene Center at Columbia University. He is the author of *The Bridge of Dreams: A Poetics of the Tale of Genji* (1987).

Robert A. F. Thurman is Professor of Indo-Tibetan Buddhism and Chair of the Department of Religion at Columbia University. He is author/translator of *The Holy Teaching of Vimalakīrti* (1976), *Tsong Khapa's Speech of Gold* (1984), *The Central Philosophy of Tibet: A Study and Translation of Jey Tsong Khapa's Essence of True Eloquence* (1991), and *The Tibetan Book of the Dead* (1994).

H. Paul Varley, formerly Professor of Japanese History at Columbia University, is currently Professor of Japanese History at the University of Hawaii. He is author or editor of a number of books on Japan, including *Japanese Culture* (3rd edition, 1984) and *Tea in Japan: Essays on the History of Chanoyu* (coedited with Kumakura Isao, 1989).

Franciscus Verellen, a former Mellon Fellow at Columbia University, is currently a member of the École Française d'Extrème Orient in Paris. He is the author of *Du Guangting (850–933): Taoiste de cour a la fin de la Chine medievale* (1989).

Burton Watson is Adjunct Professor of Chinese and Japanese at Columbia University. He is the author of *Early Chinese Literature* (1962) and the translator of *Records of the Historian: Chapters from the "Shih Chi" of Ssu-ma Ch'ien* (1961); Basic Writings of *Mo Tzu, Hsün Tzu, and Han Fei Tzu* (1967); *The Complete* Works of *Chuang Tzu* (1968); *The Columbia Book of Chinese Poetry* (1985), the *Tso-chuan* (1989) and *The Lotus Sutra* (1993).

Philip Yampolsky has taught East Asian Buddhism at Columbia University and is currently Special Lecturer in the Department of East Asian Languages and Cultures at Columbia. He is the editor/translator of *The Platform Sutra of the Sixth Patriarch* (1976), *The Zen Master Hakuin* (1971), and *Selected Writings of Nichiren* (1990).

Contributors to the Symposium

Paul Anderer is Professor of Modern Japanese Literature and Chair of the Department of East Asian Languages and Cultures at Columbia University.

Jonathan Cott is a writer, poet, and critic who has served as Contributing Editor to *Rolling Stone* and *Parabola* magazines, and was a Guggenheim Fellow, 1979–80.

Robert P. Goldman is Professor of Sanskrit at the University of California, Berkeley, and the author of *Gods, Priests, and Warriors: The Bhṛgus of the Mahābhārata* (1977) and editor and translator of *The Rāmāyaṇa of Vālmīki* (vol. 1, 1984; vol. 2, 1986).

David Johnson was a Senior Fellow in the Society of Fellows at Columbia and is now Professor of Chinese History at the University of California, Berkeley and Director of the Chinese Popular Culture Project there. He is author of *The Medieval Chinese Oligarchy* (1977) and editor, with Andrew J. Nathan and Evelyn Sakakida Rawski, of *Popular Culture in Late Imperial China* (1985).

John Van Doren is Executive Editor of *The Great Ideas Today*, published by the Great Books Foundation of the Encyclopedia Britannica.

Pauline Yu, formerly Professor of Chinese Literature at Columbia University, is currently Director of the Division of the Humanities and Professor of Chinese Literature in the Department of East Asian Languages and Cultures at the University of California at Los Angeles. She is author/translator of *The Poetry of Wang Wei* (1980), author of *The Reading of Imagery in the Chinese Poetic Tradition* (1987), and editor of *Voices of the Song Lyric in China* (1994).

Other Works in the Columbia Asian Studies Series

COMPANIONS TO ASIAN STUDIES

Approaches to the Oriental Classics, ed. Wm. Theodore de Bary	1959
Early Chinese Literature, by Burton Watson. Also in paperback ed.	1962
Approaches to Asian Civilizations, ed. Wm. Theodore de Bary and Ainslie T. Embree	1964
The Classic Chinese Novel: A Critical Introduction, by C. T. Hsia. Also in paperback ed.	1968
Chinese Lyricism: Shih Poetry from the Second to the Twelfth Century, tr. Burton Watson. Also in paperback ed.	1971
A Syllabus of Indian Civilization, by Leonard A. Gordon and Barbara Stoler Miller	1971
Twentieth-Century Chinese Stories, ed. C. T. Hsia and Joseph S. M. Lau. Also in paperback ed.	1971
A Syllabus of Chinese Civilization, by J. Mason Gentzler, 2d ed.	1972
A Syllabus of Japanese Civilization, by H. Paul Varley, 2d ed.	1972

An Introduction to Chinese Civilization, ed. John Meskill, with the assistance of J. Mason Gentzler 1973
An Introduction to Japanese Civilization, ed. Arthur E. Tiedemann 1974
Ukifune: Love in the Tale of Genji, ed. Andrew Pekarik 1982
The Pleasures of Japanese Literature, by Donald Keene 1988
A Guide to Oriental Classics, ed. Wm. Theodore de Bary and Ainslie T. Embree; third edition ed. Amy Vladeck Heinrich 1989

TRANSLATIONS FROM THE ASIAN CLASSICS

Major Plays of Chikamatsu, tr. Donald Keene. Also in paperback ed. 1961
Four Major Plays of Chikamatsu, tr. Donald Keene. Paperback text edition 1961
Records of the Grand Historian of China, translated from the Shih chi of Ssu-ma Ch'ien, tr. Burton Watson, 2 vols. 1961
Instructions for Practical Living and Other Neo-Confucian Writings by Wang Yang-ming, tr. Wing-tsit Chan 1963
Chuang Tzu: Basic Writings, tr. Burton Watson, paperback ed. only 1964
The Mahābhārata, tr. Chakravarthi V. Narasimhan. Also in paperback ed. 1965
The Manyōshū, Nippon Gakujutsu Shinkōkai edition 1965
Su Tung-p'o: Selections from a Sung Dynasty Poet, tr. Burton Watson. Also in paperback ed. 1965
Bhartrihari: Poems, tr. Barbara Stoler Miller. Also in paperback ed. 1967
Basic Writings of Mo Tzu, Hsün Tzu, and Han Fei Tzu, tr. Burton Watson. Also in separate paperback eds. 1967
The Awakening of Faith, Attributed to Aśvaghosha, tr. Yoshito S. Hakeda. Also in paperback ed. 1967
Reflections on Things at Hand: The Neo-Confucian Anthology, comp. Chu Hsi and Lü Tsu-ch'ien, tr. Wing-tsit Chan 1967
The Platform Sutra of the Sixth Patriarch, tr. Philip B. Yampolsky. Also in paperback ed. 1967
Essays in Idleness: The Tsurezuregusa of Kenkō, tr. Donald Keene. Also in paperback ed. 1967
The Pillow Book of Sei Shōnagon, tr. Ivan Morris, 2 vols. 1967
Two Plays of Ancient India: The Little Clay Cart and the Minister's Seal, tr. J. A. B. van Buitenen 1968
The Complete Works of Chuang Tzu, tr. Burton Watson 1968

Other Works in Asian Studies Series

A Chronicle of Gods and Sovereigns: Jinnō Shōtōki of Kitabatake Chikafusa, tr. H. Paul Varley	1980
Among the Flowers: The Hua-chien chi, tr. Lois Fusek	1982
Grass Hill: Poems and Prose by the Japanese Monk Gensei, tr. Burton Watson	1983
Doctors, Diviners, and Magicians of Ancient China: Biographies of Fang-shih, tr. Kenneth J. DeWoskin. Also in paperback ed.	1983
Theater of Memory: The Plays of Kālidāsa, ed. Barbara Stoler Miller. Also in paperback ed.	1984
The Columbia Book of Chinese Poetry: From Early Times to the Thirteenth Century, ed. and tr. Burton Watson. Also in paperback ed.	1984
Poems of Love and War: From the Eight Anthologies and the Ten Songs of Classical Tamil, tr. A. K. Ramanujan. Also in paperback ed.	1985
The Bhagavad-gita: Krishna's Counsel in Time of War, tr. Barbara Stoler Miller	1986
The Columbia Book of Later Chinese Poetry, ed. and tr. Jonathan Chaves. Also in paperback ed.	1986
The Tso Chuan: Selections From China's Oldest Narrative History, tr. Burton Watson.	1989
Waiting for the Wind: Thirty-Six Poets of Japan's Late Medieval Age, tr. Steven Carter	1989
Selected Writings of Nichiren, ed. Philip B. Yampolsky	1990
Saigyo, Poems of a Mountain Home, tr. Burton Watson	1990
The Book of Lieh-Tzu: A Classic of the Tao, tr. A. C. Graham. Morningside ed.	1990
The Tale of an Anklet: An Epic of South India: The Cilappatikamrom of Ilanko Atikal, tr. R. Parthasarathy	1993
Waiting for the Dawn: A Plan for the Prince, tr. and introduction by Wm. Theodore de Bary	1993
The Lotus Sutra, tr. Burton Watson. Also in paperback ed.	1993
The Classic of Changes: A New Translation of the I Ching as Interpreted by Wang Bi, tr. Richard John Lynn	1994

NEO-CONFUCIAN STUDIES

Instructions for Practical Living and Other Neo-Confucian Writings by Wang Yang-ming, tr. Wing-tsit Chan	1963
Reflections on Things at Hand: The Neo-Confucian Anthology, comp. Chu Hsi and Lü Tsu-ch'ien, tr. Wing-tsit Chan	1967

Self and Society in Ming Thought, by Wm. Theodore de Bary and the Conference on Ming Thought. Also in paperback ed. 1970
The Unfolding of Neo-Confucianism, by Wm. Theodore de Bary and the Conference on Seventeenth-Century Chinese Thought. Also in paperback ed. 1975
Principle and Practicality: Essays in Neo-Confucianism and Practical Learning, ed. Wm. Theodore de Bary and Irene Bloom. Also in paperback ed. 1979
The Syncretic Religion of Lin Chao-en, by Judith A. Berling 1980
The Renewal of Buddhism in China: Chu-hung and the Late Ming Synthesis, by Chün-fang Yü 1981
Neo-Confucian Orthodoxy and the Learning of the Mind-and-Heart, by Wm. Theodore de Bary 1981
Yüan Thought: Chinese Thought and Religion Under the Mongols, ed. Hok-lam Chan and Wm. Theodore de Bary 1982
The Liberal Tradition in China, by Wm. Theodore de Bary 1983
The Development and Decline of Chinese Cosmology, by John B. Henderson 1984
The Rise of Neo-Confucianism in Korea, by Wm. Theodore de Bary and JaHyun Kim Haboush 1985
Chiao Hung and the Restructuring of Neo-Confucianism in the Late Ming, by Edward T. Ch'ien 1985
Neo-Confucian Terms Explained: The Pei-hsi tzu-i by Ch'en Ch'un, ed. and trans. Wing-tsit Chan 1986
Knowledge Painfully Acquired: The K'un-chih chi, by Lo Ch'in-shun, ed. and trans. Irene Bloom 1987
To Become a Sage: The Ten Diagrams on Sage Learning, by Yi T'oegye, ed. and trans. Michael C. Kalton 1988
The Message of the Mind in Neo-Confucianism, by Wm. Theodore de Bary 1989

MODERN ASIAN LITERATURE SERIES

Modern Japanese Drama: An Anthology, ed. and tr. Ted Takaya. Also in paperback ed. 1979
Mask and Sword: Two Plays for the Contemporary Japanese Theater, by Yamazaki Masakazu, tr. J. Thomas Rimer 1980
Yokomitsu Riichi, Modernist, by Dennis Keene 1980
Nepali Visions, Nepali Dreams: The Poetry of Laxmiprasad Devkota, tr. David Rubin 1980

Other Works in Asian Studies Series

Literature of the Hundred Flowers, vol. 1: *Criticism and Polemics*, ed. Hualing Nieh 1981
Literature of the Hundred Flowers, vol. 2: *Poetry and Fiction*, ed. Hualing Nieh 1981
Modern Chinese Stories and Novellas, 1919–1949, ed. Joseph S. M. Lau, C. T. Hsia, and Leo Ou-fan Lee. Also in paperback ed. 1984
A View by the Sea, by Yasuoka Shōtarō, tr. Kären Wigen Lewis 1984
Other Worlds: Arishima Takeo and the Bounds of Modern Japanese Fiction, by Paul Anderer 1984
Selected Poems of Sŏ Chŏngju, tr. with intro. by David R. McCann 1989
The Sting of Life: Four Contemporary Japanese Novelists, by Van C. Gessel 1989
Stories of Osaka Life, by Oda Sakunosuke, tr. Burton Watson 1990
The Bodhisattva, or Samantabhadra, by Ishikawa Jun, tr. with intro. by William Jefferson Tyler 1990
The Travels of Lao Ts'an, by Liu T'ich-yunao, tr. Harold Shadick. Morningside ed. 1990

STUDIES IN ORIENTAL CULTURE

1. *The Ōnin War: History of Its Origins and Background, with a Selective Translation of the Chronicle of Ōnin*, by H. Paul Varley 1967
2. *Chinese Government in Ming Times: Seven Studies*, ed. Charles O. Hucker 1969
3. *The Actors' Analects (Yakusha Rongo)*, ed. and tr. by Charles J. Dunn and Bungō Torigoe 1969
4. *Self and Society in Ming Thought*, by Wm. Theodore de Bary and the Conference on Ming Thought. Also in paperback ed. 1970
5. *A History of Islamic Philosophy*, by Majid Fakhry, 2d ed. 1983
6. *Phantasies of a Love Thief: The Caurapañcāśikā Attributed to Bilhaṇa*, by Barbara Stoler Miller 1971
7. *Iqbal: Poet-Philosopher of Pakistan*, ed. Hafeez Malik 1971
8. *The Golden Tradition: An Anthology of Urdu Poetry*, by Ahmed Ali. Also in paperback ed. 1973
9. *Conquerors and Confucians: Aspects of Political Change in Late Yüan China*, by John W. Dardess 1973
10. *The Unfolding of Neo-Confucianism*, by Wm. Theodore de Bary and the Conference on Seventeenth-Century Chinese Thought. Also in paperback ed. 1975

11. *To Acquire Wisdom: The Way of Wang Yang-ming,* by Julia Ching — 1976
12. *Gods, Priests, and Warriors: The Bhṛgus of the Mahābhārata,* by Robert P. Goldman — 1977
13. *Mei Yao-ch'en and the Development of Early Sung Poetry,* by Jonathan Chaves — 1976
14. *The Legend of Semimaru, Blind Musician of Japan,* by Susan Matisoff — 1977
15. *Sir Sayyid Ahmad Khan and Muslim Modernization in India and Pakistan,* by Hafeez Malik — 1980
16. *The Khilafat Movement: Religious Symbolism and Political Mobilization in India,* by Gail Minault — 1980
17. *The World of K'ung Shang-jen: A Man of Letters in Early Ch'ing China,* by Richard Strassberg — 1983
18. *The Lotus Boat: The Origins of Chinese Tz'u Poetry in T'ang Popular Culture,* by Marsha L. Wagner — 1984
19. *Expressions of Self in Chinese Culture,* ed. Robert E. Hegel and Richard C. Hessney — 1985
20. *Songs for the Bride: Women's Voices and Wedding Rites of Rural India,* by W. G. Archer, ed. Barbara Stoler Miller and Mildred Archer — 1986
21. *A Heritage of Kings: One Man's Monarchy in the Confucian World,* by JaHyun Kim Haboush — 1988

INTRODUCTION TO ORIENTAL CIVILIZATIONS
Wm. Theodore de Bary, Editor

Sources of Japanese Tradition 1958; paperback ed., 2 vols., 1964
Sources of Indian Tradition 1958; paperback ed., 2 vols., 1964; second edition, 1988
Sources of Chinese Tradition 1960; paperback ed., 2 vols., 1964